NUTRITION OF THE VERY LOW BIRTHWEIGHT INFANT

Nestlé Nutrition Workshop Series
Paediatric Programme
Volume 43

NUTRITION OF THE VERY LOW BIRTHWEIGHT INFANT

Editors

Ekhard E. Ziegler
Department of Pediatrics
University of Iowa
Iowa City, Iowa, USA

Alan Lucas
MRC Childhood Nutrition Research Centre
Institute of Child Health
University of London
London, United Kingdom

Guido E. Moro
Center for Infant Nutrition
Macedonio Melloni Hospital
Milan, Italy

NESTLÉ NUTRITION SERVICES

Nestlé

LIPPINCOTT WILLIAMS & WILKINS

Acquisitions Editor: Beth Barry
Developmental Editor: Glenda Insua
Manufacturing Manager: Kevin Watt
Production Editor: Brandy Mui
Compositor: Maryland Composition, Inc.
Printer: Maple Press

Nestec, Ltd., 55 Avenue Nestlé,
CH-1800 Vevey, Switzerland
Lippincott Williams & Wilkins,
227 East Washington Square,
Philadelphia, Pennsylvania 19106

Printed in the United States of America

Library of Congress Cataloging-in-Publication Data

Nutrition of the very low birthweight infant / editors, Ekhard E.
    Ziegler, Alan Lucas, Guido E. Moro.
       p.   cm. — (Nestlé Nutrition workshop series ; v. 43)
    Based on the 43rd workshop held in Central Europe and Nestlé,
Poland.
    Includes bibliographical references and index.
    ISBN 0-7817-2215-2
    1. Infants (Premature)—Nutrition. 2. Birth weight, Low.
  3. Child development. I. Ziegler, Ekhard E. II. Lucas, Alan, MD.
  III. Moro, Guido E. IV. Series.
  RJ281.N88 1999
  618.92′011—dc21   99-37293
                                                   CIP

10 9 8 7 6 5 4 3 2 1

Preface

Neonatal medicine has made great strides in recent years and the result is that very small and immature infants are surviving in ever greater numbers. Nourishing these small infants presents an enormous challenge—to provide nutrition effectively and safely, to provide enough nutrition but not too much, and to do it all without undue risks. For a time after birth, the immature gastrointestinal tract must be approached with care, until it acquires the ability to handle full nutrition—hence the need for parenteral nutrition during the immediate postnatal period.

During this workshop, several speakers reviewed the encouraging progress that has been made in the use of parenteral nutrition. At its best, parenteral nutrition buys valuable time to nurture the gastrointestinal tract and does so with acceptable risk. Several presentations addressed the gastrointestinal tract: its immaturity, its vulnerability, and its peculiarities. In the past, feeding regimens designed to protect the gastrointestinal tract have emphasized the withholding of feeds, whereas in recent years, early introduction has been favored. Human milk clearly has established itself as the preferred feeding, not least because it offers greater protection for the safety of the gastrointestinal tract. Safety is an issue when iron and other essential but pro-oxidant nutrients are considered.

Does it all matter? It certainly matters in the short run. In the long run, the quality of neonatal nutrition does seem to impact later development. This finding was emphasized at the workshop, where poor growth in late infancy was shown to be a harbinger of poor development later in life. All this contributes a degree of urgency to all the questions surrounding the feeding of very low birthweight infants. Many small steps may add up to real progress. However, measuring progress objectively is one of the big challenges, along with ensuring that risks are not incurred unless they are outweighed by potential benefits.

The challenges of neonatal nutrition are many. Addressing them all during the span of the workshop would have been impossible. Selectivity was therefore inevitable. Concentrating on a few select topics meant that other important subjects would not be covered. Examples include bone growth and mineralization, body composition, and the entire topic of micronutrients. Nutrition of the very low birthweight infant is a large topic, but so is the number of potential beneficiaries of progress. This conference may have been one of the small steps that eventually add up to real progress.

Ekhard E. Ziegler
Alan Lucas
Guido E. Moro

Foreword

Feeding small premature infants is an enormous challenge for neonatologists, for nurses, and after discharge from the hospital, for the parents. Breast milk, the gold standard for feeding healthy term infants, is at best a reference for small premature infants. Their dietary needs substantially differ from those of term infants. Essential nutrients such as iron can become toxic under certain circumstances and can contribute to morbidity. Adequate intake should allow catch-up growth, avoid metabolic imbalances, and support the normal function of organs, in particular the brain. However, tolerance of oral nutrition is a limiting factor that is well known to all clinicians. Periods of abdominal distension and gastrointestinal problems are frequent and limit intake.

Substantial progress in perinatal care and neonatal intensive medicine now allows survival of a substantial number of infants with birth weights as low as 500 grams. Calculation of their nutritional requirements, clinical management during enteral nutrition, and long-term outcome are discussed during this workshop. The results of those discussions will help to further improve the quality and stimulate innovation of human milk fortifiers and formulas for small premature infants.

The programme of this workshop, which was proposed by the three Chairmen—Professor Ekhard E. Ziegler, Professor Alan Lucas, and Dr. Guido E. Moro—covers the most relevant aspects of clinical management of early enteral nutrition but also focuses on follow-up nutrition and evaluation of outcome. I thank the Chairmen and all of the speakers for their contribution to the programme. The 43rd Workshop was the first of its kind in Central Europe and Nestlé Poland provided all the logistic support that was required for a successful outcome. We thank them for their wonderful hospitality, excellent organization, and incomparable entertainment.

PROFESSOR FERDINAND HASCHKE, M.D.
Vice-President
Nestec Ltd., Vevey, Switzerland

Contents

Contributing Authors

Speakers

Howard M. Berger
Department of Pediatrics J6K195
Leiden University Medical Centre
Albinusdreef 2
P.O. Box 9600
2300 RC Leiden
The Netherlands

Carol Lynn Berseth
Department of Pediatrics/Newborn Section
Baylor College of Medicine
One Baylor Plaza
Houston, Texas 77030
USA

Susan J. Carlson
Department of Food and Nutrition
*   Services*
W 146 GH
University of Iowa Hospitals and Clinics
Iowa City, Iowa 52242
USA

Bohuslav Dvorak
Department of Pediatrics
University of Arizona
College of Medicine
1501 North Campbell Avenue
Tucson, Arizona 85724-5073
USA

Lee Frank
Department of Medicine and Pediatrics
University of Miami School of Medicine
Pulmonary Research
P.O. Box 016960
Miami, Florida 33101
USA

William C. Heird
Children's Nutrition Research Center
Baylor College of Medicine
1100 Bates Street, Suite 8066
Houston, Texas 77030-2600
USA

Berthold Koletzko
Dr. von Haunerschen Kinderspital
Lindwurmstrasse 4
München D-80337
Germany

Alan Lucas
MRC Childhood Nutrition Research
*   Centre*
Institute of Child Health
University of London
30 Guilford Street
London WC1N 1EH
UK

Jean-Léopold Micheli
Centre Hospitalier Universitaire Vaudois
Service de Pédiatrie
1011 Lausanne
Switzerland

Ruth Morley
Menzies Centre for Population Health
*   Research*
Hobart
Tasmania 7001, Australia;
University of Melbourne
Royal Children's Hospital
Flemington Road, Parkville
Victoria 3070, Australia

Guido E. Moro
Center for Infant Nutrition
Macedonio Melloni Hospital
Via Macedonio Melloni, 52
20129 Milano
Italy

Guy Putet
Hôpital Debrousse
29, rue Soeur Bouvier
69322 Lyon
France

Jacques Rigo
Department of Pediatrics
Neonatology Unit
University de Liège, CHR Citadelle
Boulevard du 12e de Ligne 1
4000 Liège
Belgium

Firmino F. Rubaltelli
University of Florence
Careggi University Hospital
85 Viale Morgagni
I-50134 Florence
Italy

Richard J. Schanler
Center for Infant Nutrition
Children's Nutrition Research Center
Baylor College of Medicine
1100 Bates Street
Houston, Texas 77030-3498
USA

W. Allan Walker
Combined Program in Pediatric
  Gastroenterology and Nutrition
Massachusetts General Hospital
149 13th Street
Charlston, Massachusetts 02129-2060
USA

Ekhard E. Ziegler
Department of Pediatrics
University of Iowa
200 Hawkins Drive
Iowa City, Iowa 52242
USA

Session Chairmen
Urszula Godula-Stuglik/*Poland*
Pawel Januszewicz/*Poland*
Ryszard Lauterbach/*Poland*
Stanislaw Nowak/*Poland*
Jerzy Szczapa/*Poland*

Invited Attendees
Klaus Albrecht/*Germany*
Omar Al-Siyud/*Saudi Arabia*
Navantino Alve/*Filho, Brazil*
Jamal Anwar Samdani/*Pakistan*
Stephanie Atkinson/*Canada*

Simon Attard Montalto/*Malta*
Elena Baibarina/*Russia*
Louise Baur/*Australia*
Driss Benjelloun/*Morocco*
Antonio Boldrini/*Italy*
Nem-Yun Boo/*Malaysia*
Maria Carreiro/*Portugal*
Irene Cheah Guat Sim/*Malaysia*
Chen Hui Jin/*China*
Philippe Chessex/*Canada*
Somporn Chotinaruemol/*Thailand*
Tamara Chuvakova/*Kazakstan*
Marcis Cirulis/*Latvia*
Richard Cooke/*UK*
Peter Cooper/*Republic of South Africa*
Christos Costalos/*Greece*
Tamara Czajkowska/*Poland*
Beata Czeszyñska/*Poland*
Malgorzata Czyzewska/*Poland*
Joan Marin Dambeanu/*Romania*
Mario De Curtis/*Italy*
Umberto De Vonderweid/*Italy*
Christian Debauche/*Belgium*
Dmitri Degtyarev/*Russia*
Sean Devane/*UK*
Hugo Devlieger/*Belgium*
Ubaldo Dimita/*Italy*
Laurent Egretau/*France*
Samir Faouri/*Jordanie*
Angela Fazzolari/*Italy*
Renato Fiore/*Brazil*
Michael Georgieff/*USA*
Christine Giannacopoulou/*Greece*
Ralitza Gueorgieva/*Bulgaria*
Mohammed Hanif/*Bangladesh*
Hahed Helal/*Egypt*
Sunthorn Horpaopan/*Thailand*
Miodrag Ignjatovic/*Yugoslavia*
Maciej Kaczmarski/*Poland*
Naima Khrouf/*Tunisia*
Khanh Dung Khu Thi/*Vietnam*
Christian Kind/*Switzerland*
Piotr Korbal/*Poland*
Naima Lamdouar-Bouazzaoui/*Morocco*
Jennifer Lightdale/*USA*
José Maria Lopes/*Brazil*
Andrea Loui/*Germany*
Marja-Liis Magi/*Estonia*
Stefanos Mantagos/*Greece*
Giovanni Francesco Marzetti/*Italy*
Diego Mieth/*Switzerland*
Mona Nabulsi-Khalil/*Lebanon*
Agathi Ntourntoufi/*Greece*

Teresa Owsianko-Podlesny/*Poland*
Luis Pereira Da Silva/*Portugal*
Frank Pohlandt/*Germany*
Jelena Polak-Babic/*Croatia*
Staffan Polberger/*Sweden*
José Augusto Pombeiro Veloso/*Portugal*
Natalya Pyasetskaya/*Ukraine*
José Quero Jimenez/*Spain*
Nabil Rashwan/*Egypt*
Hellfried Rosegger/*Austria*
Khalid Saidy/*Saudi Arabia*
Elie Saliba/*France*
Henryka Sawulicka-Oleszczuk/*Poland*
Munthir Scheikh El-Haddadin/*Syria*
Mohammed Reza Sedaghatian/*United Arab Emirates*
Iman Seoud/*Egypt*
Rita Sklepikiene/*Lithuania*
Kuldeep Suri/*Oman*
Hanna Szajewska/*Poland*
Jorge Torres Pereira/*Chile*
Ignacio Villa Elizaga/*Spain*

Beata Witoslaw/*Poland*
Wu Shi Xiao/*China*
Mei-Hui Yang/*Taiwan*
Galina Yatsyk/*Russia*

Nestlé Representatives
Roger Clemens/*USA*
Wolf Th. Endres/*Germany*
Bianca-Maria Exl/*Switzerland*
Anne-Lise Carrié Faessler/*Switzerland*
Pierre-René Guesry/*Switzerland*
Ferdinand Haschke/*Switzerland*
Linda Hsieh/*USA*
Dagmar Kreft/*Germany*
Olga Netrebenko/*Russia*
Thi Thanh Binh Nguyen/*Vietnam*
Vipapan Panitantum/*Thailand*
Delio Pichardo/*Dominicana*
Marie-Christine Secretin/*Switzerland*
Carmen Ecaterina Teodorescu/*Romania*
Audrone Vadapaliene/*Lithuania*
Louis-Dominique Van Egroo/*France*

Nestlé Nutrition Workshop Series
Paediatric Programme

NUTRITION OF THE
VERY LOW BIRTHWEIGHT
INFANT

Nutrition of the Very Low Birthweight Infant, edited by
Ekhard E. Ziegler, Alan Lucas, Guido E. Moro.
Nestlé Nutrition Workshop Series, Paediatric Programme, Vol. 43,
Nestec Ltd., Vevey/Lippincott Williams & Wilkins
Philadelphia, Pennsylvania © 1999.

Early Nutrition and Later Outcome

Alan Lucas

*MRC Childhood Nutrition Research Centre, Institute of Child Health, London WCIN IEH,
United Kingdom*

The scientific studies of the eighteenth and nineteenth centuries that underpinned the development of more recent pediatric nutritional practice occurred long before the formal development of pediatrics. Franz Simon established a rational, scientific basis for infant feeding with his landmark work in 1838 (1), when the word *pediatrics* had not even entered the English language. This was 20 years before the first chair of pediatrics in the United States and a century before pediatric chairs were created in Britain (in the 1930s). Paradoxically, however, despite the intensity of work over the past two centuries, pediatric nutrition has never emerged as an independent specialty. As a result, education and training in pediatric nutrition are poorly developed, and most pediatricians receive at most a few hours of instruction on nutrition throughout their entire formal training period. Not surprisingly, consistent standards of practice in the field have been slow to emerge, and the massive body of research has, until recently, been inadequately focused on the key questions posed by modern practice.

However, there has now been a paradigm shift in thinking about nutrition that I believe provides a compelling basis for more formal development of the field. Until recent years, the major preoccupation in nutrition was in meeting nutrient needs and preventing nutritional deficiency or excess. Although this, of course, remains important, the current focus has shifted to the rapidly increasing evidence for biological effects of nutrition on *health outcomes*. Thus key questions are now being posed and addressed that would have received much less attention 20 years ago. Among such questions are whether nutritional management matters in terms of the patients response to their disease and, perhaps of greatest biological interest, whether early nutrition matters for long-term health and development.

These issues are particularly pertinent to the relatively new population of infants surviving at low gestation following the rapid emergence of neonatal intensive care during the past 25 years. This field emphasizes the need for specialized nutrition training and provides powerful examples of the biological importance of nutrition for both short- and long-term health outcomes. In this introductory review article, I shall try to create a backcloth for the research and clinical practice issues in the nutrition of the low birthweight infant that will emerge in this timely workshop.

THE "DOES IT MATTER?" QUESTIONS

Feeding the very low birthweight preterm infant is not a natural physiological process. The cessation of placental nutrition up to 4 months too soon in biological terms and the need for rapid adaptation to postnatal life at an unphysiological stage in development create unique and challenging circumstances. In parallel with the development of neonatology as a whole, preterm nutrition is passing through the evolutionary stages of scientific research generally seen in new areas of clinical practice. It is useful to define these stages to identify the key issues for current research.

Broadly, I see research in a new clinical field as a three-stage process (2). In stage I, anecdotal observations raise the question, "Is this worth pursuing?" In stage II, epidemiological and physiological research provide descriptive and mechanistic data that raise testable hypotheses concerning the potential impact of intervention. Finally, in stage III, formal intervention experiments (generally randomized trials) test the efficacy and safety of clinical or public health practice. Thus stage III research shows whether the intervention tested *matters* in terms of improving one or more targeted health outcomes (efficacy) with acceptable risk (safety). An example would be the demonstration that the treatment of high blood pressure *matters* in terms of reducing significant morbidity without unacceptable side effects in the patient.

Until recent years, nutritional research in low-birthweight infants was largely in stage II. Research generally focused on collection of physiological and epidemiological data on growth, nutritional status, metabolic response to feeding, energy metabolism, nutrient absorption and retention, prevalence of nutrition-related disorders, and so on, which are factors of importance to our understanding of the biology and demography of infant nutrition but of uncertain relevance to outcome. It is clear, as in other areas of clinical medicine, that clinical practice in preterm nutrition can only be placed on a secure scientific footing using what I have termed *stage III research.*

What, then, are the stage III "Does it matter?" questions that are key to preterm nutrition? In the short term, such questions include whether nutritional practice has a major impact on morbidity (e.g., whether it influences critical disease processes such as necrotizing enterocolitis, infection, or mortality risk); in the long term, they include whether the way we feed low-birthweight infants has a critical impact on their health and development in later life.

Of these issues, the one that has commanded most recent attention is the idea that early nutrition could influence long-term effects on neurodevelopment or major diseases in adult life. Indeed, if the way very low-birthweight infants are fed changes their lifetime health, the implications for clinical practice are considerable. I have given this matter most attention in this chapter. I shall start by considering the broader concept of programming and its biological plausibility in the context of nutrition.

THE CONCEPT OF PROGRAMMING

Generally, events in early life might influence long-term outcome in three ways:

1. Direct damage (e.g., the loss of a limb);
2. Induction (i.e., deletion or impaired development of a somatic structure resulting from a stimulus or insult during a critical period); or

3. Physiological setting by an early stimulus or insult at a critical period, with long-term consequences for function.

Lucas (3,4) suggests that the term *programming* be applied to the latter two processes in which the programming stimulus only exerts long-term effects when applied at a critical or sensitive period.

Evidence for programming, outside the context of nutrition, is considerable (3,4). Examples are cited here. Early imprinting of behavior in birds has been recognized for centuries (5). *Hormonal* signals operating during critical windows have numerous programming effects. Thus in rats testosterone secreted by the fetal testis at a critical period programs the brain for male sexual behavior; a single dose of testosterone given at this time to a female fetus will permanently induce *male* sexual behavior (6). Teratogenic drugs, recognized since the 1920s, have powerful programming effects on somatic development. But postnatal programming by drugs may also occur: a single dose of phenobarbitone given to a neonatal rat may induce lifelong change in the activity of a key enzyme, cytochrome P450-dependent mono-oxygenase. Normal visual inputs are essential for the development of the visual pathway, hence squint amblyopia. The programming window is usually early fetal life or infancy, but, arguably, in the case of antigen-induced programming of the immune system, sensitivity may be lifelong. Whether there are other windows for programming at critical stages in life such as adolescence or menopause requires exploration.

These examples indicate that programming in fetal or postnatal life may result in initiation of normal development processes resulting from endogenous or exogenous physiological signaling during critical periods of development or that it may cause a long-term response to an environmental stimulus. Teleologically, the ability to respond to early environment to induce a lifetime change in structure or function could have evolved as a mechanism that allowed the organism to fine-tune its machinery in an adaptive way according to its early milieu. It seems likely, however, that some environmental insults could have programming effects of a nonadaptive, adverse nature.

NUTRITIONAL PROGRAMMING IN ANIMALS

Does early nutrition operate in this programming manner? McCance (7) provided key evidence for this in animals. He manipulated litter size in rats so that rats from large litters received less milk than those from small litters during the 21-day suckling period, by which time rats from large litters were substantially smaller than those from smaller litters. At this point both groups were fed normally, but the smaller animals (from large litters) continued to diverge in body size from the larger animals. Thus 3 weeks of dietary manipulation had resulted in a lifetime "programming" of growth trajectory.

McCance then showed that it was only the early weeks that constituted a critical period for such effects. Equivalent dietary manipulation for a 3-week period a few weeks later had no lasting impact. The underfed animals showed catch-up growth when they were refed; the critical window for growth programming by early nutrition had passed.

Following these key studies in the 1960s, many animal experiments on nutritional programming confirmed the wide variety of lifetime programming effects on metabolism, blood pressure, diabetes, obesity, atherosclerosis, behavior, and learning (see later); these would be of considerable public health importance were they to apply to humans.

Extensive animal data, largely on rats, show that nutrition at a vulnerable period of brain development may have permanent effects on brain size, brain cell number, behavior, learning, and memory (8,9). In Smart's review of 165 animal studies on early undernutrition on later learning (9), the number of studies in which undernourished animals fared worse than controls greatly outweighed those that favored the controls. The extent to which these animal data have relevance to human cognitive development is, however, uncertain.

With regard to health outcomes, experimental studies on fetal nutrition have shown, for instance, that protein-undernourished fetuses had long-term reduction in pancreatic cells and insulin secretion (10). Hahn (11) manipulated litter size in neonatal rats so that rats from small litters were temporarily overfed during the brief suckling period and found that in adulthood these animals had permanent elevation of plasma insulin and cholesterol. Weaning these animals onto a high-carbohydrate diet further induced lifelong elevation in the activities of HMG-CoA reductase and fatty acid synthetase (key enzymes for cholesterol and fat synthesis).

In primates (baboons), overfeeding during infancy in the female resulted in obesity that was not manifested until early adult life (12), raising the question of where the "memory" of the early event had been stored in the intervening period. In further studies (13), baboons were randomly assigned to breastfeeding or formula; then both groups were placed on a "Western-style" high-saturated-fat diet. The previously breastfed group had, in adult life, higher concentrations of plasma low-density and very-low-density lipoprotein (LDL, VLDL) cholesterol, lower protective high-density lipoprotein (HDL) cholesterol, and increased cholesterol absorption, perhaps relating to the permanent change in bile acid secretion. These data imply that breastfeeding may program these primates to be conservative with cholesterol but that this might be disadvantageous to lipid metabolism if they were subsequently placed, unphysiologically, on a high-saturated-fat diet. Indeed, at necropsy the previously breastfed baboons had significantly more atherosclerosis than those fed formula.

Our own studies in rats (14,15) showed that both pre- and postnatal nutrition may influence adult outcomes but that the critical period for programming depends on the outcome studied. Lifetime effects on body size were only seen in relation to *postnatal* nutritional manipulation; thus animals fed by mothers given a low-protein diet during lactation were permanently smaller, whereas prenatal low-protein diet given to the mother had no long-term effect on the size of the offspring. In contrast, lifetime changes in hepatic glucose metabolism (glucokinase and phosphenol pyruvate carboxykinase [PEPCK] activities) were induced only by prenatal dietary manipulation in the mother. For some outcomes, however, the critical window for programming was longer. Thus Lucas *et al.* found that *either* prenatal *or* postnatal (during lactation) low-protein diet given to the mother followed by a nutrient-enriched diet given to the offspring resulted in a programmed reduction in plasma triglycerides, HDL and total cholesterol, and systolic blood pressure in these offspring when they reached adult life (15). For some outcomes, the direction of response may depend on timing of the programming stimulus. We found lifespan was significantly *decreased* in animals born to mothers that had a low-protein diet in pregnancy but were then suckled by mothers on a normal protein diet, whereas the converse (offspring of mothers fed normally during pregnancy but suckled by mothers fed a low-protein diet) resulted in a significant *increase* in lifespan (16).

Such animal data have importance in suggesting human interventions and in defining underlying programming mechanisms (see later). However, public health policy for early nutrition in humans must ultimately depend on human studies.

NUTRITIONAL PROGRAMMING IN HUMANS

Given the evidence for programming in general and the evidence for *nutritional* programming in animals, nutritional programming in humans might be predicted. This has not been easy to prove, largely because most studies have not had an experimental design but have documented retrospective epidemiological associations often subject to alternative explanation. Collectively, the human epidemiological data are extensive, and illustrative studies are discussed here.

Early Nutrition and Later Cognitive Function: Epidemiological Evidence

Numerous investigators have attempted to test the hypothesis, using epidemiological models, that suboptimal nutrition at a vulnerable stage in brain development has permanent effects on cognitive function. Epidemiological associations found between malnutrition and reduced cognitive performance, however, might not be causal. Malnutrition, principally studied in developing countries, is inextricably associated with poverty and poor social circumstances that might explain the adverse outcomes. Prospective randomized or satisfactorily controlled studies are rare and most do not provide unequivocal data.

Several studies suggest that breastfeeding promotes long-term neurodevelopment, in some cases even after attempts to adjust for confounding factors (17), though whether or not these effects reflect residual confounding by educational and parenting differences between groups is uncertain. Our evidence that human milk may promote neurodevelopment and IQ in infants born *preterm* is stronger (17,18), with implications for practice. Human milk contains numerous factors that could influence neurodevelopment.

Nutrition and Later Disease: Epidemiological Studies

Most studies on early nutrition and later health have been epidemiological and inconclusive. Unlike the studies in baboons mentioned earlier, breastfed and bottle-fed infants have not been shown to differ in later total plasma cholesterol at 8 years (19) or total cholesterol, LDL, or HDL at up to 16 years (A Lucas *et al.*, unpublished). Early salt intake has been associated with later high blood pressure in some studies, but we and others have failed to show a causal link in preterm or normal individuals (20).

Breastfed and formula-fed babies may have potentially important differences in later health outcomes. Breastfeeding has been associated with a protective effect against insulin-dependent diabetes (21) (not observed by all) and a reduced incidence of lymphoma (22). In one epidemiological study prolonged breastfeeding in males was associated with a greater incidence of atherosclerosis in late adult life (23). Whether these associations are causal or confounded by the major demographic differences between groups needs further exploration.

Recent studies, notably by Barker and coworkers, have shown relations between anthropometric indices at birth and at one year (possible markers of early nutrition) with cardiovascular disease and its risk factors (23,24). Low body weight, head circumference, and ponderal index at birth and low weight at 1 year relate to increased risk of later cardiovascular disease. Small size at birth and up to 1 year has also been associated with higher blood pressure and adverse changes in plasma concentrations of glucose, insulin, fibrinogen, factor VII, and apolipoprotein B; abdominal circumference at birth is inversely associated with raised serum concentration of total cholesterol, LDL cholesterol, and apolipoprotein B. These provoking and important observations have been interpreted by the investigators as supporting the hypothesis that poor fetal nutrition, perhaps secondary to poor maternal nutrition, adversely programs the individual for later cardiovascular disease, hypertension, and diabetes. Their suggestion is that improvement of fetal nutrition might be an important public health measure (24). Supporting this is the evidence that early nutrition in animals has been shown to program corresponding outcomes. There are inconsistencies, however: in rats, *overnutrition* rather than undernutrition may be associated with later elevation of blood cholesterol (11), and chronic undernutrition has been associated with longevity (25). A key issue for debate is the proposed *nutritional* interpretation. Poor intrauterine growth might be associated with other, nonnutritional derangements that could be responsible for long-term programming.

AN EXPERIMENTAL APPROACH TO NUTRITIONAL PROGRAMMING IN HUMANS

The epidemiological data discussed earlier raise two critical issues: first, although such studies generate hypotheses, they do not prove nutritional cause; and second, it is speculative to use these findings to underpin public health or clinical interventions in human nutrition.

Clearly, public health and clinical policy would be most soundly based on experimental rather than on epidemiological studies. Therefore 17 years ago I elected to devote major attention of my research group to developing the use of the infant nutrition intervention experiments in a formal way, to explore the concept of nutritional programming in humans and to underpin nutritional practice. The elements of this program, which collectively were novel at that time, included the following in each clinical trial:

1. Formal randomized nutritional intervention in infancy with planned long-term follow-up.
2. Carefully calculated size to detect differences between groups for a key targeted health or developmental outcome ("efficacy") with adequate power; and trials large enough to detect differences in adverse outcome ("safety") between groups.
3. Trials conducted in a similar manner to a pharmaceutical intervention trial employing what are now termed *good clinical practice guidelines.*
4. Cohort details documented to facilitate long-term (or lifetime) follow-up.

There are several windows in which infant nutritional intervention experiments are feasible and ethical.

1. *Preterm* infants can be randomized to diet to test the importance of the perinatal period as a window for nutritional programming.
2. Formula-fed full-term infants could be randomly assigned to formulas of different nutrient content to test ways in which early infancy might be critical for nutrition. These interventions can also be targeted to infants growth-retarded at birth, who have been shown epidemiologically to be at long-term risk for growth and neurodevelopmental deficits and for ischemic heart disease and its antecedents. A key question is whether early nutritional intervention could reprogram these infants following poor intrauterine growth and ameliorate risk.
3. Infants can be randomly assigned to different weaning foods to test whether nutritional sensitivity extends into infancy or beyond.

In around 20 major outcome studies, testing a range of key hypotheses, we have more than 5,000 infants and children in all these categories, in various stages from the intervention period to long-term follow-up, the oldest subjects followed prospectively now to 16 years.

TRIALS ON THE LOW-BIRTHWEIGHT, PRETERM INFANT

Of our trials, the most long-standing (now running for 16 years) has been a five-center study on 926 infants born preterm (mean gestation of 31 weeks) (18). Such infants were considered to be valuable for nutritional programming studies for the following reasons:

1. Since it was unknown (16 years ago) which were the optimal diets for this population, it was ethical to randomly assign available diets during hospital study to address the question as to which diet was associated with a better long-term outcomes.
2. Since preterm infants are a "captive" population, intensive nutritional, physiological, biochemical, and clinical monitoring was feasible during the intervention period.
3. It might be predicted that preterm infants, born during a stage of rapid development, would be particularly sensitive to programming stimuli.

Illustrative results from this work, comprising two parallel nutritional intervention studies, are presented in this chapter. The study design has been presented elsewhere (18), and only brief details are given here. The 926 infants weighing less than 1850 g at birth represented an unselected cohort from the five centers recruited between 1982 and 1985. No parent refused consent.

In study 1 (26), conducted in three centers that had a human milk bank, subjects were randomly allocated to banked donated breast milk (from unrelated donors) or a special nutrient-enriched preterm infant formula, designed by us to meet the nutrient needs of the fast-growing immature preterm infant. Donor human milk was unsupplemented, as frequently given in the early 1980s. When mothers failed to provide their own breast milk, the infants received donor milk or preterm formula as sole diets ($n = 159$). When mothers did provide their expressed milk, donor milk and preterm formula were randomly assigned a supplement to mother's milk ($n = 343$) in volumes according to the mothers' success in providing their own milk (mean, close to 50% of intake).

In study 2 (27), the random allocation was to standard full-term formula (suitable for full-term infants, used often in the 1980s) or preterm formula, with 160 in the sole diet group and 264 in the supplement to mother's milk group. The protein (g/100 ml), energy (kcal/100 ml), and calcium (mg/100 ml) contents of the four diets were, respectively, as follows: *preterm formula*—2.0, 80, and 70; *standard formula*—1.5, 68, and 35; *banked breast milk*—1.3, <50, and 30; and *mothers' expressed milk*—1.5, 62, and 30. (Values for the latter are mean values for 6,000 pooled 24-hour samples.) The breast milk was donated by breastfeeding mothers in the community who collected milk that dripped from the contralateral breast when feeding their own infants. Many of the infants required initial parenteral nutrition, and the median number of days to attain full enteral feeds was 7 days in study 1 and 9 days in study 2. The assigned diet was given (for a median of 4 weeks) until the baby attained a weight of 2,000 g or was discharged from the neonatal unit, whichever was the sooner. After discharge from the neonatal unit, mothers fed their babies as they and their advisors chose. Follow-up staff were blind to the original dietary assignment.

Neurodevelopment

At long-term follow-up of this cohort, the principal targeted outcome was neurodevelopment. Within each study, calculated sample size was for one-third of a standard deviation (5 quotient points) for trials with randomized diet as sole diet (trial A) or breast milk supplement (trial B) combined, and half a standard deviation (8 quotient points) for the sole diet trial (trial A) alone. The subjects were seen at 18 months corrected age and at 7.5 years. Data from the 18-month follow-up only are published so far.

In study 2, babies in trial A fed standard formula had a 6-point lower mental development index and a 15-point lower psychomotor score ($p < 0.001$); and in trials A + B ($n = 310$; a balanced addition, preserving randomization), a 6-point lower psychomotor score ($p < 0.01$), despite the blunting effect of mother's milk usage (trial B) in both randomized groups. The effect size was substantially greater in males (27). Recently, we confirmed that the significant developmental disadvantage, seen principally in male preterm babies fed a standard term formula (which we now recognize does not meet the nutrient needs of this group), was also seen at 7.5 years, when IQ (notably, verbal IQ) was significantly depressed (unpublished).

Thus we showed that a brief period of dietary manipulation in the neonatal period (4 weeks on average), using a nutrient-enriched rather than a standard formula, significantly influenced neurodevelopment at 18 months. Our further follow-up at 7.5 years (unpublished), when IQ is more predictive of that in adults, indicates that the disadvantage for the standard-formula-fed group could therefore represent a permanent effect. These data provide some of the only evidence from a large long-term randomized trial that early diet, during a "critical" or vulnerable period, could "program" neurodevelopment.

Surprisingly, in study 1, despite the poor nutrient content of donor breast milk, the outcome of those individuals fed on it in the neonatal period was no worse from that seen with preterm formula. We have suggested (18) this may be due to ameliorating, beneficial factors in donor milk. Indeed, infants fed solely on donor milk (in study 1) had a substantial psychomotor advantage over those fed solely on standard formula (study 2); in this (nonrandomized) comparison, both diets were similarly low in nutrient content, yet the donor-milk-fed group had a 9-point advantage in psychomotor scores.

Health Outcomes: Bone Mineralization

These preterm studies have provided an important opportunity to test whether a period of nutritional intervention during early life could affect the propensity to disease in later life. This is currently being investigated, particularly with respect to two key endpoints: cardiovascular disease (and its markers) and bone health. Data on the latter are discussed briefly here.

Adult degenerative bone disease (osteoporosis), a major public health problem in the West, has been linked to peak bone mass attained in young adult life (28). Following attainment of peak bone mass, bone mineral content falls and may descend below the safety level for clinical disease. Most interventions to reduce the incidence of clinical disease have been in middle life. Little attention has been given until recently to the possibility that early factors could influence bone mineralization in childhood and hence peak bone mass. We have tested the hypothesis that diet in the neonatal period in preterm infants could have a long-term impact on bone mineral content and bone metabolism, of potential relevance to the propensity to bone disease in adulthood. At a 5-year follow-up we found that bone mineral content (adjusted appropriately for body size) was higher in children previously assigned randomly to human milk than in those assigned to formula (29). These data raised the possibility that either factors in human milk or, alternatively, a diet suboptimal for preterm infants (e.g., in calcium content), as human milk is, could program greater bone mineralization later in life. Our unpublished data (MF Fewtrell *et al.*) at 9- to 12-year follow-up now indicate that children fed suboptimally in the neonatal period for just 1 month on average have an increase in plasma osteocalcin (a marker for bone formation) by early adolescence. Clearly, this example of nutritional programming, determined in a strictly experimental context in humans, now needs further investigation in view of its potential implications for long-term bone health.

Programming Mechanisms

Nutritional programming has been convincingly demonstrated in animals, including primates, and there is now compelling evidence from experimental studies that this process operates in humans. More recently, attention has turned to the mechanism (3). Some programming events might have immediate effects on structural development (e.g., on dendritic arborization or glial cell growth in the brain), with long-term consequences. However, nutritional programming here might not simply reflect failure to fuel a growth process. Nutrients might be critical signals acting directly or through coupling mechanisms on "receptors" in sensitive tissues. With regard to the programming or "setting" of later function (e.g., of a key metabolic pathway), the question is how the "memory" of an early event is "stored" throughout life despite continuous cellular replication and replacement. Proposed mechanisms include adaptive effects on gene expression transmitted to the progeny of the originally programmed cells. Alternatively, the early nutritional milieu may stimulate adaptive clonal selection or differential cell proliferation so that the quantity or proportion of cell populations in a tissue is permanently affected. Indeed, in collaboration with Hales, we have obtained indirect evidence of the latter mechanism in relation to the programming of metabolically significant cell populations in the liver (14). The exploration of such fundamental processes is critical to an understanding of the biology of early nutrition.

Negative Findings

Although the foregoing examples emphasize the sensitivity of preterm infants to their early nutritional environment, not all interventions have had the hypothesized longer-term effects. We have been unable to show that early nutrition in preterm infants during the neonatal period influences long-term growth (unpublished) or blood pressure (20); and human milk fortification did not significantly promote neurodevelopment (30), though a small effect cannot be excluded and a larger study is needed.

Safety

In pharmaceutical trials of a new agent, safety is generally as important as efficacy. Although this chapter principally considers key aspects of nutritional "efficacy" (i.e., long-term benefit), our own and others' data show that safety is a surprisingly important and often neglected aspect of nutrition. Nutritional management choices may have a major influence on potentially life-threatening disease processes, including necrotizing enterocolitis and systemic sepsis (30,31; unpublished observations). For this reason regulatory bodies are now paying particular attention to safety testing of novel nutritional interventions. Interestingly, the addition of long-chain polyunsaturated fatty acids (LCPUFA) to infant formula (32) represents a watershed in the history of infant nutrition research in this respect. The standards of safety and efficacy testing of LCPUFA being required by regulatory and government bodies in the United States, Canada, and the United Kingdom are unprecedented and herald a new era in which infant nutritional research is being viewed in a pharmaceutical context. As we look back, we see that numerous new advances in infant nutrition (including the addition of LCPUFA to European low-birthweight formulas) were introduced without adequate human safety (or efficacy) trials—a situation that would have been unacceptable in the introduction of a new drug.

IMPLICATIONS

In clinical terms it is increasingly clear that nutritional management of very low-birthweight infants should be based on stage III efficacy and safety trials. Data from such trials should take precedence over stage I and II data of a more theoretical nature. Since the nutritional scientific literature is dominated by stage II data, clinicians must be selective in citing studies that influence their practice. For instance, since stage III data show that relatively brief suboptimal nutrition at a critical stage of rapid early brain development has potentially lifelong consequences for neurocognitive function, this must be weighed against stage II data on theoretically adverse metabolic consequences of meeting the very low-birthweight infants' needs in the early weeks. For instance, since meta-analyses of randomized trials indicate that transpyloric feeding may induce a higher death rate than intragastric feeding (33), this must take precedence over any more theoretical perceived benefit for the transpyloric tube feeding.

Research implications of the new approach to early nutrition are many. Two important issues are raised in this chapter. First, future clinical trials of early nutrition must be large enough to incorporate targeted clinical safety testing if this is indicated. Second, if nutrition influences long-term outcome, then it is critical that "intermediate" endpoints in clinical trials are identified to avoid the near impossibility of lifelong follow-up. Our own center is committed to exploring and using such endpoints. Cognitive function is a good example of an outcome that can be predictive of adult outcome when measured in mid-childhood. We are currently investigating whether magnetic resonance imaging and spectroscopy of the brain, when combined with functional neuropsychological testing in children, will permit noninvasive exploration of more detailed permanent effects of nutrition on the brain. With regard to health outcomes, it is important to identify tools that can detect the early origins of adult disease. Currently, we are using noninvasive vascular ultrasound to examine endothelial dysfunction dynamically as a probable measure of early atherosclerosis, with promising early results showing that growth retardation *in utero* may be associated with impaired endothelial function at age 9 to 10 years (34) and adulthood (CPM

Leeson *et al.*, unpublished). Endothelial function is currently being measured by us in a large follow-up study of preterm infants randomized to their early diet, to test the hypotheses that early suboptimal nutrition and prematurity itself adversely influences this early evidence of atherosclerotic disease.

In more general terms, the studies performed to date on preterm infants form an important part of the current experimental evidence for nutritional programming in humans, an area of major biological significance with important implications for practice.

REFERENCES

1. Simon JF. Mother's milk and its chemical and physical properties. Dissertation (in Latin), Berlin, 1838.
2. Lucas A. Does diet in preterm infants influence clinical outcome? *Biol Neonate* 1987;52:141–146.
3. Lucas A. Programming by early nutrition in man. In: *The childhood environment and adult disease.* CIBA Foundation Symposium 156. Chichester: John Wiley; 1991:38–55.
4. Lucas A. Role of nutritional programming in determining adult morbidity. *Arch Dis Child* 1994;71:288–290.
5. Spalding DA. Instinct with original observations on young animals. *Macmillan's Magazine* 1873; 27: 282–93; reprinted *Br J Anim Behav* 1954;2:2–11.
6. Angelbeck JH, DuBrul EF. The effect of neonatal testosterone on specific male and female patterns of phosphorylated cytosolic proteins in the rat preoptic-hypothalamus, cortex and amygdala. *Brain Res* 1983;264:277–283.
7. McCance RA. Food growth and time. *Lancet* 1962;ii: 271–272.
8. Dobbing J, Sands J. Vulnerability of developing brain. IX. The effect of nutritional growth retardation on the timing of the brain growth-spurt. *Biol Neonate* 1971;19:363–378.
9. Smart J. Undernutrition, learning and memory: review of experimental studies. In: Taylor TG, Jenkins NK, eds. *Proceedings of XII International Congress of Nutrition.* London: John Libbey; 1986:74–78.
10. Snoek A, Remacle C, Reusens B, Hoet JJ. Effect of a low protein diet during pregnancy on the fetal rat endocrine pancreas. *Biol Neonate* 1990;57:107–118.
11. Hahn P. Effect of litter size on plasma cholesterol and insulin and some liver and adipose tissue enzymes in adult rodents. *J Nutr* 1984;114:1231–1234.
12. Lewis DS, Bartrand HA, McMahan CA, McGill HC Jr, Carey KD, Masoro EJ. Preweaning food intake influences the adiposity of young adult baboons. *J Clin Invest* 1986;78:899–905.
13. Mott GE, Lewis DS, McGill HC. Programming of cholesterol metabolism by breast or formula feeding. In: Bock GR, Whelan J, eds. *The childhood environment and adult disease* (CIBA Foundation Symposium 156). Chichester: Wiley, 1991:56–76.
14. Desai M, Crowther NJ, Ozanne SE, Lucas A, Hales CN. Adult glucose and lipid metabolism may be programmed during fetal life. *Biochem Soc Trans* 1995;23:331–335.
15. Lucas A, Baker BA, Desai M, Hales CN. Nutrition in pregnant or lactating rats programs lipid metabolism in the offspring. *Br J Nutr* 1996;76:605–612.
16. Hales CN, Desai M, Ozanne SE, Crowther NJ. Fishing in the stream of diabetes; from measuring insulin to the control of fetal organogenesis. *Biochem Soc Trans* 1996;24:341–350.
17. Lucas A, Morley RM, Cole TJ, Lister G, Leeson-Payne C. Breast milk and subsequent intelligence quotient in children born preterm. *Lancet* 1993;339:261–264.
18. Lucas A, Morley RM, Cole TJ, Gore SM. A randomised multicentre study of human milk *vs.* formula and later development in preterm infants. *Arch Dis Child* 1994;70:F141–146.
19. Fomon ST, Rogers RR, Zeigler EE, Nelson SE, Thomas LN. Indices of fatness and cholesterol at age eight years in relation to feeding and growth in early infancy. *Pediatr Res* 1984;18:1233–1238.
20. Lucas A, Morley R, Hudson GJ, *et al.* Early sodium intake and later blood pressure in preterm infants. *Arch Dis Child* 1988;63:656–657.
21. Klingensmith GJ. Reduced risk of IDDM among breast-fed children. *Diabetes* 1988;37:1625–1632.
22. Davis MK, Savitz DA, Graubard BI. Infant feeding and childhood cancer. *Lancet* 1988;I:365–368.
23. Fall CHD, Barker DJP, Osmond C, Winter PD, Clark PMS, Hales CN. Relation of infant feeding to adult serum cholesterol concentration and death from ischaemic heart disease. In: Barker DJP, ed. *Fetal and infant origins of adult disease.* London: BMJ Publishing Group; 1992:275–288.

24. Barker DJP. Fetal nutrition and cardiovascular disease in adult life. *Lancet* 1993;341:938–941.
25. McCay CM, Maynard L, Sperling G, Barnes LL. Retarded growth, life span, ultimate body size, and age changes in the albino rat after feeding diets restricted in calories. *J Nutr* 1939;18:1–13.
26. Lucas A, Morley R, Cole TJ, *et al.* Early diet in preterm babies and development status at 18 months. *Lancet* 1990;335:1477–1481.
27. Bonjour JP, Theintz G, Law FT, Slosman D, Rizzoli R. Peak bone mass. *Osteoporosis Int* 1994;[suppl 1]:S7–13.
28. Bishop NJ, Dahlenburg SL, Fewtrell MF, Morley R, Lucas A. Early diet of preterm infants and bone mineralisation at age 5 years. *Acta Paediatr Scand* 1996;85:230–236.
29. Lucas A, Fewtrell M, Morley R, *et al.* Randomized outcome trial of human milk fortification and developmental outcome in preterm infants. *Am J Clin Nutr* 1996;64:142–152.
30. Lucas A, Cole TJ. Breast milk and neonatal necrotising enterocolitis. *Lancet* 1990;336:1519–1523.
31. Lucas A. Long-chain polyunsaturated fatty acids, infant feeding and cognitive development. In: Dobbing J, ed. *Developing brain and behaviour: the role of lipids in infant formula*. New York: Academic Press (Ross Pediatrics); 1997:1–39.
32. Steer P, Lucas A, Sinclair JC. Feeding the low birthweight infant. In: Sinclair JC, Bracken MB, eds. *Effective care of the newborn infant*. New York: Oxford University Press; 1992:94–160.
33. Leeson CPM, Whincup FH, Cook DG, *et al.* Flow mediated dilatation in 9 to 11 year old children: the influence of intrauterine and childhood factors. *Circulation* 1997;96:2233–2238.

DISCUSSION

Prof. Haschke: When comparing the two formulas, there were a lot of confounders. Would you like to comment?

Prof. Lucas: You may need to be more specific. This was certainly a randomized blinded study of two formulas, as far as we could engineer it. They were similar in their ingredients, differing only in the amounts of those ingredients. They had the same protein mix, but they differed in the amounts of protein; and they had the same fat blend, but they differed in the amounts of fat. The formulas were blinded to the investigators and were given code numbers, so the investigators or the nurses in the unit did not know which they were giving. Confounding factors may creep into any randomized trial. If you feed babies on diets which differ in nutrient content, then of course they will produce different growth rates, which then produce a different response in the attending staff. Babies who grew less well on the term formula tended to have been given slightly larger volumes than those fed on the preterm formula. However, the increase in volume was never enough to cancel out the difference in nutrient intake between the two groups. Perhaps you have some specific aspects of confounding in mind?

Prof. Haschke: You presented similar data last year, where you described three groups. One group was fed the term formula, one was fed the preterm formula, and a third was fed breast milk. As far as I remember, there was no difference between the preterm formula and the breast milk groups, whereas there was a large difference between the term formula, on the one hand, and the preterm formula and the breast milk groups, on the other. So I am confused that the data are now presented in a different way.

Prof. Lucas: We have two quite separate randomized trials, one comparing term formula with preterm formula, which is the one I presented, and another comparing banked breast milk with preterm formula, which I did not have time to present today. Both were strictly randomized trials. Thus we have two parallel independent clinical trials done in different centers, comparing two diets. However, because they have the same preterm formula in common, it has allowed us to cross-compare the two trials. The data I presented today are from a pure clinical trial conducted in two centers comparing two randomized diets.

Dr. Micheli: You opened an important window on the relation between structure and function by telling us that the size of the hippocampus could be related to memory. Do we have any means of measuring this at the bedside in extremely low-birth-weight infants?

Prof. Lucas: You are looking at the question the other way around from us. What we are interested in doing, since magnetic resonance imaging is extremely expensive and difficult, particularly in very low-birthweight babies, is to find psychometric tests that relate to particular parts of the brain, so that we can do psychometric studies that have significance for what is happening in the brain.

Some people have managed to do imaging studies in the neonatal period (e.g., Edward's group in England), but you really need to have committed machinery for that. But I would not want you to come away from this meeting thinking that I said that nutrition is the reason for the hippocampus being smaller in low-birthweight babies. That is a hypothesis, and we now need to test it prospectively. We are looking for parts of the brain where we can relate structure to function, and then we can look at the impact of nutrition on the functional outcome as a proxy for an effect on structure.

Prof. Nowak: In relation to your vascular studies, couldn't the difference in vascular function between normal and underweight babies have been related to differences in the size of the arteries you analyzed?

Prof. Lucas: You do of course have to adjust for vessel size, based on current weight. We have a number of ways of doing this; it's a very rapidly developing field. You can adjust for the area of the artery and you can apply various techniques that remove factors that you think might be confounders. Of course you can also adjust for current body size, as well as the size of the blood vessel. All I can say is that the findings I presented are robust in that none of the adjustments that we've made to take account of vessel size and body size have removed the relation between birthweight and endothelial function.

Dr. Atkinson: I want to ask you about your bone data, the osteocalcin. We know that osteocalcin fluctuates tremendously during puberty. Were the data you presented on the differences in osteocalcin corrected for pubertal status, which is, I think, rather variable among preterm infants?

Prof. Lucas: We do have detailed information on the pubertal status of these children, though not by direct examination, but by self-examination, which we feel is the most ethical approach here. From the most recent analyses, the results have stood up to adjustment for pubertal status. The actual raw data that I presented you were by randomized group, and since the groups were randomized, any confounding caused by puberty should have been balanced out. We have to take account of the possibility that one diet group put the children into earlier puberty than the other, but I can confirm that that was not so. However, I do agree with you that there is a problem in studying children as they go into adolescence.

Prof. Pohlandt: Your data on the incidence of necrotizing enterocolitis are often cited as evidence that human milk protects against necrotizing enterocolitis (NEC). But in your paper the incidence of NEC was only a secondary outcome criterion, among others. You are not able to do a confirmatory statistic, only an exploratory statistic. Your data only support the hypothesis that human milk is protective, but you always present the data as evidence. I would like you not to do that.

Prof. Lucas: I have always been quite circumspect about those data. First, it was not a randomized trial; the only randomized component of the trial that would have been suitable for this purpose was the comparison of banked breast milk *versus* preterm formula, but there were only 150 babies in that limb, which is not enough to show a difference. Having said that, however, there was a threefold difference in the incidence of NEC between those two groups. I would like to emphasize that safety aspects of diet were an important concept from the start of the study. Thus NEC was an important safety issue that we identified early in the trial planning; this is not a *post hoc* analysis. The importance of the data that we presented in *Lancet* was that they generated a hypothesis and confirmed previous findings of the protective effect of human milk. Since our publication—which I don't think would have stood alone—further data have been obtained; I presented the results of a national survey where we looked at every single case of NEC in Britain and showed that there is a relation between disease severity and the amount of human milk used. Thus even if we are not yet at the level of proof, the data are sufficiently suggestive for us to include in our advice to mothers.

Dr. Frank: Do you have any clues as to reason for the female advantage in some of your developmental studies?

Prof. Lucas: The first thing to say is that increased vulnerability of males is quite a general phenomenon. It is seen across many animal species. Nearly all the effects of early diet on neurodevelopment have been seen in male rather than female animals. Apart from neurodevelopment, there are other outcomes that are influenced selectively by gender. For instance, we published data recently in the rat showing that suboptimal nutrition programmed a change in triglycerides and cholesterol in the offspring when they reached adult life, and on close examination of the data we found that these effects only occurred in males, not in females. So we have to ask why, in evolutionary terms, should there be greater vulnerability in males than in females. One general biological argument could be that there is a greater evolutionary investment in females than in males, because of their importance for reproduction. It may be that we are not looking so much at the vulnerability of males as at the greater protection that has evolved in females to ensure their survival.

Dr. Chessex: Rather than a nutritional effect, I think there may be another explanation for gender protection and this relates to antioxidant function, which is different between the sexes. We have data showing that endothelial cells put in an environment in which the peroxide content is similar to that of parenteral nutrition solutions survive better if they are from females. And in cells from tracheal aspirates from term and preterm infants, there is also better survival of female cells. We have shown that the glutathione content of cells from girls is significantly higher than from boys, and that glutathione reductase activity is significantly greater in females than in males.

Prof. Lucas: You are looking at fundamental differences between males and females that could be related to the phenomena I was discussing; that is, a biological underlying protection favoring females. There is certainly a fundamental difference in their metabolism. As far as the nutritional effects are concerned, we are looking at randomized interventions here that produce a difference in outcome within the male group. That does not give you a mechanism. It simply says that if you randomly assign babies to diet A and diet B, there is a difference. You may well be identifying the reason that there are underlying differences, and these come to light when they interact with diet.

Dr. Walker: I was curious about your observations regarding breastfeeding *versus* formula feeding and the expression of allergy. As you know, there have been several prospective trials in the UK, the United States, and Europe suggesting that breast-feeding may delay the expression of allergy in allergy-prone infants but does not prevent it, because there are so many other factors in the environment that affect the allergic reaction. Do you think the difference in your results is because your studies dealt with preterm infants?

Prof. Lucas: One thing that *is* different about our observations is that this is the only randomized trial of human milk *versus* formula that I am aware of. One of the great problems with all breast milk *versus* formula comparisons is that they are non-randomized, because it is unethical to tell mothers to breastfeed their babies on a randomized basis. But in preterm infants, you have a unique circumstance in that it is possible to assign babies randomly to banked breast milk from unrelated donors or to formula. The nonrandomized nature of most of the comparative studies of breast milk and formula means that they are highly confounded by the large differences in demographic and social circumstances, indeed by the behavior of families as a whole, with respect to almost every aspect, including feeding practices, that might influence allergy. Thus it is very difficult to compare breast milk and formula cleanly in term infants. In the (albeit premature) babies in our study, the data are unconfounded by those social biological factors, and this represents a pure randomized comparison. However, it is also possible that what you said is true for this population as well, in the sense that we have taken a snapshot at a particular point in time, 18 months. It may well be that by 2 or 3 years of age the groups will have caught up with each other. That remains to be tested. But at 18 months there's a major difference between these randomized groups in a clean blinded study.

Prof. Koletzko: You implied that your observation of a lower prevalence of allergic manifestations in infants previously born preterm who were fed banked human milk gives us conclusive evidence that breastfeeding, at least in preterm infants, protects against allergic manifestations. I have the same concerns as Dr. Pohlandt about the *post hoc* analysis of various secondary outcomes of your studies. I also believe that feeding banked human milk may not necessarily be the same as feeding own mother's milk. The data from a large study reported by Saarinen and coworkers from Finland (1), who followed some 6,200 term infants prospectively from birth for 18 months, showed that infants who were supplemented with banked human milk during the first days after birth in hospital had a lower rate of cow's milk protein allergy than those who were fed their own mother's milk only. So the question arises as to whether factors in banked human milk, such the multitude of foreign proteins or a difference in anti-inflammatory or immunological mediators, could have different effects from unsupplemented own mother's breast milk.

Prof. Lucas: I want to emphasize that the data I presented were in babies with a positive family history of allergy. If you look at those with no family history of allergy, the effect is not shown. So we seem to have an interaction between genes and the environment.

The most serious issue you raise is the question of whether it is possible to look for multiple outcomes in one study. We had a limited number of main outcomes, and in our publications we always make it clear that our study is being used in this way. It would obviously be impossible and unethical to repeat such very large studies, so we must get the most we can out of this one. Clearly, you have to examine the data in terms of the significance of the results in relation to multiple outcomes, and you can apply your own Bonferroni procedures or whatever to the results obtained. In fact, in the case of allergy the differences between groups are really highly significant. Nevertheless, I would accept that any single randomized trial, whether you are looking at multiple outcomes or even a single outcome, simply generates a hypothesis for further testing. In the meantime, we have patients to manage and we have to base our management decisions on the best-quality data that we have at any time. I do agree that it is extremely important that further studies are done on the long-term immunological effects of diet in newborn infants, though I would emphasize again that there are no other data comparing human milk and formula in a randomized way. We must therefore regard these as potentially important data to build on in future randomized trials.

Dr. Sedaghatian: I thought there were many cells in human milk, lymphocytes and so on, that could cause an immunogenic response in babies given human milk supplements. Though you showed us a reduced allergic response at 18 months, other participants obviously feel that this may not be permanent. I think it would be wise to use mother's own milk and compare it with banked milk and premature formula in terms of the long-term outcome for allergy.

Prof. Lucas: Obviously, we can analyze the data in that way. We have got babies fed on banked breast milk, on mother's own milk, and on formula. It is quite possible to do that three-way analysis. The problem here is one of randomization. We can produce epidemiological data comparing mother's own milk with formula, but we can produce much more robust randomized data if we use banked breast milk, while recognizing the difference. I want to emphasize that in our original study both groups received their own mothers' milk. They were randomly assigned to formula as a sole diet or as a supplement to mothers' milk, or banked breast milk as a sole diet or supplement to mothers' milk. So own mother's milk is common to both groups, and what you are looking at is the difference relating to the component of the diet that was either formula or human milk. You are looking at the difference between having cow's milk protein in the diet and not having it.

Dr. Rigo: There are studies suggesting that weight gain composition is different between males and females (2). We have data showing that the increase in lean body mass in low-birthweight infants is greater in boys than in girls but that fat mass deposition is greater in girls. Do you think this suggests that the nutrient requirements of boys and girls are different during the neonatal period?

Prof. Lucas: Yes, that is possible. Ruth Morley is quite specifically looking at body composition in relation to neurodevelopment in males and females in the postdischarge period. This is so close to her topic, perhaps she would like to answer.

Dr. Morley: The data on fatness in female infants at birth are intriguing. I don't believe it is yet possible to conclude that the female infant has more fat, though I would be very interested to know whether female infants lay down fat earlier than male infants during gestation. If so, that may be one of the factors that protects female infants, because they may have greater nutrient reserves.

Prof. Lucas: That is interesting and important. One of the great problems is the difficulty in measuring body fatness in very young babies. We published two studies showing that the two ways in which you would be most likely to measure body fatness—that is, skinfold thickness and body mass index—do not correlate at all well with the gold standard measurement, deuterium dilution, during at least the first 6 months of life in healthy infants. To address the question you are posing, we need to be using quite sophisticated measures of body composition, probably isotope dilution.

Dr. Sedagathian: If I understood you correctly, you said that the preterm baby who is fed on breast milk has better bone mineralization in later childhood. Does this apply to babies who are partially fed on breast milk? We know that by 1 month, breast milk is insufficient for preterm infants, and we usually add supplements.

Prof. Lucas: Don't forget that these studies were done in the early 1980s, when human milk fortifiers were not in routine use. So you are looking at unfortified human milk during the period of randomization, uncontaminated by fortification.

I do want to emphasize another point. There were two hypotheses in our bone studies: one is that human milk has some factors in it that are important for the long-term programming of bone; the other is that it is suboptimal nutrition that has a long-term programming effect. We have better evidence in support of the latter. For example, we found a higher osteocalcin level in the term formula fed group than in the preterm formula fed group. One possible explanation for this is that if you feed babies on a nutrient-poor diet, perhaps a diet that is poor in calcium and phosphorus in early life, you may program them to be more retentive of calcium and phosphorus in later life, with an increase in bone formation. We have to consider programming as an adaptive, evolving event; the most useful reason one can think of, arguing teleologically, for having nutritional programming is that it allows you to adjust your metabolism to the nutritional environment in which you find yourself in early life. So if you are born into a nutrient-poor environment, you could argue that it would be useful to program yourself to be conservative with nutrients, and if you are born into a nutrient-rich environment, it would be useful to program yourself to be more wasteful with nutrients. So paradoxically, achieving good nutrition early on—in that particular respect—might not necessarily have the best long-term outcome.

REFERENCES

1. Saarinen K, Juntunen Backman K, Järvenplä AL, *et al.* Early feeding of cow's milk formula: a risk for cow's milk allergy. *J Pediatr Gastroenterol Nutr* 1997;24:461 (abst.).
2. Cooke RJ, Griffin IJ, McCoomick K, *et al.* Feeding preterm infants after hospital discharge: effect of dietary manipulation on nutrient intake and growth. *Pediatr Res* 1998;43:355–360.

Nutrition of the Very Low Birthweight Infant, edited by
Ekhard E. Ziegler, Alan Lucas, Guido E. Moro.
Nestlé Nutrition Workshop Series, Paediatric Programme, Vol. 43,
Nestec Ltd., Vevey/Lippincott Williams & Wilkins
Philadelphia, Pennsylvania © 1999.

Early Growth and Later Development

Ruth Morley

Menzies Centre for Population Health Research, Hobart Tasmania, Australia; and Clinical Epidemiology and Biostatistics Unit, University Department of Paediatrics, Royal Children's Hospital, Melbourne, Australia. Formerly MRC Childhood Nutrition Research Centre, Institute of Child Health, London, WC1N 1EH, United Kingdom.

There has been long-standing interest in whether a stimulus at a sensitive or critical period in development could have a long-lasting or permanent "programming" influence on later structure or function. For some types of cell (e.g., brain and muscle), differentiation and replication, or determination of cell function, occur only during limited critical periods of early development (1). Adverse factors during such a period, particularly those leading to growth failure, may therefore have a detrimental effect on an individual throughout life.

There has been recent epidemiological evidence that nutrition or growth in early life may influence long-term outcome in terms of later body size (2,3) and risk of adult disease (4–7). It is of concern to neonatologists that suboptimal nutrition during early life could have adverse long-term consequences for growth, health, or neurodevelopment in infants born preterm. Our randomized nutritional intervention trials have provided evidence that nutrition in the neonatal period affects growth (8,9). Neonatal steady-state weight gain (weight gain in g/kg·d after regaining birthweight) was significantly improved by feeding a nutrient-fortified preterm formula rather than either donor breast milk or a standard term formula. More important, our studies have also provided evidence that nutrition in the neonatal period can influence later performance, with improved developmental outcome at 9 and 18 months post term (9–12). Unpublished data suggest that this effect persists until the age of 7.5 to 8 years, particularly in respect to verbal IQ in boys.

Martyn *et al.* found no relation between fetal growth (birthweight) and adult cognitive performance among a population born between 1920 and 1943, the vast majority of whom would have been born at term (13). The brain is growing fastest around the time of full term, and it continues to grow beyond the end of the first year of life (14). Skuse *et al.* conducted a large study in term infants to investigate whether postnatal growth influences Bayley mental and motor scores at 15 months (15). They calculated a combined score and found no association between birthweight or weight at 15 months and Bayley combined score. However, they did find that early growth faltering was important. From regression models they found that a fall of 2 SD in weight between birth and 6 months was associated with a 10-point deficit in developmental score, whereas the same degree of growth faltering between 4 and 10 months was associated with a 3-point deficit. Whether these early developmental deficits result in a long-term cognitive disadvantage has not been investigated.

The possibility that early growth performance *per se* is important for later cognitive performance has not been investigated in preterm infants. We explored these issues in a large group of children born preterm who were enrolled in parallel randomized nutritional intervention trials in the United Kingdom from 1982 to 1984 and followed up through childhood (10). We tested the hypothesis that weight gain in the neonatal period or in the first 9 months post term influences outcome at 7.5 to 8 years.

Milks routinely fed to preterm infants at that time differed substantially in nutrient content, ranging from donor breast milk (from unrelated breastfeeding mothers in the community) or a standard term formula to a nutrient-enriched preterm formula designed to meet the special nutrient needs of babies born preterm, a time of rapid growth. It was both practical and ethical to undertake a randomized trial; the results were needed for informed management decisions. Because of the large differences in nutrient content between the allocated milks, we were able to investigate, in randomized prospective intervention trials, whether early nutrition influenced later development and cognitive performance (9,11,12).

Altogether, 926 infants born weighing under 1850 g in five centers in the United Kingdom in 1982 to 1984 were randomly allocated their early enteral diet. The randomization was as shown in Fig. 1. Study 1 compared banked donor milk with the preterm formula fed either as sole diets or as a supplement to the mother's expressed breast milk, if she could not provide enough milk to meet her infant's needs. Study 2 compared a standard term formula with the preterm formula, again as sole diets or as a supplement to mother's milk. The assigned diets were fed, on average, for only the first 4 weeks of life. After this period the infants were fed as their parents and medical advisers chose.

Weight was measured daily and weight gain in the neonatal period after regaining birthweight was calculated in g/kg·d. Within the population neonatal growth performance varied greatly, from 4.2 to 29.9 g/kg·d (mean 14.7, SD 3.8). Extensive social, demographic, and obstetric data were collected by trained research nurses, together with detailed prospective neonatal data, according to predefined criteria. Social class was coded into six categories (United Kingdom Registrar General's classification) and mother's educational attainments were coded according to categories published previously (16).

Surviving children in study 1 were weighed and measured at 9 months post term, 18 months post term, and 7.5 to 8 years of age. Those in study 2 were weighed and measured at 18 months post term and at 7.5 to 8 years of age, but not at 9 months post term (see Fig. 1). Of the 834 surviving subjects, 799 were still resident in the United Kingdom. Altogether 782 (98%) were assessed at 7.5 to 8 years of age using the Wechsler intelligence scale for children (revised Anglicized version: WISC-R UK). To keep testing time to a reasonable length given that we also measured various

STUDY 1.
Comparing banked donor milk with preterm formula.

Mother was asked whether she wished to provide her own expressed breast milk for her baby

↓	↓
No	Yes
↓	↓
Randomise to:	Randomise to:
Banked donor milk *vs.* Preterm formula	Banked donor milk *vs.* Preterm formula
as sole diets	*as supplements to mother's milk*
n = 159	n = 343

Follow up: 9 months post term
18 months post term
7.5 to 8 years

STUDY 2.
Comparing term with preterm formula.

Mother was asked whether she wished to provide her own expressed breast milk for her baby

↓	↓
No	Yes
↓	↓
Randomise to:	Randomise to:
Term formula *vs.* Preterm formula	Term formula *vs.* Preterm formula
as sole diets	*as supplements to mother's milk*
n = 160	n = 264

Follow up: 18 months post term
7.5 to 8 years

FIG. 1. The study design.

anthropometric and health outcomes, we used an abbreviated version of the WISC-R with five subtests: similarities, arithmetic, and vocabulary (verbal scale), block design and object assembly (performance scale). Overall WISC-R intelligence quotient (IQ) assessed from these five subscales has a correlation coefficient with the full WISC-R IQ of over 0.96 (17). We also measured word reading and arithmetic performance using the word-reading and basic number skills subscales of the British Ability Scales.

Many test items are more difficult for children with impaired manipulative skills; those with hearing impairment will have some difficulty with verbal tasks and understanding instructions, and blind children are unable to undertake most of the tasks. In these cases, test performance will be an unreliable measure of cognitive status. We therefore excluded data from children who had evidence of neuromotor or neurosensory impairment from most of the analyses reported here. We also excluded children who had insufficient data in the neonatal period to calculate steady-state weight gain reliably.

TABLE 1. *Characteristics of infants in four categories of neonatal weight gain*

	Categories of neonatal weight gain (g/kg·d)			
	<12.32	12.32 to < 14.68	14.68 to < 17.12	17.12
Mean gestation (SD) in weeks	31.4 (2.8)	31.4 (2.8)	31.1 (2.7)	31.5 (2.7)
Mean birthweight (SD) in grams	1426 (293)	1406 (306)	1381 (297)	1416 (293)
Mean (SD) birthweight ratio[a]	0.83 (0.18)	0.82 (0.18)	0.83 (0.20)	0.82 (0.20)
% male	48%	43%	49%	53%
Median (25th, 75th percentiles) days on > 30% oxygen	5 (1, 11)	3 (0, 9)	2 (0, 8)	2 (0, 6)[b]
Median (25th, 75th percentiles) total IV fluids in ml	783 (267, 2314)	900 (382, 1538)	482 (130, 1141)	474[c] (199, 810)
% on preterm formula (vs. donor milk or standard term formula)	34%	38%	53%	79%[d]

[a] Birthweight ratio is a measure of size for gestation, calculated as birthweight/mean birthweight for sex and gestation.
[b] p 0.01 by Kruskal-Wallis one-way ANOVA.
[c] $p < 0.0003$ by Kruskal-Wallis one-way ANOVA.
[d] $p < 0.00001$ by χ^2 analysis.

FACTORS ASSOCIATED WITH WEIGHT GAIN IN THE NEONATAL PERIOD

Altogether, 598 surviving children fulfilled the criteria for inclusion in these analyses and were assessed at 7.5 to 8 years. Of these, 300 were in study 1 and 298 in study 2. In Table 1, neonatal weight gain is categorized into four equal groups. Children with the lowest weight gain were less likely to have been fed preterm formula, had more intravenous fluids, and had more prolonged respiratory illness. Data are shown for days in more than 30% oxygen, but similar associations were seen with days of mechanical ventilation.

In a regression model, those factors significantly associated independently with weight gain in the neonatal period were sex of the infant (higher weight gain in boys), whether the infant was fed preterm formula, days in more than 30% oxygen, and birthweight. Preterm formula feeding improved weight gain, whereas weight gain fell with increasing days in more than 30% oxygen and with higher birthweight.

In separate analyses including only data from children whose mothers chose to provide breast milk, neonatal weight gain fell as the proportion of intake provided by maternal milk increased. From the regression coefficient, there was a 0.1 g/kg·d decrease in weight gain as the proportion of intake as mother's milk increased by 10%.

NEONATAL WEIGHT GAIN AND LATER WEIGHT

Neonatal weight gain was positively associated with weight at 9 months post term, both before and after adjusting for factors associated with neonatal weight gain in a regression model ($p = 0.009$ after adjustment).

FACTORS ASSOCIATED WITH PERFORMANCE SCORES AT 7.5 TO 8 YEARS

We have shown previously that many social and demographic factors are related to cognitive performance (18). All the scores were higher in children whose mothers had chosen to provide breast milk (16,18) or who were of higher social class or better educational attainment, and they were lower as a function of increasing birth order. Performance IQ was 3 points higher in boys ($p = 0.008$), and both reading and arithmetic scores were significantly higher in girls (by 3.4 and 1.8 points, $p < 0.001$ and < 0.03, respectively).

In separate univariate analyses, the performance measures at 7.5 to 8 years were significantly associated with some of the factors influencing neonatal weight gain. Overall, verbal, and performance IQ increased with birthweight ($p = 0.008$, 0.02, and 0.007, respectively) and decreased with the number of days in more than 30% oxygen ($p < 0.001$ in all cases). Both reading and arithmetic scores were significantly lower with increasing number of days in more than 30% oxygen ($p < 0.01$ and < 0.001, respectively).

NEONATAL WEIGHT GAIN AND PERFORMANCE SCORES AT 7.5 TO 8 YEARS

There was no significant influence of neonatal weight gain on whether the child had neuromotor impairment (Table 2). Among unimpaired children, overall and verbal

TABLE 2. *Neonatal weight gain and performance scores at 7.5 to 8 years. The proportion of children with neuromotor impairment in each neonatal weight gain category is shown. Otherwise, data are for children without neuromotor or neurosensory impairment*

	Categories of neonatal weight gain (g/kg·d)			
	<12.32	12.32 to < 14.68	14.68 to < 17.12	17.12
% with neuromotor impairment	7.5%	6.5%	5.6%	6.9%
Mean overall IQ (SD) at 7.5 to 8 years	96.5 (16.3)	99.7 (15.6)	101.3 (15.3)	101.7 (12.7)[a]
Mean verbal IQ (SD) 7.5 to 8 years	94.1 (18.1)	99.4 (17.8)	100.3 (18.5)	100.5 (14.8)[b]
Mean performance IQ (SD) at 7.5 to 8 years	103.0 (17.2)	103.3 (16.6)	104.7 (14.3)	107.0 (13.1)
Mean reading score (SD) 7.5 to 8 years	45.8 (11.1)	48.6 (12.3)	48.7 (13.2)	46.3 (11.8)
Mean arithmetic score (SD) at 7.5 to 8 years	44.4 (11.0)	45.8 (10.1)	46.8 (12.3)	46.1 (8.7)

[a] p 0.01 by ANOVA.
[b] p 0.003 by ANOVA.

TABLE 3. *Outcome measures at 7.5 to 8 years: are they significantly positively related to neonatal weight gain? (Findings from regression models)*

	All subjects	Boys	Girls
Overall IQ	—	—	—
Verbal IQ	—	—	—
Performance IQ	—	—	—
Reading score	—	—	—
Arithmetic score	—	—	—
Overall IQ ≥ 85	—	—	—
Verbal IQ ≥ 85	✓	✓	—
Performance IQ ≥ 85	—	—	—
Reading score ≥ 38	—	—	—
Arithmetic score ≥ 38	—	—	—

✓ Denotes a significant association.

IQ at 7.5 to 8 years rose significantly with increasing neonatal weight gain. There was no significant influence of neonatal weight gain on reading or arithmetic scores from the British Ability Scales.

As described earlier, there is a considerable degree of interrelationship between neonatal, social, and demographic measures with respect to their influence on later performance. To test whether weight gain in the neonatal period independently influences IQ, reading, and arithmetic scores we therefore used regression models, adjusting for other potentially influential factors. Independent factors in the initial models were birthweight, gestation, days in more than 30% oxygen, volume of intravenous fluids in the neonatal period, whether the infant was fed preterm formula (as sole diet or supplement), whether the mother chose to provide her breast milk, sex of the infant, social class, mother's educational attainments, and birth order of the child. Factors not independently related to the outcome measure ($p < 0.2$) were removed from the final models. All analyses were performed using data from both sexes, then in boys and girls separately.

In addition to investigating performance scores as continuous variables in linear regression models, we considered it important to look for predictors of good *versus* "suboptimal" outcome, the latter defined in this study as IQ scores below 85 and scores on the reading and arithmetic scales below 38. "Suboptimal" scores were more than 1 SD below the population mean of the test standardization sample, a definition that has been used by some educationalists for mild educational impairment. Analyses on these categorized variables ("good" *versus* "suboptimal" performance) were undertaken using logistic regression models.

The results of these regression analyses (excluding data from children with neuromotor or neurosensory impairment) are summarized in Table 3. The only significant finding was that there was an association between better neonatal weight gain and verbal IQ scores of 85 or higher. This was, however, largely seen in boys, not girls. In boys, the odds of a score of 85 or more were increased by 0.9 for each 1 g/kg·d increase in neonatal weight gain.

We considered the possibility that the association between neonatal weight gain and later performance in males was because of causal associations between receiving preterm formula and both better neonatal growth and better developmental outcome. Since weight gain and randomized diet are closely related, inclusion of both factors in the model is not an ideal way to decide which is the major causal factor. However, we found that after inclusion of neonatal weight gain in the model there was no significant advantage from being fed preterm formula.

In separate regression models including all subjects, there was no association between neonatal weight gain and neuromotor impairment.

POSTNEONATAL GROWTH AND LATER COGNITIVE PERFORMANCE

Regression models similar to those given earlier were constructed to include both neonatal weight gain and weight at 9 months post term, with performance scores as dependent variables. Results are summarized in Table 4. It should be noted that because only children in study 1 were seen at 9 months, these analyses are restricted to unimpaired children in that study and did not involve the whole unimpaired population as in Table 3. In the combined group of boys and girls, overall, verbal, and performance IQ increased with weight at 9 months post term. Regression coefficients and p values are shown in Table 4. In boys there was a significant positive association between weight at 9 months and overall, verbal, and performance IQ scores, as well as reading score. No influence was seen in girls. Boys were also significantly more likely to have overall or verbal IQ and reading and arithmetic scores over 85 as weight at 9 months increased (Table 4).

In further analyses we investigated whether being fatter at 9 months conferred a later cognitive advantage. Body mass index was calculated as weight/length^2 (kg/m^2). In univariate analyses there was a significant increase in all the measures, apart from

TABLE 4. *Outcome measures at 7.5 to 8 years: are they significantly positively related to weight at 9 months postterm? (Findings from regression models.)*

	All subjects	Boys	Girls
Overall IQ	+2.3 (0.02)	+3.2 (0.001)	—
Verbal IQ	+2.4 (0.002)	+3.4 (0.003)	—
Performance IQ	+2.3 (0.005)	+2.8 (0.01)	—
Reading score	—	+2.3 (0.01)	—
Arithmetic score	—	—	—
Overall IQ $\geq$ 85	—	✓	—
Verbal IQ $\geq$ 85	—	✓	—
Performance IQ $\geq$ 85	—	—	—
Reading score $\geq$ 85	—	✓	—
Arithmetic score $\geq$ 85	—	✓	—

[a] Values shown (in upper portion of table) are regression coefficient (p value) The regression coefficient indicates the influence of 1 kg increase in weight at 9 months on each outcome measure.

[b] ✓ Denotes a significant association.

Data are from study 1 only.

TABLE 5. *Outcome measures at 7.5 to 8 years: are they significantly positively related to body mass index (weight/height^2) at 9 months postterm? (Findings from regression models.)*

	All subjects	Boys	Girls
Overall IQ	+1.3 (0.01)	—	—
Verbal IQ	+1.2 (0.04)	—	—
Performance IQ	—	—	—
Reading score	+1.1 (0.009)	—	—
Arithmetic score	—	—	+1.6 (0.02)
Overall IQ ≥ 85	—	—	—
Verbal IQ ≥ 85	—	—	—
Performance IQ ≥ 85	—	—	—
Reading score ≥ 85	✓	✓	✓
Arithmetic score ≥ 85	✓	—	—

[a] Values shown (in upper portion of table) are regression coefficient (*p* value). The regression coefficient indicates the influence of 1 unit increase in body mass index at 9 months on each outcome measure.
[b] ✓ Denotes a significant association.
Data are from study 1 only.

the word-reading score, with increasing body mass index. For example, overall IQ was 96.5 (SD 14.6) in the lowest quarter for body mass index at 9 months, rising linearly to 102.4 (SD 14.5) in the highest quarter (*p* = 0.035 by analysis of variance).

In linear regression models where we applied the adjustments described earlier and included neonatal weight gain, increasing body mass index was associated with significantly higher overall and verbal IQ scores and higher reading scores in boys and girls combined (Table 5). In logistic models a higher body mass index was associated with significantly reduced odds of a reading score below 38 in males and females separately as well as combined, and reduced odds of a low arithmetic score in both sexes combined.

We also considered the possibility that head circumference gain in the neonatal period or head circumference at 9 months may be more influential than weight gain or weight in respect of later performance. This proved not to be the case. The associations were complex. Neonatal head circumference gain was negatively associated with later performance: the greater the head circumference gain, the lower were the later scores. With neonatal head circumference gain and weight and head circumference at 9 months in the regression models, weight at 9 months was still the predominant influence. When head circumference at 9 months replaced weight at 9 months in models (see Table 4), head circumference was not significantly related to any of the outcomes investigated.

COMMENT

That the influence on later performance of both neonatal weight gain and weight at 9 months is confined to males is consistent with our findings on the effect of early nutrition on later cognitive performance. At each follow-up point we have found that the advantage from being fed preterm formula (*versus* donor breast milk or term formula) is greater in boys than in girls (9–12). Animal studies have also suggested that males are more vulnerable to poor early nutrition than females. Smart (19) reviewed 165 animal studies investigating the influence of malnutrition on learning and showed that the number of studies in which undernourished animals had poorer learning than controls ($n = 80$) greatly outweighed the number of those favoring the controls ($n = 12$), but the advantage was seen predominantly in males. Also, in a study by Fitzhardinge and Steven on small-for-gestational-age full-term infants (20), only males had later cognitive deficits.

There are other possible explanations for our findings relating to weight at 9 months post term. Repeated illness and hospital admissions during that period could have influenced both growth and the ability to elicit, respond to, and learn from interactions with adults and siblings. We therefore reanalyzed these data, including the number of hospital admissions in the first 9 months post term. There was a significant independent negative association between the number of hospital admissions in the first 9 months post term and both overall and verbal IQ. With number of hospital admissions in the model, the magnitude of the effect of weight at 9 months post term on later IQ was slightly diminished but remained statistically significant in every case. For example, among boys and girls combined, inclusion of number of hospital admissions up to 9 months post term in the model reduced the regression coefficient for the influence of 9 months weight on overall IQ from 2.3 to 2.1 ($p = 0.02$ and 0.002, respectively). For every hospital admission, overall IQ at 7.5 to 9 years was reduced by 1.5 ($p = 0.02$).

Our finding that there was a small significant increase in overall and verbal IQ scores with increasing body mass index is important for clinical management. It suggests that if increasing nutrient intake in the postneonatal period results in babies becoming fatter, rather than having proportionate weight and length gain, this may still be advantageous in terms of later performance. On the grounds of adult health there is also evidence of benefit in males with increasing weight at a year. Standardized mortality ratios for death from ischemic heart disease fell from 111 in men who weighed 8.2 kg or less at 1 year to 42 in those who weighed 12.3 kg or more (21).

There were too few subjects with extremely low birthweight to permit separate analyses in that group. In analyses restricted to subjects weighing under 1,500 g we failed to replicate the preceding significant findings. However, results were very similar when we confined analyses to subjects who were in more than 30% oxygen for more than 24 hours (62% of the population).

SUMMARY

Our data suggest that weight gain both in the neonatal period and in the first year of life are important for the future cognitive performance of children born with low birthweight. Weight at 9 months post term was more influential for later cognition than neonatal weight gain, and the influence in both cases was seen predominantly in males. Increase in body mass index was also associated with a small increase in later performance scores. Our data raise the hypothesis that in boys the postneonatal period is a more critical period for brain growth and maturation than the neonatal period. In girls we were able to detect little evidence that early growth influenced later performance.

Optimizing postnatal growth of male children born preterm should be a priority. The results from randomized trials of nutrient-enriched postdischarge formula in such children should help resolve some of the issues raised here.

REFERENCES

1. Freinkel N, Metzger BE. Pregnancy as a tissue culture experience: the critical implications of maternal metabolism for fetal development. In: *Pregnancy, metabolism, diabetes and the fetus* (Ciba Foundation Symposium No 63). Amsterdam: Excerpta Medica; 1979:3–23.
2. Susser M, Stein Z. Timing in prenatal nutrition: a reprise of the Dutch Famine Study. *Nutr Rev* 1994;52:84–94.
3. Law CM, Barker DJP, Osmond C, *et al.* Early growth and abdominal fatness in adult life. *J Epidemiol Community Health* 1992;46:184–186.
4. Barker DJP, Gluckman PD, Godfrey KM, *et al.* Fetal nutrition and cardiovascular disease in adult life. *Lancet* 1993;341:938–941.
5. Leon D, Ben-Shlomo Y. Preadult influences on cardiovascular disease and cancer. In: Kuh D, Ben-Shlomo Y, eds. *A life course approach to chronic disease epidemiology.* Oxford: Oxford University Press; 1997:45–77.
6. Barker DJP, Osmond C, Simmonds SJ, *et al.* The relation of small head circumference and thinness at birth to death from cardiovascular disease in adult life. *BMJ* 1993;306:422–426.
7. Ravelli ACJ, van der Meulen JHP, Michels RPJ, *et al.* Glucose tolerance in adults after prenatal exposure to famine. *Lancet* 1998;351:173–177.
8. Lucas A, Gore SM, Cole TJ, *et al.* Multicentre trial on feeding low birthweight infants: effects of diet on early growth. *Arch Dis Child* 1984;59:722–730.
9. Lucas A, Morley R, Cole TJ, *et al.* Early diet in preterm babies and developmental status at 18 months. *Lancet* 1990;335:1477–1481.
10. Morley R, Lucas A. Nutrition and cognitive development. *Br Med Bull* 1997;53:123–134.
11. Lucas A, Morley R, Cole TJ, *et al.*. Early diet in preterm babies and developmental status in infancy. *Arch Dis Child* 1989;64:1570–1578.
12. Lucas A, Morley R, Cole TJ, Gore SM. A randomised multicentre study of human milk versus formula and later development in preterm infants. *Arch Dis Child* 1994;70:F141–146.
13. Martyn CN, Gale RC, Sayer AA, Fall C. Growth *in utero* and cognitive function in adult life: follow-up study of people born between 1920 and 1943. *BMJ* 1996;312:1393–1396.
14. Dobbing J, Sands J. Comparative aspects of the brain growth spurt. *Early Hum Dev* 1970;3:79–83.
15. Skuse D, Pickles A, Wolke D, Reilly S. Postnatal growth and mental development: evidence for a sensitive period. *J Child Psychol Psychiatry* 1994;35:521–545.
16. Morley R, Cole TJ, Lucas PJ, *et al.* Mother's choice to provide breast milk and developmental outcome. *Arch Dis Child* 1988;63:1382–1385.
17. McNemar Q. Correction to a correction. *J Consult Clin Psychol* 1974;42:145–146.
18. Lucas A, Morley R, Cole TJ, Lister G, Leeson-Payne C. Breast milk and subsequent intelligence quotient in children born preterm. *Lancet* 1992;339:261–264.
19. Smart J. Undernutrition, learning and memory: review of experimental studies. In: Taylor TG, Jenkins NK, eds. *Proceedings of XIII International Congress of Nutrition.* London: John Libbey; 1986:74–78.
20. Fitzhardinge PM, Steven EM. The small-for-date infant. II. Neurological and intellectual sequelae. *Pediatrics* 1972;50:50–57.
21. Barker DJP, Winter PD, Osmond C, Margetts B, Simmonds SJ. Weight in infancy and death from ischaemic heart disease. *Lancet* 1989;ii:577–580.

DISCUSSION

Prof. Haschke: Were the infants who were not included in the analysis treated as dropouts or as noncompliant? These represented 25% of the cohort.

Dr. Morley: These were children mostly who had some sort of motor or neurosensory problem. I made the decision not to include them in the analysis because I thought they would cloud the issue. You could argue that it was wrong to omit these children. However, these IQ tests rely on children making patterns with blocks and assembling puzzles. A child with neuromotor impairment can't do that properly, so you are not actually measuring their cognitive performance. And if they can't hear properly, this will have delayed the development of language and may impair their ability to understand instructions. I felt that if we were going to look at these questions properly, we needed a cohort with the minimum of unnecessary confounding factors.

Dr. Rigo: You had two different cohorts of infants receiving only preterm formula, one in Cambridge and one in Norwich and Sheffield. When you looked at neurodevelopmental scores at 7 years, was there a significant difference between those two cohorts? I think that you published a Bayley score at 18 months in the two groups, and if I remember correctly there was a difference between the infants who were fed preterm formula in Cambridge and those fed preterm formula in Norwich and Sheffield. It is therefore very important to know whether the two cohorts of preterm infants fed preterm formula have persisting differences in their Bayley scores and neurodevelopmental outcome.

Dr. Morley: The difference in the scores between the two preterm formula groups is accounted for by social and demographic differences between the two populations. Social class in the UK has a powerful influence. It accounts for more variance in IQ than in most other countries.

Prof. Moro: Can you tell us what kind of feeding these babies received after discharge from the neonatal department?

Dr. Morley: We had no control over that whatsoever. After they left the hospital, they were fed as their parents and their medical advisors chose. So we only knew really what happened to them in the neonatal period.

Prof. Moro: Did you find any correlation between gain in length and IQ?

Dr. Morley: There was no association. To my surprise, weight was really the most powerful influence. It was more powerful than head circumference. Head circumference gain in the neonatal period was *negatively* associated with later performance—the faster the baby's head grew in the neonatal period, the lower the later scores. Weight and head circumference at 9 months were quite closely correlated. When you have two very closely correlated factors in a model, strange things may happen. But it looked as though weight was in fact the most important influence.

Prof. Ziegler: I am tremendously interested in this type of analysis. What your remarkable study has shown is that something related to nutrition in early infancy in premature infants matters as far as long-term outcome is concerned, but we still don't know what this is. If it is protein—or maybe energy—that differs, then this should show up in the weight gain during the period of hospital inpatient management. You did the analysis, and I was delighted to see that you showed a relation between later IQ and weight gain in the nursery, but then you explained it away! Unfortunately, you presented too much information on your slides for it to be possible to identify the important confounders in your equation; maybe some are unimportant. The message I take away is that there *is* a relation between weight gain in the nursery and late IQ, which confirms for me that it is perhaps protein or energy that has made the difference.

Dr. Morley: The problem is that the children who gained weight less well were those who were most sick, and being sick does no good for the brain. For example, there was an inverse relation between later IQ and the number of days in more than 30% oxygen. We had to adjust for such factors, and when this was done the effect of weight gain was almost lost. The issue now is whether, if we give these infants more nutrients, we can get them to grow better, and whether that will improve their outcome in the long term. Maybe Dr. Lucas would like to comment?

Prof. Lucas: You need to give me another few weeks. We have just started to clean the data on a large randomized postdischarge trial. Our very preliminary findings suggest that growth is promoted beyond the period of dietary randomization. So this is going to be quite exciting, but it's too early to announce the results.

Dr. Chessex: You showed that the infants who gained weight more rapidly had received less total parenteral nutrition (TPN) by volume. I suggest a hypothesis: Maybe the volume of TPN received is important, because by infusing TPN you're infusing high doses of peroxides. Girls are better protected against peroxides, and this could explain why they appear to have a better outcome. Have you looked at that variable more closely?

Dr. Morley: TPN was not one of the factors that came out as significant in the models when I was looking at performance. We could argue about the way I did those models. What I did was to enter all the factors that I thought were of interest and then remove from the final model any where the association was less than $p = 0.02$. I plan to repeat all these analyses on the basis of how much each variable affects the regression coefficient, which is going to be extremely time-consuming. All I can say at present is that in the model chosen the volume of intravenous feeds was nowhere near being a significant factor.

Prof. Heird: I was intrigued by your association between body mass index (BMI) and neurodevelopmental scores. But I'm also impressed by the fact that most babies who grow reasonably normally on any kind of regimen probably have a high BMI, in other words they're short and fat. To what extent do you think the effect you showed really reflects the BMI? Maybe it is a reflection of the fact that the babies who aren't short and fat are the ones who had other problems along with an inadequate intake. The association may not necessarily be with BMI, but with some other factor.

Dr. Morley: I agree. More work needs to be done on this. The problem is that weight and BMI are obviously highly interrelated. Models become extremely unstable when they include a number of closely related factors.

Prof. Dimita: From a biological point of view, I cannot understand how body growth influences cognitive development positively whereas brain growth—that is, head circumference—has a negative effect on IQ. We have a great deal of epidemiological data showing that prenatal and postnatal growth of the head—that is, the brain—has a positive influence on IQ.

Prof. Lucas: Maybe I could answer that. I suggest that head circumference growth may not be as informative as other variables such as weight in preterm infants. Large head circumference gains may reflect ventricular dilatation in premature babies and therefore may be pathological rather than indicate brain growth. The other important thing is that the sickest and smallest babies have the greatest degree of skull deformation (side-to-side flattening), because they have poorly mineralized bones. Obviously, the flatter the skull is from side to side, the larger the head circumference in relation to brain volume. So the sickest babies will have spuriously large heads and will be the ones who are likely to have the worst outcome. So the effects of brain growth on neurodevelopment may be canceled out by factors that affect the apparent size of the head when you put a tape round it.

Dr. Walker: Did you use the complete WISC in some children to see if the results with the modified WISC were substantiated? And in the individuals whom you left out of the study because they had defects such as hearing loss and so on, did you do an assessment using tests for measuring IQ in handicapped people to see whether or not there was a correlation between weight gain and outcome in that group of patients?

Dr. Morley: We did not do the full WISC on any of the children, mainly because we were measuring a lot of other things, so there simply wasn't time. We did extensive anthropometry and a fair amount of motor testing, which we still haven't reported, and we also examined various cardiovascular outcomes. By the time of follow-up, the children were spread around the country, and from a logistic point of view we needed to keep the testing within 1.5 hours. So we could not do the full-scale IQ, which was a pity. I did not include here IQ data from children with neuromotor or neurosensory impairment.

Prof. Lucas: I'd like to address that a little further. Clearly, having demonstrated major differences between groups on the abbreviated form of the WISC in at least one trial, it is mandatory that we undertake much more sophisticated neurodevelopmental testing. Now that the children have reached 14 years, we can test them over a half day or even a whole day, and we can do very sophisticated neurodevelopmental testing and brain studies. If there really are quite subtle effects of diet on lifetime cognitive or motor performance, we ought to be able to identify them.

Prof. Cooper: Have you looked at the head circumference growth in the neonatal period and at 9 months in the group that you excluded because of sensorimotor handicap?

Dr. Morley: No, I haven't done any detailed analysis on that group at all, though the data are available and could certainly be analyzed.

Dr. Schanler: Do you have any information on differences in growth in the neonatal period and after discharge from hospital in infants who were fed their own mother's milk *versus* those who received banked milk or formula?

Dr. Morley: Not many of these babies actually went home breastfed, even among the ones whose mothers expressed breast milk in the neonatal period, so that was not a major issue in these cohorts. In terms of the randomized comparison between banked donor breast milk and preterm formula, there was a highly significant influence. The children who were fed banked donor breast milk grew significantly less well in terms of weight gain, length gain, and head circumference gain than those fed on the preterm formula. In the groups where the randomized diets were fed as a supplement to mother's milk, as the proportion of mother's milk in the diet increased so neonatal weight gain decreased. Thus the more mother's milk the baby got, the less was its neonatal weight gain. Of course this raises the question of the quality of the nutrition. There may be other issues at stake, apart from just growing rapidly.

Prof. Ziegler: You showed a strong association between weight at 9 months and IQ at 8 years. I wonder what that means. We know that premature babies very commonly fail to grow in the first 2 to 3 years. That in itself is a bit of a mystery. But I wonder whether weight at 9 months is simply a marker of IQ at 8 years, rather than the other way round, which is what I think you implied. In other words, if you're small, that predestines you to have a low IQ at 8 years. What are your thoughts on this?

Dr. Morley: These are basically exploratory analyses and I don't think that I would suggest that they give us any clues as to causality. All I'm telling you is that there is an association between these various measures of performances at 7.5 to 8 years and weight at 9 months post term. What the reason for that is I don't know. It is still possible that there is some confounding that I haven't adjusted for—for example, hospital admissions. Unfortunately, although we know the numbers of admissions, we don't know the lengths of stay.

Prof. Fazzolari: Have you any explanation for the differences in performance scores between males and females at 9 months?

Dr. Morley: What we have shown throughout our study is that if children were fed a suboptimal diet, or if their growth was poor, it was the boys whose performance was most affected. It was not that there was a great overall difference between boys and girls, but that the boys seemed to be more vulnerable to the adverse influences of suboptimal nutrition or poor growth. I don't know the reason for that.

Prof. Fazzolari: Was the preterm formula that you used supplemented with LC-PUFA and nucleotides?

Dr. Morley: No, these were formulas in the early 1980s.

Nutrition of the Very Low Birthweight Infant, edited by
Ekhard E. Ziegler, Alan Lucas, Guido E. Moro.
Nestlé Nutrition Workshop Series, Paediatric Programme, Vol. 43,
Nestec Ltd., Vevey/Lippincott Williams & Wilkins
Philadelphia, Pennsylvania © 1999.

Supply and Effects of Long-Chain Polyunsaturated Fatty Acids (LC-PUFA) in Premature Infants

Berthold Koletzko, Ulrike Diener, Maria Fink, Thomas Berghaus, Hans Demmelmair, Patrick von Schönaich[*] and Ulrich Bernsau[*]

Division of Metabolic Disorders and Nutrition, Dr. von Haunedes Kinderspitel, Ludwig-Maximilians-University of Munich, Germany; and [*]Department of Paediatrics, Zentralklinikum Augsburg, Germany

The feeding of preterm infants is a substitute for the placental nutrient supply that provides the substrates required for intrauterine growth and development. Though extrauterine life differs dramatically from prenatal conditions in many ways, the quantity and quality of normal intrauterine growth are considered reference points for the feeding of preterm infants, unless there is evidence for advantages of other options.

Intrauterine growth during the latter part of pregnancy is characterized by a very rapid deposition of fat (1), which greatly exceeds that of any other nutrient and accounts for about 75% of the energy retained in the newly formed tissues (2). The analysis of tissue composition from deceased infants and fetuses of different gestational ages has shown very rapid incorporation of long-chain polyunsaturated fatty acids (LC-PUFA), especially arachidonic acid and docosahexaenoic acid (DHA, C22:6n-3), into structural lipids of the brain, retina, and other tissues during the latter part of pregnancy (3,4). Particularly high LC-PUFA concentrations are found in the phospholipids of membranes with high fluidity, such as synaptosomal membranes and retinal photoreceptors (5). In view of the documented functional importance of membrane lipid composition for cellular functions, the question has been raised as to whether preterm infants, who still lack the major part of the physiological intrauterine LC-PUFA accretion, might benefit from a dietary LC-PUFA supply (6).

ESSENTIAL FATTY ACID TRANSFER ACROSS THE HUMAN PLACENTA

The understanding of the physiology of placental nutrient transfer may improve the basis for determining the optimal nutrient supply for preterm infants, whose placental substrate supply has been replaced by parenteral and enteral feeding. The human placenta allows the transmission of gases, water, and a variety of nutrients, including, to a limited degree, fatty acids. Although the fetus may synthesize saturated and monounsaturated fatty acids from glucose and ketone bodies, its supply of polyunsaturated essential fatty acids (EFA) depends entirely on placental transfer. Some previous studies on the fatty acid composition of different lipid classes in maternal and infant plasma showed that precursor EFA with 18 carbon atoms contribute markedly lower proportions to cord than maternal total plasma lipids, while higher percentage values of major LC-PUFA were found in cord blood (7–9). However, owing to methodological limitations, the available information on the fatty acid composition of various lipid classes in maternal and neonatal plasma has been rather limited. To obtain more detailed information reflecting the fatty acid transfer by the human placenta, we studied the fatty acid composition of the major lipid classes in plasma of 41 pairs of mothers and their apparently healthy infants born at full term (38 to 42 postmenstrual weeks) using high-resolution capillary gas liquid chromatography (10). Blood was drawn at the time of birth from a peripheral vein in the mother and by venipuncture from the placental portion of the umbilical cord immediately after clamping.

The analysis revealed significantly higher total fatty acid concentrations in the maternal than in the cord plasma lipid classes (Table 1). Although saturated and monounsaturated fatty acids were found at higher percentage values in cord than in maternal plasma, the median percentages of α-linolenic acid (C18:3n-3) and linoleic acid (C18:2n-6) were markedly lower in cord than in maternal plasma lipids (see Table 1). In contrast, percentage values for long-chain n-6 and n-3 LC-PUFA metabolites were significantly higher in infants than in their mothers. These results point to a preferential and selective materno-fetal LC-PUFA transfer, and the question immediately arises as to whether this selective transport might benefit the fetus.

The detailed mechanisms of placental fatty acid transfer remain to be clarified. Fatty acid transfer across the human placenta has often been considered a passive diffusion process of nonesterified fatty acids (NEFA), depending on molecular weight and concentration gradients (10). We found a correlation between the total NEFA contents in maternal and cord plasma ($r = 0.384, p = 0.014$, Fig. 1), which appears to support this hypothesis to some extent, particularly since plasma NEFA have a similar fatty acid pattern in maternal and umbilical samples, with a predominance of palmitic (C16:0) and stearic (C18:0) acids. However, the concept of simple passive diffusion of unbound fatty acids is open to question because of the approximately 2.5-fold higher maternal than cord plasma NEFA concentrations and the markedly lower percentage values of α-linolenic acid and linoleic acid in cord than in maternal plasma lipids. Higher rates of plasma clearance for the storage or metabolism of certain fatty acids in placental and fetal tissues may have contributed to the low total cord plasma NEFA levels and the differences in fatty acid pattern, in addition to a limited and possibly fatty-acid-specific placental transfer.

Although α-linolenic acid and linoleic acid can be further desaturated in the ovine placenta, no activity of both the Δ-6 and Δ-5 desaturases has been detected in human placental tissue. Therefore LC-PUFA in the fetal circulation appear to be derived either from synthesis in fetal tissues or from the mother by preferential placental trans-

TABLE 1. *Fatty acids of plasma lipids in 41 pairs of mothers and their apparently healthy infants born at full term at the time of birth (10)*

	Triglycerides		Phospholipids	
	Maternal	Cord	Maternal	Cord
Total (mg/dl)	143.31 (63.73)	24.27 (12.43)[a]	172.22 (37.63)	62.55 (18.08)[a]
C18:2n-6	11.91 (5.48)	10.05 (3.45)[a]	20.99 (3.38)	7.42 (1.37)[a]
C18:3n-6	0.14 (0.08)	0.45 (0.15)[a]	0.06 (0.04)	0.10 (0.14)[a]
C20:2n-6	0.28 (0.11)	0.31 (0.18)	0.45 (0.13)	0.35 (0.08)[a]
C20:3n-6	0.22 (0.07)	0.81 (0.43)[a]	3.37 (0.82)	4.82 (0.83)[a]
C20:4n-6	0.75 (0.29)	2.92 (1.11)[a]	7.68 (1.90)	16.14 (2.49)[a]
C22:4n-6	0.11 (0.05)	0.57 (0.31)[a]	0.31 (0.11)	0.66 (0.21)[a]
Total n-6-LC-PUFA	1.54 (0.41)	5.74 (2.20)[a]	12.37 (2.16)	22.55 (2.56)[a]
C18:3n-3	0.52 (0.19)	0.20 (0.27)[a]	0.20 (0.10)	0.00 (0.03)[a]
C20:3n-3	0.05 (0.06)	0.00 (0.00)	0.10 (0.13)	0.00 (0.00)[a]
C20:5n-3	0.06 (0.04)	0.00 (0.17)	0.35 (0.15)	0.20 (0.16)[a]
C22:5n-3	0.09 (0.04)	0.12 (0.32)	0.43 (0.11)	0.34 (0.24)[a]
C22:6n-3	0.32 (0.22)	1.33 (1.27)[a]	2.89 (0.99)	4.76 (1.70)[a]
Total n-3-LC-PUFA	0.51 (0.28)	1.59 (1.66)[a]	3.72 (1.24)	5.44 (2.12)[a]

	Cholesterol esters		Nonesterified fatty acids	
	Maternal	Cord	Maternal	Cord
Total (mg/dl)	120.13 (48.99)	33.57 (17.85)[a]	25.21 (13.04)	9.60 (6.95)[a]
C18:2n-6	48.75 (8.19)	15.28 (4.04)[a]	7.69 (4.28)	4.13 (2.94)[a]
C18:3n-6	0.52 (0.28)	0.73 (0.21)[a]	0.06 (0.17)	0.00 (0.47)
C20:2n-6	0.07 (0.06)	0.12 (0.28)[a]	0.33 (0.28)	0.00 (0.30)[a]
C20:3n-6	0.78 (0.30)	1.28 (0.39)[a]	0.33 (0.34)	0.41 (0.73)
C20:4n-6	5.66 (1.70)	11.39 (3.36)[a]	0.74 (0.56)	1.04 (1.27)[a]
C22:4n-6	0.01 (0.03)	0.00 (0.13)	0.00 (0.14)	0.00 (0.21)
Total n-6-LC-PUFA	6.69 (1.48)	14.75 (3.39)[a]	2.35 (3.47)	6.30 (7.22)[a]
C18:3n-3	0.56 (0.31)	0.08 (0.15)[a]	0.15 (0.30)	0.00 (0.06)[a]
C20:3n-3	0.00 (0.00)	0.00 (0.00)	0.00 (0.07)	0.00 (0.00)[a]
C20:5n-3	0.33 (0.20)	0.22 (0.34)[a]	0.00 (0.11)	0.00 (0.00)
C22:5n-3	0.00 (0.03)	0.00 (0.00)[a]	0.00 (0.00)	0.00 (0.00)
C22:6n-3	0.52 (0.38)	0.92 (0.52)[a]	0.18 (0.31)	0.00 (0.49)
Total n-3-LC-PUFA	0.93 (0.57)	1.26 (0.72)	0.29 (0.60)	0.00 (0.63)

Values are median (interquartile range), % wt/wt. FA = fatty acid; SAFA = saturated fatty acid; MUFA = monounsaturated fatty acid; P/S = PUFA/SAFA.
[a] $p < 0.05$.

fer. The importance of the latter is supported by experimental studies, clearly showing preferential maternal/fetal LC-PUFA transfer in the perfused human placenta (11). The major portion of radiolabeled arachidonic acid from the maternal perfusate was incorporated into fetal phospholipids, in contrast to only small amounts of α-linolenic acid and linoleic acid. It is tempting to speculate that this preferential tracer incorporation, as well as the higher proportions of n-6 and n-3 LC-PUFA in cord than in maternal plasma observed in our study, reflects a preferential supply to the fetus of selected long-chain, highly unsaturated fatty acids that may serve biologically important functions for growth and development.

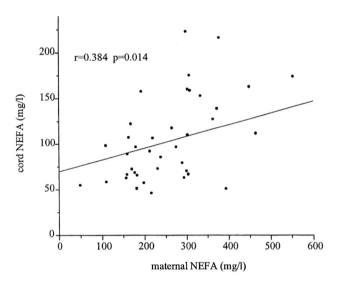

FIG. 1. Total nonesterified fatty acid (NEFA) concentrations in maternal and cord plasma (mg/l), drawn from data of Berghaus *et al.* (10).

SOURCES OF LC-PUFA FOR THE PRETERM INFANT: DIET AND ENDOGENOUS SYNTHESIS

Prematurely born infants fed with human milk receive appreciable amounts of preformed arachidonic acid and DHA with human milk lipids (12,13); these are believed to meet intrauterine accretion rates in membrane-rich tissues (14). Human milk from mothers of term and preterm infants does not differ in arachidonic acid and DHA contents and in the extent of decrease of percentage content of LC-PUFA during the first month of lactation (15) (Fig. 2). Obviously, the estimated high LC-PUFA requirement of preterm infants is not met any better by the milk of their own mothers than by mature milk of mothers of full-term infants.

Although milk LC-PUFA content is influenced to a certain extent by maternal dietary composition, compositional studies have suggested that there is some metabolic control of polyunsaturated fatty acid (PUFA) contents (12,16). Our understanding of the sources of essential fatty acids in human milk has been enhanced by metabolic studies with stable isotope techniques. In a study on six apparently healthy breastfeeding women, we gave an oral dose of 1 mg/kg bodyweight of $U^{13}C$-labeled linoleic acid and estimated its oxidation from analysis of breath gas enrichment and its transfer into milk by analysis of milk samples collected over 5 days (17). Before and at several times during a 5-day period after tracer intake, samples of breath and milk were collected and the volume of daily milk production recorded. We estimate that about 30% of milk linoleic acid is directly transferred from the diet, whereas about 11% of milk dihomo-γ-linolenic acid (DGLA) and 1.2% of milk arachidonic acid originate from direct endogenous conversion of dietary linoleic acid. In contrast, the major portion of polyunsaturated fatty acids in human milk lipids is derived from maternal body stores and not directly from the maternal diet (Fig. 3). In this way the influence of maternal dietary intake on milk composition is moderated

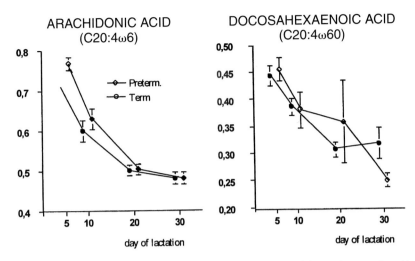

FIG. 2. Fall in human milk percentage contents of arachidonic and docosahexaenoic acids (% wt/wt) during the first month of lactation in parallel with the increase in total milk lipid secretion. Long-chain polyunsaturated fatty acid (LC-PUFA) contents of human milk from mothers of term and preterm infants show no consistent differences during the first month of lactation (15). Obviously, milk of mothers of preterm infants is not better suited to meet the higher LC-PUFA requirements of their infants than mature human milk. From Rodriguez *et al.* (13).

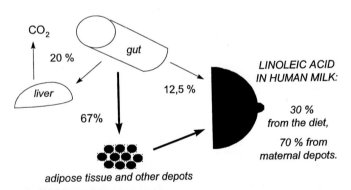

FIG. 3. Schematic depiction of linoleic acid flux in healthy breastfeeding women, based on results of a stable isotope study with oral administration of 1 mg/kg bodyweight of U-^{13}C-labeled linoleic acid and measurement of its oxidation from breath gas analyses, and its transfer into milk by analysis of milk samples collected over 5 days (17). We estimate that about 30% of milk linoleic acid is directly transferred from the diet, whereas about 11% of milk dihomo-γ-linolenic acid and 1.2% of milk arachidonic acid originate from direct endogenous conversion of dietary linoleic acid. The major portion of polyunsaturated fatty acids in human milk lipids is derived from maternal body stores and not directly from the maternal diet. Thus the influence of maternal diet on milk composition is moderated by the quantitatively larger contribution of fatty acids from maternal body pools, resulting in a relatively constant milk PUFA supply to the recipient infant. From Koletzko B (43).

by the quantitatively larger contribution of fatty acids from body compartments with a slow turnover, thus resulting in a relatively constant milk PUFA supply to the recipient infant, which might be of biological benefit.

In contrast to infants fed with human milk, those fed conventional milk formulas based on vegetable oils do not receive appreciable amounts of LC-PUFA with their diet (6,18,19) and depend on utilization of body stores or endogenous LC-PUFA synthesis from EFA precursors for delivery of LC-PUFA to membrane lipids of growing tissues. It has previously been questioned whether preterm infants could synthesize LC-PUFA themselves. Recent refinements of isotope techniques have made it possible to investigate fatty acid turnover *in vivo*, even in preterm infants (20), with the use of stable isotopes that are safe and without adverse effects (21). The availability of uniformly labeled, highly enriched tracer fatty acids and the high sensitivity and precision of gas chromatography isotope ratio mass spectrometry (GC-C-IRMS) have made it possible to perform accurate measurements on ^{13}C-enrichment in fatty acids contained in very small volumes of blood (22). We applied these techniques to enterally fed preterm infants who were given an oral bolus dose of U[13]C-labeled linoleic acid and α-linolenic acid. At 48 hours after tracer application we found a significant increase of ^{13}C content over baseline levels not only in plasma linoleic acid and α-linolenic acid but also in their long-chain n-6 and n-3 metabolites (Fig. 4). These data clearly demonstrate endogenous LC-PUFA formation in the preterm infant, but they do not indicate which proportion of LC-PUFA deposition in growing tissues may be covered by endogenous synthesis.

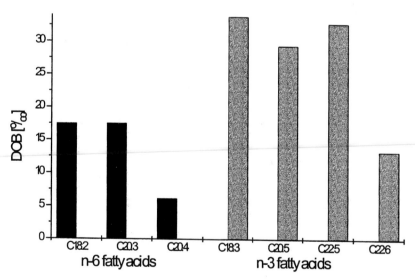

FIG. 4. Increase of ^{13}C enrichment (delta over baseline [DOB], %) of plasma phospholipid fatty acids in an enterally fed preterm infant at 48 hours after oral administration of U[13]C-labeled linoleic acid and α-linolenic acid. The increase of ^{13}C content over baseline levels not only in plasma linoleic acid and α-linolenic acid but also in their long-chain metabolites proves endogenous synthesis of long-chain polyunsaturated fatty acids by the preterm infant.

The results of the isotope analyses show a relatively high ^{13}C enrichment in the intermediary linoleic acid metabolite DGLA and the intermediary α-linolenic acid metabolites eicosapentaenoic acid (EPA) and C22:5n-3, whereas the enrichment in the biologically important end products arachidonic acid and DHA is much lower (see Fig. 3). Although these data need to be interpreted with some caution and be related to the relative pool sizes, they appear to confirm a limitation of arachidonic acid synthesis not only by Δ-6 desaturase activity but also by the activity of Δ-5 desaturation (22), and a limitation of DHA synthesis by an indirect conversion pathway through C24 intermediates and peroxisomal β oxidation (23). At this time no data are available on the amount of LC-PUFA per kilogram synthesized daily by a preterm infant. Further studies will also need to address the extent to which the activity of synthesis may be modulated by gestational and postnatal age, weight, dietary composition, and other variables.

Infants fed formulas with precursor EFA but lacking LC-PUFA show a much more pronounced decline in LC-PUFA status after birth than those receiving human milk or formula enriched with LC-PUFA (24–26), despite the demonstrable infantile LC-PUFA synthesis. These data indicate that the utilization of LC-PUFA for deposition, oxidation, and metabolic conversion to eicosanoids exceeds the infant's capability of synthesizing n-6 and n-3 LC-PUFA from the precursors linoleic acid and α-linolenic acid. Not only plasma but also tissue LC-PUFA contents are affected. In preterm infants we found mucosa cell composition to be markedly modified by dietary LC-PUFA intake (unpublished data), and in term infants who had died from sudden infant death syndrome a lower content of DHA was found in brain and retina of subjects who had been fed human milk providing preformed LC-PUFA than was found in those fed formula without LC-PUFA (27,28).

LC-PUFA ENRICHMENT OF PRETERM FORMULAS

Studies evaluating the supplementation of preterm formulas with DHA and partly also with arachidonic acid have reported normalization of LC-PUFA status in the recipient infants relative to reference groups fed human milk (24,26,29). Some double-blind randomized trials also found an LC-PUFA-associated improvement in performance of preterm infants in tests of visual and cognitive function (29–31), with results in the LC-PUFA-supplemented groups matching those of breastfed infants. However, concerns on potential adverse effects have also been raised. The use of formulas supplemented with oils comprising large amounts of EPA (C20:5n-3) relative to DHA, but no n-6 LC-PUFA, was associated both with a prolonged depletion of arachidonic acid levels throughout the first year of life and with poor growth (32,33).

Concerns have also been raised that the addition of LC-PUFA to formula may increase the vulnerability of the recipient infant to damage by reactive oxygen species, because LC-PUFA contain several methylene-interrupted double bonds that may make them more susceptible to oxidative damage (34,35). This is of particular concern in preterm infants, who are often under oxidant stress in the early postnatal period. Premature infants who required oxygen treatment and mechanical ventilation had significantly raised urinary excretion of malondialdehyde, an indicator of oxidative stress in tissues. Malondialdehyde excretion was 50% to 100% higher than found in nonventilated control infants not receiving oxygen (36). The induction of markedly enhanced peroxidation by LC-PUFA would be of serious concern because raised plasma malondialdehyde concentrations in very low-birthweight infants have been associated with adverse respiratory and ophthalmological outcomes (37).

Antioxidative protection is furnished by α-tocopherol, the major lipid-soluble chain-breaking antioxidant in the body, but preterm infants have low α-tocopherol concentrations in plasma and red blood cells compared with adults (34,36). Also, in preterm infants adipose tissue levels and concomitant tocopherol reserves are low; and they tend to have a poor ability to absorb fat and hence vitamin E (6). In contrast to the low stores, tocopherol requirements are considered higher in preterm babies, owing to greater oxidative stress (38).

To address some of these safety concerns, we studied whether the feeding of preterm infants with a formula containing LC-PUFA of both the n-6 and the n-3 series, but a somewhat lower n-6/n-3 ratio than is typically found in human milk can match the fatty acid status of preterm infants fed human milk and affect plasma vitamin E concentrations, urinary excretion of the lipid peroxidation product malondialdehyde, and growth. Preterm infants in stable clinical condition who did not require mechanical ventilation or an oxygen supply with an $FiO_2 > 0.3$ were enrolled within 3 days of established full enteral feeding (≥ 130 ml/kg·d). During the study period, the infants either received their own mother's milk fortified with 5 g/dl FM 85 (Nestlé) or were randomized in a double-blind fashion to one of two preterm infant formulas (Alprem, Nestlé) with only traces of LC-PUFA (group F), or with LC-PUFA (group LC-PUFA-F; Table 2). Both formulas contained 0.68 mg vitamin E per 100 ml. Formula-fed infants received their assigned study formula from study entry for the following 28 days. During this period, the study formula provided at least 90% of the total energy intake.

Infants of the human milk group were born with higher birthweights (1,440 ± 288 g) than infants from group LC-PUFA-F (1,145 ± 288 g, $p < 0.05$), whereas there were no significant differences compared with group F (1,177 ± 344 g). There were

TABLE 2. *Major polyunsaturated fatty acids in the study diets*

	Formula w/o LC-PUFA	Formula with LC-PUFA	Mature human milk
n-6 fatty acids			
18:2n-6	14.1	17.7	10.8
18:3n-6	n.d.	0.4	0.2
20:3n-6	n.d.	n.d.	0.3
20:4n-6	0.04	0.1	0.4
n-3 fatty acids			
18:3n-3	1.3	1.2	0.8
18:4n-3	n.d.	0.1	n.d.
20:5n-3	n.d.	0.13	0.04
22:6n-3	n.d.	0.57	0.2

Values are % wt/wt; n.d. = not detectable.

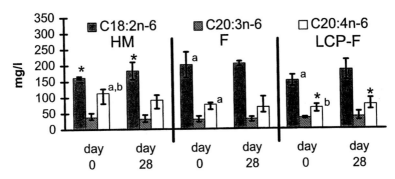

FIG. 5. Plasma phospholipid concentrations (mg/liter) of the n-6 essential fatty acids linoleic acid (C18:2n-6), dihomo-γ-linolenic acid (C20:3n-6), and arachidonic acid (C20:4n-6) in preterm infants fed human milk (HM), conventional preterm formula without LC-PUFA (F), and preterm formula with LC-PUFA (LCP-F) (median, interquartile range). Values bearing identical superscripts (a,b,c,d) indicate significant differences ($p < 0.05$) between groups; * indicates significant differences over time within groups.

no differences between groups at birth and during the study period in gestational age; clinical characteristics during pregnancy and at birth; Apgar scores at 1, 5, and 10 minutes; duration of artificial ventilation; duration of oxygen supply; type and duration of parenteral feeding; infusion of lipids; presence of disease or complications; and treatment. The mean daily formula or human milk intakes of the three groups on study days 0, 14, and 28 were about 150 ml/kg·d and did not differ at any of the three time points. All groups showed good feeding tolerances, with no significant differences in frequencies of gastric residuals, vomiting, or stools per day (data not shown), and all three groups reached similar weight gain and mean Z scores of weight, length, and head circumference during the study period, as well as changes in Z scores over time during the 4-week period.

The concentrations of major n-6 and n-3 essential fatty acids in plasma phospholipids of the three groups at study entry and the end of the study are shown in Figs. 5

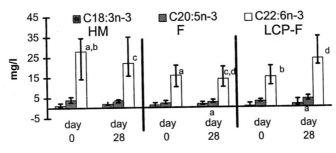

FIG. 6. Plasma phospholipid concentrations (mg/liter) of the n-3 essential fatty acids α-linolenic acid (C18:3n-3), eicosapentaenoic acid (C20:5n-3), and docosahexaenoic acid (C22:6n-3) in preterm infants fed human milk (HM), conventional preterm formula without LC-PUFA (F), and preterm formula with LC-PUFA (LCP-F) (median, interquartile range). Values bearing identical superscripts (a,b,c,d) indicate significant differences ($p < 0.05$) between groups.

and 6. Since no formula given to the infants before study entry contained LC-PUFA, only breastfed infants received LC-PUFA before study day 0. Consequently, formula-fed infants had lower values of arachidonic acid, DHA, total n-6 LC-PUFA, and total n-3 LC-PUFA in plasma phospholipids than breastfed infants at study entry. There were only minor changes of n-6 fatty acids during the study period. During the 4-week study period, arachidonic acid remained unchanged in group F, whereas it tended to decline in breastfed infants. The concentration of the principal n-3 LC-PUFA, DHA tended to decrease over the 4-week study period in breastfed infants, whereas it remained unchanged in group F. However, there was a significant increase in DHA concentration from the start to the end of the study in group LC-PUFA-F, resulting in values of DHA that were similar to those in the group fed human milk by study day 28.

At study entry, formula-fed infants showed markedly depleted levels of both n-3 and n-6 LC-PUFA. Relative to the concentrations found in infants fed human milk, the DHA level in plasma phospholipids at study entry was reduced by 45% and that of arachidonic acid was decreased by 37%. This is in agreement with our previous observations of a relatively more marked depletion of DHA than arachidonic acid (26), presumably because of the more complex pathway of endogenous DHA synthesis relative to arachidonic acid formation. It has been reported previously that preterm infants fed human milk show falling DHA levels after birth, which then tend to stabilize at a lower level. In group F, the most marked decline in DHA apparently occurred before study entry, whereas DHA concentrations remained unchanged over the entire study period. Consequently the unsupplemented infants remained highly depleted in DHA, with only 64% of the DHA level of breastfed infants at the end of the study. This emphasizes the importance of dietary DHA supplementation for preterm infants if plasma fatty acid profiles of infants fed human milk are to be matched. This goal was achieved in infants fed the supplemented formula. Despite the low DHA concentrations found in these infants at study entry, values similar to those of breastfed infants were reached by day 14 and remained stable thereafter.

The DHA concentrations of the formulas used in the present study, as well as in the other supplementation studies cited, are all within the range reported for human milk (12). However, if the plasma and body fatty acid pools of infants fed human milk could be matched using formulas containing less DHA, reducing the concentration would not only provide technological advantages and reduce the cost of the formula but also limit potential risks of DHA supplementation such as increased lipid peroxidation or potential effects on the metabolism of n-6 LC-PUFA and growth. With the supplement used in this study no such adverse effects were observed. Total n-6 LC-PUFA levels were stable in both formula groups.

The fact that growth rates did not differ among the study groups might be related to the stable arachidonic acid levels observed in all the groups. The supplemented formula given here contained only minor amounts of EPA (0.14% of total fatty acids). This low EPA content, together with the simultaneous provision of n-6 LC-PUFA, seems to lead to stable n-6 FA levels and thus to normal growth. However, group sizes were too small to draw definitive conclusions about growth effects. Although lower arachidonic acid levels have been correlated with poorer intrauterine

(39,40) and extrauterine (32,33) growth, a preterm infant formula containing both DHA and arachidonic acid was recently reported to enhance growth. Hansen *et al.* (41) studied the effects of LC-PUFA supplementation on growth in a large number of preterm infants and found enhanced weight gain during the hospital stay in infants supplemented with both DHA and arachidonic acid compared with unsupplemented infants. Moreover, body weight at 2 and 4 months corrected age was reported to be greater in infants supplemented with both DHA and arachidonic acid than in infants fed formulas containing no LC-PUFA, or only DHA. These results suggest that formulas containing both n-6 and n-3 LC-PUFA might promote better growth.

Recently, data were reported in abstract form (42) which suggested that immune phenotypes of premature infants are also influenced by the dietary LC-PUFA supply (Table 3). Cell types in peripheral blood were identified by monoclonal antibodies and interleukin-10 production after mitogen stimulation of peripheral lymphocytes was measured by enzyme-linked immunosorbent assay. Immune phenotypes at age 42 days were significantly different in infants fed formula without LC-PUFA than in infants who received preformed arachidonic and docosahexaenoic acids from either formula or human milk (see Table 3).

In our trial, over the 28-day feeding period there was no change in the plasma α-tocopherol concentrations in the human milk group or in the LC-PUFA-F group (Fig. 7). In infants fed either of the infant formulas at day 28, plasma α-tocopherol concentrations were similar to those found in infants fed human milk. Compared with human milk, the change in α-tocopherol concentration over the 28 days was significantly greater in the standard formula-fed group but not in the LC-PUFA-F group. Urinary malondialdehyde excretion of formula-fed infants was significantly greater than in infants fed human milk but did not differ between the two formula groups.

Since the LC-PUFA content of infant formula might contribute to oxidative stress, the formula must contain sufficient vitamin E both to prevent oxidation of the formula and, once ingested, to protect the infant from oxidation reactions within the body that might have potentially harmful consequences. The European Society for Gastroenterology, Hepatology, and Nutrition (ESPGHAN) recommends at least 0.9 mg vitamin E/g PUFA furnished in the formula (35), and the formulas used in this

TABLE 3. *Immunological variables in preterm infants at the age of 42 days after feeding with randomly assigned infant formula without (formula w/o LC-PUFA) or with arachidonic and docosahexaenoic acid (formula with LC-PUFA), or with human milk**

	Formula w/o LC-PUFA	Formula with LC-PUFA	Human milk (with LC-PUFA)
CD4/CD8 ratio	4.1 ± 0.5^a	2.9 ± 0.2^b	2.9 ± 0.2^b
CD4+CD45RO+ (% total)	5.6 ± 0.4^a	7.1 ± 1.0^b	7.0 ± 0.7^b
CD4+CD45RA+ (% total)	85 ± 2^a	77 ± 4^b	72 ± 3^b
IL10 (pg/ml)	11 ± 32^a	167 ± 38^b	296 ± 44^b

* Immune phenotypes of infants fed formula without LC-PUFA differ significantly from those of infants receiving LC-PUFA either from formula or from human milk. From Field et al. (42).

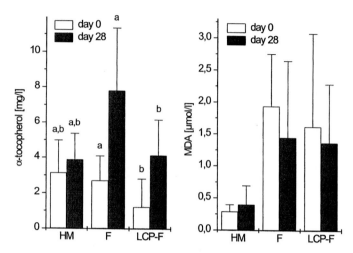

FIG. 7. Plasma α-tocopherol and urinary malondialdehyde (MDA) concentrations in preterm infants fed human milk (HM), conventional preterm formula without LC-PUFA (F), and preterm formula with LC-PUFA (LCP-F) (median, interquartile range). Values bearing identical superscripts (a,b,c,d) indicate significant differences ($p < 0.05$) between groups.

study contained 2.8 mg vitamin E/g PUFA. These levels appear adequate to support plasma vitamin E, since this plasma index in infants fed either of the two formulas at day 28 was equivalent to that in infants fed human milk. However, at the end of the study α-tocopherol concentrations in the standard formula group tended to be higher than in the LC-PUFA-F group. Since both formulas contained the same amount of vitamin E, this observation may indicate a greater turnover of vitamin E in the presence of LC-PUFA. A previous study from our laboratory showed a tendency for α-tocopherol concentrations in plasma and erythrocytes in preterm infants to be lower when they were fed fish oil–supplemented formulas (34). In contrast, concentrations of plasma or erythrocyte α-tocopherol increase after birth in preterm and term infants fed standard or LC-PUFA-supplemented formulas, just as they did with breastfeeding. It is also possible that LC-PUFA themselves may act as antioxidants in the body if they are not located at critical sites in the cell (e.g., the membrane) and if they are immediately replaced after auto-oxidation. If these fatty acids were to be oxidized, they might protect more important membrane-bound fatty acids from oxidation. This intriguing possibility deserves further investigation.

In any case, the data obtained in this trial show that the LC-PUFA-enriched formula tested here is effective in improving the plasma LC-PUFA status of preterm infants and does not have appreciable adverse effects.

DOCOSAHEXAENOIC ACID SUPPLY AND THE DEVELOPMENT OF VISUAL FUNCTION

A major question in addition to the evaluation of biochemical efficacy and safety is whether the provision of preformed LC-PUFA in diets for preterm infants provides any functional advantage. As one biomarker of neurocellular function, we studied whether early visual acuity is influenced by LC-PUFA supplementation.

In a further double-blind clinical trial, 26 preterm infants (birthweight 1,682 ± 267 g; gestational age 32.6 ± 2.3 weeks) were randomized to receive one of three preterm infant formulas that differed in their DHA contents only, ranging from 0.03% to 0.5% of total fatty acids. Feeding of the formulas started within the first 2 weeks of life, at a mean age of 12 days of life. Ten breastfed preterm infants with a birthweight of 1,625 ± 235 g and a gestational age of 33.6 ± 2.3 weeks were included as a nonrandomized reference group. On study day 28 a blood sample was obtained and the concentration of plasma phospholipid DHA was determined by high-resolution gas chromatography. Exclusive feeding with human milk or the assigned study formula was continued until 48 weeks of postconceptional age.

At 48 weeks of postconceptional age visual acuity was tested by transient visual evoked potentials (VEP). Transient VEP are recorded when the stimulus is reversing at a slow rate. In this case a complete response of the occipital cortex is recorded. There is no superimposition on the subsequent VEP resulting from the next pattern reversal. A typical transient VEP waveform is shown in Fig. 8.

Infants were placed on their mother's lap 1 m away from a monitor that presented high-contrast black-and-white checkerboard pattern stimuli at a reversal rate of 1 Hz (two reversals a second). The VEP were recorded in a dark room with the stimulator screen being the only light source. Recording of the potentials only occurred when the infant was alert and looking at the monitor displaying the pattern. Potentials were recorded with three electrodes placed on the head of the infant, using specially designed hardware and software. Two recordings were made with each pattern size (11-, 15-, 23-, 30-, 38-, 46-, and 57-min arc). The peak-to-peak amplitude of the VEP was measured and plotted against the log of the angle subtended by each pattern size. The

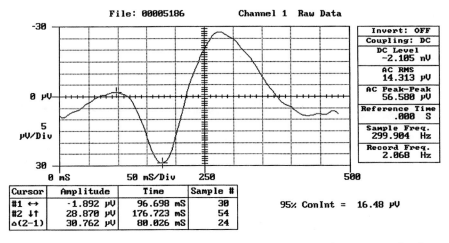

FIG. 8. Transient visual evoked potential (VEP) of a preterm infant at the postconceptional age of 48 weeks.

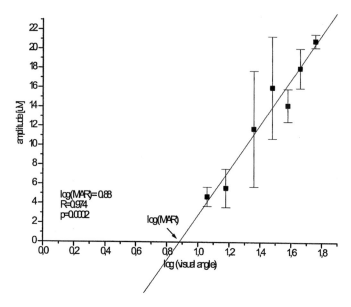

FIG. 9. Visual evoked potential (VEP) amplitudes *versus* pattern size function in a preterm infant (48 weeks postconceptional age).

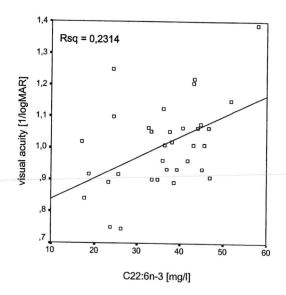

FIG. 10. Plasma phospholipid DHA concentration on study day 28 is significantly correlated with visual acuity measured by visual evoked potentials (VEP) at 48 weeks postconceptional age.

linear part of the curve was extrapolated to 0 μV to obtain the logarithm of the minimum angle of resolution (logMAR), which expresses visual acuity (Fig. 9).

Plasma phospholipid DHA concentrations at 28 days after study entry were significantly correlated with VEP acuity at 48 weeks postconceptional age (Pearson $r = -0.486$, $p = 0.002$, Fig. 10). Thus there is a clear dose/response relation between DHA status and visual acuity achieved at this age: Infants with higher DHA concentrations in their plasma phospholipids have better VEP acuities than infants with lower DHA concentrations.

We conclude that in view of this direct relation between DHA availability and the early development of a neurophysiological function, it appears desirable to approach ways of feeding premature infants that avoid DHA depletion.

ACKNOWLEDGMENTS

Our work was supported by Bundesministerium für Forschung und Technologie, Bonn, Germany; Deutsche Forschungsgemeinschaft, Bonn, Germany; Nestec SA, Vevey, Switzerland; and Nestle Alete GmbH, München, Germany.

REFERENCES

1. Widdowson EM, Southgate DAT, Schutz Y. Comparison of dried milk preparations for babies on sale in 7 European countries. *Arch Dis Child* 1954;49:867–873.
2. Ziegler EE, O'Donnell AM, Nelson SE, Fomon SJ. Body composition of the reference fetus. *Growth* 1976;40:329–341.
3. Clandinin MT, Chappell JE, Leong S, Heim T, Swyer PR, Chance GW. Intrauterine fatty acid accretion in human brain: implications for fatty acid requirements. *Early Hum Dev* 1980;4:121–129.
4. Martinez M. Tissue levels of polyunsaturated fatty acids during early human development. *J Pediatr* 1992;120:S129–138.
5. Innis SM. n-3 Fatty acid requirements of the newborn. *Lipids* 1992;27:879–885.
6. Koletzko B, Tsang R, Zlotkin SH, Nichols B, Hansen JW, eds. Importance of dietary lipids. In: *Nutrition during infancy: principles and practice*. Cincinnati: Digital Educational Publishing; 1997:123–153.
7. Olegard R, Svennerholm L. Effects of diet on fatty acid composition of plasma and red cell phosphoglycerides in three-month-old infants. *Acta Paediatr Scand* 1971;60:505–511.
8. Friedman Z, Danon A, Lamberth ELJ, Mann WJ. Cord blood fatty acid composition in infants and in their mothers during the third trimester. *J Pediatr* 1978;92:461–466.
9. Hendrickse W, Stammers JP, Hull D. The transfer of free fatty acids across the human placenta. *Br J Obstet Gynaecol* 1985;92:945–952.
10. Berghaus T, Demmelmair H, Koletzko B. Fatty acid composition of lipid classes in maternal and cord plasma at birth. *Eur J Pediatr* 1998;157:763–768.
11. Kuhn DC, Crawford MA, Stevens P. Transport and metabolism of essential fatty acids by the human placenta. *Controv Gynecol Obstet* 1985;13:139–140.
12. Koletzko B, Thiel I, Abiodun PO. The fatty acid composition of human milk in Europe and Africa. *J Pediatr* 1992;120:S62–70.
13. Rodriguez M, Koletzko B, Kunz C, Jensen RG. Nutritional and biochemical properties of human milk. II. Lipids, micronutrients and bioactive factors. *Clin Perinatol* (*in press*).
14. Koletzko B, Thiel I, Springer S. Lipids in human milk: a model for infant formulae? *Eur J Clin Nutr* 1992;46:S45–55.
15. Genzel-Boroviczeny O, Wahle J, Koletzko B. Fatty acid composition of human milk during the first month after term and preterm delivery. *Eur J Pediatr* 1997;156:142–147.
16. Koletzko B, Thiel I, Abiodun PO. Fatty acid composition of mature human milk in Nigeria. *Z Ernährungswiss* 1991;30:289–297.
17. Demmelmair H, Baumheuer M, Koletzko B, Dokoupil K, Kratl G. Metabolism of U^{13}C-labelled linoleic acid in lactating women. *J Lipid Res* 1998;39:1389–1396.

18. Decsi T, Behrendt E, Koletzko B. Fatty acid composition of Hungarian infant formulae revisited. *Acta Paediatr Hung* 1994;34:107–116.

19. Koletzko B, Bremer HJ. Fat content and fatty acid composition of infant formulae. *Acta Paediatr Scand* 1989;78:513–521.

20. Demmelmair H, Sauerwald T, Koletzko B, Richter T. New insights into lipid and fatty acid metabolism via stable isotopes. *Eur J Pediatr* 1997;156 [Suppl 1]:S70–74.

21. Koletzko B, Sauerwald T, Demmelmair H. Safety of stable isotope use. *Eur J Pediatr* 1997;156 [Suppl 1]:S12–17.

22. Demmelmair H, von Schenck U, Behrendt E, Sauerwald T, Koletzko B. Estimation of arachidonic acid synthesis in full term neonates using natural variation of ^{13}C content. *J Pediatr Gastroenterol Nutr* 1995;21:31–36.

23. Sauerwald T, Hachey DL, Jensen CL, Chen H, Anderson RE, Heird WC. Intermediates in endogenous synthesis of C22: 6ω3 and C20: 4ω6 by term and preterm infants. *Pediatr Res* 1997;41:183–187.

24. Koletzko B, Schmidt E, Bremer HJ, Haug M, Harzer G. Effects of dietary long-chain polyunsaturated fatty acids on the essential fatty acid status of premature infants. *Eur J Pediatr* 1989;148:669–675.

25. Carlson SE, Wilson WW. Docosahexaenoic acid (DHA) supplementation of preterm (PT) infants: effect on the 12-month Bayley mental developmental index (MDI). *Pediatr Res* 1994;35:20A (abst.).

26. Koletzko B, Edenhofer S, Lipowsky G, Reinhardt D. Effects of a low birthweight infant formula containing docosahexaenoic and arachidonic acids at human milk levels. *J Pediatr Gastroenterol Nutr* 1995;21:200–208.

27. Makrides M, Neumann MA, Byard RW, Simmer K, Gibson RA. Fatty acid composition of brain, retina, and erythrocytes in breast- and formula-fed infants. *Am J Clin Nutr* 1994;60:189–194.

28. Farquharson J, Cockburn F, Patrick WA, Jamieson EC, Logan RW. Infant cerebral cortex phospholipid fatty-acid composition and diet. *Lancet* 1992;340:810–813.

29. Carlson SE, Werkman SH. A randomized trial of visual attention of preterm infants fed docosahexaenoic acid until two months. *Lipids* 1996;31:85–90.

30. Carlson SE, Ford AJ, Werkman SH, Peeples JM, Koo WK. Visual acuity and fatty acid status of term infants fed human milk and formulas with and without docosahexaenoate and arachidonate from egg yolk lecithin. *Pediatr Res* 996;39:882–888.

31. Uauy R, Birch DG, Birch EE, Tyson JE, Hoffman DR. Effect of dietary omega-3 fatty acids on retinal function of very-low-birth-weight neonates. *Pediatr Res* 1990;28:485–492.

32. Carlson SE, Cooke RJ, Werkman SH, Tolley EA. First year growth of preterm infants fed standard compared to marine oil n-3 supplemented formula. *Lipids* 1992;27:901–907.

33. Carlson SE, Werkman SH, Peeples JM. In: Galli C, Simopoulos AP, Tremoli E, eds. Growth and development of premature infants in relation to n 3 and n 6 fatty acid status. In: *Fatty acids and lipids: biological aspects.* Basel: Karger, 1994:63–69.

34. Koletzko B, Decsi T, Sawatzki G. Vitamin E status of low birthweight infants fed formula enriched with long-chain polyunsaturated fatty acids. *Int J Vitam Nutr Res* 1995;65:101–104.

35. ESPGHAN Committee on Nutrition. Comment on the vitamin E content in infant formulas, follow on formulas and formulas for low birthweight infants. *J Pediatr Gastroenterol Nutr* 1998;26:351–352.

36. Schlenzig JS, Bervoets K, von LV, Bohles H. Urinary malondialdehyde concentration in preterm neonates: is there a relationship to disease entities of neonatal intensive care? *Acta Paediatr* 1993;82:202–205. [Published erratum in *Acta Paediatr* 1993;82:630.]

37. Inder TE, Darlow BA, Sluis KB, *et al.* The correlation of elevated levels of an index of lipid peroxidation (MDA-TBA) with adverse outcome in the very low birthweight infant. *Acta Paediatr* 1996;85:1116–1122.

38. Ripalda MJ, Rudolph N, Wong SL. Developmental patterns of antioxidant defense mechanisms in human erythrocytes. *Pediatr Res* 1989;26:366–369.

39. Koletzko B, Braun M. Arachidonic acid and early human growth: is there a relation? *Ann Nutr Metab* 1991;35:128–131.

40. Leaf AA, Leighfield MJ, Costeloe KL, Crawford MA. Long chain polyunsaturated fatty acids and fetal growth. *Early Hum Dev* 1992;30:183–191.

41. Hansen J, Schade D, Harris C. Docosahexaenoic acid plus arachidonic acid enhance preterm infant growth. *Prostaglandins Leukot Essent Fatty Acids* 1997;57:196 (abst.).

42. Field CJ, Thomson C, van Aerde J, *et al.* The effects of supplementing preterm formula with long-chain unsaturated fatty acids on immune phenotypes and cytokine production. *J Pediatr Gastroenterol Nutr* 1998;26:590 (abst.).

43. Koletzko B, Demmelmair H, Soda P. Nutritional support of infants and children: supply and metabolism of lipids. *Baillière's Clin Gastroenterology* 1998;12:671–696.

DISCUSSION

Dr. Rashwan: At what age did you test visual acuity? And were children with retinopathy of prematurity excluded?

Prof. Koletzko: The data I presented were obtained at 48 weeks post conception (i.e., at 2 months corrected age). We also have later measurements that have not been fully evaluated yet. The study protocol implied that infants with subnormal visual acuity had detailed ophthalmological examination and refraction measurements, and infants with confirmed abnormalities were excluded from the study.

Dr. Szajewska: Is there any scientific evidence for how long supplementation with LC-PUFA should last? At what age would you stop it?

Prof. Koletzko: No, I don't think there is any such evidence available to allow final conclusions. You can show that a longer duration of supplementation will have a more lasting effect on, for example, plasma phospholipid profiles, but the question then is whether or not that is related to function.

Prof. Haschke: What happens during DHA depletion of the mother? Is there DHA depletion during pregnancy? Are there any data on how the mother uses supplementary DHA during a depleted-state storage, oxidation, and so on?

Prof. Koletzko: There are data from the Maastricht group reporting that there is a reduction in DHA in plasma lipids during pregnancy. It is difficult to interpret that information without looking at tissue levels, because we know that lipid metabolism is markedly altered during pregnancy. I am aware of at least two intervention studies in which pregnant women were supplemented with DHA, but I don't know the outcome. We have studied lactating women given labeled ω-3 fatty acids and have recently presented the results in abstract form [1]. To our surprise, we found that oxidation of our ω-3 fatty acid supplement during lactation was not different from the oxidation of C18 fatty acids. There is thus apparently no sparing of ω-3 fatty acids from oxidation during lactation. Whether that also holds true during pregnancy could be tested.

Prof. Haschke: Are there data to show that if the mother is depleted of DHA, her infant is born with low DHA values in plasma, or in any other tissue that could be analyzed?

Prof. Koletzko: This really depends on what you are looking at. If you look at a 1,000-g infant that has about 20 g of fat in all, most of which is structural lipid, there is almost a complete absence of white adipose tissue, and therefore there is little available DHA. The greater the birthweight and gestational age, of course, the greater is the increase in reserves. It is a good question that is implied in your comment: "Does it matter whether or not there is available DHA?" Would it be sensible to do studies in which different population groups were examined? There is one interesting study from Carlson [2], who compared preterm infants without and with bronchopulmonary disease. She found functional effects of DHA in infants who were relatively healthy and without bronchopulmonary disease, but infants with bronchopulmonary dysplasia did not react to DHA supplementation. I assume that the difference was associated with a different growth pattern.

Prof. Lucas: I am sure you would expect me to be slightly provocative! You are looking at the results of relatively small physiological studies. If I were going to be critical, I would say that you put things in the best possible light by selecting those studies that support the view that you should add long-chain lipids to infant formulas. But as you know, world regulatory bodies are much divided on this. The Canadian, American, and British authorities have not yet made a recommendation because they are still concerned about the literature. For instance, if you take Carlson's first study rather than her second one, you find that it seemed to make babies worse rather than better, if anything, when fish oil was added to the diet; or you could take the Auestad study, which admittedly was in term infants that, though it did not show any difference overall in development, showed that at 14 months the babies fed additional arachidonic acid and DHA had worse vocabulary scores. You could of course put that down to chance.

If you look overall at the relation between LC-PUFA levels in the plasma and function, you would have to say that it is not consistently good. And safety has obviously been raised, to the extent that regulatory bodies are concerned. In the Carlson study, for example, there were nine cases of necrotizing enterocolitis in the LC-PUFA supplemented group and three in the control group, which was bordering on significance ($p = 0.06$). There was also a difference in infections that wasn't significant in its own right but if, as I have provocatively done, you combine those with the NEC cases, then you actually have significantly more NEC plus sepsis withdrawals in the LC-PUFA group than in the control group.

What I'm saying is that one could stand up and present the counterarguments to many of your conclusions. I would wish people to be left with more confusion rather than with more certainty, since regulatory bodies are certainly confused at present.

Prof. Koletzko: I could not agree more. We certainly all welcome more data, there's no question about that. But my point of view is not that of a regulatory body. As you well know, decisions by regulatory bodies are influenced by many factors, and much lobbying is invested to influence decision making. But that is not our issue. You raised differences in outcomes both with respect to efficacy and with respect to safety in different studies. Remember that we are not supplementing with LC-PUFA as such, but we are employing different types of intervention in different studies, involving supplements of specific oils under specific conditions. I don't find it surprising that not all results are identical because in any intervention studies there are different effects in different studies. We should also be aware that people use different methodologies. You referred to the study by Auestad [3] and coworkers in term infants where no effect was found on some of the efficacy parameters selected. This was a multicenter study with different methodologies applied in different centers. Carlson used exactly the same formula, also with term infants, in a single-center study with consistent methodology, and she found an advantage of this very same supplementation. I'm not claiming that only she was right; I'm just saying that questions of study design and methodology are very relevant.

With respect to the adverse effects of Carlson's first study, that was an intervention with a high-EPA fish oil that led to depletion of arachidonic acid. Even though we don't have the final scientific evidence at this point, it is reasonable to assume that we should avoid arachidonic acid depletion because it may well affect growth. We need more data on that.

In view of your concern on a proposed increased risk for NEC, I would like to point your attention to the study by Carlson et al. [4], who reported a significantly reduced incidence of NEC in a double-blind controlled trial in the group of preterm infants who received a formula with phospholipids providing LC-PUFA as compared with a regular formula without LC-PUFA.

Prof. Lucas: We are just in the middle of analyzing a study on LC-PUFA supplements, albeit in term infants. The analysis of safety in outcome trials requires larger numbers of subjects than the analysis of efficacy. You need very large numbers of subjects to reassure people that there is not a differential instance of adverse effects, and none of the published studies is big enough to do this. The study we are just analyzing is on 447 subjects, so it does have a reasonably robust sample size.

Prof. Koletzko: Of course it should be our first concern to ensure the safety of interventions and an adequate safety-to-benefit ratio. Yes, we do need large trials to look at that. If you look at the taurine story, for example, some years ago very few data were available. If the data were re-examined today, who knows what conclusions we would arrive at? But at that time, the situation was very different. Taurine was easy to add, it was cheap, and nobody in the infant food industry complained about the suggestion of adding it. My only concern now, and particularly with respect to preterm infants, is that it will be very difficult to demonstrate the unequivocal safety of every intervention if you need a thousand infants to do so. If the criteria are too rigorous, it could work against the interests of the infants because it would impede any kind of innovation.

Dr. Walker: In relation to allergy, one cannot interpret the data you gave as showing effects on allergy. At most one can say that fatty acids can affect cytokine release and possibly inflammation, but not allergy. I just don't want that to be overinterpreted.

One of the most important components or functions of fatty acids is their incorporation into membranes within cells. From my perspective, enterocytes are very important. Is there a developmental difference when fatty acids are ingested in the very immature infant compared with the less immature infant with respect to incorporation into membranes?

Prof. Koletzko: With respect to your comment on allergy, I absolutely agree. I was just citing the authors' speculative conclusion. I agree that no conclusions about allergy can be drawn.

With respect to the developmental differences, I am not aware of any detailed studies. What we can see is that in both term and preterm infants at different gestational ages, even down to very immature infants, there is a rapid response of plasma and cell lipid composition to dietary intake. However, we don't know anything about the relative distribution.

Dr. Walker: Have you looked at membrane fluidity, which is a very important function of the enterocyte membrane with respect to molecular transport?

Prof. Koletzko: Yes, we've done that in one of the early studies where we tried to squeeze red blood cells through a capillary and then measured the speed of transition with a laser device. We did not find any effect.

Dr. Sedaghatian: In one of your slides, you clearly showed that as gestational age increases, so LC-PUFA increases in the baby. Perhaps babies at different stages of development need different LC-PUFA intakes. Maybe this accounts for some of the conflicting results that have been published.

Prof. Koletzko: That's a good question. I don't think we have any data to answer it as yet.

Prof. Heird: The accumulation of DHA and arachidonic acid in the brain of the developing fetus is roughly the same, somewhere in the region of 4 to 5 mg/d. So per kg body weight, the accumulation is obviously greater for the preterm infant. This continues for some time past full-term gestation. In our studies of the conversion of linolenic and linoleic acids to DHA and arachidonic acid, respectively, the actual rate of conversion is higher in preterm infants than in term infants and seems to decrease somewhat with age. It is very difficult to estimate the fractional rates of conversion or the fractional rates of synthesis, so even though those rates are higher, the pool sizes in the preterm infants are obviously lower. So whether the preterm infant actually makes as much or more than the term infant remains to be seen.

Prof. Fazzolari: Could you clarify the relation between maternal and cord lipids and the risk of intracranial bleeding?

Prof. Koletzko: In the comparison of maternal and infant blood we found that the precursors linoleic and α-linolenic acids were lower in these infants, who had higher levels of long-chain metabolites than their mothers. With respect to bleeding, there is of course great concern that if we add the wrong pattern or the wrong amount of ω-3 fatty acids, we might inhibit thrombocyte aggregation, as has been shown in adults, and increase the risk of bleeding. There have been studies examining this issue. One was published a few years ago by Uauy *et al.* [5]. He found that an intervention rich in ω-3 fatty acids caused a significant change in bleeding time in premature infants, but although this was statistically significant, the values were still well within the normal range. Thus the authors considered that the effect was not clinically important. However, that was a study supplying ω-3 fatty acids only, and we have good reason to think that the effect of bleeding is not so much dependent on the total intake of ω-3 fatty acids as on the ratio between EPA and arachidonic acid.

Dr. Micheli: Do you have data on the placental transfer of LC-PUFA in human fetuses at around 30 weeks of gestation?

Prof. Koletzko: I believe Dr. Crustes de Paulet from Marseille has data on fetal blood samples taken during different periods of gestation, from about 20 weeks onward through the whole of gestation, looking at fetal and maternal blood. The basic conclusion was that the pattern in the infant is similar to the mother, but there is a change in fatty acid composition during gestation.

Prof. Berger: Was the vitamin E content similar in the two formulas? It has been argued that you should not look at the ratio of vitamin E to PUFA per gram weight, but rather at the ratio of vitamin E to active hydrogen—in other words, how many unsaturated bonds there are.

Prof. Koletzko: The vitamin E content was identical at 0.68 mg/100 ml formula. Since the additional amount of LC-PUFA was relatively small compared with the content of precursor PUFA, the ratio between vitamin E and number of double bonds was only changed to a very minor degree. There was about 20% linoleic + α linolenic acid in the formula and only 0.5% of the long-chain metabolites. Thus the ratio changed very little.

REFERENCES

1. Sauerwald TU, Fidler N, Pohl A, *et al.* Docosahexaenoic acid (DHA) recovery in human milk after dietary supplementation. *Pediatr Res* 1998;43:268A.
2. Carlson SE, Werkman SH, Tolley EA. Effect of long chain n-3 fatty acid supplementation on visual acuity and growth of preterm infants with and without bronchopulmonary dysplasia. *Am J Clin Nutr* 1996;63(5):687–697.
3. Auestad N, Montalto MB, Hall RT, *et al.* Visual acuity, erythrocyte fatty acid composition, and growth in term infants fed formulas with long chain polyunsaturated fatty acids for one year. Ross Pediatric Lipid Study. *Pediatr Res* 1997;41(1):1–10.
4. Carlson SE, Montalto MB, Ponder DL, *et al.* Lower incidence of necrotizing enterocolitis in infants fed a preterm formula with egg phospholipids. *Pediatr Res* 1998;44:491–498.
5. Uauy R, Hoffman DR, Birch EE, *et al.* Safety and efficacy of omega-3 fatty acids in the nutrition of very low birth weight infants: soy oil and marine oil supplementation of formula. *J Pediatr* 1994;124(4):612–620.

Nutrition of the Very Low Birthweight Infant, edited by
Ekhard E. Ziegler, Alan Lucas, Guido E. Moro.
Nestlé Nutrition Workshop Series, Paediatric Programme, Vol. 43,
Nestec Ltd., Vevey/Lippincott Williams & Wilkins
Philadelphia, Pennsylvania © 1999.

Early Use of Parenteral Amino Acids

William C. Heird

USDA/ARS Children's Nutrition Research Center, Baylor College of Medicine, Houston, Texas, USA

The potential importance of the early nutritional management of low-birthweight (LBW) infants, including the early use of parenteral amino acids, is best illustrated by the pattern of their early growth. Figure 1 shows the increase in weight and length of two groups of such infants from birth to a postmenstrual age of 43 weeks. One group weighed between 750 and 1,250 g at birth; the other weighed between 1,250 and 1,750 g. Of note is the fact that the curves have two components—an initial, relatively flat component and a subsequent, curvilinear component. Imbedded within the flat component of the weight curve is an initial 10% to 20% weight loss during the first 7 to 10 days of life and a subsequent slow period of weight gain resulting in the eventual return to birthweight. This usually occurs about the time that sufficient enteral intake to support normal growth is tolerated, but by this time, the mean weight and length of both groups, although near the 50th centile at birth, is below the third centile (1). The curvilinear component of the curves depicts the rapid rate of increase in weight and length after birthweight is regained, such that the mean weight of the larger group of infants is near the 50th centile by 43 weeks postmenstrual age (PMA) and that of the smaller group is no longer below the third centile. Interestingly, the length curves show little "catch-up" in either group of infants; at 43 weeks PMA, the mean length of both groups relative to the intrauterine length curve (1) is only minimally improved.

Some of the initial weight loss represents loss of excess extracellular fluid (2) and probably is of little consequence to the infant. However, the proportion of this initial weight loss that is secondary to loss of endogenous protein and fat stores plus accompanying intracellular fluid could have untoward consequences. This component of initial weight loss of LBW infants is obviously related to inadequate nutrient intake secondary to the widely recognized difficulties of feeding these infants, particularly the increasing number of surviving infants who weigh less than 1,250 g at birth. Such infants have immature and/or uncoordinated sucking and swallowing mechanisms. Many other aspects of gastrointestinal function also are poorly developed (e.g., motility). In addition, several metabolic pathways are immature, creating a number of special nutrient requirements. Equally important, these infants often have other problems that interfere with, or are thought to interfere with, nutrient de-

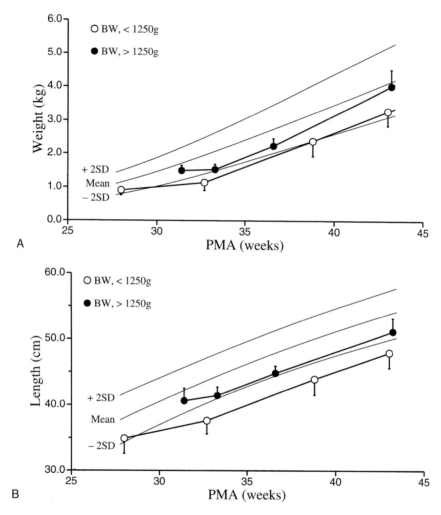

FIG. 1. Increase in weight (**A**) and length (**B**) from birth to 43 weeks postmenstrual age of preterm infants weighing less than (*n* = 12) and more than (*n* = 16) 1,250 g at birth. The first three points of each curve depict weight and length at birth, at achievement of full feeds (150 ml/kg·d), and at discharge. The lighter lines depict the 3rd, 50th, and 97th centiles of intrauterine growth (1).

livery. More subtle problems are concerns that enteral feeding during this early period of life may contribute to the development of necrotizing enterocolitis and that aggressive enteral or parenteral nutrition during this time will result in undesirable metabolic disturbances. As a result, feedings are often withheld and nutrient intake is inadequate for varying periods of time. In general, as illustrated in Fig. 1, this period is longer for smaller, more immature, and sicker infants.

Most infants who weigh less than 1,250 g at birth receive only minimal, if any, enteral intake during the first week of life, and in some, enteral intake is low for the first several weeks of life. During this time, many receive nutrients parenterally, but the quantity of such nutrients delivered is usually well below any reasonable estimate of requirements. Thus, as illustrated in Fig. 1, most infants who weigh less than 1,250 g at birth, although at or near the 50th centile for weight and length at birth, are well below the third centiles by the time birthweight is regained. Although not shown in Fig. 1, it is obvious that the infant whose weight and length are below the 10th centile at birth will be even more growth retarded by the time birthweight is regained.

These observations and considerations raise a number of questions, some of which are addressed in this chapter. These include the consequences of this early period of undernutrition and poor growth, the extent to which the early growth deficits can be recouped after birthweight is regained, and whether the early period of growth can be prevented or reduced.

CONSEQUENCES OF EARLY UNDERNUTRITION

Data from a number of studies (Table 1) show that the low-birthweight (LBW) infant who receives no protein or amino acid intake during early life experiences urinary nitrogen losses of between 90 and 180 mg/kg·d (3–10). Data from individual infants participating in one of the studies in which I was involved (10) are summarized in

TABLE 1. *Nitrogen balance of LBW infants while receiving glucose alone vs. glucose and amino acids during the first week of life*

Study	Birthweight (g)	Energy intake (kcal/kg·d)	Amino acid intake (g/kg·d)	Nitrogen balance (mg/kg·d)
Anderson et al., 1979 (3)	1600	60	0	−132
		60	2.5	178
Saini et al., 1989 (4)	1087	36	0	−133
		45	1.8	120
Mitton et al., 1991 (5)	1470	34	0	−91
	1480	35	0	−125
van Lingen et al., 1992 (7)	1400	47	0	−96
	1510	48	2.3	224
Mitton & Garlick, 1992 (6)	1280	31	0	−139
		83	2.6	259
	1330	30	0	−137
		88	2.6	283
Rivera et al., 1993 (8)	1090	35	0	−135
	1050	54	1.6	88
van Goudoever et al., 1995 (9)	1439	26	0	−110
	1356	29	1.2	10
Kashyap and Heird, 1994 (10)	996	30	0	−183
	996	50	2.0	114

TABLE 2. *Urinary nitrogen excretion and blood urea nitrogen (BUN) concentration before and after addition of amino acids to parenteral nutrition regimens (10)*

Infant	Birthweight (g)	Urinary nitrogen excretion (mg/kg·d)		BUN concentration (mg/dl)	
		Before[a]	After[b]	Before[a]	After[b]
1	745	198	160	16	9
2	1260	214	135	21	14
3	765	158	181	33	21
4	1070	128	150	8	12
5	970	162	325	22	25
6	1100	271	199	21	25
7	1070	142	188	19	228
8	850	155	207	23	20
9	1140	287	312	21	28
10	985	117	153	16	18
Mean		183 ± 58	201 ± 66	20 ± 6	19.3 ± 6.2

[a] Duration ranged from 2 to 9 days (mean = 3 days); nitrogen intake = 0; mean energy intake = 30 ± 8.5 kcal/kg·d.
[b] Duration ranged from 2 to 9 days (mean = 4.8 days); mean nitrogen intake = 315 ± 58 mg/kg·d; mean energy intake = 50 ± 8 kcal/kg·d.

Table 2. In this study, urinary nitrogen excretion was measured daily for the first 10 to 14 days of life. The infants received no amino acid intake during the initial few days (mean = 3 days); during the subsequent period (mean = 5 days), amino acid intake averaged about 2 g/kg·d. The mean nitrogen excretion of these infants while they were receiving no exogenous nitrogen intake was about 180 mg/kg·d, which equates to a daily loss of approximately 1% of body protein stores. Interestingly, urinary nitrogen excretion did not increase dramatically when amino acids were added to the parenteral nutrition regimen. Blood urea nitrogen concentration also did not increase; in many infants, in fact, it decreased. Moreover, plasma amino acid concentrations, which were quite low during the early period of no nitrogen intake, did not exceed cord plasma concentrations of infants born at about the same gestational age (11).

These studies (3–10) show that an amino acid intake of about 1.0 g/kg·d reverses the usual negative nitrogen balance of these infants and that a higher amino acid intake results in positive nitrogen balance. They also illustrate that an early parenteral amino acid intake of as much as 2 g/kg·d, even with a modest concomitant energy intake, does not result in metabolic disturbances. Those studies that included estimates of whole-body protein synthesis and breakdown (6–9,12) indicate that the effect of amino acids is to increase endogenous synthesis; effects of parenteral amino acids on endogenous breakdown are minimal or nonexistent.

Theoretically, reversing the negative nitrogen balance of about 160 mg/kg·d (equivalent to 1 g/kg·d of protein) to zero will decrease the magnitude of weight loss during this period of life by approximately 5 g/kg·d (i.e., 1 g of endogenous protein plus an accompanying 4 g of intracellular fluid). Achievement of a positive balance of 160 mg/kg·d should result in lean body mass deposition of about 5 g/kg·d (again, 1 g/kg·d of protein plus accompanying intracellular fluid). An even higher parenteral amino acid intake, particularly if positive energy balance is achieved, will result in greater rates of lean body mass deposition and, perhaps, earlier resumption of normal growth.

An amino acid intake of at least 3 g/kg·d is likely to be required to support a rate of lean body mass deposition approaching the intrauterine rate. However, an amino acid intake of this magnitude has not been evaluated in infants with poor tolerance of parenteral glucose and lipid and, hence, limited energy intake. Although the data summarized in Tables 1 and 2 show that positive amino acid and protein balance can be achieved with energy intakes as low as 30 to 35 kcal/kg·d, a higher energy intake will clearly improve utilization of the administered amino acids and protein and help promote anabolism.

The functional consequences of an early period of inadequate nutrition are less clear. On the one hand, prolonged mobilization of endogenous protein stores will eventually result in muscle weakness and perhaps failure. This could be particularly hazardous for infants with pulmonary problems. In addition, the known detrimental effects of malnutrition on host defense mechanisms could further increase these infants' susceptibility to infection. Unfortunately, data to confirm or refute these possibilities are lacking.

The impact of inadequate early nutrition on growth and development of the central nervous system is of particular concern. In large part, this concern stems from a body of data, primarily from animals but also from human infants, showing that malnutrition during a "critical" period of central nervous system growth and development, if not corrected during the "critical" period, results in deficits that cannot be recouped (13). In the human infant, the "critical" period for growth of the entire central nervous system is thought to span at least the first 18 months of life (14). Thus correction of early malnutrition within this period should circumvent overall deficits. However, specific developmental events occur in various regions of the central nervous system throughout this time, and little is known about the effects of malnutrition during the reasonably short critical period for these events. Since growth and development of the central nervous system are particularly rapid during the third trimester of gestation, it seems reasonable to assume that the impact of inadequate nutrition during any portion of this period is likely to be particularly detrimental. However, data to support this assumption are lacking.

Lucas *et al.* have shown that LBW infants fed a preterm formula, and hence a higher protein intake, during the period after birthweight was regained until discharge had higher neurodevelopmental indices at both 18 months (15) and at 7 to 8 years of age (16) than infants fed a term formula with a lower content of protein (and other nutrients) during this period. Moreover, Hack *et al.* (17) have shown that one of the primary predictors of poor neurodevelopmental outcome at 8 years of age is a lower than normal head circumference at 8 months of age. These investigators have also shown that head circumference at 8 months of age is related to early growth.

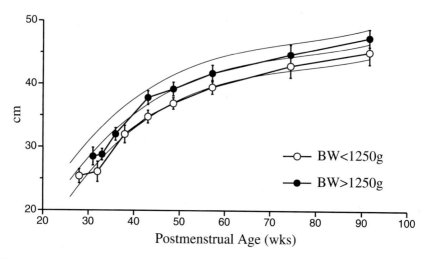

FIG. 2. Increase in head circumference from birth to 74 weeks postmenstrual age of preterm infants weighing less than (*n* = 12) and more than (*n* = 16) 1,250 g at birth. The first three points on each curve depict head circumference at birth, at attainment of full feeds (150 ml/kg·d), and at discharge. The lighter lines depict the 3rd, 50th, and 97th centiles as compiled from intrauterine data (18) and of breast-fed female infants (19).

Figure 2 shows the head circumferences of the two groups of infants whose weight and length are depicted in Fig. 1. It is obvious that the mean head circumference of the smaller infants, who were also sicker and did not regain birthweight as quickly, was significantly lower than that of the larger infants throughout the first year of life. In fact, as shown in Table 3, the head circumference of 20% of these infants was less than two standard deviations below the expected circumference at 1 year of age (19). In addition, at all ages evaluated, there was a strong correlation between head circumference at that age and both weight and length at that age (r^2 values for correlation between head circumference and weight at 43, 48, 56, 74, and 92 weeks PMA, respectively, were 0.668, 0.838, 0.456, 0.719, and 0.704; r^2 values for correlation

TABLE 3. *Percentage of LBW infants weighing less than and greater than 1250 g at birth with head circumference below the third percentile at various ages over the first year of life*

Age	BW < 1250 g	BW > 1250 g
Birth	8%	12%
Full feeds	92%	18%
Discharge	50%	24%
43w, PMA	67%	6%
48w, PMA	42%	6%
56w, PMA	42%	6%
74w, PMA	42%	19%
92w, PMA	20%	0%

between head circumference and length at 43, 48, 56, 74, and 92 weeks PMA were 0.622, 0.717, 0.455, 0.662, and 0.731).

Thus it is clear that inadequate early nutrition, particularly inadequate protein or amino acid intake, is accompanied by loss of endogenous protein stores. Since the LBW infants' endogenous protein stores are limited (20), it is clear that a prolonged period of unopposed endogenous protein loss will eventually result in death. However, the duration of this period remains undefined. More important, perhaps, are the long-term consequences of a shorter period of unopposed endogenous protein breakdown. Although it is usually assumed that any such consequences can be overcome if adequate nutrient intakes are eventually achieved, the poorer long-term neurodevelopmental outcomes of infants fed term *versus* preterm formulas for a period of approximately 4 weeks during early life, as reported by Lucas *et al.* (15,16), suggest otherwise. *A priori*, there is little reason to believe that a shorter period of an even more inadequate nutritional intake than term formula during early life will not affect subsequent neurodevelopmental outcome.

EXTENT TO WHICH EARLY GROWTH FAILURE OF LBW INFANTS CAN BE RECOUPED

As discussed earlier, infants weighing more than as well as less than 1,250 g at birth usually experience some catch-up growth after birthweight is regained. However, at 43 weeks PMA, the mean weight, length, and head circumference of the smaller infants depicted in Figs. 1 and 2 remain two standard deviations or more below the means expected for this age. In the larger infants, much of the weight and head circumference deficit, but little of the length deficit, was recouped by 43 weeks PMA. Thus neither group, although managed quite well according to current nutritional guidelines, experienced complete catch-up growth by 43 weeks PMA. It is important therefore to examine the feasibility of later catch-up.

The nutrient requirements for catch-up growth *per se* are roughly the same as the requirements for normal growth. However, these requirements are superimposed upon those for normal growth. Forbes (21) has shown that catch-up occurs when the magnitude of growth above the normal growth curve equals the magnitude of growth below the normal curve as the growth deficit was incurred. In other words, the requirements for catch-up growth are a function of the amount of catch-up to be achieved and the duration over which it is achieved. For example, the requirements to produce catch-up of 500 g over 50 days are those necessary to produce an additional 10 g of weight gain daily (which, of course, will vary, depending upon the composition of the weight gain). The daily requirements to achieve this catch-up growth within 25 days obviously will be greater, and those for achieving it in 100 days will be less. In all cases, the requirements for catch-up are additional to those for normal growth.

Kashyap *et al.* (22) have shown that the protein and energy intakes required, on average, to produce both specific rates and specific compositions of weight gain can be predicted and that the predicted intakes result, on average, in the expected outcomes.

The exercise summarized in Table 4 shows these principles applied to an infant who weighs 690 g at birth and regains birthweight at 3 weeks of age (23), an optimistic expectation based on the curves of Fig. 1. For complete catch-up (i.e., for the infant to weigh the same and have the same body composition as a fetus of the same post-conceptional age by the time of discharge at a weight of 1,830 g), the infant must increase in weight from 690 to 1,830 g in 35 rather than in 56 days, as would have occurred had premature birth not occurred. The protein and energy intakes predicted to support this rate of weight gain with the same composition as that which would have occurred *in utero* are 5 g/kg·d and 123 kcal/kg·d. A lower protein intake and a higher energy intake might produce the desired rate of weight gain, but the fat content of this weight gain would be greater than that deposited *in utero*.

The protein intake predicted to result in catch-up by the time weight reaches 1,830 g (i.e., 5 g/kg·d) is not likely to be tolerated as well at the predicted energy intake (i.e., 123 kcal/kg) as a lower protein intake (22,24). However, at least some of the weight deficit incurred during the 3-week period required to regain birthweight can be recouped before discharge. Theoretically, a protein intake of 3.4 g/kg·d and an energy intake of approximately 100 kcal/kg·d will support a rate of weight gain of sufficient magnitude to result in the infant's being only 2 weeks behind the fetus of the same postconceptional age at discharge (Table 4). Continuing this combination of protein and energy intakes after discharge should make it possible to recoup the remaining 2-week delay in regaining birthweight by the time the infant reaches a postmenstrual age of 40 weeks.

It also is possible that even greater protein and energy intakes will result in greater rates of weight gain and, hence, more catch-up before discharge. For example, a protein intake of 4 g/kg·d with a concomitant energy intake of 109 kcal/kg·d should allow the theoretical infant to recoup two-thirds of the weight deficit incurred during the first three weeks of life before discharge at 1,830 g (see Table 4). Although a protein intake of 4 g/kg·d is unlikely to be utilized completely at an energy intake of only 109 kcal/kg·d, this combination of protein and energy intakes is also unlikely to

TABLE 4. *Protein and energy intakes predicted to result in different rates of catch-up growth*

Weight gain	Predicted protein intake (g/kg·d)	Predicted energy intake (kcal/kg·d)
690 g → 1830 g:		
in 56 days*	2.9	91
in 49 days	3.4	98
in 42 days	4.0	109
in 35 days	4.9	123
1830 g → 3450 g:		
in 56 days*	2.7	89
in 49 days	3.0	93
in 42 days	3.4	99
in 35 days	4.0	109

* Time required in utero.

result in disturbing metabolic abnormalities (22,24). A greater energy intake will improve utilization of this protein intake and result in a somewhat greater rate of weight gain (in theory, about 1 g/kg·d for each 10 kcal/kg·d increase in energy intake). However, this additional weight gain will be predominantly fat. Whether this should be of concern remains to be established (25).

More modest protein and energy intakes after discharge, but more than provided by term formulas on which most LBW infants are currently fed after discharge, may also enhance catch-up (26,27). Whether it is preferable to catch up over a shorter period (i.e., by discharge) or by a postmenstrual age of 40 weeks remains to be established. Although it is clear that catch-up can occur throughout childhood and particularly during adolescence, the extent to which very small LBW infants catch up is not clear (28). Most available studies, in fact, suggest that many such infants remain small relative to their growth potential.

The smaller group of infants depicted in Figure 1 did not regain birthweight until approximately 5 weeks after birth, and although they experienced catch-up growth from this time through to a postmenstrual age of 43 weeks, the amount of catch-up growth was not sufficient to allow them to completely recoup the deficit incurred during the first 5 weeks of life. Clearly, if birthweight had been regained sooner, as was true for the larger group of infants, the amount of catch-up required would have been less and the likelihood of the infant's catching up and returning to its "expected" growth channel would have been enhanced. However, reducing the time required to regain birthweight will almost certainly require more aggressive nutritional management during this period. Since more aggressive enteral or parenteral feeding during this period may result in other problems, it seems wise to withhold specific recommendations until more information is available about the consequences of inadequate early nutrition and growth as well as the hazards of more aggressive early enteral or parenteral nutrition. Nonetheless, it is important to examine the evidence that more aggressive nutritional management during early life will prevent or reduce early growth failure, as the foregoing theoretical considerations suggest.

PREVENTION AND/OR REDUCTION OF EARLY GROWTH FAILURE

Few studies have addressed the issue of whether the early growth failure of LBW infants can be prevented or reduced. In one such study (29), which was conducted at a single regional neonatal center over a 25-month period, 125 infants weighing less than 1,200 g at birth or between 1,200 and 1,499 g at birth and requiring mechanical ventilation within 24 hours of birth were assigned randomly to receive aggressive nutritional management ($n = 64$) or standard management ($n = 61$). Outcome variables included nutrient intakes, growth, and clinical morbidity during the study period (i.e., from enrollment until death or discharge home).

The two modes of nutritional management differed in the timing of the introduction of parenteral amino acids, carbohydrate, and lipid as well as in the maximum amount of each nutrient infused. In general, each nutrient was introduced sooner, the amount of each was increased more rapidly, and the maximum amount of each was greater in the aggressively managed group. Enteral feedings were also introduced earlier in this group. Although the volume of enteral feeding was not necessarily increased more rapidly, criteria for withholding feeds or stopping feeds were less stringent for this group.

As hypothesized, the parenteral intakes of all major nutrients were higher in the aggressively managed group. Enteral intake also was started sooner in this group, but full enteral feeding was not attained sooner (21 and 22 days in the aggressively managed and control groups, respectively). Total energy intake of the aggressively managed group was higher for the first 42 days of life, and enteral intake was higher for the first 21 days of life. The maximum initial weight loss of the aggressively managed group was less than that of the conventionally managed group (5.1% *versus* 8.4% of body weight), and the aggressively managed group, on average, regained birthweight 3 days sooner than the control group. The weights of the two groups at death or discharge did not differ, but fewer of the aggressively managed group were below the 10th centile of expected weight, length, and head circumference at discharge. Moreover, although the mean weight of both groups was below the 10th centile of expected weight at 10 and 12 weeks and postnatal age, the mean weight of the aggressively managed group was significantly greater than that of the control group at these ages. This suggests that the aggressively managed group was discharged sooner.

Despite stratified randomization, the aggressively managed group was sicker at enrollment. However, neither morbidity nor mortality during the study period differed between groups. After adjusting for disease severity, gestational age, and birthweight, aggressive nutritional management reduced the odds of having a weight, length, or head circumference below the 10th centile at discharge by more than half. The odds of developing bronchopulmonary dysplasia were also halved by aggressive nutritional management, and the odds of developing infection were reduced by 70%.

Overall, this study shows conclusively that the early nutritional intake of sick, LBW infants as well as their intake throughout hospitalization can be improved considerably without increasing the incidence of adverse clinical or metabolic sequelae. Whether this improves long-term growth and development remains to be determined. In this regard, it is important to note that a modest improvement in early growth is unlikely to result in a detectable effect on subsequent weight or length. This is because the extent of growth before discharge is quite small in comparison with that normally occurring between discharge and 12 months of age. Consider, for example, two groups of infants having the same mean birthweights but growing differently before discharge, such that discharge weights of the two groups are 2,500 g and 2,000 g, a difference of 25%. If both groups gain 7,500 g between discharge and 12 months of age, the difference in mean weights of the two groups at 12 months of age will still be 500 g, a difference of only 5.3%. Clearly, the 25% difference at discharge will be much easier to detect than the 5% difference at 12 months of age.

Regardless of detectable effects of improved early nutritional management, and hence better early growth, on subsequent size, it is reasonable to assume that the infant whose early weight loss is less and who regains birthweight sooner is less likely to have later sequelae of inadequate early nutrition. However, data to support this assumption are lacking. In this regard, as part of the same study that showed beneficial effects of preterm *versus* term formula on subsequent neurodevelopmental performance (15,16), another group of infants was fed banked human milk, which has an even lower nutrient content than term formula, and the subsequent neurodevelopmental performance of this group was similar to that of the group fed preterm formula (30). Thus factors other than nutrition *per se* seem to be important with respect to subsequent neurodevelopmental performance. However, since these factors have not been completely identified, it is difficult to modify them. Improved early nutrition, on the other hand, can be achieved and can at least partially reverse the extent and duration of early growth failure experienced by most LBW infants. Further, there are strong reasons to expect that it may also improve subsequent growth and, particularly, development.

REFERENCES

1. Usher R, McLean F. Intrauterine growth of live born Caucasian infants at sea level: standards obtained from measurements in 7 dimensions of infants born between 25 and 44 weeks of gestation. *J Pediatr* 1969;74:901–910.
2. Van Der Wagen A, Okken A, Zweens J, Zulstra WG. Composition of postnatal weight loss and subsequent weight gain in small for dates newborn infants. *Acta Paediatr Scand* 1985;74:57–61.
3. Anderson TL, Muttart C, Bieber MA, Nicholson JF, Heird WC. A controlled trial of glucose *vs.* glucose amino acids in premature infants. *J Pediatr* 1979;94:947–951.
4. Saini J, MacMahon P, Morgan JB, Kovar IZ. Early parenteral feeding of amino acids. *Arch Dis Child* 1989;64:1362–1366.
5. Mitton SG, Calder AG, Garlick PJ. Protein turnover rates in sick, premature neonates during the first few days of life. *Pediatr Res* 1991;30:418–422.
6. Mitton SG, Garlick PJ. Changes in protein turnover after the introduction of parenteral nutrition in premature infants: comparison of breast milk and egg protein-based amino acid solutions. *Pediatr Res* 1992;32:447–454.
7. Van Lingen RA, van Goudoever JB, Luijendijk IHT, Wattimena JLD, Sauer PJJ. Effects of early amino acid administration during total parenteral nutrition on protein metabolism in pre-term infants. *Clin Sci* 1992;82:199–203.
8. Rivera A, Bell EF, Bier DM. Effect of intravenous amino acids on protein metabolism of preterm infants during the first three days of life. *Pediatr Res* 1993;33:106–111.
9. Van Goudoever JB, Colen T, Wattimena JLD, Huijmans JGM, Carnielli VP, Sauer PJJ. Immediate commencement of amino acid supplementation in preterm infants: effect on serum amino acid concentrations and protein kinetics on the first day of life. *J Pediatr* 1995;127:458–465.
10. Kashyap S, Heird WC. Protein requirements of low birthweight, very low birthweight, and small for gestational age infants. In: Räihä, Niels CR, eds. *Protein metabolism during infancy.* New York: Raven Press; 1994:133–146.
11. Pittard WB, Geddes KM, Picone TA. Cord blood amino acid concentrations from neonates of 23–41 weeks gestational age. *J Parenter Enter Nutr* 1988;12:1673–1679.
12. Denne SC, Karn CA, Ahirichs JA, Dorotheo AR, Wang J, Liechty EA. Proteolysis and phenylalanine hydroxylation in response to parenteral nutrition in extremely premature and normal newborns. *J Clin Invest* 1996;3:746–754.
13. Dobbing J. Nutritional growth restriction and the nervous system. In: Davison AN, Thompson RHS, eds. *The molecular bases of neuropathology.* London: Edward Arnold; 1981:221–233.
14. Dobbing J, Sands J. Comparative aspects of the brain growth spurt. *Early Human Dev* 1970;3:79–83.
15. Lucas A, Morley R, Cole TJ, *et al.* Early diet in preterm babies and developmental status at 18 months. *Lancet* 1990;335:1477–1481.
16. Lucas A. Long chain polyunsaturated fatty acids, infant feeding and cognitive development. In: Dobbing J, ed. *Developing brain and behaviour.* London: Academic Press; 1997:3–39.
17. Hack M, Breslau N, Weissman B, Aram D, Klein N, Borawski E. Effect of very low birth weight and subnormal head size on cognitive abilities at school age. *NEJM* 1991;325:231–237.

18. Yudkin PL, Aboualfa M, Eyre JA, Redman CWG, Wilkinson AR. New birthweight and head circumference centiles for gestational ages 24 to 42 weeks. *Early Hum Dev* 1987;15:45–52.
19. WHO Working Group on Infant Growth. *An evaluation of infant growth*. Geneva: World Health Organization; 1994.
20. Widdowson E. Changes in body proportions and composition during growth. In: Davis JA, Dobbing J, eds. *Scientific foundations of paediatrics*. Philadelphia: WB Saunders; 1974:153–163.
21. Forbes GB. A note on the mathematics of catch-up growth. *Pediatr Res* 1974;8:929–931.
22. Kashyap S, Schulze KF, Ramakrishnan R, Dell RB, Heird WC. Evaluation of a mathematical model for predicting the relationship between protein and energy intakes of low-birth-weight infants and the rate and composition of weight gain. *Pediatr Res* 1994;35:704–712.
23. Heird WC, Wu C. Are we discharging preterm infants in a suboptimal nutritional state? In: Hay WW, Lucas A, eds. *Posthospital nutrition in the preterm infant*. Columbus: Ross Laboratories; 1996:7–20.
24. Kashyap S, Schulze KF, Forsyth M, *et al.* Growth, nutrient retention, and metabolic response of low-birth-weight infants fed supplemented and unsupplemented preterm human milk. *J Pediatr* 1988;113:713–721.
25. Dietz WH. Critical periods in childhood for the development of obesity. *Am J Clin Nutr* 1994;59:955–9.
26. Lucas A, Bishop NJ, King FJ, Cole TJ. Randomized trial of nutrition for preterm infants after discharge. *Arch Dis Child* 1992;67:324–327.
27. Carver JD, Wu, PYK, Hall RT, Baggs GE, Bienneman B. Growth of preterm infants fed Similac Neocare or Similac with iron after hospital discharge. *Pediatr Res* 1997;41:229A (abst.).
28. Hack M, Weissman B, Borawski-Clark E. Catch-up growth during childhood among very low-birth-weight children. *Arch Pediatr Adolesc Med* 1996;150:1122–1129.
29. Wilson DC, Cairns P, Halliday HL, *et al.* Randomised controlled trial of an aggressive nutritional regimen in sick very low birthweight infants. *Arch Dis Child* 1997;77:F4–11.
30. Lucas A, Morley R, Cole TJ, Gore SM. A randomised multicentre study of human milk *versus* formula and later development in preterm infants. *Arch Dis Child Fetal Neonatal Ed* 1994;70:F141–146.

DISCUSSION

Dr. Walker: I am not a neonatologist, so I am asking this for information. It is my understanding that one of the problems with catch-up growth, both in the very small premature infant and in the malnourished child, is that there is barrier at cell level to taking up sufficient substrate to allow the required turnover. What do we know about that in the very small premature infant, in relation to how much they can absorb when you're providing them with excess energy?

Prof. Heird: Obviously, there is a limit. We studied protein intakes ranging from 2.25 to 4.5 g/kg·d and energy intakes ranging from 100 to 150 kcal/kg·d. With a protein intake of around 4 g/kg·d and an energy intake of 120 kcal/kg·d, there was some inhibition of protein utilization, but over most of that range the babies we studied seemed to "soak up" whatever nutrients were provided. Granted, these were not sick babies; they were babies who had regained birth weight, so they were reasonably stable. The upper limit seems to us to be about 4 g/kg·d and 120 kcal/kg·d; at a protein intake of 4 g/kg·d and an energy intake of 150 kcal/kg·d there will be increased fat deposition.

Prof. Lucas: It is impressive that it was possible to give a protein intake of 3.5 g/kg·d, which is far more than the average neonatologist would give, without any obvious adverse effect. Was the failure to achieve growth because they were not given enough energy to utilize the protein? How far can we go to test this hypothesis?

Prof. Heird: I certainly have no ethical qualms about pushing the intake to 3 g/kg·d. There are nurseries around the United States that are doing this; I even know of some who have gone up to 4 g/kg·d. We talk a lot about a limiting energy intake, but this, I believe, is overdone. There are few data about the actual limiting energy intake. It is true that urinary nitrogen excretion increases as the protein/energy ratio of the diet increases, which can occur simply by increasing the protein and keeping the energy constant, or by changing both. But this is a fairly small effect. You can calculate the effects of a 0.5-g amino acid increase *vs.* 20-kcal increase and regardless of the fact that the additional 0.5 g of amino acid intake is not used as completely, it still has a greater effect on nitrogen and protein deposition than the 20 kcal.

Dr. Sedaghatian: Nobody has looked longitudinally at babies who have gained their birthweight after 20 or 30 days. Maybe these small babies really need more days to catch up their birthweight. Is it really physiological to push them to catch up?

Prof. Heird: Obviously, some of the early weight loss is water, and I don't think loss of water is going to hurt the baby in any way. However, a baby *in utero* does not go 3 weeks with no protein intake. I am not totally pleased with the intrauterine rate of weight gain argument, but I know of no better substitute. I think that the creation of growth curves for preterm infants based on how they grow postnatally is just silly; this is just perpetuating the unsatisfactory situation. I quite agree with you that we don't have all the studies necessary to determine if growth in the early weeks affects neurodevelopmental outcome, though we are beginning to get that with some of the data you heard from Prof. Morley.

Dr. Micheli: What is the rationale for reducing the amino acid supply and glucose supply after birth in extremely low-birthweight infants? Surely we should try to mimic what the placenta does.

Prof. Heird: In the early days of TPN, it was soon realized that you could not start with a 25% solution of glucose on day 1 without developing rather dramatic hyperglycemia, osmotic diuresis, and so on. So someone conceived the bright idea of having different strength parenteral nutrition solutions. They simply took a full-strength infusate and made it into half strength, quarter strength, or what have you. This obviously reduced both the glucose and the amino acid concentration. As far as I can tell, this is the origin of the practice of giving a low intake of amino acids on day 1 and then increasing it gradually to the desired value by the end of the first week of life or later. I also think there is an almost irrational fear of protein in this early period. The reason for that derives from early studies using protein intakes of 6–8 g/kg·d.

Dr. Rashwan: Is there any information on the effects of aggressive nutrition on renal function?

Prof. Heird: I can't think of any specific studies of the effect of aggressive protein therapy on renal function. In the data I presented, some studies measured urea nitrogen, some measured acidosis, and some measured other indicators of renal function, and there were no seriously abnormal results. The primary effect of a high protein intake on whole body protein metabolism in these infants seems to be to increase synthesis, rather than to increase breakdown. When the synthesis component increases, the balance is more positive and there is less excretion of breakdown metabolites.

Dr. Putet: It is surprising to me that in the second part of the Wilson study (i.e., after 2 to 3 weeks), there was absolutely no catch-up. I wonder why. A lot of these infants had bronchopulmonary dysplasia, so the fact that some will have been treated with corticosteroids may have been responsible for this inadequate catch-up. As far as growth is concerned, what is important is lean body mass. What do you think is the minimum protein and energy intake during the first 10 days of life necessary to prevent a fall in lean body mass in these infants? Weight loss during the first weeks of life is partly or mostly water, but we need to protect against loss of lean body mass. I don't mind losing a little more than 5% as water, as long as lean body mass is protected.

Prof. Heird: I don't mind some loss of water either. But if you are losing at least 1 g/kg of protein and the intracellular water that goes with it, that is not a good situation. That is going to decrease lean body mass. That was the type of weight loss I was suggesting should be prevented, not necessarily the simple loss of extracellular fluid, which seems to be there in excess to start with. I am concerned about the timing of catch-up growth. If it doesn't matter whether losses are recouped over the next 3 or 4 weeks, or over the next 4 years, then one could just ignore the first few days. If, on the other hand, the loss of lean body mass during these first few days is important for brain development, that may not be such a wise approach. You asked for suggestions on minimum intakes: I would be reasonably pleased with about 3 g/kg·d amino acids and 60 kcal/kg·d energy.

Prof. Moro: You mentioned head circumference growth. Results from various groups in the United States suggest there is a positive correlation between head circumference growth and neurodevelopmental outcome. But today, in this room, we heard exactly the opposite from Prof. Morley. As this measurement is very easy to perform in neonatal departments and after the baby has been discharged, most neonatologists should have enough data to answer this question definitively. Can you tell us whether or not there is a positive correlation between these two variables?

Prof. Heird: I had not heard the data that were presented this morning until today, so I cannot comment on them. My impression was that in that set of data there was a strong correlation between the size of the baby and its head circumference. The same was true in the data I showed you. Thus small babies and short babies have smaller head circumferences. If Prof. Morley tells me, on the basis of a large sample, that there is not a good correlation between head circumference and neurodevelopmental outcome, then I shall have to accept that so long as she is convinced that she has separated the effects of head circumference from those of weight or length. Also, as Prof. Lucas pointed out, a large head circumference is not always a good thing; for example, if it is due to hydrocephalus or other pathological cause. It is a complicated issue.

Dr. Morley: The question of why we find different results in the United Kingdom is important. There is one issue here that I would like to emphasize again, and that is the influence of social class in the United Kingdom. This has a very powerful effect on outcome and accounts for about 25% of variance in the models; it is also related to head circumference. Because social class is a prior factor, I had it in the model. It may be that this is actually taking out some of the effect of head circumference, simply because it is correlated with head circumference. If I run the model just with head circumference at 9 months, it does have a significant effect on several of the outcomes. If I run it just with weight, it has a highly significant effect. If I then put them both in, it is almost always weight that comes out predominant. This is a complex issue, because if you put two related variables in a model, you may get serious distortion of the effects.

Dr. Guesry: You spent most of your time speaking about the quantitative aspects of amino acid supply. I want to know about the qualitative aspects. None of the papers I've read have addressed the issue of qualitative differences in amino acid supply between very low-birthweight and low-birthweight infants. Do you know anything about differences in amino acid patterns, or in the conditionally essential amino acids, between VLBW and LBW infants?

Prof. Heird: In our studies, there really does not seem to be much difference between requirements for low-birthweight infants and term infants. When you get down to very low-birthweight infants, there is much less information. I am reasonably sure that there is no completely ideal parenteral amino acid solution available today. None contain cysteine and none contain tyrosine; granted, tyrosine should not be an essential amino acid since the rate-limiting enzyme for its synthesis is there from the start, but studies have repeatedly shown that babies and animals that receive tyrosine in some form do better. Glutamine also is not present in available parenteral amino acid mixtures. If these "quality" problems could be solved, the quantities of amino acids required may change considerably. In other words, the reason that 3 g/kg·d are needed may be that the overall quality of the amino acid mixture is not ideal.

Dr. Chessex: People are starting to look at outcome measures relating to amino acid quality. We have just published a paper in *Pediatric Research* that looks at a completely different side of the problem [1]. Instead of looking at the amount of energy and the amount of protein, we're looking at the way we're giving these substrates. We have shown that if you protect the amino acid solution from light, you will affect the quality of the amino acids. I refer particularly to cysteine. In Europe, where such solutions do contain cysteine, its rate of disappearance is about 50% over 24 hours if left in a bag in ambient light.

Prof. Heird: Are you referring to glucocysteine?

Dr. Chessex: We haven't measured whether it was glucocysteine, but in the two solutions, the only difference was the fact that they were put in the presence or the absence of light. Protecting the solution with a bag reduced the disappearance of the final amount of cysteine that you can measure in the solution.

Prof. Heird: You will definitely find some glucocysteine. Of course, light also has an effect on tryptophan, which is another major problem. With regard to European amino acid mixtures, it is true that some contain cysteine, but it is a fraction of the amount that most people would assume reasonable.

Prof. Lucas: We all recognize that this is an extremely heterogeneous group of babies, with different energy needs. There are differences in the work of ventilation, different protein needs for catch-up growth according to how growth retarded they are at birth, different needs related to gestation, some have got sepsis, some are in a catabolic state, some are on steroids, and indeed we know from experience that these babies grow very differently—some grow very well and others take weeks to catch up. The obvious question is how much we should be attempting to individualize intakes on the basis of an objective measurement of need. When I have been asked to look at infants who are growing very poorly and have done energy expenditure measurements, I have often found that growth-retarded babies require much more energy than people ever dare to give them. Don't you think we should be trying to get babies to grow according to their individual needs rather than thinking in terms of rigid regimens?

Prof. Heird: I totally agree with you. But we have to start somewhere. In most nurseries around the world, babies are getting only 0.5 g/kg·d of amino acids in the first week of life. The suggestion that one should start by increasing this early intake to a more reasonable amount and then individualize intakes makes some sense to me. I am impressed that if you look at the group means of almost any study, the standard deviation is usually less than 20%. But once that is translated into values for individual babies, variation increases considerably.

Prof. Devlieger: With regard to water, I think very premature babies differ greatly in their water content. Perhaps weight is not the best denominator for calculations of nutrient requirements or weight loss. Should we not apply a correction factor for edema or take into account fluid tolerance of the baby?

Prof. Heird: Those things need to be taken into account. Unfortunately, as you know, it is virtually impossible to measure extracellular water at the bedside in a way that can enable you to make decisions. Some of that information can be obtained, but certainly not on an entire nursery population. There are studies that suggest that about half of the early weight loss is excess extracellular loss and the other half is lean body mass.

Dr. Schanler: With respect to the aggressive approach paper, it seems as though we were discussing the first few weeks only. I think that the aggressive approach, as he calls it, should be continued throughout the hospital stay, when the babies are on full enteral feeds. There should be a target at that time too. I think the simplest target is the rate of weight gain on a daily basis. If the period of enteral nutrition also received emphasis, there might be more positive outcomes. I also want to put in a plea to change the term *aggressive.* When we talk to neonatologists, they get nervous about that term *aggressive nutrition,* so I think we should call it the *rational nutrition approach.*

Prof. Heird: They did follow the baby until discharge, so their study covered the entire period of admission. What was different after full feeds were tolerated is not clear to me. As I pointed out, I would not call the approach aggressive.

REFERENCES

1. Laborie S, Lavoie JC, Chessex P. Paradoxical role of ascorbic acid and riboflavin in solutions of total parenteral nutrition: implication in photoinduced peroxide generation. *Pediatr Res* 1998;48(5):601–606.

Nutrition of the Very Low Birthweight Infant, edited by
Ekhard E. Ziegler, Alan Lucas, Guido E. Moro.
Nestlé Nutrition Workshop Series, Paediatric Programme, Vol. 43,
Nestec Ltd., Vevey/Lippincott Williams & Wilkins
Philadelphia, Pennsylvania © 1999.

Early Administration of Intravenous Lipids: Still under Debate

Guy Putet

Service de Réanimation Néonatale, Hôpital Debrousse, 69322 Lyon, France

Intravenous lipid (IL) emulsions are important constituents of total parenteral nutrition (TPN) because they provide essential fatty acids and allow an increase in energy intake without giving an excess of glucose, which may be associated with an increase in carbon dioxide production. In the very low-birthweight (VLBW) infants, who often cannot be fed enterally for days or weeks in the early neonatal period, IL emulsions are considered a major source of energy for adequate nutrition.

However, the utilization of IL emulsions during the very first days of life is still debated, especially during the early stage of respiratory distress, since unwanted effects have been described, including hypertriglyceridemia, possible impairment of the immune system, a negative effect on bilirubin albumin binding, impaired coagulation, and intolerance of the lipid during stress. Such unwanted side effects have often been described at doses or infusion rates that may not be appropriate for VLBW infants or extremely low-birthweight (ELBW) infants in clinical practice because of their metabolic immaturity.

It is well known and accepted that intravenous glucose or amino acids have to be given at a constant rate and in amounts that do not induce metabolic disturbances or exceed the metabolic capacity of the infant. It is obvious that a similar argument must be applied when intravenous lipids are infused.

Triglyceride clearance from the bloodstream is the first step in the metabolic utilization of IL emulsions and is dependent on lipoprotein lipase activity, which is the rate-limiting enzymatic step in the hydrolysis of circulating triglycerides. Free fatty acids (FFA) released by this hydrolysis recirculate bound to albumin, causing an increment in plasma FFA that can be used as a metabolic fuel in liver, heart, or skeletal muscle. In liver these FFA may also be converted to VLDL and enter the lipoprotein cycle. FFA may also enter adipose tissue, where they can be re-esterified to triglycerides and stored.

Plasma lipid clearance is less efficient in VLBW infants than in term infants, especially in those who are small for gestational age (SGA) (1,2). It is also variable from one infant to another and—for the same dosage regimen—is improved when IL emulsions are given as a continuous infusion over 24 hours (3). Clearance capacity is evaluated by measuring the serum triglyceride concentration, though the allowable upper limit of serum triglyceride has not yet been established. In infants fed pooled human milk, triglyceride concentrations of 100 to 200 mg/dl are usual. Because significant increases in plasma cholesterol, phospholipids, and very low-density lipoproteins have been described when plasma triglyceride values exceed 100 to 150 mg/dl in infants receiving intravenous lipids, it seems reasonable to take this as the upper limit for unstable VLBW infants.

The most important factor to consider is not the overall daily intake of intravenous lipid given to the infant but the infusion rate—that is, the amount given in unit of time (g/kg per minute or hour), so as not to exceed the plasma clearance capacity. This was well illustrated in a study by Kao et al. (3). Thus instead of saying that 1 or 2 g/kg·d of intravenous lipid may be given to a particular infant, it is preferable to say that a rate of 0.4 or 0.8 g/kg·h can be infused and to remember that increasing this infusion rate may be harmful, just as it is harmful to make a sudden increase in the infusion rate of glucose. The clearance capacity may also be modified by stress of any type (infection, inflammation, surgery, and so on) (4), and in these circumstances utilization of intravenous lipids must be restricted or even halted.

The use of 10% and 20% lipid emulsions has been investigated in recent studies. These have shown that excessive quantities of phospholipid liposomes contained in 10% lipid emulsions impede the removal of triglycerides from plasma and are associated with higher plasma triglyceride concentrations and raised cholesterol and phospholipid levels. It is now clear that 20% lipid emulsions should be used rather than 10% emulsions (5,6).

Oxidation of infused fat will depend on the total energy expenditure of the infant and on the concomitant carbohydrate intake. If the amount of energy given as carbohydrate is greatly above the level of energy expenditure, the amount of perfused lipid that will be oxidized will be low (7). Data show that above a glucose intake of 20 g/kg·d, most of the infused lipid may be stored and not oxidized. Thus utilization (oxidation) of IL emulsion as an energy source will depend on the total energy intake, on the total glucose intake, and on the level of energy expenditure.

It is not clear whether supplementation with carnitine can increase fat oxidation, and studies evaluating carnitine supplementation in VLBW infants have been controversial (8,9). However, as the need for added carnitine for better fat oxidation is still not established, it may be wise to try to keep tissue carnitine stores or plasma carnitine concentrations at the levels observed in human milk-fed VLBW infants.

EARLY INTRAVENOUS LIPID STILL DEBATED

Can we start intravenous lipid in the first 3 to 4 days of life, or do we have to wait until the end of the first week? Few studies have focused on this point. Hammerman and Aramburo (10) compared two groups of VLBW infants (less than 1,750 g at birth) randomly assigned to receive TPN with or without 10% lipid emulsion for 5 days. One group received 10% lipid emulsion after the third day of life, and the other received it only after the eighth day. Lipids were started at 0.5 g/kg·d and progressively increased to 2.5 g/kg·d. All infants received 1 ml/d of a multivitamin preparation. Chronic lung disease appeared to be increased in duration and tended to be more severe after lipid intake, as the number of days of ventilation (37 ± 35 *versus* 21 ± 18 days) and of oxygen therapy (51 ± 39 *versus* 28 ± 23 days) was increased significantly in the lipid group. The vasoconstrictor metabolite thromboxane B2 was raised in the IL group in comparison with the group receiving no lipids.

Sosenko *et al.* (11) randomly assigned 133 infants to receive 20% Intralipid or not during the first week of life, separating the infants in two weight strata: 600 to 800 g (42 infants receiving IL *versus* 37 control), and 801 to 1,000 g (28 IL *versus* 26 control). The IL groups were given lipids at less than 12 hours of age, starting at 0.5 g/kg·d, increasing to 1.5 g/kg·d maintained through to day 7. Control groups received no Intralipid until after day 7. Both groups received the same amount of a multivitamin solution. The results showed that in the overall population there was no significant difference in mortality (32.9% *versus* 25.4%, IL *versus* control) but that the mortality was higher in the 600- to 800-g stratum in infants receiving IL (47.5% *versus* 24.3% in the control group). Though the clinical data were similar in the two groups, it may be important to observe that the numbers of infants whose mother received corticosteroids was significantly higher in the controls (30%) than in the IL group (7%), and this may have introduced bias (relating to the influence of antenatal corticosteroid administration on the survival of ELBW infants). It is also important to emphasize that in the 801- to 1,000-g group there were more than twice as many deaths in the controls (7/26) as in the IL group (3/28). In that stratum, maternal corticosteroid administration was 11% in the IL group *versus* 19% in the controls. No significant difference was observed for chronic lung disease, but there was a significant increase in pulmonary hemorrhage, and a larger number of infants required supplemental oxygen at day 7 in the lipid groups. However, it was shown that by day 28 the number of infants requiring supplemental oxygen was greater in the control groups for both weight strata, and the number of infants requiring oxygen at 60 days was more than twice as high in the control group as in the IL group.

Similarly, Gilbertson *et al.* (12) studied 29 VLBW infants of less than 1,500 g receiving isocaloric, isonitrogenous parenteral feeding from day 1 with either intravenous lipid given at 1 g/kg·d from day 1 increasing to 3 g/kg·d by day 4 (IL group, n = 16) or intravenous lipid given only after day 8 (control group, n = 13). Lipids were given over 20 hours. At the end of the trial, there was no difference between the two groups for chronic lung disease, jaundice, septicemia, periventricular hemorrhage, necrotizing enterocolitis, or any other selected variables. The authors concluded that when lipids are infused at rates not exceeding 0.15 g/kg·h (3 g/kg·d over 24 hours), with stepwise dose increases from the first day of life, they can be tolerated by sick VLBW infants without an increase in the incidence of adverse effects.

More recently, Fox *et al.* (13) undertook a meta-analysis of six randomized clinical trials designed to assess the effect of early (day 1 to 5) *versus* late (day 5 to 14) introduction of intravenous lipids. They found no significant trend or effect on the incidence of death or chronic lung disease (at 28 days or at 36 weeks).

INTRAVENOUS LIPIDS AND JAUNDICE

In jaundiced newborn infants caution has been advised over the use of lipid emulsions because the fatty acids released during hydrolysis can displace bilirubin from albumin binding sites, producing unbound bilirubin and increasing the risk of kernicterus.

In vitro studies have shown that at a molar ratio of free fatty acids to serum albumin (FFA/Alb) of 4, no free bilirubin is released (14). *In vivo*, no generation of unbound bilirubin is demonstrated if the FFA/Alb ratio is below 6 (1). There are even some data (15) showing that Intralipid binds bilirubin and may serve as a potential vehicle for serum transport of bilirubin. In the study by Sosenko *et al.* (11), jaundice was not an exclusion criterion. In the study by Hammerman and Aramburo (10) severe hyperbilirubinemia (not defined more precisely) was an exclusion criterion. However, in the patients studied there was no detectable difference in bilirubin levels between the lipid group and the control group on days 1, 3, or 5 (IL group *versus* control: day 3, 7.3 ± 3.9 *versus* 7.7 ± 2.8 mg/dl; day 5, 5.6 ± 2.6 *versus* 6.0 ± 2.9 mg/dl).

In the study by Gilbertson *et al.* (12) it was stated that the molar ratio of fatty acid to serum albumin remained below 3 in all cases. The incidence of significant jaundice—defined as serum bilirubin concentrations above 200 μmol/liter (11.7 mg/dl) and days of phototherapy (2.46 ± 0.40 days *versus* 2.23 ± 0.51 days, IL *versus* control)—was similar in the two groups.

Adamkin *et al.* (16) specifically studied the effect of administration of 10% lipid emulsion on triglycerides, free fatty acids, albumin, and unconjugated bilirubin in 26 VLBW infants weighing ≤ 1,500 g at birth, six being less than 750 g. Lipid emulsion was started on the fourth postnatal day at 0.5 g/kg·d. This was increased by 0.5 g/kg·d from postnatal day 7 in infants below 1,200 g. In infants above 1,200 g, lipid intake was advanced to 1 g/kg·d on postnatal day 5 and increased by 0.5 g/kg·d from postnatal day 7. A maximum lipid intake of 3.5 g/kg·d was achieved by postnatal day 10. The lipid infusion time was 18 hours in each 24-hour period. Data were provided for 8 days of TPN that included lipid administration. Five VLBW infants had a single serum triglyceride value above 200 mg/dl (defined as hypertriglyceridemia). All infants had FFA/Alb ratios below 3. A mean peak serum unconjugated bilirubin of 5.8 mg/dl occurred on postnatal day 3 (baseline) and was stable or fell during the next 10 days of lipid infusion.

Brans *et al.* (17) studied 38 neonates below 1,500 g on TPN, divided into three groups: group I received fat emulsion at a constant rate over 24 hours, starting at 1 g/kg·d and increasing by 1 g/kg·d to a maximum of 4 g/kg; group II received the same intake of fat emulsion but over 16 hours; group III received fat emulsion over 24 hours but starting at a dose of 4 g/kg·d. The study was stopped if a baby was unable to tolerate the fat emulsion (plasma frankly creamy). Blood samples were obtained every 24 hours (i.e., 8 hours after the end of fat infusion in group II). One infant in group II and one in group III had severe hyperlipemia. In all groups the FFA increased significantly. Serum total bilirubin concentrations were not statistically different from preinfusion levels and were similar between groups for a given day.

Serum apparent unbound bilirubin ranged from 1 to 45 μmol/liter, and the authors found no correlation with the FFA concentrations.

Most of these studies show that IL emulsion can be given in jaundiced VLBW infants if the serum level of FFA stays within the permitted range. Once again, the infusion rate of the IL emulsion is the key issue.

INTRAVENOUS LIPIDS, GAS EXCHANGE, AND PULMONARY VASCULAR RESISTANCE

Numerous studies have addressed the issue of the potentially deleterious effect of fat emulsions on pulmonary function in VLBW infants. This deleterious effect may be the result of alteration in vascular tone leading to a state of pulmonary hypertension or of infiltration of pulmonary tissue by lipids. It is obvious that most cases of pulmonary side effects described have been associated with high rates of lipid infusion.

The study by Brans *et al.* (18), where VLBW infants (less than 1,500 g at birth) were given intravenous lipids according to the protocol described previously (17), showed that infants receiving 4 g/kg·d of IL over 16 hours had an increased pulmonary alveolar/arteriolar gradient of oxygen (A-aDO$_2$) when compared with infants receiving the same amount over 24 hours. Their data suggest that the continuous administration of fat emulsions at a constant rate over 24 hours was safer than intermittent infusion, thus showing yet again that infusion rate is more important than the total daily amount infused.

Shulman *et al.* (19) made a retrospective comparison of necropsy data on neonates (not all were VLBW) who received or did not receive lipid infusions. Lipids were infused continuously over 24 hours, and the rate of infusion was decreased when triglyceride levels were above 150 mg/dl. Fourteen of 26 infants in the lipid group and two of 13 in the nonlipid group were found to have pulmonary vascular lipid deposition. The fact that pulmonary vascular lipid deposits were present even in infants who had never received intravenous fat suggests the need for caution before drawing definite conclusions about a relation between intravenous fat infusions and lung lipid deposition. However, in their conclusion the authors pointed out that their results suggested that vascular deposits were at least partly determined by the amount and duration of intravenous fat administration.

Prasertsom *et al.* (20) used two-dimensional echocardiography to estimate pulmonary vascular resistance from the ratio of right ventricular pre-ejection period to ejection time (RVPEP/ET) in 11 preterm infants with respiratory distress syndrome receiving a 20% lipid emulsion. Intravenous lipid was started on the second postnatal day at a dose of 0.0625 g/kg·h (1.5 g/kg·d) for 24 hours and increased to 0.125 g/kg·h (3 g/kg·d) on the third day. Intravenous lipid was discontinued for 24 hours on the fourth day and then restarted for 24 hours on the sixth day at 0.0625 g/kg·h. The RVPEP/ET ratio increased by 20% after 24 hours of intravenous lipid at 1.5 g/kg·d, by 45% after 24 hours at 3 g/kg·d, and returned to baseline 24 hours after the lipid infusion had been discontinued. The increases in RVPEP/ET ratio were not observed immediately after starting or restarting intravenous lipids but after several hours of infusion, and the authors discussed the role of changes in eicosanoid metabolism, suggesting that the dose-dependent increase in pulmonary arterial pressure was thromboxane mediated. None of their infants was said to be hyperlipemic (though serum triglyceride concentrations were not quoted).

Similar data were published by Lloyd and Boucek (21) from a study on six premature infants (birthweight between 1,500 and 2,500 g) receiving 0.1 to 0.45 g/kg·h of intravenous lipid (2.4 to 10.8 g/kg·d), but in that study the increase in RVPEP/ET ratio was observed within 2 hours of infusion onset, the faster response being assumed to be due to the high lipid infusion rate.

INTRAVENOUS LIPID AND PEROXIDATION

Unsaturated fatty acids are highly susceptible to peroxidation, and the products (hydroperoxides) can interfere with arachidonic acid metabolism or react to form organic free radicals, which can initiate peroxidative injury in tissues. Stimulation of cyclooxygenases may also result, causing increased production of prostaglandin H2, and then prostacyclin (PGI2) and thromboxane (Tx) A2, which are important vasoactive products.

Several studies have shown that lipid peroxidation occurs in intravenous lipid emulsions used in preterm infants (22–24). The concentration of lipid hydroperoxides is variable between bottles and is said to increase under light exposure, especially under phototherapy lights (23,25). Protecting the emulsions from light with aluminum foil or by adding antioxidant products such as ascorbic acid directly to the bottles eliminates the phototherapy effect (25).

However, other factors or nutrients may contribute to the *in vitro* generation of peroxides. Lavoie *et al.* (26) showed that multivitamin preparations (MVI) mixed in parenteral nutrition solutions were the major contributor to the generation of peroxides, with a 10-fold increase in fat-free TPN solutions but only a fourfold increase in lipid-containing TPN solutions. They showed a dose/response relation between the concentration of MVI and the peroxide level. The effect of light was the strongest in the presence of multivitamins. These investigators found that lipid emulsions had a significant but minor additive effect compared with multivitamin preparations. According to these data, it may be desirable to protect intravenous emulsions from light, particularly phototherapy light, until more data are available on the consequences of peroxide production in TPN preparations.

CONCLUSION

Intravenous lipid infusions are an important component of TPN during the early days of life in VLBW infants, at a time when enteral feeding is impossible or poorly tolerated, since they provide both essential fatty acids and high-density energy. Better current knowledge of the metabolic fate of the infused lipids permits their use during the first week of life if the infusion rate does not exceed the immature metabolic capacity of these infants. This may be difficult to assess, especially in very sick and unstable infants, and explains why we still have to be cautious. However, there is a further debate that still has not been entirely resolved by current published studies, and that is over the quality of lipid emulsions. There is reason to believe that the quality of the available emulsions needs to be improved to obtain a more suitable fatty acid composition and a lower phospholipid content; we also need a better understanding of how to prevent lipid peroxidation.

REFERENCES

1. Andrew G, Chan G, Schiff D. Lipid metabolism in the neonate. The effect of Intralipid infusion on plasma triglyceride and free fatty acid concentrations in the neonate. *J Pediatr* 1976;88:273–279.
2. Griffin EA, Bryan MH, Angel A. Variations in Intralipid tolerance in newborn infants. *Pediatr Res* 1983;17:478–481.
3. Kao LC, Cheng MH, Warburton D. Triglycerides, FFA, FFA/albumin molar ration and cholesterol levels in serum of neonates receiving long-term lipid infusions: controlled trial of continuous and intermittent regimen. *J Pediatr* 1989;104:429–435.
4. Hulman G, Pearson HJ, Fraser I, Bell PRF. Agglutination of Intralipid by sera of acutely ill patients. *Lancet* 1982;ii:1426–1427.
5. Haumont D, Deckelbaum RJ, Richelle M, *et al.* Plasma lipid and plasma lipoprotein concentrations in low birth weight infants given parenteral nutrition with twenty or ten percent lipid emulsion. *J Pediatr* 1989;115:787–793.
6. Bach AC, Férézout J, Frey A. Phospholipid-rich particles in commercial parenteral fat emulsions. An overview. *Prog Lipid Res* 1996;35:133–153.
7. Putet G, Verellen G, Heim T, Smith JM, Swyer PR. Energy intake and substrates utilization during total parental nutrition. In: Wesdorp RC, Soeters PB, eds. *Newborn clinical nutrition.* Edinburgh: Churchill Livingstone; 1982:63–70.
8. Bonner C, Debrie KL, Hug G, Landrigan E, Taylor BJ. Effect of parenteral L-carnitine supplementation on fat metabolism and nutrition in premature neonates. *J Pediatr* 1995;126:287–292.
9. Helms RA, Mauer EC, Hay WW, Christensen ML, Storm MC. Effect of intravenous L-carnitine on growth parameters and fat metabolism during parenteral nutrition in neonates. *J Parenter Enter Nutr* 1990;14:448–453.
10. Hammerman C, Aramburo MJ. Decreased lipid intake reduces morbidity in sick premature neonates. *J Pediatr* 1988;113:1083–1088.
11. Sosenko RS, Rodriguez-Pierce M, Bancalari E. Effect of early initiation of intravenous lipid administration on the incidence and severity of chronic lung disease in premature infants. *J Pediatr* 1993;123:975–982.
12. Gilbertson N, Kovar IZ, Cox DJ, Crowe L, Palmer NT. Introduction of intravenous lipid administration on the first day of life in the very low birth weight neonate. *J Pediatr* 1991;119:615–623.
13. Fox GF, Wilson DC, Ohlsson A. Effects of early *versus* late introduction of intravenous lipid to preterm infants on death and chronic lung disease. Results of meta-analysis. *Pediatr Res* 1988;43:214A (abst.).
14. Thiessen H, Jacobsen J, Brodersen R. Displacement of albumin-bound bilirubin by fatty acids. *Acta Paediatr Scand* 1972;61:285–288.
15. Thaler MM, Wennberg RP. Influence of intravenous nutrients on bilirubin transport. Emulsified lipid solutions. *Pediatr Res* 1977;11:167–171.
16. Adamkin DH, Radmacher PG, Klingbeil RL. Use of intravenous lipid and hyperbilirubinemia in the first week. *J Pediatr Gastroenterol Nutr* 1992;14:135–139.
17. Brans YW, Ritter DA, Kenny JD, Andrew DS, Dutton EB, Carrillo DW. Influence of intravenous fat emulsion on serum bilirubin in very low birthweight neonates. *Arch Dis Child* 1987;62:156–160.
18. Brans YW, Dutton EB, Andrew DS, Menchaca EM, West DL. Fat emulsion tolerance in very low birth weight neonates: effect on diffusion of oxygen in the lungs and on blood pH. *Pediatrics* 1986;78:79–84.
19. Shulman RJ, Langston C, Schanler RJ. Pulmonary vascular deposition after administration of intravenous fat to infants. *Pediatrics* 1987;79:99–102.
20. Prasertsom W, Phillipos EZ, Van Aerde JE, Robertson M. Pulmonary vascular resistance during lipid infusion in neonates. *Arch Dis Child* 1996;74:F95–98.

21. Lloyd TR, Boucek MM. Effect of Intralipid on the neonatal pulmonary bed: an echographic study. *J Pediatr* 1986;108:130–133.
22. Helbock HJ, Motchnik PA, Ames BN. Toxic hydroperoxides in intravenous lipid emulsions used in preterm infants. *Pediatrics* 1993;91:83–87.
23. Pitkänen O, Hallman M, Andersson S. Generation of free radicals in lipid emulsion used in parenteral nutrition. *Pediatr Res* 1991;29:56–59.
24. Inder TE, Darlow BA, Sluis KB, *et al.* The correlation of elevated levels of an index of lipid peroxidation (MDA-TBA) with adverse outcome in the very low birthweight infant. *Acta Paediatr* 1996;85:1116–1122.
25. Neuzil J, Darlow BA, Inder TE, Slins KB, Winterbourn CC, Stocker R. Oxidation of parenteral lipid emulsion by ambient and phototherapy lights: potential toxicity of routine parenteral feeding. *J Pediatr* 1995;126:785–790.
26. Lavoie JC, Belanger S, Spalinger M, Chessex P. Admixture of a multivitamin preparation to parenteral nutrition: the major contributor to in vitro generation of peroxides. *Pediatrics* 1997;99:e6.

DISCUSSION

Prof. Koletzko: I would like to stimulate you to comment a bit more on the question of the quality of lipids. You rightly emphasized your concern about peroxidation with soybean oil emulsion. Many of us have been concerned about exposing very small premature infants to these high concentrations of PUFA, and soybean oil emulsion does not contain much in the way of biologically active antioxidants. Also, the very marked disturbance of the fatty acid patterns of endogenous lipids, both in plasma and tissue, with soybean oil emulsion may well be directly related to the disturbances of thromboxane levels that you've shown. We have just completed a randomized trial comparing Intralipid with olive oil–based emulsion in small premature infants. I found the results very encouraging, because with the olive oil emulsion there is a much more physiological fatty acid pattern, a more physiological lipoprotein pattern, and maybe most important, a much improved vitamin E status with less peroxidative stress.

Dr. Putet: It's clear that there is too much polyunsaturated fatty acid in the available lipid infusion solutions, which increases the possibility of peroxidation. There are enough published data to show that peroxidation can occur in ambient light, and even more so under phototherapy. The peroxidation rate of TPN containing protein, multivitamins, and lipids may increase to such an extent that it could be harmful. For example, it could disturb arachidonic acid metabolism and interfere with prostaglandin and prostacyclin/thromboxane production. This would cause vasoconstriction in the pulmonary bed, as has been shown in almost every study that has investigated peroxidative phenomena. All the data suggest that we should try to improve lipid solutions by reducing their content of polyunsaturated fatty acids. You mentioned a new solution with oleic acid, but we already have a solution made from a 50:50 mix of medium-chain triglycerides and long-chain triglycerides. This solution has 50% less polyunsaturated fatty acid and consequently less peroxidation. We also know that the cholesterol level is reduced in infants who are infused for several days or a week with this solution, so this is obviously already one way toward an improved intravenous lipid solution.

Prof. Koletzko: Do you think we have enough information on the safety of MCT emulsion in premature infants? I'm concerned, in view of data of Deckelbaum and coworkers [1], that a very high proportion of MCT emulsion is apparently not split by lipoprotein lipase and is incorporated into cells intact, at least *in vitro*. Is that not a concern in relation to preterm infants?

Dr. Putet: There may be cause for concern if too much MCT is given. However, there is no evidence at present that a 50:50 solution MCT/LCT given at, say, 1.5 or 2 g/kg·d causes any problems. I would say that the advantages of this form of lipid infusion, in relation to reduced peroxidation, would outweigh any possible disadvantages.

Prof. Moro: Do you think that the levels of peroxidation described may be associated *in vivo* with liver damage, and so with TPN-associated cholestasis?

Dr. Putet: Maybe Prof. Chessex could answer that question. In any event, I think that if we can show that there is a substantial increase in peroxidation in either parenteral or enteral feeds, it may be harmful.

Dr. Chessex: We have been looking at animal models. We have shown a decrease in lung glutathione in such models perfused with either multivitamin solution or peroxides at the same concentration, and we have also shown a fall in the liver content of glutathione. We are currently looking at these livers, which show a relative increase in weight compared with the body weight of the animals. Thus we are looking at precisely the issue that Prof. Moro asked about: Could this be one of the factors explaining cholestasis? Then we have begun to look at what happens in children. We have been measuring urinary peroxide excretion in babies before and after giving a multivitamin solution, and there is a doubling of the urinary excretion of peroxides and other markers of peroxidation such as isoprostins. The next step was to look at the effect of light. When we protect the solution from light (i.e., just the tubing coming down from the bag; the bag is already covered), we have a 50% fall in urinary peroxide excretion. We are now trying to determine whether this may have any functional effect in the infants in the long term.

Prof. Berger: I'd also like to comment on peroxidation. I think it is important to investigate the possibility that parenteral feeding produces a decreased output of free radicals. As Prof. Heird emphasized, we know we have trouble giving enough cysteine, and we have problems with vitamin E. If there is not enough cysteine, we're probably not allowing these babies to make enough glutathione. In 1987, we postulated that cholestasis was the result of a free radical process. On looking at the literature, we were interested to find reports of the compound lipofuscin, which had been named *intravenous fat pigment* and was commonly found in biopsies from babies with cholestasis in the United States, where they had not been using Intralipid. We therefore suggested that lipofuscin was a clue that this cholestasis was in fact a peroxidation process. This emphasizes that the problem isn't related only to lipids but is related to many other factors—trace elements, amino acids, and other antioxidants that influence the output of free radicals. If we want to understand this process, it is important to look at the factors influencing the input, the output, and the target organ sensitivity.

Prof. Heird: As you know, MCT-containing emulsions are not available in the United States, but they would seem to have some advantages with respect to oxidation, and thus as an immediate energy source for babies whose total energy intake is decreased—for example, in the first few days of TPN. Is anything known about the effects of MCT *versus* LCT in promoting nitrogen retention or nitrogen utilization?

Dr. Putet: This is a controversial subject. We know that MCT are oxidized more readily than LCT. This has been shown in adults and even in infants, using labeled carbon. There may ultimately be little difference between these two forms of lipid with respect to the amount of energy actually utilized by the body, since there appears to be some futile cycling with MCT, but the amounts involved are very small. I doubt whether, in a situation where not more than 20% of the energy will be given as fat, there will be much difference in utilization between LCT and MCT/LCT solutions.

Dr. Rashwan: When should you stop giving lipid infusions? Some say you should stop when 50% of the intake is enteral. Do you agree with this?

Dr. Putet: I think this is mainly a question of the total nonprotein energy intake. If you are giving enough enteral feeding to give, say, at least 70 to 80 kcal/kg·d, I think you can then stop parenteral nutrition. I think in terms of the total amount of lipid given either enterally or parenterally, and the total amount of glucose given either enterally or parenterally. When I give TPN along with some enteral nutrition, I calculate the overall lipid and glucose intake, and try not to include more than 30% to 40% of the energy as lipids. When the infant is weaned onto enteral nutrition, the proportion of lipid in the energy intake will be higher, around 40% to 50%. With TPN, I do not increase the lipid part of the total nonprotein energy intake above 20% to 25%.

Dr. Filijo: Do you think it is necessary to use intravenous L-carnitine to assist the metabolism of parenteral lipids at the mitochondrial level?

Dr. Putet: The carnitine question is still controversial. I think it reasonable to try to ensure that the carnitine level is at least at the lower end of the range found in babies fed with breast milk. I would be in favor of giving it because I see no reason for letting it be low, and we know that plasma carnitine becomes very low in infants on TPN for more than a week or so. However, we have no evidence that it increases the oxidation rate of the lipids given, though it has been shown that ketone bodies are increased, even in small infants. In all, I think there are more arguments in favor of giving it than against.

Prof. Moro: A very practical question: should Intralipid be given in a separate bag or in the same bag with other nutrients?

Dr. Putet: The problem of putting lipids, glucose, vitamins, proteins, calcium, and phosphorus in one solution is a galenic one. If the pharmacist is able to produce a stable solution, which is in fact feasible, then I think there is no problem in using this. We have done several studies to ensure that lipid solutions do not interfere with calcium, phosphorus, and other nutrients, and it is probably simpler to use a single solution than a Y connector. You do have to be careful about particles, however, when you put lipids in a solution. If the solution is unstable, you may get large particles in it, so it is best to use a filter.

Dr. Schanler: The problem of particulates arises if you try to increase the calcium and phosphorus content of IV solutions. At high concentrations of calcium and phosphorus, we occasionally do see precipitates, so I would be very cautious about that. On the other hand, you get better vitamin A and E levels in babies when you mix the vitamins with the intravenous lipid.

Dr. Putet: I agree. You really have to be sure that your pharmacist can produce a stable preparation.

Prof. Lucas: I am confused about oleic acid. When it was first shown that Intralipid could cause lung damage, there were many studies trying to get to the bottom of the problem. As you know, oleic acid is a major component of Intralipid. Studies by Grossman on experimental animals showed that infusion of oleic acid had very detrimental effects on a number of aspects of lung function. Now you are promoting it as an important lipid. Are you saying that these animal studies don't apply to humans?

Dr. Putet: Most of these studies have relevance to humans, but I would emphasize again that what is important is the infusion rate—the amount given per unit of time. As with glucose, if you infuse too much too fast, you will get a lot of trouble.

Prof. Endres: There are several old reports of pulmonary intra-arterial thromboses after high-rate Intralipid infusions. Do you think this is linked to chronic lung disease in premature babies?

Dr. Putet: There may be lipid deposition in the lungs of individuals who have never received lipids. This has been shown in infants, in adults, and in animals, *in vitro* and *in vivo*. Where lipid infusions are given, if the infusion rate exceeds the clearance capacity of the plasma, lipid particles will be taken up by the reticuloendothelial system in the endothelium. So under those circumstances, when you exceed the metabolic capacity of the infant, you may get problems. That is my understanding, at least.

REFERENCES

1. Deckelbaum RJ, Carpentier Y, Olivecrona T, Moser A. Hydrolysis of medium vs. long chain triglycerides in pure and mixed intravenous lipid emulsion by purified lipoprotein lipases *in vitro. Clin Nutr* 1986;5 [suppl. 54].

Nutrition of the Very Low Birthweight Infant, edited by
Ekhard E. Ziegler, Alan Lucas, Guido E. Moro.
Nestlé Nutrition Workshop Series, Paediatric Programme, Vol. 43,
Nestec Ltd., Vevey/Lippincott Williams & Wilkins
Philadelphia, Pennsylvania © 1999.

Fortification of Human Milk

Guido E. Moro and Iolanda Minoli

*Center for Infant Nutrition to Prevent Illnesses in Adult Life, Department of Perinatal
Pathology, Macedonio Melloni Maternity Hospital, Milan, Italy*

Human milk may confer nutritional and nonnutritional advantages in feeding the
preterm infant, including protection against infections and enhanced intestinal development. In addition, recent studies have suggested that human milk is superior to formula for feeding preterm infants with respect to both short-term and long-term outcome data (1,2). However, many studies have shown that preterm milk and banked
term milk do not provide adequate quantities of several nutrients, specifically protein
and minerals, to meet the nutritional needs of the preterm infant (3–5).

HUMAN MILK FORMULA

To overcome the nutritional inadequacies of human milk, Lucas *et al.* introduced the
term *lactoengineering* and produced a "human milk formula"—that is, a formula
made entirely with human milk components (6). The original formula prepared by
Lucas was based on fortification of human milk with protein, fat, calcium, and phosphorus. However, since it has been shown that increasing the energy intake of very-
low-birthweight (VLBW) babies to more than 115 to 120 kcal/kg·d does not improve
linear growth but only increases fat accretion (7,8), current fortification schedules are
designed primarily to increase the protein content of human milk, while also providing an additional source of minerals and vitamins (9–12).

In our Center for Infant Nutrition in Milan, Italy, a human milk protein concentrate
is obtained by an ultrafiltration process (13). Briefly, defatted milk is pasteurized at
72°C for 15 seconds, ultrafiltrated, freeze-dried, and stored in small, sealed-glass am-
poules (Fig. 1). The concentrate is composed of 65% to 70% protein, 12% lactose,
9% fat, and small quantities of minerals. The final concentrate is used to supplement
human milk and produce a "human milk formula" for feeding VLBW infants. The infants assigned to receive our human milk formula also receive a daily supplement of
calcium (30 mg/kg from calcium lactate) and phosphorus (20 mg/kg from sodium
phosphate). Beginning on the 15th day of life, all infants also receive a daily vitamin
supplement providing 1,200 IU of vitamin A, 1,200 IU of vitamin D, 30 mg/kg of vitamin E, and 50 mg/kg of vitamin C. Starting at 30 days of age, all infants also receive supplemental iron (2 mg/kg from ferrous sulfate).

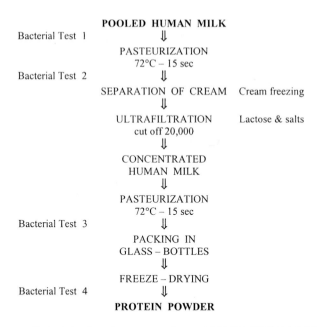

FIG. 1. Human milk lactoengineering: processing used in the Center for Infant Nutrition, Maternity Hospital Macedonio Melloni, Milan, to separate protein concentrate from human milk.

HUMAN MILK FORTIFIERS

Human milk enriched with human milk protein, salts, and vitamins seems to meet the protein requirements of the VLBW infant, preserves the unique immunological and nutritional properties of human milk, and produces growth, metabolism, and plasma amino acid concentrations that should be considered the basis for feeding VLBW infants (11–14).

No human milk protein preparation is currently commercially available. Furthermore, it is not likely that one will become available in the future owing to the high cost of processing human milk and the difficulty in collecting adequate amounts of milk without the risk of transmitting viral infections. These problems have necessitated the development of fortifiers based on other sources of protein, primarily bovine milk proteins or protein hydrolysates, with or without the addition of amino acids (11,12,15–18). Although some differences in plasma amino acid concentrations have been observed, other metabolic responses and growth have generally been similar, regardless of the source of protein.

There are several different forms (liquid and powder) of cow's milk based human milk fortifiers available (Table 1). Powdered fortifiers have the advantage of providing supplementation without displacing milk volume, thus allowing a larger intake of human milk. However, adding a powdered source of protein and minerals to preterm milk could result in excessive intake of one or more of these nutrients, depending on the nutrient content of the milk itself. Liquid supplementation randomly dilutes the higher levels of nutrients contained in some mothers' milks. A disadvantage of a

TABLE 1. Commercial human milk fortifiers for preterm infants

Packaging (Added to 100 ml human milk)	NENATAL-F and COW & GATE (Nutricia) Powder 1.5 g packets (2 packets)		EOPROTIN (Milupa) Powder can (3 g)		FM–85 (Nestlé) Powder can (5 g)		ENFAMIL HUMAN MILK FORTIFIER (Mead Johnson) Powder 0.96 g packets (4 packets)		SIMILAC NATURAL CARE (Ross Laboratories) Liquid 24 cal/fl oz, 4 fl oz bottle (100 ml)	
Nutrients:	Per 100 kcal	Added to 100 ml HM	Per 100 kcal	Added to 100 ml HM	Per 100 kcal	Added to 100 ml HM	Per 100 kcal	Added to 100 ml HM	Per 100 kcal	Mixed 1:1
Energy (kcal)	100	10	100	11	100	18	100	14	100	100
Protein (g)	7.0	0.7	5.4	0.6	5.0	0.8	5.0	0.7	2.71	2.6
Carbohydrate (g)	20	2	18.8	2.1	20.1	3.6	19.3	2.7	10.6	10.8
Fat (g)	0	0	0.4	0.04	0.1	0.01	0.28	<0.1	5.43	5.4
Minerals	Present		Present		Present		Present		Present	
Vitamins	Present		Present		Present		Present		Present	

HM = human milk.

liquid supplement is that it contributes to the total volume of the intake, thus decreasing the amount of human milk ingested.

ANALYSIS OF HUMAN MILK BEFORE FORTIFICATION

In many neonatal units, human milk is routinely enriched in a fixed proportion with commercial fortifiers containing protein, carbohydrates, and electrolytes. Because of the large variation in human milk concentrations of protein and fat—particularly in the mother's own milk but also in banked milk—there is an obvious risk of under- or overnutrition of the vulnerable VLBW infant (19). Unfortunately, routine analysis of the macronutrient composition of the human milk given to VLBW infants is rarely performed before fortification, despite recommendations that it should be (10,20–22). Thus quality control of human milk used for VLBW infant feeding is mandatory, both to monitor the nutritional value of the milk supplied and to decide on the amount of fortifier to be added. To monitor the macronutrient composition of human milk, we use an infrared analyzer, as suggested by Michaelsen et al. (23,24). The infrared technique has been used for the routine analysis of bovine milk for several years. The equipment has a higher precision and accuracy than direct methods and is very simple to use. The classical analysis of protein, fat, and carbohydrate content in human milk is time-consuming and requires three different analytical approaches. Infrared analysis overcomes this problem and allows almost real-time results to be obtained (with a milk sample of 6 ml, the measurement takes less than 1 minute). We evaluated the precision and accuracy of this method using a Milko-Scan 133 B infrared analyzer (Foss Electric, Denmark). A comparative study was performed on 62 samples of milk (33 human, 29 bovine). The results of the infrared analysis were compared with those of reference methods (25,26). No differences were found between infrared analysis and reference methods both for human and bovine milk, and the coefficients of variation (CV) were similar to those already reported by Michaelsen et al. (23). Figure 2, panel A, shows the linear regression for all 62 milk samples for protein determination. The equation of the curve was $y = 0.64 + 0.62x$ and the correlation coefficient (R) was 0.79. The equations and the correlation coefficients calculated for the linear regression were, respectively, $y = 0.08 + 0.86$ and $R = 0.90$ for human milk, and $y = 1.35 + 0.27x$ and $R = 0.55$ for bovine milk (see Fig. 2, panel B). The data obtained confirm that infrared analysis may be a valuable method for measuring macronutrients in milk, especially in human samples, since precision and accuracy seem to be better for human milk than for bovine milk. Moreover, this method offers the advantage of being quicker and simpler than reference methods, and for this reason it may be recommended for use in neonatal intensive care units.

Protein analysis of human milk before fortification offers the possibility of improving the nutritional management of VLBW infants—with a few simple calculations the protein concentration of human milk can be adjusted to achieve the desired daily protein intake (generally 3.5 g/kg).

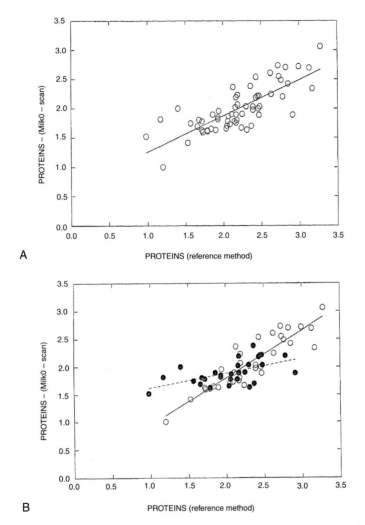

FIG. 2. Relation between protein content measured by infrared analysis and by Lowry reference method for all 62 samples (panel A) and for human (O) and bovine (●) milk samples considered separately (panel B). The correlation coefficient (R) for all 62 milk samples was 0.79 (panel A). The correlation coefficients calculated separately for human milk and bovine milk were 0.90 and 0.55, respectively (panel B).

VARIABLE FORTIFICATION REGIMEN

Because the nutrient needs of the VLBW infant change markedly as the infant grows and because the composition of human milk is variable, fortification of milk with predetermined, fixed amounts of nutrients is apt to result in a mismatch between nutrient needs and nutrient intakes during at least part and probably most of an infant's rapid growth period. To increase the likelihood of obtaining a good match between intake and requirement, a variable fortification regimen has been proposed that uses the metabolic response of the infant (serum urea concentration) to guide the level of fortification (27).

Using this regimen in an initial cautious study, we showed (27) that the new regimen did lead to higher nutrient intakes, and these in turn led to a somewhat higher rate of growth. An experimental bovine milk protein–based fortifier (BMF) prepared from ultrafiltrated bovine whey protein concentrate (casein-to-whey-protein ratio = 40/60) was used either in the new fashion, with amounts determined by serum urea monitoring (regimen VAR), or in the conventional fixed proportion (regimen FIX). Using the fixed proportion, we also compared the new fortifier with a fortifier based on human milk protein (regimen HMP). Twelve infants were studied on each of the three regimens.

At study entry, fortification in regimen VAR was the same as in regimen FIX; that is, 3.5 g of BMF were added to each 100 ml of breast milk (fortification level 0). In regimen VAR, fortification was subsequently adjusted on the basis of twice-weekly determinations of corrected serum urea nitrogen (SUN): SUN $\times$ 0.5/SCr, where 0.5 is the "normal" serum creatinine concentration and SCr is serum creatinine concentration determined at the same time as serum urea nitrogen.

Adjustment of the fortification level after each determination of corrected serum urea nitrogen was performed as shown in Table 2. Fortification level was not changed from the standard 3.5 g per 100 ml of milk when corrected serum urea nitrogen was between 9.1 and 12.0 mg/dl (fortification level 0); fortification level was increased by one level (+0.6 g) if the corrected urea nitrogen was less than 9 mg/dl, and decreased by one level (−0.6 g) if it was more than 12 mg/dl. The fortification level was not changed by more than one level at a time. Levels −3 and +3 were the limits of adjustment (see Table 2).

As a result of this fortification schedule, fortification levels greater than level 0 were used most of the time in the regimen VAR. During study weeks 1 and 2, fortification levels of +1 and +2 were used with few exceptions, and mean fortification levels were +1.54 and +1.79, respectively. During study week 3, fortification was lower, with a mean value of +0.86 (Table 3).

As expected, fortification with the VAR regimen led to a higher energy and protein intake, mainly in the first 2 weeks of the study, with the difference for protein

TABLE 2. *Adjustment of fortification*

Fortification level	CSUN (mg/dl)	Amount of fortifier (g/100 ml)
+3	<3.0	5.3
+2	3.1–6.0	4.7
+1	6.1–9.0	4.1
0	9.1–12.0	3.5
−1	12.1–15.0	2.9
−2	15.1–18.0	2.3
−3	>18.0	1.7

CSUN = corrected serum urea nitrogen.

TABLE 3. *Fortification level in the variable group*

Week of study	Mean fortification level
Week 1	+ 1.54
Week 2	+ 1.79
Week 3	+ 0.86

intake reaching statistical difference ($p < 0.01$) during week 2 (Table 4). Weight gain, whether expressed as g/d or g/kg·d, was lowest with regimen HMP (27.8 g/d or 17.2 g/kg·d), higher with regimen FIX (30.0 g/d or 18.3 g/kg·d), and highest with regimen VAR (32.3 g/d or 18.8 g/kg·d). Differences in gains in length and head circumference were small and not statistically significant. The difference in weight gain among the feeding groups resulted in earlier discharge of infants in the VAR group. Since a body weight of 2,200 g is required in our department before discharge of VLBW infants, a difference in weight gain of 4.5 g/d between HMP and VAR groups led to a 4.5-day reduction in hospital stay in the infants in the VAR group; the difference between FIX and VAR groups resulted in a 2-day reduction in hospital stay in the VAR group. Plasma concentrations of several amino acids were higher in the VAR group than in the FIX group, but none, including threonine, was outside the range reported by other investigators in infants receiving fortified breast milk (28–30). Thus, it appears that in VLBW infants protein fortification of human milk beyond the standard fixed level is metabolically safe.

CONCLUSIONS

The results of our study and data from published reports strongly support the use of fortified human milk in VLBW infant feeding. Considering all the clinical and neurodevelopmental implications of the nutritional management of these infants, we

TABLE 4. *Intakes of energy and protein*

	HMP	FIX	VAR
Intake of energy (kcal/kg·d)			
Week 1	118 (6)	116 (9)	125 (3)
Week 2	121 (7)	119 (7)	125 (7)
Week 3	119 (6)	117 (7)	120 (7)
Intake of protein (g/kg·d)			
Week 1	3.50 (0.26)	3.35 (0.46)	3.69 (0.40)
Week 2	3.67 (0.29)	3.45 (0.34)*	4.00 (0.46)*
Week 3	3.55 (0.27)	3.44 (0.42)	3.73 (0.28)

Mean (SD).
* $p < 0.01$.

make the following practical suggestions:

- Human milk may confer nutritional and nonnutritional advantages to VLBW infants, including protection against infections, enhanced intestinal maturation, and improved long-term developmental outcome.
- Human milk alone cannot meet the considerable nutrient needs of the VLBW infant. Thus, human milk fed to VLBW infants must be fortified with protein, minerals, and vitamins.
- Human milk protein should be considered the gold standard for human milk fortification.
- In view of the practical problems of preparing and using human milk protein for fortifying human milk, mother's own milk (when available) or banked milk fortified with protein of nonhuman origin should constitute the basis for feeding VLBW infants.
- To improve the nutritional management of VLBW infants fed human milk, an individualized feeding system should be used, based on infrared analyses of human milk before fortification.
- The simple addition of a fortifier to human milk in fixed proportion, as is the current practice, is not entirely satisfactory because it often leads to inadequate nutrient intakes.
- Individual differences among VLBW infants call for precise interindividual and intraindividual adjustments of protein intake during the stay in the nursery. This means a variable protein intake based on the metabolic responses of each premature infant.
- When a variable fortification regimen is used in feeding VLBW infants, metabolic monitoring of the protein intake is mandatory.
- Serum urea nitrogen responds promptly to changes in protein intake and is proportional to protein intake, so it could be considered the most suitable metabolic indicator of protein adequacy.
- Different strategies of variable fortification should probably be applied to different categories of VLBW infants.

REFERENCES

1. Lucas A, Morley R, Cole TJ, Lister G, Leeson-Payne C. Breast milk and subsequent intelligence quotient in children born preterm. *Lancet* 1992;339:261–264.
2. Lucas A, Fewtrell MS, Morley R, *et al.* Randomized outcome trial of human milk fortification and developmental outcome in preterm infants. *Am J Clin Nutr* 1996;64:142–151.
3. Fomon SJ, Ziegler EE, Vázquez HD. Human milk and the small premature infant. *Am J Dis Child* 1977;131:463–467.
4. Atkinson SA, Radde IC, Anderson GH. Macromineral balances in premature infants fed their own mothers milk or formula. *J Pediatr* 1983;102:99–106.
5. Putet G, Senterre J, Rigo J, Salle B. Nutrient balance, energy utilization, and composition of weight gain in very low birthweight infants fed pooled human milk or a preterm formula. *J Pediatr* 1984;105:79–85.
6. Lucas A, Lucas PJ, Chavin SI, Lyster RLJ, Baum JD. A human milk formula. *Early Hum Dev* 1980;4:15–21.
7. Moro GE, Minoli I, Heininger J, Cohen M, Gaull G, Räihä N. Relationship between protein and energy in the feeding of preterm infants during the first month of life. *Acta Paediatr Scand* 1984;73:49–54.

8. Kashyap S, Forsyth M, Zucker C, Ramakrishnan R, Dell RB, Heird WC. Effects of varying protein and energy intakes on growth and metabolic response in low birth weight infants. *J Pediatr* 1986;108:955–963.
9. Schanler RJ, Garza C, Nichols BL. Fortified mother's milk for very low birth weight infants: results of growth and nutrient balance studies. *J Pediatr* 1985;107:437–445.
10. Polberger SKT, Axelsson IE, Räihä NCR. Growth of very low birth weight infants on varying amounts of human milk protein. *Pediatr Res* 1989;25:414–419.
11. Moro GE, Minoli I, Fulconis F, Clementi M, Räihä NCR. Growth and metabolic responses in low-birth-weight infants fed human milk fortified with human milk protein or with a bovine milk protein preparation. *J Pediatr Gastroenterol Nutr* 1991;13:150–154.
12. Boehm G, Borte M, Bellstedt K, Moro GE, Minoli I. Protein quality of human milk fortifier in low birth weight infants: effects on growth and plasma amino acid profiles. *Eur J Pediatr* 1993;152:1036–1039.
13. Moro GE, Fulconis F, Ferrari L, Marzioli S, Coppalini B, Minoli I. Tecniche di preparazione di derivati del latte umano da aggiungere al latte di donna nell alimentazione del prematuro. *Minerva Pediatr* 1983;35:853–858.
14. Boehm G, Müller DM, Senger H, Borte M, Moro GE. Nitrogen and fat balances in very low birth weight infants fed human milk fortified with human milk or bovine milk protein. *Eur J Pediatr* 1993;152:236–239.
15. Tönz O, Schubiger G. Feeding of very-low-birth-weight infants with breast-milk enriched by energy, nitrogen and minerals: FM85. *Helv Paediatr Acta* 1985;40:235–247.
16. Putet G, Rigo J, Salle B, Senterre J. Supplementation of pooled human milk with casein hydrolysate: energy and nitrogen balance and weight gain composition in very low birth weight infants. *Pediatr Res* 1987;21:458–461.
17. Greer FR, McCormick A. Improved bone mineralization and growth in premature infants fed fortified own mother's milk. *J Pediatr* 1988;112:961–969.
18. Moyer-Mileur L, Chan GM, Gill G. Evaluation of liquid or powdered fortification of human milk on growth and bone mineralization status of preterm infants. *J Pediatr Gastroenterol Nutr* 1992;15:370–374.
19. Lucas A, Hudson GJ. Preterm milk as a source of protein for low birthweight infants. *Arch Dis Child* 1984;59:831–836.
20. Hibberd CM, Brooke OG, Carter ND, Hang M, Harzer G. Variation in the composition of breast milk during the first 5 weeks of lactation: implications for the feeding of preterm infants. *Arch Dis Child* 1982;57:658–662.
21. Lönnerdal B, Smith C, Keen CL. Analysis of human milk: current methodologies and future needs. *J Pediatr Gastroenterol Nutr* 1984;3:290–295.
22. Polberger S, Lönnerdal B. Simple and rapid macronutrient analysis of human milk for individualized fortification: basis for improved nutritional management of very-low-birth-weight infants? *J Pediatr Gastroenterol Nutr* 1993;17:283–290.
23. Michaelsen KF, Pedersen SB, Skafte L, Jæger P, Peitersen B. Infrared analysis for determining macronutrients in human milk. *J Pediatr Gastroenterol Nutr* 1988;7:229–235.
24. Michaelsen KF, Skafte L, Badsberg JH, Jørgensen M. Variation in macronutrients in human milk bank: influencing factors and implications for human milk banking. *J Pediatr Gastroenterol Nutr* 1990;11:229–239.
25. Lowry OH, Rosembrough NJ, Farr AL, Randall RJ. Protein measurement with folin phenol reagent. *J Biol Chem* 1951;193:265–275.
26. Folch J, Lees M, Sloane Stanley GH. A simple method for the isolation and purification of total lipids from animal tissues. *J Biol Chem* 1957;226:497–509.
27. Moro GE, Minoli I, Ostrom M, *et al.* Fortification of human milk: evaluation of a novel fortification scheme and of a new fortifier. *J Pediatr Gastroenterol Nutr* 1995;20:160–172.
28. Schanler RJ, Garza C. Plasma amino acid differences in very low birth weight infants fed either human milk or whey-dominant cow milk formula. *Pediatr Res* 1987;21:301–305.
29. Kashyap S, Schulze KF, Forsyth M, Dell RB, Ramakrishnan R, Heird WC. Growth, nutrient retention, and metabolic response of low-birth-weight infants fed supplemented and unsupplemented preterm human milk. *Am J Clin Nutr* 1990;52:254–262.
30. Polberger SKT, Axelsson IE, Räihä NCR. Amino acid concentrations in plasma and urine in very low birth weight infants fed protein-unenriched or human milk protein-enriched human milk. *Pediatrics* 1990;86:909–915.

DISCUSSION

Prof. Koletzko: In your experience with measuring human milk composition with the infrared system, do you find it helpful to preferentially select milks with a high lipid content and energy content, to provide an increased energy intake?

Prof. Moro: When we evaluate milk by infrared analysis, we determine the whole macronutrient composition. This means that we know the protein content, the fat content, and the carbohydrate content of the milk. So we are able to separate milks of different energy densities and use them appropriately. Sometimes it is not even necessary to add a fortification; for example, milk from mothers who have given birth preterm may be quite rich in protein—up to 2 g/100 ml, and in fat also.

Prof. Koletzko: My second question relates to the vitamin content of human milk fortifiers. The available fortifiers contain different amounts of vitamins. Has there been any evaluation of the potential benefit of vitamin supplementation of human milk fortifiers?

Prof. Moro: I think all the vitamin preparations are suitable for VLBW infants. In our unit we seldom use artificial fortifiers. We routinely use human milk protein fortifiers and we add vitamins and minerals separately.

Prof. Cooper: Could you explain why the group that was fortified with human milk protein had a slightly lower weight gain.

Prof. Moro: The mean growth rate was numerically somewhat lower, but the difference was not significant. When you use human milk protein for fortification, a proportion of the measured protein is immunoglobulin. The immunologic components have obvious advantages but are not absorbed. So you need to exclude this component from the calculations of growth rate.

Prof. Cooper: If you could measure the actual amount of protein given with infrared, why didn't you use serum urea nitrogen as your indicator to evaluate how much fortifier to add?

Prof. Moro: Infrared analysis gives you only the protein content of the milk, not the metabolic response of the baby. If you want to know whether the protein intake you are giving is well tolerated, you need a metabolic index. We decided on serum urea nitrogen, because it was most responsive to variations in the protein intake.

Dr. Walker: In the process of preparing your fortified milk, you put it through several stages that would have considerably reduced its protective value—that is, you freeze dried it and you put it through two pasteurization cycles. Have you looked at the fecal flora in the infants, and is there any difference in necrotizing enterocolitis incidence compared with infants fed their own mothers' raw milk?

Prof. Moro: We generally use fresh breast milk from the infant's own mother as the basic feed. The human milk fortification that we add is only a supplement to the protein intake. Thus the fresh maternal milk can operate in the usual way to defend the baby from necrotizing enterocolitis. The pasteurization that is performed during the separation of the protein will result in the loss of some nutritional properties, such as lipase activity, but there is plenty of evidence that at least some of the immunologic properties are retained.

Prof. Heird: I am uncertain why the fortifiers contain an energy source. In your analysis, did you really find human milk that had a sufficiently low energy content to require the addition of both protein and energy?

Prof. Moro: The problem is to give the correct protein energy ratio. If you decide to increase the protein intake above, say, 4 g/kg·d, you will have to enrich the milk with some other source of energy.

Prof. Heird: How often does human milk contain less than, say, 67 kcal/dl?

Prof. Moro: Generally, preterm milk contains about 70 kcal/dl in the first weeks.

Prof. Endres: How often do you perform the infrared analyses? And who does the work?

Prof. Moro: Nurses do the analyses at the start of each day in the department. Analyses are done for each baby, and feed is prepared for 24 hours.

Dr. Rigo: When you use human milk fortifiers, you increase the osmolality of the milk. When we use fortifiers, the increase is about 100 mOsm/kg H_2O. But because of the dextrin content of some human milk fortifiers and the amylase activity of human milk, the increase could be greater. What do you feel about feeding preterm infants on milk with osmolality reaching, say, 400 mOsm/kg H_2O?

Prof. Moro: We measured the osmolality of the feeds at the beginning of our clinical studies. With human milk protein fortifier, it never exceeded 350 mOsm/kg H_2O.

Dr. Filho: In Brazil we are very aware of the problem of osmolality. The only human milk fortification product available causes a large increase in osmolarity. Thus unsupplemented milk from our milk bank has an osmolality of about 270 mOsm/kg, but when we add the fortifier, it increases to 396 mOsm H_2O. We are very concerned that this may cause problems.

Prof. Moro: The value of 350 mOsm H_2O refers to human milk fortified with human milk protein, not with a commercially available fortifier. Commercially available fortifiers are enriched with protein, carbohydrates, and minerals, so you must be very careful about their composition. When you add them to human milk you must check the osmolality. We give minerals and vitamins separately.

Prof. De Vonderweid: There is a big difference if you add the fortifier to banked milk that has been pasteurized and to fresh human milk. If you add the fortifier to fresh human milk, the enzyme activity is much higher and you may reach osmolalities of 600 to 800 mOsm/kg H_2O. This is not the case when you use banked pasteurized human milk.

Prof. Haschke: You showed us a study where you compared a variable and a fixed fortification regimen. You said that it is absolutely necessary to measure the protein content in human milk when you fortify it. Let's go back to practical issues. Most hospitals do not have these facilities, so my question concerns safety. Are there any safety studies that have raised concern over the fixed model as compared with the flexible model you are using?

Prof. Moro: If you can measure the macronutrient composition of human milk, you can look at the metabolic responses of the baby to evaluate whether the protein intake you are giving is suitable or not. If you measure serum urea nitrogen twice a week, you can see whether the baby is tolerating the protein intake from a metabolic point of view. You can't then decide whether to increase or decrease the protein intake without knowing exactly how much you are giving.

Prof. Haschke: This is exactly the point I was making. Did you see any problem with the fixed supplementation regimen in terms of the metabolic outcome?

Prof. Moro: No, the metabolic responses were practically the same.

Prof. Haschke: The efficacy of the fortification did not seem very impressive. The weight gain was almost the same as in the unsupplemented babies.

Prof. Moro: Well, the number of babies studied was small, only 12 in each group. In spite of this, the weight difference between the variable group and the group fed with human milk protein fortification was 4.5 g/day. This brought to a reduction in hospital stay of about 4 days. I think that is important.

Prof. Haschke: But you showed that the weight gain in g/kg body weight/day was the same.

Prof. Moro: But if you look at the weight increment per day, the babies fed with variable fortification were able to reach discharge weight, which is 2,200 g in our department, 4 days before the group fed with human milk protein fortifier and 2 days before the group fed with fixed fortifier.

Prof. Lucas: In response to Prof. Haschke's question about safety, when we did our own fortification trial, which we published in the *American Journal of Clinical Nutrition* [1], we did not do monitoring, and we used a fixed fortification schedule. Our previous analytic data based on breast milk suggested that fortification would take a certain number of infants into the particularly high-protein-intake range in the early weeks. We decided to accept that but to monitor plasma amino acids. Though I accept that it is difficult to define hyperaminoacidemia in the newborn preterm infant, we did not identify any cases with our policy of fortifying human milk with 0.7 g of protein per 100 ml right from the start.

Prof. Pohlandt: If you measure serum urea several times a week, which I think is reasonable because it reflects the individual metabolic situation in the baby, then I doubt whether you also have to do the infrared measurement. Have you seen any benefit from doing both? I think that a better basis for increasing the amount of fortifier would be twice weekly urea measurements rather than the average protein concentration of the milk.

Prof. Moro: You can use the metabolic response of the baby to evaluate whether the protein intake is appropriate, but you don't know how much protein the baby is receiving.

Prof. Pohlandt: But all you need to do is to increase the protein intake stepwise until you reach the appropriate blood urea.

Prof. Moro: I agree, but you will never know how much protein the baby is receiving.

Prof. Pohlandt: I'm not interested in that!

Prof. Ziegler: I think there is some confusion about what Prof. Moro actually did. He did a study comparing fixed to variable fortification, but in that study he did *not* use the infrared analyzer. I think Prof. Pohlandt assumed that he did both, but he did not. He is now recommending that infrared analysis should be used routinely, but that was not done in that study, so he cannot say whether it would have made any difference to the results.

Prof. Moro: That is correct.

Dr. Sedaghatian: Has anybody determined the amount of protein needed at different gestational ages in premature babies? Surely we should be recommending an appropriate intake according to gestational age rather than a fixed amount of protein from 24 to 36 weeks gestation, which I can't imagine is really physiological. Doesn't maternal milk protein content reflect the premature infant's requirements?

Prof. Moro: Papers from Atkinson and other groups [2,3] evaluated the composition of human milk from mothers delivering at different gestational ages, and it was clearly shown that there was a correlation between gestational age and the macronutrient composition of the milk. The protein content of preterm milk is at least 20% higher than that of term milk. This difference lasts for 3 to 4 weeks.

Prof. Lucas: The high protein of preterm milk is a volume artifact. That has been shown very clearly. The more milk the mother produces, the lower the protein content; it's as if there was a fixed protein synthetic rate. This is not an evolutionary phenomenon in preterm milk. It is only that mothers of preterm infants produce very little milk, so it has a high protein content. You would do better to relate the protein level to the volume of milk produced rather than to gestation.

Prof. Fazzolari: Could you describe the amino acid profile you find on your different dietary regimens. Did you find any difference in amino acids that can affect the central nervous system—I mean tryptophan, tyrosine, phenylalanine, and so on?

Prof. Moro: In the variable group the values of practically all the amino acids were higher than in the other groups. In spite of that, all the levels remained in the normal range.

Prof. Heird: What is the cost of the infrared system, and how much does that add to the daily cost of providing milk for a baby.

Prof. Moro: The equipment costs about $30,000 in US currency. Each sample costs about $13.

Prof. Heird: The whole issue of cost and effectiveness is going to have to be addressed. I can see the advantages of such a system for research purposes, but I wonder if a better use of the resources might not be to do a thorough evaluation of the effects of a fixed supplementation program.

Prof. Nowak: Could you tell us about viral safety of your milk fortifier? I believe that in certain countries there has been controversy about the use of banked milk, because of the risk of cytomegalovirus transmission.

Prof. Moro: We performed Holder pasteurization that is heating the milk at 63°C for 30 minutes. With that schedule you don't have any risk of viral contamination. All viruses are inactivated.

Dr. Schanler: Short, high-temperature processing kills viruses, and specifically kills cell-associated CMV. I think such a procedure is virally safe.

Prof. Haschke: Are you sure that it is safe in terms of hepatitis C?

Dr. Schanler: We haven't tested that. When we did the studies we did not know about it.

Prof. Polberger: The question about pasteurization and the killing of viruses is a tricky one. Holder pasteurization, 63°C for 30 minutes, seems to be the most valid method at present. There has been some concern about other methods. I also would like to mention the issue of cytomegalovirus infection. There have been reports that you should always freeze mother's own milk before supplying her own infant because of the risk of CMV. I don't know if everybody is doing that. It is stated that you should not use fresh milk at all in preterm infants, even if it is from the infant's own mother.

REFERENCES

1. Lucas A, Fewtrell MS, Morley R, *et al.* Randomized outcome trial of human milk fortification and developmental outcome in preterm infants. *Am J Clin Nutr* 1996;64(2):142–151.
2. Atkinson SA, Bryan MH, Anderson GH. Human milk: difference is nitrogen concentration in milk from mothers of term and preterm infants. *J Pediatr* 1978;93:67–69.
3. Atkinson SA, Bryan MH, Anderson GH. Human milk feeding in premature infants: protein, fat and carbohydrate balances in the first two weeks of life. *J Pediatr* 1981;99:617–624.

Nutrition of the Very Low Birthweight Infant, edited by
Ekhard E. Ziegler, Alan Lucas, Guido E. Moro.
Nestlé Nutrition Workshop Series, Paediatric Programme, Vol. 43,
Nestec Ltd., Vevey/Lippincott Williams & Wilkins
Philadelphia, Pennsylvania © 1999.

Clinical Benefits of Human Milk for Premature Infants

Richard J. Schanler

Section of Neonatology and USDA/ARS Children's Nutrition Research Center, Department of Pediatrics, Baylor College of Medicine, Houston, Texas

The American Academy of Pediatrics recommends breastfeeding throughout the first year after birth for the full-term neonate and acknowledges the benefits of human milk in the management of premature infants (1). The beneficial effects generally relate to improvements in host defense, digestion and absorption of nutrients, neurodevelopment, gastrointestinal function, and psychological effects for the mother. The goal for nutritional support of the premature infant is to meet the intrauterine rates of growth (2). In doing so, several specialized needs of the premature infant must be considered, including metabolic and gastrointestinal immaturity, immunological compromise, and associated medical conditions that affect nutritional support. Human milk is capable of satisfying many of those needs for premature infants (3). However, careful attention to nutritional status is necessary. In this chapter I will focus on the benefits of human milk for the premature infant, comment on the need for nutrient fortification of human milk, and discuss the outcomes of feeding fortified human milk.

UNFORTIFIED HUMAN MILK

Clinical studies in nurseries throughout the world have suggested a decrease in infection in premature infants fed human milk compared with formula. Narayanan *et al.* (4) reported a lower incidence of a variety of infections in premature infants fed their mothers' milk during the daytime (and formula at night) compared with similar infants fed formula exclusively. The lower rate of infection is reported irrespective of whether fresh or pasteurized human milk is fed (3). Early feeding of colostrum is also associated with a lower rate of infection compared with the early feeding of formula (3). Most recently, data from Mexico City suggest that premature infants have fewer episodes of necrotizing enterocolitis, diarrhea, and urinary tract infection, and needed less antibiotic treatment when fed their own mothers' milk compared with similar infants fed term formula (5).

Necrotizing enterocolitis (NEC), a devastating acute intestinal inflammatory disease in premature infants, is less likely to occur in infants fed human milk. A very large, nonrandomized study of premature infants in hospital reported that the incidence of NEC was significantly lower in infants fed human milk, either exclusively or partially, than in infants fed formula (6). That study reported clinical cases as well as confirmed cases, and in both circumstances the incidence of NEC was significantly higher in infants fed solely on formula. In another report, the disease appeared to be less severe and there was a lower incidence of intestinal perforation during the course of the disease in infants who had received human milk before diagnosis (7%) compared with those fed formula (39%) (7). These data suggest that the use of human milk may help prevent NEC in premature infants.

Specific factors such as secretory IgA (sIgA), lactoferrin, lysozyme, oligosaccharides, growth factors, and cellular components may affect the host defense of the premature infant. One of the major protective effects of human milk on the recipient infant operates through the entero-mammary immune system. It is reasonable to expect that exposure of the mother to the environment of the neonatal nursery through skin-to-skin contact with her premature infant may be advantageous to the infant. In this manner, mothers can be induced to make specific antibodies against the nosocomial pathogens in the nursery environment.

The reason for the protective role of human milk in NEC is unclear. One study associated a decreased incidence of NEC in premature infants with the feeding of a preparation of immunoglobulins A and G (IgA–IgG) derived from serum (8). The infants fed the IgA–IgG preparation had a significantly higher fecal excretion of IgA than controls, suggesting a local protective effect throughout the gastrointestinal tract. Our studies at the Children's Nutrition Research Center in Houston also showed greater fecal excretion of IgA as well as greater excretion of lactoferrin in feces and both IgA and lactoferrin in urine of premature infants fed human milk compared with similar infants fed formula (9,10). In our studies, fecal excretion accounted for 9% of the IgA and 5% of the lactoferrin intake. Additional studies suggest that human milk–derived lactoferrin may be absorbed intact and excreted in the urine of premature infants (11). These results suggest that human milk may enhance the premature infant's host defenses through local and systemic actions.

Diet also may affect fecal flora. Feeding of human milk to a compromised premature infant may result in a fecal flora that is less pathogenic than that of a bovine-derived formula. A less pathogenic flora would change the predominant nursery-acquired fecal pathogens to more beneficial, less pathogenic microorganisms.

Thus the relation between the feeding of human milk and the reduced incidence of infection or NEC reported in these descriptive studies indicates the particular suitability of human milk for premature infants.

However, the exclusive feeding of unfortified human milk in premature infants, generally infants with birthweights of less than 1,500 g, has been associated with poorer rates of growth and with nutritional deficits, during and beyond the period of hospital inpatient care (5,12–17). Because of the availability of commercial formulas designed to meet the nutritional needs of the premature infant, the use of unfortified human milk has declined. The recognition that growth and nutrient deficits can be improved with the use of nutrient supplements has led to a renewed enthusiasm for the use of human milk for premature infants (18–21).

Unfortified human milk may not supply sufficient quantities of nutrients for several reasons. The concentrations of several nutrients (e.g., protein and sodium) decline through lactation. The nutrient needs of the premature infant, however, do not decline until approximately 40 weeks of postmenstrual age. Therefore the decline in milk concentration results in an inadequate nutrient supply to the infant. The content of other nutrients (such as calcium and phosphorus) is too low to meet the considerable needs of the premature infant. Technical reasons associated with the collection, storage, and delivery of milk to the infant also result in a decreased quantity of available nutrients (e.g., fat, vitamin C, vitamin A, riboflavin). Lastly, the premature infant is usually tube-fed, making *ad libitum* feeding unlikely. Furthermore, fluid restriction is often imposed as part of the clinical management. Given the reasons cited, it should not be a surprise that inadequacies of calcium, phosphorus, protein, sodium, vitamins, and energy are observed in the premature infant fed unfortified human milk (5,12–17).

HUMAN MILK FORTIFICATION

Single and multinutrient supplementation of human milk has been associated with improvements in short-term growth and nutritional status. Mineral supplementation of unfortified human milk during the hospital stay increases bone mineralization during and beyond the neonatal period and prevents a decrease in linear growth (22–24). Supplementation with both calcium and phosphorus results in normalization of biochemical indices of mineral status—serum calcium, phosphorus, and alkaline phosphatase activity; urinary excretion of calcium and phosphorus (25,26). Sodium supplementation results in normalization of serum sodium (27). Supplementation with protein and energy is associated with improved rates of weight gain and improved indices of protein nutritional status—blood urea nitrogen, serum albumin, prealbumin (16,21).

Current practice suggests the use of multinutrient fortification of human milk. Nutritional outcomes of feeding fortified human milk in the United States indicate that premature infants receive less volume but greater intakes of protein and minerals, and experience greater gain in weight and increments in linear growth than infants fed unfortified human milk exclusively (19,28,29). Balance study data indicate that the use of fortified human milk results in net nutrient retention that approaches or is greater than the expected intrauterine rates of accretion. Fat absorption, however, has been lower than expected in some reports (26,30).

Lucas *et al.* (31) compared growth and nutritional status in premature infants who received fortified human milk *versus* partially supplemented (control) human milk. Premature infants fed human milk (birthweight < 1,850 g) were assigned to receive either a multinutrient fortifier (Enfamil Human Milk Fortifier, Mead Johnson Nutritional Group, Evansville, Indiana) or a control supplement (phosphorus 4.8 mmol/liter, sodium 0.3 mmol/liter, and multivitamins) mixed with their mothers' milk. Many mothers were unable to sustain lactation for the duration of the study (average 40 days), so preterm formula comprised more than 50% of the milk consumed in both groups. Therefore the primary comparisons between groups may have been affected by the large quantity of formula given to the study infants. Nevertheless, there were no differences between fortified and control supplement human milk groups in growth outcome measures at 18 months of follow-up. Short-term differences were observed that were more apparent in an analysis of the data from infants who received more than 50% of their enteral feeding as human milk. The data suggested that the feeding of fortified human milk was associated with greater weight gain and a higher blood urea nitrogen (an index of normal protein nutritional status) than control supplemented human milk.

The growth and nutritional status of premature infants fed fortified human milk *versus* preterm formula has been examined (29). The growth rates of infants (birthweight ~1 kg, gestational age ~28 weeks) fed fortified human milk (Enfamil Human Milk Fortifier, Mead Johnson) were significantly lower (18 *versus* 22 g/kg·d) than in infants fed preterm formula (Enfamil Premature Formula, Mead Johnson). Premature infants fed fortified human milk also had lesser increments in linear growth (0.8 *versus* 1.0 cm/week) and in average skinfold thickness (0.17 *versus* 0.25 mm/week) than infants fed preterm formula. To meet projected daily weight gains, the infants fed fortified human milk required milk intakes of more than 180 ml/kg·d compared with infants fed preterm formula, who needed 150 to 160 ml/kg·d to achieve those goals. The fluid intakes of infants fed fortified human milk were significantly greater than those usually recommended. Nutrient absorption and retention were measured by 72-hour balance studies at two time periods during the hospital stay, at 6 and 9 weeks of postnatal age. The fortified human milk provided nutrient intakes that approached or surpassed the estimates for intrauterine nutrient accretion (2,32). A correlation between calcium retention and bone mineral content of the radius was observed, suggesting that a greater quantity of minerals may affect bone mineralization. The data further suggested that the addition of magnesium, copper, and possibly zinc to human milk may not be necessary, as respective retentions were significantly above the intrauterine nutrient accretion rates.

The most marked difference between fortified human milk and preterm formula was in the absorption of fat. The infants fed fortified human milk had significantly lower rates of fat absorption than those fed preterm formula (62% *versus* 91% and 78% *versus* 92% at 6 and 9 weeks, respectively). The lower rates of fat, and therefore energy, absorption may have been the reason for the lower rates of growth in the infants fed fortified human milk (15,26,30).

It is unclear why fat absorption was so low. The addition of a large quantity of minerals to human milk may have created an unfavorable milieu for the human milk lipid system. The fat globule may have been disrupted by osmotic forces generated by the high mineral content of the fortifier. Such forces may affect the fat globule and liberate fatty acids. Moreover, free fatty acids may bind minerals. In the intestinal tract, soap formation caused by fatty acid binding to minerals may hinder fat absorption. Interactions between calcium and fatty acids have been reported during calcium supplementation of human milk for premature infants (33). Clinical data suggest that the large quantity of minerals in the fortifier affect fat absorption. Premature infants

TABLE 1. *Comparison of selected fortifiers for human milk (prepared per 100 ml milk)*

	PrHM*	EHMF†	SNC‡	Eoprotin§	SMAHMF‖	FM85#
Energy (kcal)	71	85	76	85	86	89
Fat (g)	3.6	3.6**	4.0	3.6**	3.6**	3.6
Carbohydrate (g)	7.0	9.7	7.8	9.8	9.4	10.6
Protein (g)	1.8	2.5	2.0	2.6	2.8	2.6
Calcium (mg)	22	112	97	72	112	73
Phosphorus (mg)	14	59	50	48	59	48
Magnesium (mg)	2.5	3.5	6.3	5.3	4.0	4.5
Sodium (mmol)	0.7	1.0	1.1	1.9	1.1	1.9
Zinc (μg)	320	1030	760	320**	450	320**
Copper (μg)	60	122	130	60**	60**	60**
Vitamins††	Yes	††	††	†	††	†

* PrHM = Preterm Human Milk (46).

† EHMF = Enfamil Human Milk Fortifier (Mead Johnson Nutritionals, Evansville, IN); partial vitamin supplement.

‡ SNC = Similac Natural Care (Ross Labs, Columbus, OH): mixed 1:1 (vol:vol) with PrHM.

§ Eoprotin (Milupa, Friedrichsdorf, Germany).

‖ S-26 SMA Human Milk Fortifier (Wyeth Nutritionals International, Philadelphia, PA).

FM85 (Nestlé, Vevey, Switzerland).

** Indicates nutrient not contained in fortifier.

†† Complete multivitamins mixture: A, D, E, K, B-1, B-2, B-6, C, niacin, folate, B-12, pantothenate, biotin.

receiving a human milk fortifier (Eoprotin, Milupa, Friedrichsdorf, Germany) containing less minerals than the Enfamil Human Milk Fortifier have mean rates of fat absorption of 92% and rates of weight gain and linear growth greater than those reported for similar infants fed Enfamil Human Milk Fortifier (29,34). A comparison of the nutrient content of human milk fortifiers is given in Table 1. Although it is difficult to make comparisons between studies, the lower mineral content fortifier tends to favor better fat absorption and growth. Thus it appears that when fat absorption is improved, growth rates increase, and this may be achieved at lower milk intakes. The improvement of fat absorption would most probably favor even better mineral absorption.

Differences in rates of growth in premature infants receiving fortified human milk *versus* preterm formula have been reported, even for formulas containing lower quantities of protein and minerals than those available in the United States (35). However, in those studies bone mineralization did not differ significantly. Thus the slower rate of growth may not be a marker of poorer nutritional status. None of the studies suggested that the slower rate of growth of the fortified human milk–fed premature infant is detrimental. Indeed, it has been shown that these infants have a shorter period of hospital admission and less infection and necrotizing enterocolitis than infants fed preterm formula (35,36).

NONNUTRITIONAL OUTCOMES OF FEEDING FORTIFIED HUMAN MILK

Questions have been raised as to whether the addition of bovine-derived human milk fortifiers affects feeding tolerance in premature infants. Gastric residual volumes are often used to assess feeding tolerance. The residual volume may be affected by gastric emptying. The data on gastric emptying, however, are controversial. Novel ultrasound techniques to assess gastric cross-sectional areas have yielded conflicting results (37,38). In contrast, Lucas *et al.* (31) clearly observed that the use of fortified human milk was not associated with feeding intolerance as manifest by abdominal distension, vomiting, changes in stool frequency, or volume of gastric aspirate when compared with control-supplemented human milk.

The feeding of unfortified human milk to preterm infants during their time in the hospital has been associated with greater intellectual performance scores at 7.5 to 8 years than in similar infants fed formula (39). The relation between diet and developmental outcome at 3 years of age also was reported for Australian premature infants who were born at less than 33 weeks of gestation (40). Human milk feeding had a beneficial effect on scores of intelligence and distractibility hyperactivity. Neurodevelopmental outcomes at 18 months, however, were not affected by human milk fortification in the study of Lucas *et al.* (31).

Visual function may be improved by feeding human milk to premature infants, possibly owing to the high concentration of very long-chain polyenoic fatty acids in the milk (41). Human milk also has significant antioxidant activity, including but not limited to such compounds as beta carotene, taurine, and vitamin E. Because of the antioxidant activity, the relation between diet and retinopathy of prematurity was examined (42). In this retrospective review of medical records, factors associated with the development of retinopathy of prematurity were studied and the diagnosis of retinopathy of prematurity was found to be significantly more common in formula-fed infants than in human milk–fed infants. The severity of retinopathy also was reported to be less in human milk–fed premature infants. Fewer infants fed human milk (exclusively or partially) progressed to advanced retinopathy, and none required cryotherapy or laser surgery (42). Most of the later studies were conducted in infants receiving fortified human milk. These results support the potential beneficial effects of human milk on neurodevelopmental function in the premature infant, whether receiving unfortified or fortified human milk.

A major concern with human milk fortification is that the added nutrients may affect the complex system of host defense. The relation between diet and the incidence of infection in premature infants has been examined. Human milk–fed infants had a 26% incidence of documented infection compared with 49% in formula-fed infants (43). The relation between necrotizing enterocolitis and human milk feeding has been discussed. Lucas *et al.* (31) determined that the use of fortified human milk was not associated with either confirmed infection or necrotizing enterocolitis. When the latter two events were combined, however, the group fed fortified human milk had more events than the control supplement group. Although it is difficult to conclude that the use of fortifiers is harmful, these data indicate the need for continued surveillance of these events (44).

In a review of prospectively collected data on morbidity and diet in premature infants in Houston, those infants fed exclusively on fortified human milk had a significantly lower incidence of necrotizing enterocolitis and sepsis, fewer positive blood cultures, and less antibiotic usage than infants fed preterm formula or a regimen of alternate feedings of fortified human milk and preterm formula (36). Infants fed exclusively on fortified human milk had more episodes of skin-to-skin contact with their mothers and a shorter hospital stay. These data suggest that feeding premature infants with fortified human milk had a marked effect on the cost of medical care. The data further suggest that skin-to-skin contact may be the necessary link to promote an entero-mammary response in the premature infant. It may well become the practice to encourage mothers to have skin-to-skin contact to enhance their capacity to synthesize specific factors that counter the pathogens in the nursery environment.

The effects of nutrient fortification (Enfamil Human Milk Fortifier, Mead Johnson) on some of the general host defense properties of the milk have been evaluated. Fortification did not affect the concentration of IgA (45). Bacterial colony counts, however, increased over time of storage of fortified human milk (45). When fortified human milk was evaluated under simulated nursery conditions, bacterial colony counts were not significantly different after 20 hours of storage at refrigerator temperature but did increase from 20 to 24 hours when maintained at incubator temperature. The overall increase in bacterial colony counts by 24 hours, however, was small (approximately a 10-fold difference). These data did not suggest that changes are necessary in regard to the current practice of how fortifiers are used in the nursery, but they do suggest caution in handling human milk and the need to evaluate environmental effects as they arise.

CONCLUSION

Various methods have been reported and used clinically to augment the nutrient supply for the human milk fed premature infant. These methods include specialized multinutrient powdered mixtures ("fortifiers"), complete liquid formulas designed to be mixed with human milk, complete powdered formulas to be mixed with human milk, or alternate feeding of human milk and preterm formula. Although the optimum form of nutrition of premature infants is unknown, data are accumulating to suggest that human milk, fortified with additional nutrients, is appropriate for the tube-fed infant.

- The use of fortified human milk generally ensures adequate growth, nutrient retention, and biochemical indices of nutritional status in the premature infant when fed at approximately 180 ml/kg·d.
- Data are needed to determine the precise quantity of nutrients to be added as supplements. Nutrient interactions have not been explored in detail.
- Although large quantities of calcium appear to be needed, the exogenous calcium may affect fat absorption adversely.
- Although manipulation of milk may affect the intrinsic host defense properties of the milk, when compared with preterm formula, the feeding of fortified human milk may provide significant protection from infection and necrotizing enterocolitis.
- Lastly, the potential stimulation of an entero-mammary pathway through skin-to-skin contact may be a means of providing species specific antimicrobial protection for the premature infant. Several of these areas require further exploration.

Thus for premature infants, neonatal centers should encourage the feeding of forti-fied human milk, along with skin-to-skin contact, as a reasonable method of enhanc-ing milk production while potentially facilitating the development of an entero-mam-mary response.

ACKNOWLEDGMENT

This review was supported by the National Institute of Child Health and Human Development, Grant No. RO-1-HD-28140, and the General Clinical Research Center, Baylor College of Medicine/Texas Children's Hospital Clinical Research Center, Grant No. MO-1-RR-00188, National Institutes of Health. Partial funding also has been provided from the USDA/ARS under Cooperative Agreement No. 58-6250-1-003. This work is a publication of the USDA/ARS Children's Nutrition Research Center, Department of Pediatrics, Baylor College of Medicine and Texas Children's Hospital, Houston, TX. The contents of this publication do not necessar-ily reflect the views or policies of the USDA, nor does mention of trade names, com-mercial products, or organizations imply endorsement by the U.S. government.

REFERENCES

1. American Academy of Pediatrics, Work Group on Breastfeeding. Breastfeeding and the use of human milk. *Pediatrics* 1997;100:1035–1039.
2. Ziegler EE, O Donnell AM, Nelson SE, Fomon SJ. Body composition of the reference fetus. *Growth* 1976;40:329–341.
3. Schanler RJ. Suitability of human milk for the low birthweight infant. *Clin Perinatol* 1995;22:207–222.
4. Narayanan I, Prakash K, Bala S, Verma RK, Gujral VV. Partial supplementation with expressed breast-milk for prevention of infection in low-birth-weight infants. *Lancet* 1980;ii:561–563.
5. Contreras-Lemus J, Flores-Huerta S, Cisneros-Silva I, *et al.* Disminucion de la morbilidad en neonatos pretermino alimentados con leche de su propia madre. *Biol Med Hosp Infant Mex* 1992;49:671–677.
6. Lucas A, Cole TJ. Breast milk and neonatal necrotizing enterocolitis. *Lancet* 1990;336:1519–1523.
7. Covert RF, Barman N, Domanico RS, Singh JK. Prior enteral nutrition with human milk protects against intestinal perforation in infants who develop necrotizing enterocolitis. *Pediatr Res* 1995;37:305A (abst.).
8. Eibl MM, Wolf HM, Furnkranz H, Rosenkranz A. Prevention of necrotizing enterocolitis in low-birth-weight infants by IgA–IgG feeding. *N Engl J Med* 1988;319:1–7.
9. Schanler RJ, Goldblum RM, Garza C, Goldman AS. Enhanced fecal excretion of selected immune factors in very low birth weight infants fed fortified human milk. *Pediatr Res* 1986;20:711–715.
10. Goldblum RM, Schanler RJ, Garza C, Goldman AS. Human milk feeding enhances the urinary ex-cretion of immunologic factors in low birth weight infants. *Pediatr Res* 1989;25:184–188.
11. Hutchens TW, Henry JF, Yip T. Origin of intact lactoferrin and its DNA-binding fragments found in the urine of human milk–fed preterm infants. Evaluation by stable isotope enrichment. *Pediatr Res* 1991;29:243–250.
12. Atkinson SA, Radde IC, Anderson GH. Macromineral balances in premature infants fed their own mothers milk or formula. *J Pediatr* 1983;102:99–106.
13. Tönz O, Schubiger G. Feeding of very-low-birth-weight infants with breast-milk enriched by energy, nitrogen and minerals: FM85. *Helv Paediatr Acta* 1985;40:235–247.
14. Cooper PA, Rothberg AD, Pettifor JM, Bolton KD, Devenhuis S. Growth and biochemical response of premature infants fed pooled preterm milk or special formula. *J Pediatr Gastroenterol Nutr* 1984;3:749–754.
15. Atkinson SA, Bryan MH, Anderson GH. Human milk feeding in premature infants: protein, fat and carbohydrate balances in the first two weeks of life. *J Pediatr* 1981;99:617–624.

16. Kashyap S, Schulze KF, Forsyth M, Dell RB, Ramakrishnan R, Heird WC. Growth, nutrient retention, and metabolic response of low-birth-weight infants fed supplemented and unsupplemented preterm human milk. *Am J Clin Nutr* 1990;52:254–262.
17. Gross SJ. Growth and biochemical response of preterm infants fed human milk or modified infant formula. *N Engl J Med* 1983;308:237–241.
18. Schanler RJ, Garza C, Smith EO. Fortified mothers milk for very low birth weight infants: results of macromineral balance studies. *J Pediatr* 1985;107:767–774.
19. Greer FR, McCormick A. Improved bone mineralization and growth in premature infants fed fortified own mother's milk. *J Pediatr* 1988;112:961–969.
20. Horsman A, Ryan SW, Congdon PJ, Truscott JG, Simpson M. Bone mineral accretion rate and calcium intake in preterm infants. *Arch Dis Child* 1989;64:910–918.
21. Polberger SKT, Axelsson IA, Raiha NCR. Growth of very low birth weight infants on varying amounts of human milk protein. *Pediatr Res* 1989;25:414–419.
22. Abrams SA, Schanler RJ, Garza C. Bone mineralization in former very low birth weight infants fed either human milk or commercial formula. *J Pediatr* 1988;112:956–962.
23. Lucas A, Brooke OG, Baker BA, Bishop N, Morley R. High alkaline phosphatase activity and growth in preterm neonates. *Arch Dis Child* 1989;64:902–909.
24. Abrams SA, Schanler RJ, Tsang RC, Garza C. Bone mineralization in former very low birth weight infants fed either human milk or commercial formula: one year follow-up observation. *J Pediatr* 1989;114:1041–1044.
25. Rowe JC, Wood DH, Rowe DW, Raisz LG. Nutritional hypophosphatemic rickets in a premature infant fed breast milk. *N Engl J Med* 1979;300:293–296.
26. Schanler RJ, Garza C. Improved mineral balance in very low birth weight infants fed fortified human milk. *J Pediatr* 1987;112:452–456.
27. Kumar SP, Sacks LM. Hyponatremia in very-low-birth-weight infants and human milk feedings. *J Pediatr* 1978; 93: 1026–1027.
28. Schanler RJ, Abrams SA. Postnatal attainment of intrauterine macromineral accretion rates in low birth weight infants fed fortified human milk. *J Pediatr* 1995;126:441–447.
29. Schanler RJ, Shulman RJ, Lau C. Growth of premature infants fed fortified human milk. *Pediatr Res* 1997;41:240A (abst.).
30. Schanler RJ, Garza C, Nichols BL. Fortified mothers milk for very low birth weight infants: results of growth and nutrient balance studies. *J Pediatr* 1985;107:437–445.
31. Lucas A, Fewtrell MS, Morley R, *et al.* Randomized outcome trial of human milk fortification and developmental outcome in preterm infants. *Am J Clin Nutr* 1996;64:142–151.
32. Reifen RM, Zlotkin S. Microminerals. In: Tsang RC, Lucas A, Uauy R, Zlotkin S, eds. *Nutritional needs of the preterm infant: scientific basis and practical guidelines.* Baltimore: Williams & Wilkins, 1993:195–208.
33. Chappell JE, Clandinin MT, Kearney-Volpe C, Reichman B, Swyer PW. Fatty acid balance studies in premature infants fed human milk or formula: effect of calcium supplementation. *J Pediatr* 1986;108:439–447.
34. Boehm G, Muller DM, Senger H, Borte M, Moro GE. Nitrogen and fat balances in very low birth weight infants fed human milk fortified with human milk or bovine milk protein. *Eur J Pediatr* 1993;152:236–239.
35. Wauben IP, Atkinson SA, Grad TL, Shah JK, Paes B. Moderate nutrient supplementation of mother's milk for preterm infants supports adequate bone mass and short-term growth: a randomized, controlled trial. *Am J Clin Nutr* 1998;67:465–472.
36. Schanler RJ, Shulman RJ, Lau C. Fortified human milk improves the health of the premature infant. *Pediatr Res* 1996;40:551.
37. McClure RJ, Newell SJ. Effect of fortifying breast milk on gastric emptying. *Arch Dis Child* 1996;74:F60–62.
38. Ewer AK, Yu VYH. Gastric emptying in pre-term infants: the effect of breast milk fortifier. *Acta Paediatr* 1996;85:1112–1115.
39. Lucas A, Morley R, Cole TJ, Lister G, Leeson-Payne C. Breast milk and subsequent intelligence quotient in children born preterm. *Lancet* 1992;339:261–264.
40. Hagan R, French N, Evans S, *et al.* Breast feeding distractibility and IQ in very preterm infants. *Pediatr Res* 1996;39:266A (abst.).
41. Carlson SE, Werkman SH, Rhodes PG, Tolley EA. Visual-acuity development in healthy preterm infants: effect of marine-oil supplementation. *Am J Clin Nutr* 1993;58:35–42.
42. Hylander MA, Strobino DM, Dhanireddy R. Human milk feedings and retinopathy of prematurity (ROP) among very low birth weight (VLBW) infants. *Pediatr Res* 1995;37:214A (abst.).

43. Hylander MA, Strobino DM, Dhanireddy R. Human milk feedings and infection among very low birth weight (VLBW) infants. *Pediatr Res* 1996;39:295A (abst.).
44. Schanler RJ. Human milk fortification for premature infants. *Am J Clin Nutr* 1996;64:249–250.
45. Jocson MAL, Mason EO, Schanler RJ. The effects of nutrient fortification and varying storage conditions on host defense properties of human milk. *Pediatrics* 1997;100:240–243.

DISCUSSION

Dr. Putet: Can you comment on the difference in weight gain between the two groups. Do you think it is only a question of energy absorption?

Dr. Schanler: There were marked differences in fat and energy absorption in the two groups, and together with the differences in skinfold thickness this seems to be the reason why those babies were growing slower.

Dr. Rigo: When we analyzed our data comparing Enfamil human milk fortifier with preterm formula using metabolic balance techniques, we were surprised to find that the weight gain composition seemed somewhat different in preterm infants fed human milk fortifier than in those fed preterm formula. Although the protein deposition was similar, the water content of the tissue deposited seemed to be lower in the infants fed human milk fortifier. Do you have any idea why this should be? Is it to do with the sodium intake?

Dr. Schanler: In our study sodium intakes were roughly the same in the two groups.

Dr. Rigo: But the weight gain was significantly different not only because of differences in fat deposition. We think the lean mass deposition is also different, probably because of the different amount of tissue water.

Dr. Schanler: Nitrogen balance was slightly greater in the preterm infants fed fortified human milk. Probably there was more lean tissue deposition in that group.

Prof. Haschke: Necrotizing enterocolitis was only found in 1% of the infants fed the fortifier? This contradicts previous results where a substantially higher incidence was found. Could you comment on that?

Dr. Schanler: This could be a spurious result based on relatively small numbers. We are looking at this now prospectively. Also, you need to remember that distinct from other studies these infants were fed larger volumes of feed. Their diet was predominantly human milk. We only studied babies who were receiving more than 50 ml/kg·d of fortified human milk, babies who were receiving a mixture of fortified human milk and formula were not included. A problem with analyzing data from babies receiving fortified human milk is that it is hard to get pure groups of infants fed either fortified human milk or human milk exclusively. Babies usually receive formula and to some extent that complicates the observations.

Prof. Haschke: Fat absorption and retention and to some extent calcium and phosphorus retention were low. Do you think these were interrelated?

Dr. Schanler: I think they are related. Either the minerals are binding the fat or damaging the fat globule and binding the fatty acids in the milk, so making them unavailable to the infant, or this process is going on in the gut and the calcium is binding fat there. But it is probably the overall mineral content magnesium as well that affects fat absorption.

Dr. Faouri: Did you observe any differences between your two groups regarding bilirubin levels and the duration of jaundice?

Dr. Schanler: No, there was no difference in hyperbilirubinemia or the use of phototherapy.

Dr. Sedaghatian: How do you use your human milk? Do you store it, or do you give it fresh?

Dr. Schanler: We use mothers own milk. The milk is frozen after collection and then thawed and fortified before use for feeding. We don't pasteurize it.

Prof. Lucas: We have been looking at our human milk data in relation to infection and found, surprisingly, that sepsis in premature babies was social class related. You might have expected that it would not be, as they are all looked after by the same nurses. But that of course creates potential confounding when you compare breastfed and formula-fed groups in a nonrandomized way, because of the greater positive health behavior of the social classes who breastfeed. Did you attempt to see whether your infection data were robust after adjusting for the early socioeconomic factors?

Dr. Schanler: No, we did not. But that's an interesting point to study.

Prof. Cooke: Do you employ any form of bacteriological surveillance on human milk that you use to feed preterm babies, either if it is fresh or frozen or if it is processed in another way, and if so, what is that policy?

Dr. Schanler: We don't have a strict policy. We culture milk in the first week it is brought into the nursery as an indicator of whether or not the mother is complying with the collection procedures. We almost never discard milk because of the results of a culture, but it has helped us re-emphasize to the mothers what technique should be applied.

Prof. Cooke: But if you don't throw it away, then presumably you feed it, no matter what it has got in it. Our own work seems to suggest that from one collection to another on the same day, you can have positive and negative samples. So I wonder what you feel the value of occasion sampling is.

Dr. Schanler: We don't have an answer to that question. What is your opinion about that? What should we do?

Prof. Cooke: Does anybody else in the room have a policy backed by any sort of science?

Dr. Schanler: The Human Milk Bank Association of North America has the same type of policy—that is, no routine surveillance, but do it to monitor collection technique.

Prof. Lucas: Neither the Human Milk Bank Association of North America nor the recent British directive recommends routine screening of mother's own milk. The scientific rationale behind that is first that infection rates are, if anything, lower on unpasteurized human milk than on formula, and second that a Canadian study showed a very poor relation between the presence of organisms in the milk and infection in the baby. There really is no compelling data that human milk is a source of infection for premature babies.

Dr. Walker: Your collaborators in previous studies have defined a mechanism by which mothers produce antibodies in their milk against flora in their own environment, suggesting that there is a built-in protective process against infection. Have you looked at the milk sample to determine if there are antibodies directed against the organisms that colonize the infant?

Dr. Schanler: That is what we are doing right now.

Prof. Pohlandt: We heard from the audience and the panel that there is no scientific basis for bacteriological surveillance of human milk. But there have been several papers on the vertical transmission of CMV. Do you think we can still use raw breast milk without checking the mother for CMV, taking into account the risk of vertical transmission to her baby? We have eight cases in our unit.

Dr. Schanler: We know that CMV is destroyed by freezing. I look for guidance in the audience. We are not really sure what is the best course of action.

Prof. Pohlandt: We have tested this in the lab. We found that a temperature of −20°C does not destroy the infectious agent.

Dr. Schanler: Please report that. It is important.

Prof. Nowak: You said that you give your babies their mother's own milk, which means that there may be a significant delay before they receive their first milk feed. Do you think this gap should be filled, perhaps with an IgA preparation? [1].

Dr. Schanler: In our nursery, the staff are reluctant to feed very early. By the time the babies start feeds, on day 4 or 5, there is breast milk available in the volumes that we are going to use. So, in our case, that is not a concern. The IgA study needs to be replicated; those data were almost too surprising to be believed. I know that an attempt was made to repeat it but it was stopped because of the hepatitis C scare.

Dr. Walker: There have been some follow-up studies in the United States [2], but they have not shown as good results as were originally reported in the *New England Journal of Medicine*.

Dr. Nowak: You have shown many benefits of human milk, particularly in relation to the occurrence of necrotizing enterocolitis. What kind of feed would you recommend when enteral feeding is reestablished after necrotizing enterocolitis? Human milk? Regular formula? Hydrolyzed formula?

Dr. Schanler: We routinely use human milk for all our babies post-NEC, moving to fortified human milk thereafter. I don't know of any trials on this, but it's an important area. Every textbook you read has one sentence on the nutritional support post-NEC, which is to use hydrolysate formula. There are few data to back that up. We routinely use human milk in those infants, and the only ones who don't tolerate it are the ones who don't tolerate any milk and need prolonged parenteral nutrition.

Dr. Rashwan: Is there any evidence of delayed gastric emptying when using fortifiers?

Dr. Schanler: We did not see any difference in indices of feeding tolerance between fortified human milk and formula. There is one report showing better gastric emptying with unfortified human milk than with formula [3]. There are a couple of very confusing reports looking at gastric emptying with ultrasound techniques: one showed no difference with fortified human milk and the other showed delayed emptying with fortified milk [4,5], but we did not see any difference.

REFERENCES

1. Eibl MM, Wolf HM, Furnkranz H, Rosenkranz A. Prevention of necrotizing enterocolitis in low-birth-weight infants by IgA-IgG feeding. *N Engl J Med* 1988;319:1–7.
2. Groer M, Walker WA. What is the role of preterm breast milk supplementation in the host defenses of preterm infants? *Adv Pediatr* 1996;43:335–358.
3. Cavell B. Gastric emptying in infants fed human milk or infant formula. *Acta Paediatr Scand* 1981;70:639–641.
4. Ewer AK, Yu VYH. Gastric emptying in pre-term infants: the effect of breast milk fortifier. *Acta Paediatr* 1996;85:1112–1115.
5. McClure RJ, Newell SJ. Effect of fortifying breast milk on gastric emptying. *Arch Dis Child* 1996;74:F60–62.

Nutrition of the Very Low Birthweight Infant, edited by
Ekhard E. Ziegler, Alan Lucas, Guido E. Moro.
Nestlé Nutrition Workshop Series, Paediatric Programme, Vol. 43,
Nestec Ltd., Vevey/Lippincott Williams & Wilkins
Philadelphia, Pennsylvania © 1999.

Development of Lung Defenses Against Free Radical Injury

Lee Frank

University of Miami School of Medicine, Pulmonary Research Center (R-120), PO Box 016960, Miami, Florida 33101

OXYGEN TOXICITY

All respiring organisms are caught in a cruel bind in that oxygen which supports their lives is a toxic substance in which presence they survive only by virtue of an elaborate system of defenses.

—I. Fridovich (1975)

Oxygen represents one of the more fascinating biological paradoxes, for, while life-giving in normal concentrations, it becomes universally toxic to cells and organisms at hyperoxic levels. Although oxygen itself is nontoxic, its atoms are capable of sequential one-electron reduction reactions that create highly reactive O_2 intermediates such as superoxide free radical (O_2^-), hydrogen peroxide (H_2O_2), singlet oxygen ($^1O_2$), and the extremely reactive hydroxyl free radical ($OH\cdot$). These cytotoxic oxygen species are normal byproducts of oxygen metabolism in our cells, especially metabolism through the mitochondrial respiratory enzyme chain and the mixed function microsomal enzyme system [1,2]. Importantly, also, the production rate of oxygen radicals greatly increases with increases in O_2 tension so that under 95% O_2 conditions mitochondrial and microsomal oxygen radical generation will increase 10-fold or more [3]. These reactive oxygen species (ROS) are cytotoxic because they can interact with and damage all the principal components of aerobic cells, including proteins (oxidation of protein sulfhydryl groups with subsequent loss of enzyme activities), carbohydrates (depolymerization), lipids (lipid peroxidation reactions and loss of membrane integrity), and even genetic material (DNA cross-linking and scission of DNA strands). Additionally, radicals block normal biosynthesis of cellular protein and DNA [1,2].

To prevent these damaging interactions from ROS produced under normoxic conditions, cells have evolved an elaborate series of defenses to block their potential cytotoxic effects on vital cell components. Foremost of these are the antioxidant enzymes—superoxide dismutase (SOD), catalase (CAT), and the glutathione peroxidase (GP) enzyme system that also includes the enzymes glutathione reductase

TABLE 1. *The catalytic antioxidant enzyme defense system*

AOES	Function
Superoxide dismutase (SOD) 　MnSOD—mitochondrial 　CuZnSOD—cytosolic	$O_2^- + O_2^- + 2H^+ \rightarrow O_2 + H_2O_2$
Catalase (CAT)	$2\,H_2O_2 \rightarrow O_2 + 2H_2O$
Glutathione peroxidase (GP)	$H_2O_2 + 2GSH \rightarrow 2H_2O + GSSG$ $2ROO^\cdot + 2\,GSH \rightarrow 2\,ROH + O_2 + GSSG$
Glutathione reductase (GR)	$GSSG + NADPH + H^+ \rightarrow 2\,GSH + NADP^+$
Glucose-6-PO_4-dehydrogenase	$Glucose\text{-}6\text{-}PO_4 + NADP^+ \rightarrow NADPH + H^+$ $+$ 6-phosphogluconate

O_2^- = superoxide free radical; H_2O_2 = hydrogen peroxide; $ROO^\cdot$ = peroxyl radical; ROH = nontoxic lipid alcohol; GSH = reduced glutathione; GSSG = oxidized glutathione. From reference 4, with permission of publisher.

(GR) and glucose-6-phosphate dehydrogenase (G-6-PD). Table 1 shows how these enzymes protect by scavenging and detoxifying reactive oxygen intermediates at catalytic rates (4). In addition to this primary antioxidant defensive system, cells have evolved a secondary, nonenzymatic or stoichiometric antioxidant defensive system (Table 2) that, because many of its components are present in high intracellular concentrations, is believed to have an important role in the overall antioxidant armamentarium of aerobic cells. Some of these secondary antioxidants include vitamins A, C, and E; sulfur-containing amino acids for glutathione production; metal chelators such as ceruloplasmin and transferrin and others (4).

The so-called oxygen free radical theory of oxygen toxicity, which has been formulated over the past 30 years, is summarized in Fig. 1 (5). It is believed that under

TABLE 2. *Secondary or noncatalytic antioxidant defense system*

Antioxidant	Function
Glutathione	$2GSH + 2ROO^\cdot \rightarrow GSSG + 2ROH + O_2$ May also directly scavenge O_2 radicals May also regenerate oxidized vitamin E
Ascorbate (vitamin C)	May directly scavenge O_2 radicals and/or regenerate oxidized vitamin E
β-carotene (vitamin A)	Scavenger of singlet oxygen, $^1O_2$
Vitamin E (α-tocopherol)	Interrupts chain-reaction lipid peroxidation by reducing peroxyl, alkoxyl radicals $Vit\,E + (ROO^\cdot)\,(RO^\cdot) \rightarrow (ROOH)\,(ROH) + Vit\,E^\cdot$ May also scavenge $OH\cdot$ directly
Ceruloplasmin	Binds Cu to prevent $OH\cdot$ formation. Ferroxidase function ($Fe^{++} \rightarrow Fe^{+++}$) to prevent $OH\cdot$ formation.
Others: Cysteamine, cysteine, nonessential PUFAs, other thiols, transferrin	

Abbreviations: O_2^- = superoxide free radical; H_2O_2 = hydrogen peroxide; $ROO^\cdot$ = peroxyl radical; ROH = nontoxic lipid alcohol; GSH = reduced glutathione; GSSG = oxidized glutathione; $RO^\cdot$ = alkoxyl radical; Vit $E^\cdot$ = vitamin E radical; $OH\cdot$ = hydroxyl free radical. From reference 4, with permission of publisher.

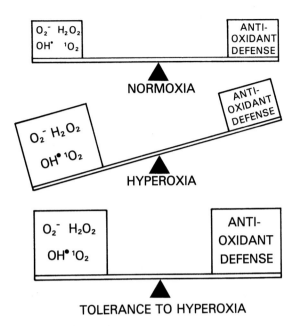

FIG. 1. Oxygen free radicals and the antioxidant defense system. Under normoxic conditions, equilibrium exists between the production of potentially cytotoxic O_2 radicals and the antioxidant defense system of the cell, so that reactive O_2 metabolites are rapidly detoxified. Under hyperoxic conditions, the O_2 radical production rate markedly increases and effectively overwhelms the cell's normal complement of antioxidant defenses. The oxidant/antioxidant imbalance results in cytotoxic O_2 radicals interacting with and damaging important cell components. Tolerance to hyperoxia is associated with augmentation of the antioxidant defenses of the cell by either endogenous means (e.g., induction of increased antioxidant enzyme synthesis) or exogenous means (e.g., treatment with antioxidant agents). Tolerance to hyperoxia therefore depends on an increased capacity of the cell to detoxify the increased O_2 radicals produced under hyperoxic conditions, and a restoration of oxidant/antioxidant equilibrium. (From ref. 5, with permission of the publisher.)

ambient oxygen tensions the cellular antioxidant defenses are sufficient to handle the normal flux of ROS production, leading to a state of oxidant/antioxidant balance or equilibrium. Cytotoxic problems arise under hyperoxic conditions when the increased production rate of oxygen radicals at some point overwhelms the normal detoxifying capacities of the antioxidant constituents of the cell (especially the antioxidant enzymes), leading to a state of oxidant/antioxidant imbalance or disequilibrium. Under such troubling conditions, some means of augmenting the normal antioxidant enzyme defensive system may be sufficient to restore partial or complete oxidant/antioxidant equilibrium again and produce a state of "oxygen tolerance" under hyperoxic conditions, or relative protection from oxygen radical–induced cell injury and lethality.

Multiple experimental studies have by now established that when increased antioxidant enzyme activities can be induced in lung cells there is relative protection of the lung from pulmonary oxygen toxicity (i.e., marked lung edema and hemorrhage). On the other hand, when antioxidant enzyme activities are artificially lowered by chemical inhibitors or by immunological means, accelerated hyperoxic toxicity is the expected outcome (5–9).

OXYGEN TOXICITY AND THE NEWBORN

> They enter the new world naked,
> Cold, uncertain of all
> Save that they enter. All about them
> The cold, unfamiliar wind.
>
> —*William Carlos Williams*, "Spring and All"

Birth presents the newborn with a host of new problems and for the very low-birth-weight (VLBW) premature newborn these problems are intensified. Prepared cardiovascular and pulmonary systems are critical for the survival of the newborn. It is important to recall that the fetus grows and matures *in utero* in a relatively hypoxic milieu (pO_2 = 20 to 25 mm Hg) and that birth represents an immediate

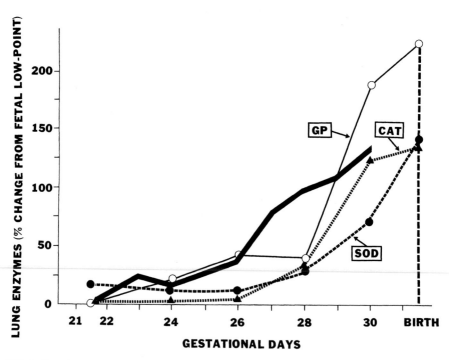

FIG. 2. Developmental changes in antioxidant enzyme activities in lungs of rabbits in late gestation and the newborn period. Enzyme values were calculated as activity units/mg DNA and are expressed here as percentage increase in activity above baseline value (activities at 21 to 22 days). The late gestational increase in activity of the three antioxidant enzymes—superoxide dismutase (SOD), catalase (CAT), and glutathione peroxidase (GP)—parallel the late gestational pattern of elevation of lung surfactant concentration (*thick solid line*) in the rabbit. (From ref. 11, with permission of the publisher.)

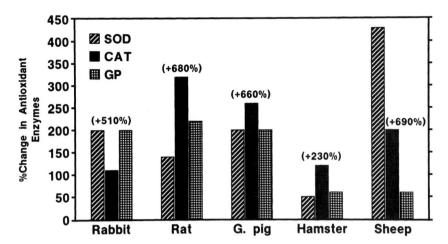

FIG. 3. Developmental changes in pulmonary antioxidant enzyme activities in fetal lungs of five species. Enzyme values are calculated as activity units/mg DNA and are expressed here as percentage increase in activity occurring over the final 15% of gestation. Numbers in parentheses are sums of activity increases for the three antioxidant enzymes—superoxide dismutase (SOD), catalase (CAT), and glutathione peroxidase (GP). (From ref. 5, with permission of the publisher.)

transition into the cold, unfamiliar wind of a relatively hyperoxic world (blood pO_2 = 100 mm Hg; alveolar pO_2 = 140 mm Hg) (10). Just as the late gestational maturation of the surfactant system can be viewed as nature's way of preparing the lung for its immediate new role as an efficient respiratory organ, nature must have provided some means to protect the lung of the newborn from the approximately five- to sevenfold increase in O_2 tension and the manyfold increases in oxygen free radical production that the air-breathing lung will experience immediately at birth. The first studies to test this hypothesis relied on the delivery of premature rabbit pups throughout the third trimester of pregnancy and measuring the lung activities of the important antioxidant enzymes (11). It was found that during the final ~15% of gestation there was a marked and spontaneous increase in the activities of SOD, CAT, GP, and G-6-PD in the premature pup lungs, confirming the hypothesis that nature does indeed prepare the newborn lung for its sudden transition into a relatively oxygen-rich world at the moment of birth (Fig. 2). These findings have since been confirmed in four other laboratory animal species—the rat, guinea pig, hamster, and sheep (12,13). Of added interest, in each of the five species tested, the time course of prenatal maturation of the lung antioxidant enzyme protective system (in the last 10% to 20% of gestation) coincided very closely with the chronology of development of the important pulmonary surfactant system (as assessed by the disaturated phosphatidylcholine concentration). Figure 3 illustrates the extent of rise of the antioxidant enzymes during late gestation in the five experimental animal species tested (average total rise ~600%) (5).

To date, there have been three studies examining the question of whether or not the human fetal lung also participates in this same preparation-for-birth phenomenon of the protective antioxidant enzyme system (14–16). Table 3 shows the results of the initial human infant study. All three studies have measured either antioxidant enzyme activities or antioxidant enzyme mRNA levels from mid-gestation to term and have reported definite several-fold increases in human fetal lung SOD (both CuZnSOD and MnSOD) and CAT activities.

Thus these findings can help to explain several important associations between very premature birth and the distressingly high incidence of bronchopulmonary dysplasia (BPD) or chronic lung disease. As well as missing the late gestational rise in surfactant synthesis, the VLBW infant is probably born too prematurely for maturation of the primary lung antioxidant enzyme defense system, making it clearer why oxygen toxicity is well accepted as a factor in the pathogenesis of BPD. Whether or not 21% oxygen represents a cytotoxic insult to the lung of the very prematurely born, it would seem biochemically inevitable that rapid pulmonary oxygen toxicity will result when vigorous hyperoxic treatment with FIO_2 values of 0.50 to 0.70 or higher is required for the VLBW infant with respiratory distress shortly after birth. This is especially pertinent when one realizes that the VLBW infant is also known to be deficient in key elements of its secondary antioxidant system, including vitamins A and E, the sulfur-containing amino acids, glutathione, ceruloplasmin, transferrin, and the transition metals Cu, Zn, Fe, Mn, and Se, which are the metal groups required for synthesis and activation of the individual antioxidant enzymes. All these factors are present at very low levels in the VLBW infant because each is dependent on maternal-to-fetal transfer in the latter part of the third trimester (17–19). Thus the known tendency of the VLBW infant to develop BPD ($\sim$50% incidence) should come as no surprise, nor should the clinical finding that although artificial surfactant treatment can reduce the incidence of acute respiratory distress syndrome in the VLBW infant, the overall incidence of BPD has scarcely been affected by this therapy (20).

Another factor also enters the scheme of oxygen toxicity illustrated in Fig. 1. This is that oxygen toxicity, or relative oxygen tolerance under hyperoxic conditions, depends to a large extent on whether or not the cells of the lung can augment their basic complement of antioxidant enzymes during hyperoxic challenge. It is well established that a primary reason that full-term newborn animals can tolerate prolonged exposure to high concentrations of oxygen much better than adult animals of the same species is that the full-term neonatal lung can rapidly increase its antioxidant enzyme activities (and mRNA) during hyperoxia, a capability that the lungs of adult

TABLE 3. *Superoxide dismutase (SOD) activity in human lung*

Group	SOD (units/mg DNA)
Fetus (18–20 weeks) (6)	17 + 1
Respiratory distress infants (26–32 weeks) (4)	37 + 4[a]
Normal term infants (38–40 weeks) (4)	46 + 6[a]

[a] $p < 0.05$ compared with preceding group value. From reference 14, with permission of the publisher.

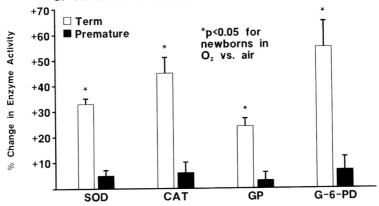

FIG. 4. Comparative pulmonary antioxidant enzyme responses of full-term (*empty bars*) *versus* prematurely born rabbits (*solid bars*) to hyperoxia (>90% O_2, 48 hours). Enzyme activities were calculated as activity units/mg DNA and are expressed here as percentage change in O_2-exposed *versus* air-exposed lung enzyme values. Unlike the term newborn animals, the premature animals show essentially no lung superoxide dismutase (SOD), catalase (CAT), glutathione peroxidase (GP), or glucose-6-phosphate dehydrogenase (G-6-PD) response to hyperoxia. (*$p <$ 0.05 or less for term hyperoxic values *versus* air controls; and for O_2-exposed term rabbits *versus* premature rabbits). (From ref. 21, with permission of the publisher.)

animals have lost (5,7,9). But how about the lung in the preterm animal? Initial studies in premature *versus* full-term newborn rabbit pups showed that the premature rabbit pups at 29 days of gestation (term = 31.5 days) responded much worse to hyperoxia than the full-term pups, with much earlier and greater pathological evidence of oxygen toxicity and a lethal time (LT50) of less than 4 days *versus* more than 10 days for the simultaneously exposed term newborn pups. As Fig. 4 shows, although the relatively O_2-tolerant term animals were consistently able to increase their lung antioxidant enzyme complement during hyperoxia, the prematurely born animals consistently failed to show any augmentation of their protective antioxidant enzyme system (21).

Subsequent studies in premature sheep and in the excellent premature baboon model of BPD have also failed to show any evidence that the lung of the prematurely born mammal can mount an appropriate increase in protective antioxidant enzyme activity when challenged with potentially cytotoxic oxygen concentrations (22). If the same were found to be true for the oxygen-requiring premature human infant, its already compromised antioxidant defense state would be even more unprotective than currently suspected.

POSSIBLE ANTIOXIDANT TREATMENT

If the ability to augment its own endogenous pulmonary antioxidant enzyme protective system is denied to the VLBW premature infant, could exogenous means be employed to achieve a greater measure of oxidant/antioxidant equilibrium during hyperoxic treatment? Several years ago just such a direct attempt was made in a population of VLBW infants who were treated with repeated parenteral injections of purified bovine SOD enzyme (23). While the clinical trial was reported to be successful (a BPD incidence of 3/14 [21%] in SOD treated *versus* 12/17 [71%] in untreated controls), the trial was subsequently criticized for several reasons, including the BPD criteria used, and there has been no reported attempt to repeat the study in the subsequent 14 years. Also, no explanation was provided as to how the administered SOD got to the intracellular sites of ROS generation where it was needed, since it has been shown repeatedly that (lung) cells are impermeable to the large antioxidant enzyme molecules (24). Subsequently, a means to "trick" cells into becoming permeable to antioxidant enzymes was developed. By incorporating purified antioxidant enzymes into lipid liposomes that can easily penetrate cell membranes it could be shown that cell levels of the administered liposome-encapsulated antioxidant enzymes did increase. In subsequent studies, significant protection of both adult and neonatal rats from prolonged hyperoxic exposure was achieved by daily dosing with these antioxidant enzyme preparations (25,26). Unfortunately, a potential problem with antioxidant enzyme liposome preparations is infection, since the liposomes are also rapidly taken up by cells of the reticuloendothelial system, interfering with efficient bacterial clearance.

Recently, two groups of investigators have developed an exciting new way of introducing exogenous antioxidant enzymes into the lining cells of the lung. These investigators found that by premixing purified antioxidant enzymes with a commercially available surfactant preparation (Survanta) it was possible, after intratracheal instillation, to show both a very homogeneous lung distribution of (radiolabeled) SOD and CAT (probably owing to the spreading properties of the surfactant) and an increase in lung antioxidant enzyme activity within 1 hour of administration. By 24 hours after administration, the lung cellular antioxidant enzyme content had risen even further (27,28). Subsequent studies on neonatal piglets exposed to hyperoxia have shown dramatic protective effects against oxygen toxicity in treated neonates with augmented antioxidant enzyme activity. Recently under way is a clinical trial of surfactant plus human recombinant SOD in VLBW infants prone to developing BPD (approximately 100 patients have already been enrolled) (Davis J, personal communication).

Molecular biology techniques have also been applied recently to the antioxidant enzymes and their role in protecting against clinically important hyperoxia. For example, in transgenic mice expressing a 50% increase in pulmonary MnSOD activity, the mean survival time in 95% O_2 was improved from 130 hours to 230 hours (29). *In vitro* transfection studies using adenovirus vectors to transfer the genetic material (cDNA) for the antioxidant enzymes into cultured lung cells have been successful in both increasing the lung cell antioxidant enzyme activity levels and markedly improving cell survival rates on later hyperoxic challenge (30,31). Recently, an exciting *in vivo* lung transfection study was reported at last year's American Lung Association meetings. Using adenovirus vectors and the cDNAs from human recombinant SOD and CAT, the investigators found raised lung cell SOD and CAT activities 3 days after treatment, thus showing that transfection by the intratracheal route was successful.

(This meant that not only did the transfected genetic material become intranuclear, but also that the antioxidant enzyme cDNAs were both successfully transcribed and translated into new antioxidant enzyme protein.) In the single hyperoxic exposure experiment attempted to date, seven out of 10 transfected adult rats survived in hyperoxia, compared with three out of 10 control rats (32). Thus at least two possible means of augmenting pulmonary antioxidant enzymes could shortly become clinically feasible and both could provide for the first time a potent means of protecting patients from the paradoxically toxic effects of life-giving oxygen treatment.

UNDERNUTRITION, OXYGEN TOXICITY, AND BRONCHOPULMONARY DYSPLASIA

Several years ago an NIH study group on nutrition and the respiratory system concluded with the statement that "sufficient evidence is available to recommend that greater clinical priority be given to nutrition as a vigorous part of total support in premature infants" (33). Clinically, so much attention is usually given to establishing respiratory stability in the VLBW newborn infant with respiratory distress that adequate nutritional support often becomes a low priority. This is unfortunate because the meager energy reserves of the VLBW infant (24 to 28 weeks) of $\sim$110 kcal/kg (2.0% body fat and negligible stores of glycogen) compared with the full-term newborn (1,500 kcal/kg; $\sim$15% body fat and 1.5% glycogen stores) means that a very detrimental early catabolic state may be established in the VLBW infant (34). Since BPD is considered to be a disease determined largely by the degree of imbalance between ongoing lung injury and lung repair capacities, inadequate nutrition and a catabolic state will have a detrimental effect on each of the factors implicated in the pathogenesis of BPD listed in Table 4 (35). In addition to the known inhibitory

TABLE 4. *The potential consequences of undernutrition in the premature VLBW newborn*

1. Poor energy reserves	→	Early onset of catabolic state.
2. Effects on respiratory distress syndrome	→	Inhibited/delayed surfactant production ↓ respiratory muscle function
3. Effects on protection from hyperoxia/barotrauma	→	↓ epithelial integrity (vitamin A) ↓ defense against O_2 free radicals (↓ AOE synthesis, vitamins E and C, etc.) ↓ lung biosynthesis, cell replication
4. Effects on lung repair and development of BPD	→	↓ lung biosynthesis ↓ replacement of damaged cells ↓ replacement of normal extracellular components (collagen, elastin)
5. Effects on lung growth	→	↓ lung biosynthesis/cell replication ↓ lung structural maturation (alveolarization)
6. Effects on susceptibility to infection	→	↓ cellular, humoral defenses against pathogens (IgA, alveolar macrophages, leukocytes, lymphocytes) ↓ epithelial cell integrity ↓ mucociliary clearance mechanisms

BPD = bronchopulmonary dysplasia; VLBW = very low birthweight. From reference 35, with permission of the publisher.

action of undernutrition on surfactant biosynthesis, a catabolic state plus low lung content of the metal cofactors for antioxidant enzyme synthesis (Cu, Zn, Fe, Mn, Se) can be expected to impair the normal late gestational development of the lung's protective antioxidant enzyme system. In addition, deficiency of other specific nutrients—including vitamins A and E, ascorbate, sulfur-containing amino acids such as cysteine, and so on—will further compromise a poor antioxidant armamentarium in the very prematurely born. Several experimental studies have shown the marked detrimental effect of undernutrition in newborn animals exposed to hyperoxia, including a doubling of mortality rates (56% mortality from pulmonary oxygen toxicity in malnourished rat pups *versus* only a 27% mortality in normally nourished pups exposed to 95% O_2 for 7 days [36]). During that study the growth-inhibiting and biochemical effects of hyperoxia and undernutrition were found to be additive (Table 5)—including a remarkable decline of 65% in normal lung DNA content (implying a very poor ability to repair lung cell damage and replace lost lung cells) (36).

Specific lipid nutrition could have a variety of positive effects in the setting of hyperoxic lung injury:

- It has a high energy density and is iso-osmotic;
- It provides essential fatty acids to only marginally replete or fatty acid deficient VLBW infants;
- It probably improves the absorption of lipid-soluble vitamins A and E;
- It may reduce lipogenesis from glucose and subsequent excess CO_2 production for excretion;
- A balanced fat and carbohydrate intake may allow more optimal nitrogen retention;
- There may be a beneficial effect of polyunsaturated fatty acids (PUFA), since they have specific antioxidant effects of their own (37).

This last suggestion is based on a hypothesis by the British food chemist Dormandy, who theorized that "intracellular PUFA, located in noncritical nonmembrane sites and immediately replaced after their own auto-oxidation, could serve to avidly scavenge excess O_2 radicals and prevent their interaction with critical membrane PUFA," thus protecting cells from membrane lipid peroxidation damage (37). To test this long-neglected hypothesis, pregnant rats were fed throughout gestation and early nurturing with either a normal rodent diet (polyunsaturated to saturated fatty acid [P/S] ratio of 1.2), a safflower oil–based diet rich in PUFA (P/S ratio = 9.0), or a

TABLE 5. *Combined effects of hyperoxia and undernutrition on newborn rats*

Parameter	Hyperoxia	Undernutrition	Hyperoxia + undernutrition
Lethality	27%	0 in air controls	56%
Body weight	↓ 14%	↓ 21%	↓ 34%
Lung weight	↓ 24%	↓ 23%	↓ 42%
Lung protein	↓ 24%	↓ 11%	↓ 34%
Lung DNA	↓ 44%	↓ 20%	↓ 65%

From reference 36, with permission of the publisher.

palm oil–based diet rich in saturated fatty acids (P/S ratio = 0.2). Using gas chromatography measurements, both maternal milk and neonatal animal lungs had P/S ratios closely reflecting the three respective diets. When challenged with hyperoxia, the safflower oil group had a significantly improved survival (80/84; 95%), whereas the palm oil group had a worse survival (38/84; 45%), compared with the regular diet group (56/84; 67%) (38). A subsequent study using PUFA-rich Intralipid as the maternal dietary source confirmed the safflower oil (high P/S ratio) findings, with improved hyperoxic survival (89/95; 94%), further confirming the Dormandy PUFA protection theory (39).

REFERENCES

1. Freeman BA, Crapo JD. Biology of disease. Free radicals and tissue injury. *Lab Invest* 1982;47:412–426.
2. Halliwell B, Gutteridge JMC. Protection against oxidants in biological systems: the superoxide theory of oxygen toxicity. In: Halliwell B, Gutteridge JMC, eds. *Free radicals in biology and medicine.* Oxford: Clarendon Press; 1989:86–187.
3. Freeman BA, Crapo JD. Hyperoxia increases oxygen free radical production in rat lung and lung mitochondria. *J Biol Chem* 1981;256:10986–10992.
4. Frank, L. Antioxidants, nutrition, and bronchopulmonary dysplasia. In: Holzman RB, Frank L, eds. *Clinics in perinatology: bronchopulmonary dysplasia.* Volume 19. Philadelphia: WB Saunders; 1992:541–562.
5. Frank L. Developmental aspects of experimental pulmonary oxygen toxicity. *Free Radic Biol Med* 1991;11:463–494.
6. Sies H. Strategies of antioxidant defense. *Eur J Biochem* 1993;215:213–219.
7. White CW. Pulmonary oxygen toxicity: cellular mechanisms of oxidant injury and antioxidant defenses. In: Bancalari E, Stocker JT, eds. *Bronchopulmonary dysplasia.* Cambridge, MA: Hemisphere; 1988:22–41.
8. Frank L, Summerville J, Massaro D. Protection from oxygen toxicity with endotoxin: role of the endogenous antioxidant enzymes of the lung. *J Clin Invest* 1980;65:1104–1111.
9. Frank L, Wood D, Roberts RJ. The effect of diethyldithiocarbamate (DDC) on oxygen toxicity and lung enzyme activity in immature and adult rats. *Biochem Pharmacol* 1978;27:251–254.
10. Dejours, P. *Principles in comparative respiratory physiology,* 2nd ed. Amsterdam: Elsevier/North Holland; 1981:147–171.
11. Frank L, Groseclose EE. Preparation for birth into an O_2-rich environment: the antioxidant enzymes in the developing rabbit lung. *Pediatr Res* 1984;18:240–244.
12. Frank L, Sosenko IRS. Prenatal development of lung antioxidant enzymes in four species. *J Pediatr* 1987;110:106–110.
13. Frank L, Sosenko IRS. Development of lung antioxidant enzyme system in late gestation: possible implications for the prematurely-born infant. *J Pediatr* 1987;110:9–14.
14. Autor AP, Frank L, Roberts RJ. Developmental characteristics of pulmonary superoxide dismutase: relationship to idiopathic respiratory distress syndrome. *Pediatr Res* 1976;10:154–158.
15. Dobashi K, Asayama K, Hyashibe H, *et al.* Immunochemical study of copper-zinc and manganese superoxide dismutases in the lungs of human fetuses and newborn infants: developmental profile and alterations in hyaline membrane disease and bronchopulmonary dysplasia. *Virchows Arch A: Pathol Anat Histopathol* 1993;423:177–189.
16. Asikainen TM, Saksela M, Heikinheimo M, *et al.* Expression of antioxidant enzymes during human lung development. *Pediatr Res* 1997;41:40A (abst.).
17. Hustead VA, Gutcher GR, Anderson SA, Zachman RD. Relationship of vitamin A (retinol) status to lung disease in the preterm infant. *J Pediatr* 1984;105:610–615.
18. Gutcher GR, Raynor WJ, Farrell PM. An evaluation of vitamin E status in premature infants. *Am J Clin Nutr* 1984;40:1078–1089.
19. Rosenfeld W, Concepcion L, Evans H, *et al.* Serial trypsin inhibitory capacity and ceruloplasmin levels in prematures at risk for bronchopulmonary dysplasia. *Am Rev Respir Dis* 1986;134:1229–1232.
20. Hudak BB, Egar EA. Impact of lung surfactant therapy on chronic lung diseases in premature infants. *Clin Perinatol* 1992;19:591–602.

21. Frank L, Sosenko IRS. Failure of premature rabbits to increase antioxidant enzymes during hyperoxic exposure: increased susceptibility to pulmonary oxygen toxicity compared to term rabbits. *Pediatr Res* 1991;29:292–296.
22. Jenkinson SG, Roberts RJ, DeLemos RA, *et al.* Allopurinol-induced effects in premature baboons with respiratory distress syndrome. *J Appl Physiol* 1991;70:1160–1167.
23. Rosenfeld W, Evans H, Concepcion L, *et al.* Prevention of bronchopulmonary dysplasia by administration of bovine superoxide dismutase in preterm infants with respiratory distress syndrome. *J Pediatr* 1984;105:781–785.
24. Huber W, Saifer MGP, Williams LD. Superoxide dismutase pharmacology and orgotein efficacy: new perspectives. In: Bannister WH, Bannister JV, eds. *Biological and clinical aspects of superoxide and superoxide dismutase.* Amsterdam: Elsevier/North Holland; 1980:395–407.
25. Turrens JF, Crapo JD, Freeman BA. Protection against oxygen toxicity by intravenous injection of liposome-entrapped catalase and superoxide dismutase. *J Clin Invest* 1984;73:87–95.
26. Tanswell AK, Freeman BA. Liposome-entrapped antioxidant enzymes prevent lethal O_2 toxicity in the newborn rat. *J Appl Physiol* 1987;63:347–352.
27. Nieves-Cruz B, Rivera A, Cifuentes J, *et al.* Clinical surfactant preparations mediate SOD and catalase uptake by type II cells and lung tissue. *Am J Physiol (Lung Cell Mol Physiol)* 1996;270:L659–667.
28. Davis JM, Rosenfeld WN, Sanders RJ, Gonenne A. Prophylactic effects of recombinant human superoxide dismutase in neonatal lung injury. *J Appl Physiol* 1993;74:2234–2241.
29. Wispe JR, Warner BB, Clark JC, *et al.* Human Mn-superoxide dismutase in pulmonary epithelial cells of transgenic mice confers protection from oxygen injury. *J Biol Chem* 1992;267:23937–23941.
30. Huang T-T, Carlson EJ, Leadon SA, *et al.* Relationship of resistance to oxygen free radicals to Cu/Zn-superoxide dismutase activity in transgenic, transfected, and trisomic cells. *FASEB J* 1992;6:903–910.
31. Erzunum SC, Lemarchand P, Rosenfeld MA, *et al.* Protection of human endothelial cells from oxidant injury by adenovirus mediated transfer of the human catalase cDNA. *Nucleic Acids Res* 1993;21:1607–1612.
32. Prayssac P, Erzunum SC, Danel C, *et al.* Adenovirus-mediated transfer to the lungs of catalase and superoxide dismutase cDNAs prevents hyperoxia toxicity but not ischemia reperfusion injury in rats. *Am J Respir Crit Care Med* 1997;155:A265 (abst.).
33. Edelman NH, Rucker RB, Peavy HH. NIH workshop summary. Nutrition and the respiratory system. *Am Rev Respir Dis* 1986;134:347–352.
34. Widdowson EM. Chemical composition and nutritional needs of the fetus at different stages of gestation. In: Aebi H, Whitehead R, eds. *Maternal nutrition during pregnancy and lactation.* Berne: H Huber; 1980:39–48.
35. Frank L, Sosenko IRS. Undernutrition as a major contributing factor in the pathogenesis of bronchopulmonary dysplasia. *Am Rev Respir Dis* 1988;138:725–729.
36. Frank L, Groseclose EE. Oxygen toxicity in newborns: the adverse effect of undernutrition. *J Appl Physiol* 1982;53:1248–1252.
37. Dormandy, TL. Biological rancidification. *Lancet* 1969;ii:684–686.
38. Sosenko IRS, Innis SM, Frank L. Polyunsaturated fatty acids and protection of newborn rats from oxygen toxicity. *J Pediatr* 1988;112:630–635.
39. Sosenko IRS, Innis SM, Frank L. Intralipid increases lung polyunsaturated fatty acids and protects newborn rats from oxygen toxicity. *Pediatr Res* 1991;30:413–417.

DISCUSSION

Dr. Guesry: Do you know if the enzymes superoxide dismutase, catalase, and glutathione peroxidase are inducible by corticosteroids given to the mother to stimulate surfactant production, or are they inhibited?

Dr. Frank: The fact that both these hormonal systems seem to have a common time course for maturation suggested that they might be under the same control mechanisms. When pregnant rats were given dexamethasone, the expected increases in surfactant were found. At the same time, there were very marked increases in all the antioxidant enzymes.

Dr. Guesry: When you propose giving antioxidants to pregnant women at the end of gestation, are you sure about the relationship between the different antioxidants? So far, all the experiments that have been done to try to prevent cancer or aging have been quite disappointing. May it not be dangerous to give vitamin E, vitamin C, beta-carotene, selenium, and so on, all together if we have not yet understood the synergy between these different antioxidants. There could be some countereffect.

Dr. Frank: That is an important point. Several of these—vitamin E, vitamin C, vitamin A—have been given separately to premature infants specifically to try to avoid chronic lung disease, and none has been effective. Therefore the question is whether, since they have slightly different biological effects—for example, the free radicals they interact with, the fact that some are lipid-based and some are in the cytosol—it might be better to combine them, but I have no information about possible complications.

Prof. Lucas: You have given us some compelling arguments for preventing undernutrition in relation to lung disease in animals. What I'm interested in is whether there is any hard evidence in humans. In our randomized studies where we manipulated nutritional status with enteral feeding, we found no evidence that this influenced any of the standard indices of respiratory illness—days on ventilation, days on oxygen, and so forth. Perhaps the more important period is the very early period, but that is difficult to study because it is confounded, and low intakes are often correlated with sickness. I wonder whether in the Wilson study, for instance, there was evidence of improved respiratory outcomes? Do you have any evidence that manipulating diet in preterm infants in the early part of life actually reduces respiratory illness?

Dr. Frank: I don't have any direct information, but everything we know about oxygen free radicals tells us that they start attacking immediately after birth, and the complications of undernutrition will also start immediately after birth.

Dr. Chessex: Yesterday we were discussing LC-PUFAs as baddies in the peroxidation story, but now you tell us they are goodies, and you propounded a theory about them being antioxidants. Could you explain that a bit more?

Dr. Frank: This theory was developed many years ago by Thomas Dormandy, a British nutritional chemist. He hypothesized that if you could get polyunsaturated fatty acids into nonmembrane-containing areas of cells, they would act as efficient free radical trapping agents, because of the affinity of unsaturated fatty acids for oxygen radicals. Unfortunately, his theory was ignored for a long time, but eventually it was tested in a rat model designed to determine whether a diet rich in polyunsaturated fatty acids would increase survival in newborn rats in high ambient oxygen. There were three groups: a control group, which had a survival rate of 75% after 7 days on oxygen; a group given saturated fatty acids, which had a 45% survival; and a group given safflower oil with a very high PUFA content, the PUFAs being located in the triglyceride fraction and not the phospholipid or membrane fraction, which had a survival rate of about 97%. So his theory seems to work—that is, PUFAs enter the cell and become expendable targets, as it were, for oxygen free radical attack.

Dr. Walker: In 1993, Goldman proposed that one of the major functions of breast milk was its anti-inflammatory properties, including antioxidants [1]. Do you have any information on whether the ingestion of this highly anti-inflammatory substance has any impact on some of the problems in the lung?

Dr. Frank: No, except that I would expect the protein molecules to be destroyed in the stomach, if this was a purely nutritional way of increasing the enzyme defenses.

Prof. Berger: We have looked at this in well babies, not in ill ones. A couple of years ago, in the *American Journal of Clinical Nutrition*, we reported differences in antioxidants in babies fed breast milk or formula feeds [2]. We looked at a number of plasma antioxidants, and also at trapping capacity. The only difference we found was the delayed fall in plasma bilirubin in the breastfed babies, which is well known. Over recent years this has been recognized as a very powerful antioxidant mechanism.

Dr. Micheli: Is there any way of measuring oxidative stress at the bedside?

Dr. Frank: The best way is probably to measure exhaled pentane and ethane as a measure of lipid peroxidation. That has been shown to increase with increasing oxygen tension in premature infants. It is also shown that prematures in general have higher excretion of these substances than term newborns and adults. There is an association between the incidence of bronchopulmonary dysplasia and increased production of pentane or ethane, which are breakdown products of lipid peroxides [3,4]. There are also blood measurements. You can measure the total antioxidant content of the blood, but correlations with the clinical situation are not very good.

Dr. Chessex: Could you expand on what induces the activation of these antioxidants at the end of gestation? If we could understand that, we might be able to induce them earlier in small preterm infants.

Dr. Frank: At least in animal studies, and in this last human study I've mentioned, it seems that there are genes that are turned on at a certain period in development.

Dr. Chessex: But what is the triggering mechanism? Haven't you shown that it was at the level of the mitochondrion?

Dr. Frank: We've looked at mitochondrial free radical production and we've looked at superoxide production and found that both those factors are increased just before the rise in antioxidant enzymes. But whether that is a cause/effect relationship I'm not prepared to say right now. It looks like that.

Dr. Micheli: I was intrigued by your slide showing the relation between oxygen partial pressure and oxygen consumption. If I understood it, that was an animal experiment and you showed that at the mitochondrial level oxygen consumption was greatly increased. But when you measure oxygen consumption in preterm babies receiving high inspired oxygen it is not greatly increased.

Dr. Frank: Those were isolated mitochondria and microsomes. The results have been duplicated in whole lung homogenates. I don't know about the oxygen consumption of preterm infants receiving oxygen. I heard of a study several years ago that said they had a 25% increase in consumption, but I don't know whether those results are regarded as valid [5].

REFERENCES

1. Goldman AS. The immune system of human milk: antimicrobial, anti-inflammatory and immunomodulating properties. *Pediatr Infect Dis J* 1993;12(8):664–671.
2. van Zoeren-Grobben D, Lindeman JH, Houdkamp E, *et al.* Postnatal changes in plasma chain-breaking antioxidants in healthy preterm infants fed formula and/or human milk. *Am J Clin Nutr* 1994;60:900–906.
3. Pitkanen OM, Hallman M, Andersson SM. Correlation of free oxygen radical-induced lipid peroxidation with outcome in very low birth weight infants. *J Pediatr* 1990;116:760–764.
4. Varsila E, Pitkanen O, Hallman M, *et al.* Immaturity-dependent free radical activity in premature infants. *Pediatr Res* 1994;36:55–59.
5. Weinstein MR, Oh W. Oxygen consumption in infants with bronchopulmonary dysplasia. *J Pediatr* 1981;99:958–961.

Nutrition of the Very Low Birthweight Infant, edited by
Ekhard E. Ziegler, Alan Lucas, Guido E. Moro.
Nestlé Nutrition Workshop Series, Paediatric Programme, Vol. 43,
Nestec Ltd., Vevey/Lippincott Williams & Wilkins
Philadelphia, Pennsylvania © 1999.

Pro-oxidant Effects of Iron in the Newborn Period

H. M. Berger, R. M. W. Moison, D. Van Zoeren-Grobben,
N. Conneman, and J. Geerdink

*Division of Neonatology, Department of Pediatrics, Leiden University Medical Center,
Universitait Leiden, Leiden, The Netherlands*

Iron, a transition metal, can take part in redox processes by undergoing reversible valency changes. It plays an essential role in oxygen transport by hemoglobin in erythrocytes, oxygen storage by myoglobin in muscle, and electron transfer and energy metabolism in mitochondria. It is also a cofactor in various enzymes. Iron deficiency can produce adverse effects because of anemia in all age groups, but in the child it may also impair neurodevelopment. Worldwide attempts are made to prevent iron deficiency, and iron supplementation is recommended for at-risk groups (1).

Recently, concern has arisen that universal supplementation may also sometimes be harmful (1,2). Excess iron supply has been linked to heart disease and malignancy in older patients (1,3).

These problems do not appear to have direct implications for the pediatrician. Iron deficiency is the main problem in children, especially when they are growing rapidly. However, iron overload may occur more frequently in neonatal nurseries than we generally realize. Although inherited neonatal hemochromatosis is a rare disease, other causes of iron overload may be more common. One example may occur in preterm babies. Because of their poor endogenous reserves and rapid postnatal growth, it is recommended that such infants begin iron supplementation from the eighth postnatal week. However, if they are fed on preterm formula, usually iron fortified, their iron supplementation starts much sooner. This early dietary supplementation may be harmful to some of the babies. Another example is often encountered in our perinatal unit, the center for rhesus hemolytic disease in The Netherlands. Babies with hemolysis and raised ferritin levels nevertheless receive dietary iron if fed on formula feeds (4). Specific contraindications to iron supplementation may need to be agreed upon and the timing of the start of supplementation more stringently controlled (2).

In this chapter we review the role of iron in the pathogenesis of free radical damage in the newborn baby. The available evidence on how nutrition may influence the pro-oxidant activity of iron in the baby is discussed.

ROLE OF REACTIVE OXYGEN SPECIES IN THE PATHOGENESIS OF DISEASE IN THE NEWBORN

Reactive oxygen species (ROS), by damaging proteins, lipids, and DNA, can play a role in the pathogenesis of diseases such as hypoxic/ischemic encephalopathy, intraventricular hemorrhage, retinopathy of prematurity, chronic lung disease, and necrotizing enterocolitis. Preliminary work also implicates ROS in parenteral nutrition induced cholestasis and rhesus hemolytic disease (5). Recent research suggests that the redox status of cells can also influence disease processes by influencing membrane receptors, enzyme activity, signal transduction and transcription, and gene expression (6). Antioxidant defenses, made up of intracellular and extracellular components, work synergistically to prevent oxidative damage and help maintain the optimal redox balance of tissues for normal metabolic activity, growth, and development.

The ROS include inorganic and organic oxygen-derived compounds, some of which are free radicals (one or more unpaired electrons in their atomic orbits)—that is, superoxide radical ($\cdot O_2$), hydrogen peroxide (H_2O_2), hydroxyl radical ($\cdot OH$), hypochlorous acid (HOCl), nitric oxide radical (NO$\cdot$), and alkoxyl and peroxyl radicals (RO$\cdot$ and ROO$\cdot$). NO$\cdot$ reacts rapidly with $\cdot O_2$ to form the strong oxidant peroxynitrite (ONOO$^-$) (7,8).

The ROS pool depends on the balance between their input (exogenous and endogenous sources) and their output (rate of removal), and a sink model is useful in analyzing the processes that can influence this pool (Fig. 1) (5).

Input

Although the diatomic oxygen molecule (O_2) is itself a radical with two unpaired electrons, its reaction with biomolecules is spin restricted: the parallel spin of the two electrons restricts its ability to oxidize other nonradical molecules containing atoms that are usually bound covalently by electrons in opposite spin (7). However, O_2 can be converted to highly active ROS. During energy production in the mitochondria most of the O_2 undergoes a four-electron reduction to water, but a normal small, accidental leak of electrons does occur, producing a single-electron reduction of O_2 to $\cdot O_2$. Eicosanoid metabolism also produces $\cdot O_2$. Much larger and potentially damaging amounts of $\cdot O_2$ are released when mitochondria are damaged or when xanthine oxidase in various cells or NADPH oxidase in neutrophils is activated by ischemia/reperfusion injury. The $\cdot O_2$ can be further reduced to H_2O_2, either spontaneously or through superoxide dismutase activity. If it is not catabolized the H_2O_2 will, in the presence of nonprotein-bound transition metals in the reduced form (e.g., ferrous [Fe^{2+}] ions) be converted to $\cdot OH$, the most reactive oxygen metabolite. Nonprotein-bound iron (NPBI) is normally present in only minute amounts in cells and is not present in plasma. Ceruloplasmin oxidizes iron, which is then rigorously bound to transferrin in plasma, whereas ferritin—the intracellular iron binding protein—has an intrinsic ferroxidase activity (7). These proteins are referred to as preventive antioxidants, since they inhibit $\cdot OH$ production.

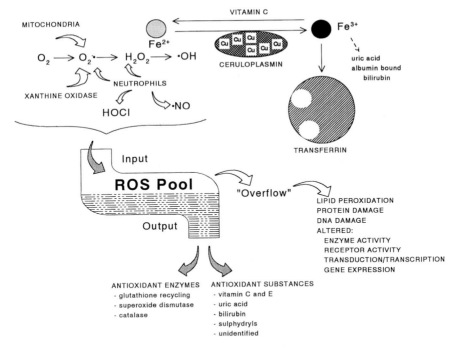

FIG. 1. Simplified sink model showing how an imbalance in the input or output of reactive oxygen species (ROS) may result in an overflow, causing molecular damage or alterations in redox-dependent essential cell activities (e.g., signal transduction). The production of ROS (e.g., by mitochondria, xanthine oxidase, and neutrophils) contributes to the input of ROS. The preventive antioxidant capacity of ceruloplasmin and transferrin, which, respectively, oxidize and bind iron and thus inhibit conversion of H_2O_2 to OH, are emphasized. The role of antioxidant enzymes and chain-breaking antioxidant substances (e.g., vitamin E) in controlling the output of ROS is shown. Note that uric acid and bilirubin can act as preventive and chain-breaking antioxidants, whereas vitamin C may have pro-oxidant as well as antioxidant activity.

Another important ROS is ·NO, which is produced by endothelial cells, neurons, and activated macrophages and neutrophils. ·NO can react with $\cdot O_2$ to produce the powerful oxidant $ONOO^-$.

Output

The output of ROS depends on antioxidant enzymes and antioxidant substances. $\cdot O_2$ is converted by superoxide dismutase to H_2O_2, which is catabolized by catalase, glutathione peroxidase, or both. The synergistic action of chain-breaking antioxidants (e.g., vitamins E and C, uric acid, bilirubin, sulfhydryl groups, and various "unidentified" antioxidants) also prevents oxidative damage (5). These antioxidants sacrifice themselves by forming stable radicals, thus inhibiting propagation of the oxidative process—that is, continuation of a chain of radical reactions between more reactive unsaturated lipids and proteins (see later).

Imbalance Between Input and Output

An increased production and/or decreased removal of ROS—that is, an imbalance between input and output results in accumulation of ROS. Intracellular antioxidant enzymes form the major component of the antioxidant system; however, immaturity may increase the relative importance of extracellular antioxidants (5). In this review we will concentrate on the role of plasma antioxidants in preventing iron-induced oxidative damage in the preterm and term newborn infant.

THE MECHANISM OF IRON-INDUCED OXIDATIVE DAMAGE

Transition metals (e.g., iron and copper) are found at the active sites of oxidase and oxygenase enzymes because they can accept and donate single electrons and thus overcome the spin restriction of O_2. However, this ability can cause harm if the iron is "free": NPBI in the reduced ferrous form (Fe^{2+}) can reduce H_2O_2 to $\cdot OH$ (Fenton reaction): $Fe^{2+} + H_2O_2 \rightarrow Fe^{3+} + \cdot OH + OH^-$. The Fe^{2+} can also react with (i) lipids, (ii) proteins, and (iii) DNA.

Reaction with Lipids

Fe^{2+} reacts with lipid peroxides (ROOH) (and endoperoxides produced by cyclooxygenase) to form damaging $RO\cdot$ and $ROO\cdot$ radicals that can extract H from polyunsaturated fatty acids (RH) and thus initiate a chain reaction of peroxidation:

$$Fe^{2+} + ROOH \rightarrow Fe^{3+} + ROO\cdot + OH^-$$

$$ROO\cdot + RH \rightarrow ROOH + R\cdot$$

$$R\cdot + O_2 \rightarrow ROO\cdot$$

Reaction with Proteins

Although initially most attention was paid to the effects of iron-induced damage on lipids, it is clear that iron-induced oxidative damage of amino acids (e.g., histidine, tyrosine, phenylalanine, or cysteine) can also have major repercussions such as inactivation of glutamine synthetase in the brain or α-1-proteinase inhibitor in plasma (8).

Reaction with DNA

Iron-induced DNA damage can occur: $\cdot OH$ radical can oxidize the DNA bases to produce compounds such as 8-oxoguanine and 2-hydroxyadenine, as well as causing strand scission. Low-molecular-weight iron can passively diffuse from the cytoplasm across the nuclear pores, but there is also an active nuclear iron transport system. The normal function of nuclear iron has not been established, but iron overload could damage DNA by the Fenton reaction (3).

PROTECTION AGAINST IRON INDUCED OXIDATIVE DAMAGE

Production of OH, through the catalytic action of NPBI, must be prevented. Thus iron is predominantly incorporated into proteins (e.g., enzymes) and is rigorously bound when transported by transferrin in plasma or lactoferrin in milk, or when it is stored in ferritin or hemosiderin. Normally, NPBI is absent in extracellular fluids and is only present in very small concentrations in cells—as chelates of citrate, ATP, or ADP—during transfer from transferrin or ferritin into hemoglobin or enzymes. The iron content of plasma normally depends on the balance between input (from exogenous supply through absorption from the intestine and release from the endogenous storage depots ferritin and hemosiderin) and endogenous output into tissues such as bone marrow. Except during menstruation, little iron is normally lost exogenously (through skin and intestinal mucosal cell turnover).

The iron must be in the oxidized Fe^{3+} form before it can be bound by transferrin, lactoferrin, and ferritin. The Fe^{2+} is oxidized in plasma to Fe^{3+} by the ferroxidase activity of ceruloplasmin, but ferritin has an intrinsic ferroxidase activity. This oxidizing activity can be antagonized by reducing agents, in particular high concentrations of vitamin C (Figs. 1 and 2A). It has been suggested that megadoses of vitamin C taken by iron-repleted adults for antioxidant protection might therefore act as a pro-oxidant and initiate peroxidative damage (9). Transferrin and lactoferrin bind iron more rigorously than ferritin. Ferritin iron, unlike iron in transferrin and lactoferrin, is released in the presence of reducing substances such as $\cdot O_2$ and vitamin C. However, transferrin, unlike lactoferrin, will release its iron in an acidic environment (pH <5.5). There is evidence that uric acid and bilirubin, as well as being powerful chain-breaking antioxidants, may also bind iron (Fig. 1) (5,10). This could offer some additional protection against iron-induced oxidative damage in the newborn, but the levels of these two substances often fall rapidly postnatally owing to renal immaturity and phototherapy, respectively (5).

Clinical studies to investigate iron-induced stress have concentrated on extracellular measurements. Gutteridge has developed methods to assess the iron-oxidizing (ceruloplasmin) and iron-binding (transferrin) antioxidant capacity of plasma, as well as to test for the presence of NPBI (Fig. 2A and 2B; Fig. 3) (7). The antioxidant capacities of ceruloplasmin and transferrin are measured *in vitro* as their ability to inhibit peroxidation of unilamellar liposomes containing unsaturated lipids. By altering the concentrations of either iron or vitamin C in the test system, the capacity of either ceruloplasmin or transferrin in a patient's plasma can be tested (Figs. 2A and 2B). Various methods are available to measure NPBI ("free iron") (7,11); the commonly used bleomycin test is illustrated in Fig. 3 (7). The test is based on the well-described pharmacological action of bleomycin, an antitumor antibiotic, that initiates strand breaks in DNA by oxidative damage. It binds to DNA and then chelates NPBI, which, if then reduced by vitamin C, produces oxidative DNA damage. The breakdown products react with

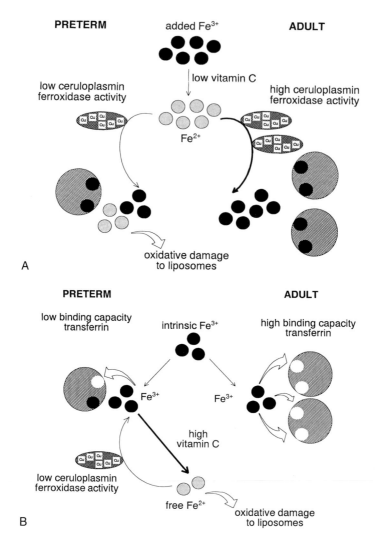

FIG. 2. *In vitro* tests to assess the iron-oxidizing and iron-binding antioxidant capacities of, respectively, plasma ceruloplasmin and transferrin. The percent inhibition of peroxidation of polyunsaturated fatty acids, in liposomes, by plasma is assessed (i.e., the fall in malondialdehyde production as measured by the thiobarbituric acid [TBA)] reaction). (**A**) Ceruloplasmin ferroxidase activity. Plasma is incubated in the presence of liposomes and a high concentration of iron. The excess of added Fe^{3+} will occupy all available transferrin binding sites in adults as well as babies and free (non-protein-bound [NPBI]) iron will always occur. Pro-oxidant Fe^{2+} will form if the ferroxidase capacity of ceruloplasmin is limited despite the low vitamin C concentration. Plasma with low ceruloplasmin levels (e.g., in preterm babies) can only partly inhibit oxidative damage of liposomes compared with plasma of adults. (**B**) Transferrin iron-binding capacity. Plasma is incubated in the presence of liposomes and a high concentration of vitamin C. The free iron-binding sites on transferrin bind the trace amounts of intrinsic iron (from glassware). The excess of added vitamin C antagonizes the ferroxidase activity of ceruloplasmin, and any free iron will be reduced to Fe^{2+} and catalyze lipid peroxidation. Plasma with low concentrations of transferrin and/or highly iron-saturated transferrin (e.g., from preterm babies) can only partly inhibit lipid peroxidation compared with plasma of adults.

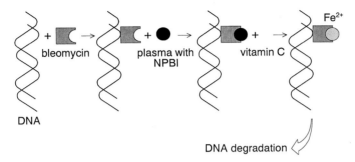

FIG. 3. The bleomycin assay for non-protein-bound iron in extracellular fluids (e.g., plasma). Bleomycin requires the presence of iron to degrade DNA. Bleomycin does not remove iron from proteins, and a positive test indicates the presence of non-protein-bound iron (NPBI, free iron). Bleomycin attaches to DNA and binds NPBI, which if reduced by added vitamin C will degrade DNA to malondialdehyde, which can be measured spectrophotometrically as a pink thiobarbituric acid adduct.

thiobarbituric acid to form a pink chromagen that can be measured. Thus the presence of NPBI in extracellular fluid can be measured by the degree of DNA damage using this *in vitro* test. Gutteridge *et al.* have confirmed the biological relevance of the test: when the NPBI test is positive in babies' plasma, the "free iron" present is also available for use as a cofactor by aconitase (12). These tests have been used to compare normal and iron-overloaded children and adults (e.g., in kwashiorkor, thalassemia, and hereditary hemochromatosis) as well as in healthy and ill newborn babies.

EVIDENCE OF LIMITED PROTECTION AGAINST IRON-INDUCED OXIDATIVE DAMAGE IN THE NEWBORN BABY

Plasma NPBI is only detected in older patients when they are ill and have excess iron or decreased iron-binding capacity. However, plasma NPBI is commonly present in cord blood, even in well babies (13,14). This is probably related to their relatively low transferrin and ceruloplasmin concentrations as well as to the very active transplacental iron and vitamin C transport (15). The possible role of this NPBI in the pathogenesis of various diseases in babies is increasingly attracting attention.

Scott *et al.* first drew attention to the fact that transferrin was highly loaded with iron in cord blood plasma (16). Because certain pathogenic microorganisms are iron dependent, this group speculated that early iron supplementation could increase the risk of neonatal sepsis. More recently, it has been realized that iron overload may also cause damage by initiating oxidative processes, and Sullivan was the first to suggest that this process could be important in the newborn infant (17). He hypothesized that iron-induced oxidative damage could lead to retinopathy of prematurity, intraventricular hemorrhage, bronchopulmonary dysplasia, and necrotizing enterocolitis. Despite the steadily increasing number of *in vitro* and *in vivo* studies, the role of iron-induced oxidative damage in neonatal diseases and its interaction with nutrition and other treatments in the neonatal period is still poorly understood.

Cord blood plasma transferrin concentrations correlate positively with gestational age, but even at term they are much lower than in adults (16). The levels in growth-retarded babies are similar to those in well-nourished newborn babies. In the baby, transferrin is much more highly loaded with iron than in later life. The calculated transferrin saturation is around 60% in babies, compared with 40% in adults (16); however, in a recent study where babies' transferrin saturation was measured, it was found to be even higher, with levels of 100% being common (18). The formula to calculate transferrin saturation uses the molecular mass of transferrin and may not be appropriate for babies. Transferrin is not a homogeneous substance and variations in the polypeptide and glycan chains contribute to its heterogeneity. Different subtypes occur in the preterm and term newborn baby (19), and this could affect the iron-binding capacity. Recently, NPBI has been detected in the plasma of healthy preterm and term babies (13,14). The need to build up adequate iron reserves in the last trimester may be the teleological explanation for the highly iron-loaded transferrin, and this may carry little risk in the low-oxygen environment *in utero*. However, after birth the situation changes dramatically and the presence of NPBI may be dangerous in the high-oxygen environment of terrestrial life.

Recent studies show that both the preterm and the term baby have diminished ability *in vitro* to inhibit lipid peroxidation owing to the limited iron-binding capacity of their transferrin and limited iron-oxidizing capacity of their ceruloplasmin (Figs. 1 and 2) (15). The decreased iron-binding capacity is related to their low transferrin concentrations as well as to the high iron saturation. The role of qualitative factors (e.g., amino acids, glycans, and bicarbonate ion in transferrin) is unknown. The decreased iron-oxidizing capacity is due not only to their low plasma ceruloplasmin levels but also to the high plasma vitamin C level at birth, which antagonizes the ferroxidase activity of ceruloplasmin (Figs. 1 and 2A) (15). The vitamin C concentration falls rapidly and is much lower by the third day in even fairly mature preterm babies (5). There is a negative correlation between ferroxidase activity and the vitamin C/ceruloplasmin ratio in babies (11). Thus any NPBI would then theoretically exist in the pro-oxidant Fe^{2+} form, and Berger *et al.* have recently shown that the NPBI was indeed present in cord blood plasma as Fe^{2+} (20). Little is known about how the postnatal changes in iron and vitamin C levels and transferrin and ceruloplasmin activities may affect the presence and toxicity of NPBI. An important clinical study has shown that babies with NPBI even in the presence of high vitamin C levels do not have increased concentrations of F_2-isoprostane and carbonyl, oxidative products of lipids and proteins, respectively, in their cord blood plasma (21). On the basis of further *in vitro* studies the authors suggested that, although vitamin C can act as a double-edged sword and have either pro-oxidant or antioxidant effects, the very high levels in the newborn, even in the presence of NPBI, have a net antioxidant effect (21). However, we have shown that vitamin C levels fall dramatically postnatally (5). Thus we suggest that the situation might change to a pro-oxidant state postnatally if NPBI persists. We are in the midst of analyzing the serial postnatal changes in NPBI in babies who participated in a feeding trial. Preliminary results suggest that NPBI levels in plasma do fall rapidly postnatally (22).

THE CLINICAL EVIDENCE THAT IRON PLAYS A ROLE AS A PRO-OXIDANT IN NEONATAL DISEASE

There is now preliminary evidence incriminating iron-induced oxidative damage in the pathogenesis of rhesus hemolytic disease (4), neonatal respiratory distress syndrome (RDS) (14), bronchopulmonary dysplasia (23), hypoxic/ischemic encephalopathy (24), and retinopathy of prematurity (25). There appear to be no clinical studies relating iron to the development of necrotizing enterocolitis, but iron does play an important role in animal models of this disease (26). There is a clear link between nutrition and necrotizing enterocolitis (27), and the potential interaction in the intestinal lumen of iron, vitamin C, and long-chain polyunsaturated fats requires clinical and experimental investigation.

In rhesus hemolytic disease, excess iron release from hemolysis may overload the transferrin and damage the liver and endothelial cells, producing hydrops fetalis by oxidative mechanisms (4) analogous to those occurring in thalassemia, and hemochromatosis in older patients (28). Babies with rhesus hemolytic disease have raised ferritin levels, a lowered latent iron-binding capacity, increased lipid peroxidation products, and decreased vitamin C concentrations in their plasma.

In RDS, leakage of plasma containing NPBI into the alveolar space could aggravate surfactant losses by inducing peroxidation (14). The ability of plasma from preterm babies to inhibit iron-catalyzed lipid peroxidation of pulmonary surfactant *in vitro* was lower than that of term babies and was related to the presence of NPBI. Babies with RDS who subsequently develop chronic lung disease have lower transferrin levels than those who recover uneventfully from RDS. The fall in transferrin (a smaller molecule than ceruloplasmin) may be due to leakage into the alveoli (23) caused by oxidative damage, and this could aggravate oxidative damage in the alveolar space (11,14).

In hypoxic/ischemic encephalopathy the energy depletion, acidosis, and superoxide production may release iron from tissue stores in the brain and liver (24). Plasma NPBI is present in asphyxiated babies; this may not only reflect the unbound iron status in the brain but also directly contribute to ischemic reperfusion injury (24). Extracellular oxidative events may, for example, damage endothelial cell membranes, aggravate the cerebral edema, and adversely contribute to the long-term outcome of the babies.

Thus even brief temporary disturbances in iron binding could have serious long-term effects on the growth and development of many tissues in the baby.

THE POSSIBLE INTERACTION OF VARIOUS TREATMENTS AND/OR DIET ON IRON-INDUCED OXIDATIVE DAMAGE IN THE NEWBORN

At present, treatment of ill or preterm babies probably inadvertently inhibits or aggravates iron-induced oxidative stress, but in future, specific prevention of this problem may be possible (4) for a number of important neonatal (and pediatric) diseases. Possible therapeutic steps could include lowering iron and raising vitamin C concentrations, or iron-binding and iron-oxidizing activity of the plasma. The iron content of plasma is controlled by input from exogenous and endogenous sources, but the only significant output is through cell uptake, as exogenous losses are minimal. The large number of transfusions that preterm babies receive can more than compensate for their missed transplacental supplies. Furthermore, intrauterine transfusions in rhesus hemolytic disease may cause iron overload, and babies with this disease should not receive preterm formulas containing extra iron in early life (4). It appears that, unlike in older patients, iron overload from blood transfusions does not result in downregulation of intestinal iron absorption in preterm infants (29). Therefore early feeding of iron-supplemented formulas to babies could aggravate any iron overload in those requiring transfusions. Blood transfusions in babies with bronchopulmonary dysplasia did increase the incidence of NPBI, although there was no increase in lipid peroxidation products in the plasma (30). Formulas with a high iron, low vitamin E, and high polyunsaturated fatty acid content can cause hemolytic anemia (31). We compared the effect of early iron supplementation through preterm formulas on NPBI levels and oxidative stress in preterm infants (gestational age 27 to 34 weeks) fed an iron-fortified preterm formula (0.8 mg/dl iron) with a group of infants fed the same formula without added iron (0.08 mg/dl iron). Formulas were given as soon as the infants tolerated enteral feeds. Iron supplementation did not result in a different incidence of NPBI, or different levels of lipid peroxidation products and antioxidants such as vitamins C and E. However, ferritin concentrations were lower in the non-supplemented group, and 17% of these infants had deficient values at the end of the study period, compared with none in the supplemented group (22). Parenteral iron may increase oxidative stress when used in all-in-one solutions (32) or when provided with erythropoietin treatment to prevent early anemia in preterm babies. However, when given alone, erythropoietin actually protects the lung of premature rabbits by decreasing the iron loading of transferrin (33).

The iron-oxidizing and iron-binding capacity may also be inadvertently influenced by therapeutic measures. The possible clinical consequences of the antagonistic effect of vitamin C on ferroxidase activity were discussed in the preceding discussion and have been reviewed recently (5). Peroxynitrite, a powerful oxidant product of nitric oxide, releases copper from ceruloplasmin (34). This could increase the risk of free plasma Fe^{2+} in babies treated with nitric oxide for pulmonary hypertension. Antenatal corticosteroids appear to increase ceruloplasmin concentrations, whereas transfusions and exchange transfusions using fresh-frozen plasma may increase both ceruloplasmin and transferrin concentrations and activity (5). Because of the possible risks of viral infection, we are wary of using fresh-frozen plasma unless it is specifically indicated (e.g., in bleeding diathesis or exchange transfusions). However, in future the use of recombinant transferrin proteins may offer the advantages of increased iron binding without the risks of infection (5,14). As well as quantitative changes in transferrin concentration, qualitative changes in its ability to bind iron could occur. Transferrin binding of iron requires the synergistic action of an anion (bicarbonate); therefore acidosis and its treatment could, respectively, decrease or increase plasma iron binding (24). Transferrin can also bind other metals such as aluminum. It appears that iron successfully competes against aluminum for the binding sites on transferrin (35); however, these studies have not been carried out with the isoforms of transferrin present in the newborn (see earlier). We speculate that the well-recognized aluminum contamination of feeds and infusions could further limit the iron-binding capacity of transferrin in the neonatal period and perhaps initiate iron-induced peroxidation of the unsaturated lipid intake seen in babies on intravenous fat and the newer preterm formulas.

CONCLUSION

Attention has only recently turned to the possible harmful effects of iron. Overload with this transition metal appears to play a major role in inducing oxidative damage in many diseases in all age groups. Newborn infants have a limited antioxidant capacity and may be more sensitive to iron-induced oxidative damage. There is no clear clinical evidence that postnatal iron supplementation contributes to oxidative damage in the newborn studies, but systematic study of this potential problem has only just begun. Iron toxicity may be one of the factors explaining how illness, therapy, and diet interact to influence morbidity and mortality in the newborn.

SUMMARY

Non-protein-bound iron in the reduced ferrous form can act as a powerful pro-oxidant and damage lipids, proteins, and DNA. *In vitro* and *in vivo* evidence suggests that these processes play a role in the pathogenesis of diseases such as hypoxic/ischemic encephalopathy, retinopathy of prematurity, respiratory distress syndrome, and rhesus hemolytic disease in the newborn infant. Immaturity, disease, and nutrition can influence iron and vitamin C concentrations as well as the iron-oxidizing capacity of ceruloplasmin and the iron-binding capacity of transferrin, thereby predisposing the baby to iron-induced oxidative damage. It may, however, be possible by providing optimal nutrition and other therapeutic steps to inhibit iron-induced oxidative damage in the newborn period.

ACKNOWLEDGMENTS

The advice and support of Professor John Gutteridge, from the very start of our research into ROS metabolism in the newborn at the Leiden University Medical Centre, has been of crucial importance. Dr Frans Walther and Alexandra Schrama critically reviewed the manuscript.

REFERENCES

1. Report of the British Nutrition Foundation Task Force. *Iron: nutritional and physiological significance.* London: Chapman & Hall; 1995:1–185.
2. Wharton BA. Iron nutrition in childhood: the interplay of genes, development and environment. *Acta Paediatr Scand Suppl* 1989;361:5–11.

3. Meneghini R. Iron homeostasis, oxidative stress, and DNA damage. *Free Radic Biol Med* 1997; 23:783–792.
4. Berger HM, Lindeman JHN, van Zoeren-Grobben D, Houdkamp E, Schrijver J, Kanhai HH. Iron overload, free radical damage, and rhesus haemolytic disease. *Lancet* 1990;335:933–936.
5. Berger HM, Molicki JS, Moison RM, van Zoeren-Grobben D. Extracellular defence against oxidative stress in the newborn. *Semin Neonatol* 1998;3:183–190.
6. Palmer HJ, Paulson KE. Reactive oxygen species and antioxidants in signal transduction and gene expression. *Nutr Rev* 1997;55:353–361.
7. Gutteridge JM, Halliwell B. Iron toxicity and oxygen radicals. *Baillières Clin Haematol* 1989;2:195–256.
8. Dean RT, Fu S, Stocker R, Davies MJ. Biochemistry and pathology of radical-mediated protein oxidation. *Biochem J* 1997;324:1–18.
9. Gutteridge JM. Plasma ascorbate levels and inhibition of the antioxidant activity of caeruloplasmin. *Clin Sci* 1991;81:413–417.
10. Hulea SA, Wasowicz E, Kummerow FA. Inhibition of metal-catalyzed oxidation of low-density lipoprotein by free and albumin-bound bilirubin. *Biochim Biophys Acta* 1995;1259:29–38.
11. Kime R, Gibson A, Yong W, Hider R, Powers H. Chromatographic method for the determination of non-transferrin-bound iron suitable for use on the plasma and bronchoalveolar lavage fluid of preterm babies. *Clin Sci* 1996;91:633–638.
12. Gutteridge JM, Mumby S, Koizumi M, Taniguchi N. Free iron in neonatal plasma activates aconitase: evidence for biologically reactive iron. *Biochem Biophys Res Commun* 1996;229:806–809.
13. Evans PJ, Evans R, Kovar IZ, Holton AF, Halliwell B. Bleomycin-detectable iron in the plasma of premature and full-term neonates. *FEBS Lett* 1992;303:210–212.
14. Moison RM, Palinckx JJ, Roest M, Houdkamp E, Berger HM. Induction of lipid peroxidation of pulmonary surfactant by plasma of preterm babies. *Lancet* 1993;341:79–82.
15. Lindeman JH, Houdkamp E, Lentjes EG, Poorthuis BJ, Berger HM. Limited protection against iron-induced lipid peroxidation by cord blood plasma. *Free Radic Res Commun* 1992;16:285–294.
16. Scott PH, Berger HM, Kenward C, Scott P, Wharton BA. Effect of gestational age and intrauterine nutrition on plasma transferrin and iron in the newborn. *Arch Dis Child* 1975;50:796–798.
17. Sullivan JL. Iron, plasma antioxidants, and the oxygen radical disease of prematurity. *Am J Dis Child* 1988;142:1341–1344.
18. Lentjes EG, Lindeman JH, van de Bent W, Berger HM. Measured versus calculated latent iron binding capacity in plasma of newborns. *Ann Clin Biochem* 1995;32:478–481.
19. de Jong G, van Dijk JP, van Eijk HG. The biology of transferrin. *Clin Chim Acta* 1990;190:1–46.
20. Berger HM, Mumby S, Gutteridge JM. Ferrous ions detected in iron-overloaded cord blood plasma from preterm and term babies: implications for oxidative stress. *Free Radic Res* 1995;22:555–559.
21. Berger TM, Polidori MC, Dabbagh A, *et al.* Antioxidant activity of vitamin C in iron-overloaded human plasma. *J Biol Chem* 1997;272:15656–15660.
22. Van Zoeren-Grobben D, Moison RMW, Haasnoot AA, Berger HM. Iron containing feeding formula and oxidative stress in preterm babies. *Pediatr Res* 1998;43:270A.
23. Moison RM, Haasnoot AA, van Zoeren-Grobben D, Berger HM. Plasma proteins in acute and chronic lung disease of the newborn. *Free Radic Biol Med* 1998;25:321–328.
24. Dorrepaal CA, Berger HM, Benders MJ, van Zoeren-Grobben D, Van De Bor M, Van Bel F. Nonprotein-bound iron in postasphyxial reperfusion injury of the newborn. *Pediatrics* 1996;98:883–889.
25. Inder TE, Clemett RS, Austin NC, Graham P, Darlow BA. High iron status in very low birth weight infants is associated with an increased risk of retinopathy of prematurity. *J Pediatr* 1997; 131:541–544.
26. Lelli JLJ, Pradhan S, Cobb LM. Prevention of postischemic injury in immature intestine by deferoxamine. *J Surg Res* 1993;54:34–38.
27. Lucas A, Cole TJ. Breast milk and neonatal necrotising enterocolitis. *Lancet* 1990;336:1519–1523.
28. Hershko C, Peto TE. Non-transferrin plasma iron [editorial]. *Br J Haematol* 1987;66:149–151.
29. Shaw JC. Iron absorption by the premature infant. The effect of transfusion and iron supplements on the serum ferritin levels. *Acta Paediatr Scand Suppl* 1982;299:83–89.
30. Cooke RW, Drury JA, Yoxall CW, James C. Blood transfusion and chronic lung disease in preterm infants. *Eur J Pediatr* 1997;156:47–50.
31. Williams ML, Shott RJ, O'Neal PL, Oski FA. Role of dietary iron and fat on vitamin E deficiency anemia of infancy. *N Engl J Med* 1975;292:887–890.

32. Lavoie JC, Chessex P. Bound iron admixture prevents the spontaneous generation of peroxides in total parenteral nutrition solutions. *J Pediatr Gastroenterol Nutr* 1997;25:307–311.
33. Bany-Mohammed FM, Slivka S, Hallman M. Recombinant human erythropoietin: possible role as an antioxidant in premature rabbits. *Pediatr Res* 1996;40:381–387.
34. Swain JA, Darley-Usmar V, Gutteridge JM. Peroxynitrite releases copper from caeruloplasmin: implications for atherosclerosis. *FEBS Lett* 1994;342:49–52.
35. Van Landeghem GF, D'Haese PC, Lamberts LV, De Broe ME. Competition of iron and aluminum for transferrin: the molecular basis for aluminum deposition in iron-overloaded dialysis patients? *Exp Nephrol* 1997;5:239–245.

DISCUSSION

Prof. Heird: I was struck by the fact that the problem seems to be maximal during the first few days of life. Do you think there is a relation between early nutritional management and levels of transferrin and therefore of iron binding?

Prof. Berger: That's an important aspect. We have been looking at well babies in particular. We are analyzing our babies with chronic lung disease, but I don't have the results yet. Even though you are probably giving a minimal amount in these first days, there is buildup in that critical period. People are now suggesting that if we give erythropoietin, we need to give intravenous iron as well. That's as iron dextran, which is rapidly converted to iron. I am concerned that this new therapeutic measure might have an important pro-oxidant effect. This might also be aggravated in babies who are releasing endogenous iron, such as those with asphyxia and acidosis, where plasma iron may be increased.

Prof. Heird: I was more interested in protein and the effects on synthesis of the iron-binding proteins.

Prof. Berger: The half-life of transferrin is 8 days, and that of ceruloplasmin is twice as much, 14 days as I recall. I don't know whether there is a fall in transferrin in newborn babies with illness because of undernutrition. We have a paper coming out [1] where we followed transferrin levels, ceruloplasmin, and albumin sequentially in babies with and without chronic lung disease after respiratory distress syndrome. It is well known that babies who have RDS have low protein levels because of lung leakage. We were interested in what would happen in chronic lung disease with continuation of the leaky lung problem, or where we're feeding them poorly. We found a low albumin and transferrin in these babies, which persisted to day 10. Looking at total protein-to-transferrin ratios, we think this was related to leakage into the lung and increased output rather than to decreased production because of poor nutrition.

Prof. Cooke: Like you, we've had some experience in measuring free iron using the bleomycin assay. One of our concerns has been that we've been unable to demonstrate that in the presence of free iron there are other indicators of excessive lipid peroxidation. One possibility is that the bleomycin assay may be measuring iron that is actually bound, but not to transferrin. It can be very loosely bound to a number of other proteins and be displaced by the assay itself. Alternatively, maybe we don't have adequate measures of lipid peroxidation that are useful in the newborn. We've measured breath pentane and found that it is not correlated with chronic lung disease, paradoxically; it seems to be correlated mainly with brain injury. The brain obviously is a source of large amounts of lipid, and children with brain injury have very high breath pentane. Lipid infusions in TPN produce huge levels of breath pentane, presumably unrelated to lung damage. The other measures that have been used are things like malondialdehyde (MDA), but these are very general and very crude measures of lipid peroxidation. The answer may be to look at something much more localized, perhaps measuring MDA or similar markers in lung fluid. We have started doing that and have shown high levels of MDA and very low levels of antioxidants in lung fluid. I think we need to get closer to the source of the damage. Iron may be important, but we've been looking at the wrong outcome markers.

Prof. Berger: Bleomycin is not an easy test. That's one of the problems. When you speak to people of different parts of the world you find they don't use it. Gutteridge has recently been looking at aconitase activity. Aconitase is an enzyme concerned with citrate metabolism, and it needs iron to be activated. He showed that in babies with free iron present in the plasma you can induce aconitase activity, and this correlates with the bleomycin iron present [2]. So there is some confirmation that the bleomycin test is backed up by newer tests. What we then did in our babies was to actually measure iron-binding capacity and showed there was a very strong correlation between the bleomycin iron and the presence of iron-binding capacity or free iron [3]. So there is confirmation that this iron test is reasonable. What I'm concerned about is the possibility that it is not always true that heme iron and hemoglobin iron do not participate in the test. It may be true in adults, but in the baby there could be interference. I agree we need more sensitive markers. As Dr. Frank pointed out, perhaps we should be looking not only at fat peroxidation products, but also at DNA and protein products in plasma as markers of peroxidation.

Prof. Haschke: Does transferrin receptor help to define iron requirements or iron toxicity?

Prof. Berger: There was a recent abstract [4] looking at transferrin receptor in terms of analyzing the hemolytic process and iron overload in rhesus hemolytic disease, but I'm not aware of anything specifically on preterm infants.

Prof. Haschke: Many people may now be concerned about the ratio of vitamin C to iron. In most formulas the molar ratio is about 10:1. Do you see any disadvantage or even potential dangers if such formulas are given to premature infants, especially when there is danger of iron overload?

Prof. Berger: That question is now beginning to be asked, but we don't have an answer as yet. I know that some research is under way in New Zealand looking at the influence of vitamin C supplementation and iron-induced peroxidation.

Dr. Walker: We have been concerned about the possibility that, as an inappropriate response to luminal stimuli, the NFκB transcription factor excessively regulates the upswing of interleukin-8, which causes an inflammatory response. So your hypothesis is that iron is necessary to release NFκB may not be a very good thing in the immature enterocyte and may create further damage. The absence of iron may be an important factor.

Prof. Berger: On looking up the literature on this subject I came across five articles showing that iron can influence the activation of NFκB, though I agree this was not in the intestine but mainly in cultured liver cells. It is, however, going to be a fascinating prospect to alter redox potential in newborn babies and possibly alter not only NFκB but also apoptosis, which we know goes on for weeks after perinatal asphyxia.

Prof. Nowak: Can ferritin-bound iron be displaced under certain clinical situations, such as acidosis or drugs that we use in the nursery?

Prof. Berger: Transferrin iron is very well bound, whereas ferritin iron is more easily released. But transferrin iron can be released with acidosis; in fact, the basis of the latent iron-binding capacity tests is to make the plasma very acid so that even the transferrin loses its iron. Ferritin is another story. The work of Koster from Rotterdam suggests that ferritin iron release occurs in ischemia reperfusion damage and heart infarcts [5]. He showed that in the presence of superoxide radicals, ferritin releases its iron. So where you have ischemia reperfusion there will be both an increase of free radical superoxide and a release of iron, which the superoxide then can reduce. The superoxide then also contributes hydrogen peroxide, which the reduced iron will convert to hydroxyl radical. So the release of iron from ferritin, which contains a great excess of iron atoms compared with transferrin, might be very important. We see a dramatic rise in iron release in asphyxiated newborns.

Prof. Ziegler: You mentioned the use of intravenous iron dextran in conjunction with recombinant human erythropoietin. Is anything known about what this does to free iron concentrations in plasma?

Prof. Berger: This was the subject of an editorial in the *Journal of Pediatrics* recently [6]. Dr. Chessex showed last year in the *Journal of Pediatric Gastroenterology and Nutrition* [7] that when iron sulfate was present in parenteral fluids, there was ongoing peroxidation in the solution, but with iron dextran there was no increase in peroxide production. So iron dextran seems to be inactive and this fits in with the chemical detail. However, when it is taken up by the reticuloendothelial system, it is rapidly converted to iron and then bound to transferrin. Thus, depending on your input *vs.* your output, it is theoretically possible that there could be free iron in transit, not yet bound to transferrin.

Dr. Chessex: We found that iron dextran actually had a protective effect against peroxide generation in TPN solutions—the opposite of free iron. We don't understand why. We tested the effect of dextran alone, and it does not have any antiperoxide activity. So it's the iron dextran complex that has this activity. We thought it might be a spurious *in vitro* finding, but we found a fall in urinary peroxide excretion in five pediatric patients receiving intravenous dextran iron after they started treatment. So this seemed to confirm what we were finding *in vitro*. However, most people now use other sources of complex iron since iron dextran can cause anaphylactic reactions.

Prof. Berger: A parallel could be drawn with desferrioxamine, which also chelates iron which is then not normally active. There was a paper in *Lancet* a couple of years ago describing patients with thalassemia who were being treated with intravenous desferrioxamine who ended up with severe adult respiratory distress syndrome [8]. It was suggested then that, depending on the site, even these iron-chelating agents could release iron.

Dr. Georgieff: We published some relevant research in the *American Journal of Physiology* a couple of months ago [9]. This was a study on newborn lambs who were phlebotomized and put into iron balance with saccharated intravenous iron at various doses. These ranged from 0 in the control group through 1 mg/kg·d, 2 mg, 5 mg, and 15 mg. The iron was given as boluses every 3 days, so the highest group received 45 mg/kg every 3 days. The experimental blood loss was equivalent to that found in the newborn intensive care unit, about 2 ml/kg daily. We found that we were able to put the animals back into iron balance at 2 mg/kg·d of IV iron. Assuming that a baby absorbs about 33% from the gut, that would be equivalent to an enteral dose of about 6 mg/kg·d, which is consistent with the dose given to babies receiving erythropoietin. We found no evidence of peroxidative damage until we reached the highest dose of

15 mg/kg·d (45 mg/kg bolus every 3 days). The one animal that received that large amount of iron died after the second dose. At 5 mg/kg·d we saw mild changes that were not really very significant. So although in the lamb the transferrin is saturated at a different percentage than in the human baby, it obviously takes a fair amount of iron to get peroxidative damage.

Prof. Haschke: This interaction between vitamin C and ceruloplasmin seems to be a very sensitive issue. Is there any situation where a high copper intake together with low ceruloplasmin synthesis could be pro-oxidative?

Prof. Berger: It is now believed that copper transport is mainly by albumin, and copper on ceruloplasmin is for ferroxidase activity. Could excess copper play a role in oxidative damage? *In vitro*, copper is a more powerful pro-oxidant than iron, but its role in the newborn has not been explored. It has been shown that copper may be present in excess in some intravenous fluids, particularly albumin preparations, depending on the maker or the source. So there could be an increased input from this source, perhaps more than we realize. However, the major factor is probably a decreased copper output in some babies. Copper is excreted in the bile and it has been shown that in babies with cholestasis there is increased serum copper. We heard yesterday that there may be peroxidative damage in cholestasis, so it may be that copper is playing a role. We studied copper as a pro-oxidant in preterm babies and showed that babies with low albumin levels had a decreased ability to inhibit copper-induced peroxidation [10]. So it is possible that an excess of copper in the presence of a low albumin could give rise to a pro-oxidant state.

Dr. Georgieff: There are certain conditions that result in babies being born with either low or high ferritin. Low ferritin is often seen in babies with intrauterine growth retardation, probably as a reflection of decreased placental transport. And between 50% and 60% of infants of diabetic mothers are also born with low-ferritin iron. I wonder if there is any information on their susceptibility to oxidative diseases?

Prof. Berger: I don't know anything about the diabetic group, but we were interested in the intrauterine growth retardation, particularly when people started suggesting that necrotizing enterocolitis has a high incidence in intrauterine growth retardation. I wondered whether this might have something to do with iron. We carried out a study in Cape Town on mothers with preeclampsia who had cesarean sections, looking at the babies' cord blood levels of iron and non-protein-bound iron. The babies were divided into those with intrauterine growth retardation and those of appropriate weight, but we found no difference in transferrin, ceruloplasmin, or non-protein-bound iron levels.

Prof. Lucas: There is concern about iron intake in adults in relation to ischemic heart disease. Could you comment on our management of preterm infants from an iron point of view? These infants will be sent home with an amount of medicinal iron to be taken daily, and this may be doubled with the iron that they also get in an iron-fortified formula; then within weeks of going home, they may also start receiving iron-fortified weaning feeds. So there are multiple sources of iron.

Prof. Berger: That's an important question. We have grown up with the idea that iron absorption is regulated and that the amount of absorption depends on iron status. But in the preterm baby, at least in the early weeks of life, that may not be so [11]. The iron absorption regulating mechanism appears not to be well developed, and even when a baby is getting blood transfusions there appears to be undiminished iron absorption from the gut. So it's certainly possible that we could overload these babies. I'm concerned about the possible effects of this if the baby becomes ill. To draw a parallel with the adult, one theory about iron and atherosclerosis is that a high iron level is not in itself related to increased atherosclerosis, but if there is excess iron in the tissues at the time of myocardial ischemia, this iron is released and triggers oxidative damage. It is a worrying possibility that the preterm baby who suddenly gets ill may suffer in a similar way from release of iron.

Dr. Georgieff: To give the other side of the coin, we are seeing many children in our clinic with extremely low ferritin and TIBC and with hemoglobins of around 5 g/liter. I don't know how common this is, but I want to make the point that there is probably a very wide range of iron sufficiency and insufficiency in premature infants after discharge home. The children we see with low iron status tend to have been healthy babies of perhaps 26 or 28 weeks of gestation who did not have lung disease, who did not get transfusions, and who were fed either with a low-iron formula or, more commonly, with their own mother's milk without iron supplementation. On the other hand, there was the article recently in the *Journal of Pediatrics* [12] documenting ferritins of 500 to 700 ng/ml in babies discharged from neonatal intensive care. So here we have a fairly toxic compound with narrow therapeutic range, and I think we need to pay more attention to iron balance, both in the NICU and at follow-up.

Prof. Berger: This is exactly the point I was trying to make. We need something rather more sensitive than stool gazing.

REFERENCES

1. Moison RM, Haasnoot AA, van Zoeren-Grobben D, Berger HM. Plasma proteins in acute and chronic lung disease of the newborn. *Free Radic Biol Med* 1998;25:321–328.
2. Mumby S, Koizumi M. Taniguchi N, Gutteridge JM. Reactive iron species in biological fluids activate the iron sulfur cluster of aconitase. *Biochim Biophys Acta* 1988;1380(1):102–108.
3. Moison RM, Palinckx JJ, Roest M, Houdkamp E, Berger HM. Induction of lipid peroxidation of pulmonary surfactant by plasma of preterm babies. *Lancet* 1993;341:79–82.
4. Kivivuori S, Siimes MA, Andersson S, Teramo K. The serum transferrin receptor concentration in a fetus with hemolytic disease. *Pediatr Res* 1998;43:239A.
5. Biemond P, Swaak AJ, van Eijk HG, Koster JF. Superoxide dependent iron release from ferritin in inflammatory diseases. *Free Radic Biol Med* 1988;4:185–198.
6. Strauss RG. Recombinant erythropoietin for the anemia of prematurity: still a promise not a panacea. *J Pediatr* 1997;131:653–655 (editorial).
7. Lavoie JC, Chessex P. Bound iron admixture prevents the spontaneous generation of peroxides in total parenteral nutrition solutions. *J Pediatr Gastroenterol Nutr* 1997;25:307–311.
8. Tenebein M, Kowalski S, Sienko A, Bowden DH, Adamson IY. Pulmonary toxic effects of continuous desferrioxamine administration in acute iron poisoning. *Lancet* 1992;339:699–701.
9. Guiang SF III, Georgieff MK, Lambert DJ, Schmidt RL, Widness JA. Intravenous iron supplementation effect on tissue iron and hemoproteins in chronically phlebotomized lambs. *Am J Physiology* 1997;273:R2124–21231.
10. Lindeman JH, Lentjes EG, Berger HM. Diminished protection against copper-induced lipid peroxidation by cord blood plasma of preterm and term infants. *J Parenteral Enter Nutr* 1995;19:373–375.
11. Shaw JC. Iron absorption by the premature infant. The effect of transfusion and iron supplements on the serum ferritin levels. *Acta Paediatr Scand Suppl* 1982;299:83–89.
12. Inder TE, Clemett RS, Austin NC, Graham P, Darlow BA. High iron status in very low birth weight infants is associated with an increased risk of retinopathy of prematurity. *J Pediatr* 1997; 131:541–544.

Nutrition of the Very Low Birthweight Infant, edited by
Ekhard E. Ziegler, Alan Lucas, Guido E. Moro.
Nestlé Nutrition Workshop Series, Paediatric Programme, Vol. 43,
Nestec Ltd., Vevey/Lippincott Williams & Wilkins
Philadelphia, Pennsylvania © 1999.

Nitrogen Balance and Plasma Amino Acids in the Evaluation of Protein Sources for Extremely Low Birthweight Infants

Jacques Rigo[a], G. Putet[b], J.C. Picaud[c], C. Pieltain[a], M. De Curtis[d],
B.L. Salle[c], J. Senterre[a]

[a]*Department of Neonatology, University of Liège, Hôpital de la Citadelle, Liège, Belgium.*
[b]*Department of Neonatology, Hôpital Debrousse, Lyon, France;* [c]*Department of
Neonatology, Hôpital Edouard Herriot, Lyon, France;* [d]*Istituto Materno Infantile, University
of Palermo, Italy*

The nutritional problems of preterm babies have become particularly relevant in the last decade because of the increased survival of extremely low birthweight (ELBW) infants and the numerous studies underlining the importance of early feeding on short- and long-term development (1). It is well known that the nutritional requirements of extremely premature infants are greater than those of other, larger premature and full-term neonates and that nutritional support should be initiated early in the neonatal period, combining the use of parenteral and enteral feeding (2). The reduction of gut motility, enzyme function, and intestinal nutrient absorption in these very small babies has led to the use of total parenteral nutrition as a prolonged exclusive feeding process during the first weeks of life. However, "minimal enteral feeding" has been shown to enhance gut motility and accelerate establishment of full enteral feeding (3,4). There is now some evidence that early enteral nutrition may be well tolerated without adverse effects in ELBW infants, but precise guidelines on early enteral support need to be established.

Enteral feeding is generally initiated with the baby's own mother's milk, with or without fortification with energy, minerals, and proteins, or with a preterm formula. More recently, to improve gastric emptying and gastrointestinal digestibility and to prevent atopic diseases, the use of partially hydrolyzed protein formulas has been suggested (5). There are insufficient published data for accurate evaluation of the influence of protein quality on nitrogen absorption, nitrogen utilization, and plasma amino acid concentrations in ELBW infants. This information therefore needs to be obtained by extrapolation from the results of the numerous studies that have been carried out on larger preterm infants studied at various gestational ages and body weights.

NITROGEN ABSORPTION

Various factors may affect nitrogen absorption in preterm infants (6). The stomach does not contribute significantly to overall protein digestion (7). The breakdown of most large-molecular-weight proteins into smaller peptides and amino acids is the result of luminal hydrolysis and subsequently of peptidase activity, located at the level of the microvillus membrane or within the enterocyte (7). In human milk, antibodies, enzymes, and growth factors appear to survive the gastrointestinal environment and can be detected in the stool, decreasing the apparent nitrogen absorption rate (7). Studies in animal preterm neonates suggest that bovine and human whey proteins are hydrolyzed more slowly than casein (8). In addition, the decreasing level of immunoreactive human α-lactalbumin found in the serum of preterm infants with increasing gestational age suggests a relative impairment of protein hydrolysis at the earlier stages of development (9). Because of this, the use of formulas containing partially or more extensively hydrolyzed proteins has been suggested, but their effect on nitrogen absorption is still questionable as the transport of small peptides or individual amino acids may not be as efficient as it is when they have been initially hydrolyzed by microvillus membrane peptidases (10).

Over a period of more than 20 years, we have performed 356 metabolic balance studies (11–16) in preterm infants fed human milk, either unsupplemented or supplemented with various human milk fortifiers (HMF; $n = 88$), European whey-predominant formulas designed before 1980 (WPF1; $n = 72$) and after 1980 (WPF2; $n = 49$), American whey-predominant formulas (WPF3; $n = 58$), hydrolyzed whey formulas (HWF; $n = 31$), and casein-predominant formulas also designed before 1980 (CPF; $n = 58$) (Table 1). In all, almost 30 different regimens were evaluated.

Fecal nitrogen excretion represents the sum of endogenous fecal nitrogen derived from the gastrointestinal tract (desquamation, secretion) and the nonabsorbed fraction of the nitrogen intake. The apparent nitrogen absorption rate may be estimated as the ratio between absorbed nitrogen and nitrogen intake. The apparent nitrogen absorption rate differs significantly according to the feeding regimen. It was higher with WPF1 (89.9%), WPF2 (90.7%), or CPF (89.5%) than with HMF (82.7%), WHF (84.3%), or WPF3 (86.0%) (Table 1). The fractional nitrogen absorption rate (true digestibility) can be estimated by regression analysis between nitrogen absorbed and nitrogen ingested, as the nitrogen coefficient (Fig. 1). Calculated values for this coefficient are (see Fig. 1) 83.4 ± 3.0% for HMF; 93.3 ± 1.0% for WPF1, WPF2, and CPF combined; 76.9 ± 6.1% for WPF3; and 80.6 ± 7.9.% for WHF. From these data, the endogenous nitrogen excretion was estimated in the group with the highest nitrogen absorption rate. The mean value lies between 30 and 40 mg/kg body weight per day.

When we evaluated the American whey-predominant formulas (WPF3), which are essentially in-can liquid formulas sterilized with heat treatment that induced a Maillard reaction, our data confirm that the technical process may impair nitrogen absorption (17). Similarly, the technologies necessary to perform partial protein hydrolysis appear to reduce nitrogen absorption significantly in preterm infants.

Reanalyzing the results of numerous metabolic balance studies reported by various groups, Micheli and Schutz (6) suggested that nitrogen absorption could be di-

TABLE 1. *Metabolic balances in preterm infants fed various formulas: population**

	Milk group					
	HMF	WPF 1	WPF 2	WPF 3	WHF	CPF
N	88	72	49	58	31	58
Birthweight (g)	1368 ± 255^{bf}	1792 ± 231^{acdef}	1460 ± 382^{bf}	1343 ± 295^{bf}	1376 ± 276^{b}	1859 ± 264^{acde}
Gestat. age (wks)	30.5 ± 1.8^{btb}	32.3 ± 1.6^{acdef}	30.6 ± 2.8^{bdf}	29.7 ± 2.1^{abfc}	30.5 ± 2.3^{b}	31.8 ± 1.4^{abcde}
Postnatal age (d)	28 ± 11b^{df}	18 ± 6^{acde}	28 ± 15^{bf}	32 ± 12^{abef}	28 ± 12^{bd}	19 ± 8^{acde}
Cor. GA wks	34.5 ± 1.5^{b}	34.9 ± 1.4^{adf}	34.6 ± 1.7	34.1 ± 1.7^{b}	34.4 ± 1.3	34.6 ± 1.3
Weight (g)	1730 ± 247^{bcf}	2005 ± 254^{acdef}	1860 ± 280^{abf}	1880 ± 269^{bef}	1765 ± 224^{bd}	2097 ± 272^{abcde}
Intake (mg/kg/d)	517 ± 86^{ef}	545 ± 102^{df}	522 ± 70^{ef}	506 ± 58^{bef}	553 ± 56^{acdf}	688 ± 143^{abcde}
Fecal excretion (mg/kg/d)	90 ± 28^{bcdf}	53 ± 16^{adef}	49 ± 19^{adef}	71 ± 29^{abce}	87 ± 26^{bcdf}	70 ± 18^{abce}
Absorption (mg/kg/d)	428 ± 76^{bcef}	492 ± 104^{adf}	474 ± 65^{adf}	434 ± 52^{bcef}	466 ± 51^{adf}	618 ± 135^{abcde}
Absorption (% of intake)	82.7 ± 4.8^{bcdf}	89.9 ± 3.7^{ade}	90.7 ± 3.3^{adef}	86 ± 5^{abcf}	84 ± 4.0^{bcf}	89.5 ± 2.7^{acde}
Urinary excretion (mg/kg/d)	121 ± 45^{bdf}	191 ± 95^{acdef}	106 ± 36^{bdf}	98 ± 21^{abef}	122 ± 39^{bdf}	319 ± 108^{abcde}
Retention (mg/kg/d)	307 ± 56^{cde}	3 01 ± 67^{cde}	368 ± 57^{abdef}	337 ± 46^{abcf}	343 ± 42^{abcf}	299 ± 82^{cde}
Net prot. utilsat.# (%)	59.7 ± 7.7^{bcdf}	56.0 ± 11^{acdef}	71.5 ± 6.5^{abdef}	66.6 ± 5.8^{bcef}	62.4 ± 6.5^{bcdf}	44.1 ± 10.5^{abcde}
Prot. efficiency @ (%)	72.1 ± 7.6^{bcdf}	62.6 ± 13.2^{acdef}	77.7 ± 6.4^{abef}	77.5 ± 4.4^{abef}	74.0 ± 6.9^{bcdf}	49.3 ± 11.9^{abcde}

* Values are expressed as mean ± 1 SD.
^{a} p < 0.05 versus HMF
^{b} p < 0.05 versus WPF 1
^{c} p < 0.05 versus WPF 2
^{d} p < 0.05 versus WPF 3
^{e} p < 0.05 versus WHF
^{f} p < 0.05 versus CPF
nitrogen retention/nitrogen intake
@ nitrogen retention/nitrogen absorbed

Nitrogen balance

Absorption

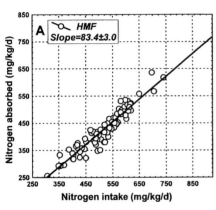

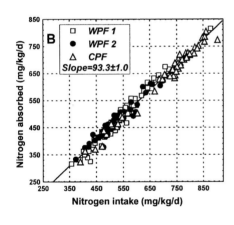

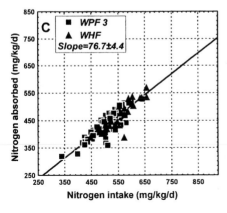

Retention

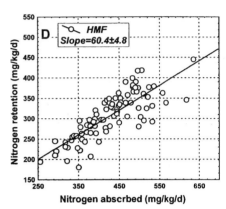

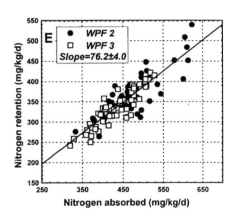

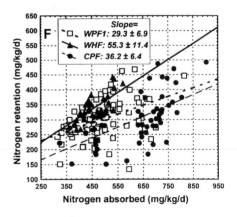

rectly related to gestational age and that immaturity of ELBW infants could significantly reduce metabolizable nitrogen. Multivariate analysis of our data does not confirm this hypothesis but suggests that nitrogen absorption is independent of weight or gestational age at the time of the balance study (Fig. 2). Thus data we obtained in VLBW infants could probably be extrapolated to ELBW infants.

NITROGEN UTILIZATION

During the second part of gestation, lean body mass and protein accretion increase faster than weight gain owing to a progressive reduction in total water content (18). The fetus has a much higher fractional protein turnover rate than the term infant, because of the increased ratio of organs with high rates of protein synthesis over other tissues. Body nitrogen content increases exponentially during this period, whereas protein gain represents around 20% to 25% of protein synthesis (18).

Many factors are known to affect protein utilization in ELBW infants: protein and nitrogen intakes, energy-to-protein ratio, biological value of ingested proteins, nutritional status, hormones, and clinical factors (6). Various studies have shown that daily protein gain increases linearly with protein supply up to around 4 g/kg·d, at which point the effect of protein gain appears to decrease. However, an additional effect of metabolizable energy has been demonstrated. This effect appears to be more pronounced at suboptimal energy intakes (<100 kcal/kg·d). The efficiency of protein gain can be estimated by the ratio between retained and absorbed nitrogen, as well as by the slope of the regression line calculated between nitrogen retained and nitrogen absorbed (see Fig. 1D–F).

In our results the efficiency of protein gain differs according to the feeding regimen (Table 1); the highest values were obtained in preterm infants fed WPF2 (77.7%) and WPF3 (77.5%). The efficiency of protein gain was significantly reduced in infants fed WHF (74.0%) and HMF (72.1%). The lower value obtained with HMF may be related to the nonprotein nitrogen (NPN) fraction of human milk, representing 20% to 25% of the total nitrogen content of human milk but 13.5% to 17% of the total nitrogen content of HMF. As demonstrated for urea nitrogen, the contribution of this metabolizable NPN fraction to protein gain is lower than that of α-lactalbumin or casein in human milk (19). By contrast, the significantly lower value obtained with WHF suggests that the process of hydrolysis itself reduces the bioavailability of whey protein. The low efficiency values obtained with the use of WPF1 (62.6%) and CPF (49.3%) may be related, on the one hand, to the higher nitrogen supply provided by those formulas reaching the protein gain plateau and, on the other hand, by a relative reduction in metabolizable energy caused by the use of a poorly absorbed cow's milk fat blend in most of the formulas made before 1980.

◀───

FIG. 1. *Left:* Relation between nitrogen absorption and intake in preterm infants according to feeding regimen: (**A**) HMF; *n* = 88; (**B**) WPF1, WPF2, and CPF; *n* = 179; (**C**) WPF3 and WHF, *n* = 89. *Right:* Relation between nitrogen retention and absorption in preterm infants according to feeding regimen: (**D**) HMF, *n* = 88; (**E**) WPF2 and WPF3, *n* = 107; (**F**) WPF1, WHF, and CPF; *n* = 161.

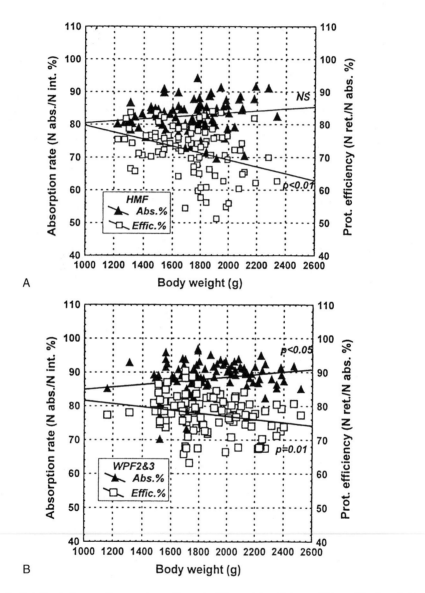

FIG. 2. Relation between nitrogen absorption rate (%), protein efficiency (%), and body weight in preterm infants fed HMF (**A**) and WPF2 and WPF3 (**B**).

The efficiency of whey-predominant and casein-predominant formulas has been demonstrated more recently by Cooke *et al.* (20), who compared three preterm formulas with 60:40, 35:65, and 20:80 whey/casein ratios. The absorption rate was slightly lower with the whey-predominant formula (83% *versus* 86% and 85%), whereas efficiency was around 80% and similar in the three groups.

Thus, with respect to net protein utilization (N retained/N ingested), cow's milk protein formulas, whether whey-predominant or casein-predominant, appear to be more efficient than human milk, with or without protein supplementation. However, our studies confirm that in formulas the protein bioavailability can be altered by various technical processes such as heat treatment or hydrolysis (21).

The fractional protein synthesis rate decreases with gestational age in fetal sheep at a greater rate than the fractional growth rate, but both curves indicate a much higher protein turnover and presumably a greater utilization in ELBW infants (18). Animal studies and metabolic balances performed in preterm infants show that the rate of protein accretion per unit body weight decreases throughout gestation (18). Reanalyzing the results of numerous metabolic balance studies in preterm infants, Micheli and Schutz (6) showed that there is a gestational-age-related change in the percentage of protein energy needed to achieve optimal protein gain. However, the efficiency of protein gain—the ratio between protein gain and metabolizable protein—seems to be independent of gestational age. In contrast, in preterm infants fed HMF or formulas with the highest protein efficiency (WPF2, WPF3), we calculated that protein gain was dependent not only on the absorbed protein supply but also on the body weight at the time of the balance study. The efficiency of protein gain (ratio of protein retained to protein absorbed) was inversely related to body weight (see Fig. 2), suggesting a greater efficiency of protein deposition in ELBW infants.

PLASMA AMINO ACID CONCENTRATIONS

ELBW infants have incomplete development of several amino acid metabolic pathways and require high-quality protein with an adequate nitrogen supply to prevent deficiency or overload of various essential or semi-essential amino acids. It is still a matter of debate whether the plasma amino acid disturbances commonly observed in preterm infants on oral or parenteral nutrition are harmful for development.

Optimal values for plasma amino acid concentrations in preterm infants are also a matter of discussion. At least three different gold standards have been proposed for premature infants:

1. amino acid concentrations from the umbilical cord obtained at fetal cord puncture or after birth;
2. amino acid concentrations obtained in rapidly growing preterm infants receiving their own mother's milk or human milk supplemented with human milk proteins;
3. amino acid concentrations in healthy breastfed term infants (22–27).

For ELBW infants, levels that obtain during the last trimester of gestation or in growing infants with optimal intake of human milk protein appear to be safe. However, since large differences are observed for some amino acids (threonine, valine, tyrosine, phenylalanine, lysine, and histidine) between fetal and postnatal values, a combined reference standard has been proposed (Fig. 3), taking into account the mean ± 1 SD of the values obtained in cord blood and in preterm infants fed human milk supplemented with human milk protein (28,29).

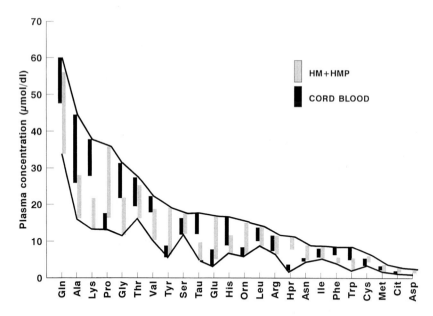

FIG. 3. Plasma amino acid reference values for preterm infants. Cord blood amino acid concentrations (mean ± 1 SD) were combined with the values obtained in preterm infants fed human milk fortified with human milk protein (mean ± 1 SD).

According to this reference, preterm infants fed human milk fortified with whole cow's milk protein or casein hydrolysate have plasma amino acid concentrations within the normal range. On the other hand, the use of whey hydrolysate as a fortifier induces a significant increase in plasma threonine and a relative reduction in phenylalanine (29,30).

In view of the fact that bovine casein has a different amino acid composition from human milk, that bovine whey is quite different from human whey, and that human milk contains a relatively large proportion of nonprotein nitrogen partially available for protein synthesis, it is virtually impossible in cow's milk-based formulas to obtain a nitrogen and amino acid pattern identical to that found in human milk. Thus there have been numerous studies evaluating indices of protein metabolism and plasma amino acid concentrations in preterm infants fed formula with various whey/casein ratios (20,31–33). Recent data (20,32,33) suggest that the type of protein has no effect on metabolic acidosis, uremia, or hyperammonemia, in contrast to data reported in preterm infants receiving older preterm formulas (34). However, the supply of individual amino acids differs significantly according to the whey/casein ratio, thereby influencing the plasma amino acid concentrations. Thus, compared with reference values, threonine is increased and histidine is relatively decreased in infants fed WPF, whereas methionine and aromatic amino acids are increased in infants fed CPF. However, these disturbances of plasma amino acid concentrations do not reach the level previously reported with older formulas (35,36).

Whey-hydrolyzed formulas have recently been evaluated in preterm infants (5,37). Indeed, various technological processes necessary to reduce protein antigenicity may modify amino acid content and amino acid bioavailability (21). The use of a higher percentage of whey in protein-hydrolyzed formulas aggravates the distortion of plasma amino acids previously observed with the use of whey-predominant formulas, with an increase in threonine and a decrease in aromatic amino acid concentrations. Moreover, a sharp decrease in plasma histidine and tryptophan concentrations was also observed, which could be related to a relative reduction in amino acid bioavailability. Therefore histidine and tryptophan supplementation seems to be required for these formulas (37).

Whey protein separation is obtained by acidic or enzymatic casein precipitation from cow's milk proteins. In contrast to enzymatic precipitation, in the acidic precipitation process the κ-casein and its glycomacropeptide rich in threonine are eliminated from the soluble phase with the casein (38). Therefore it is now possible to design whey-predominant or whey-hydrolyzed formulas with a lower threonine content.

Using a crossover study design, we recently evaluated plasma amino acid concentrations in 14 preterm infants receiving either a conventional enzymatic or an acidic whey-predominant formula (39). A sharp reduction in plasma threonine concentration was observed in infants fed the acidic WPF (27.9 ± 8.5 μmol/dl) compared with those receiving the conventional WPF (37.5 ± 8.4 μmol/dl). All the other plasma amino acid concentrations were similar with the exception of valine, which was also reduced in the infants fed with acidic WPF. Similarly, in another study in preterm infants receiving an acidic whey-hydrolyzed formula (40), the plasma threonine concentration was significantly lower (35.7 ± 9.2 μmol/dl; $n = 13$) than the value observed in those fed the enzymatic whey-hydrolyzed formula (48.7 ± 11.3 μmol/dl; $n = 11$). Considering that threonine metabolism is highly dependent on gestational age (41) and that the increase of brain threonine concentration related to plasma concentrations is higher than that of the other essential amino acids (42), it is highly advisable to use acidic whey rather than enzymatic whey in formulas for ELBW infants.

Glutamine is the most abundant amino acid in the human body and the predominant amino acid supplied to the fetus through the placenta. It is thought to be an important fuel for rapidly dividing cells such as enterocytes and lymphocytes. In ELBW infants who undergo numerous stresses during the first weeks of life and are fed by parenteral and oral nutrition, the provision of glutamine is limited at a time of increased demand. It could indeed be a conditionally essential amino acid. It has recently been suggested that glutamine supplementation in formula may decrease hospital-acquired sepsis and improve tolerance of enteral feedings in ELBW infants (43). Therefore glutamine supplementation in formulas specially designed for ELBW infants should be considered and carefully evaluated.

CONCLUSION

There is much evidence that early enteral feeding, by enhancing the maturation of the gastrointestinal tract, decreases the number of days of feeding intolerance without adverse effect in ELBW infants. However, owing to the immaturity of numerous metabolic pathways and their precarious state, there is a need for more appropriate guidelines on early enteral support. Several studies support the use of human milk, but attention needs to be focused on specific nutrient limitations. Calcium, phosphorus, proteins, and energy supplements are available, but they markedly increase the osmolality of the feed. When human milk is not available, specifically designed formulas can be used. A review of numerous metabolic balance studies has shown that nitrogen absorption and utilization appear satisfactory. However, absorption and utilization may be impaired by the technical processes involved in protein isolation, protein hydrolysis, or sterilization. The immaturity of amino acid metabolic pathways in ELBW infants may easily induce an amino acid overload or deficiency, which may be deleterious for development. Therefore protein sources, amino acid composition, and the bioavailability of amino acids require careful evaluation and adaptation to optimize plasma amino acid concentrations.

REFERENCES

1. Lucas A. Programming by early nutrition: an experimental approach. *J Nutr* 1998;128:401–406.
2. Pereira GR. Nutritional care of the extremely premature infant. *Clin Perinatol* 1995;22:61–75.
3. Berseth CL. Minimal enteral feeding. *Clin Perinatol* 1995;22:195–205.
4. Denne SC, Clark SE, Poindexter BB, *et al.* Nutrition and metabolism in the high-risk neonate. In: Fanaroff AA, Martin RJ, eds. *Neonatal-perinatal medicine: disease of the fetus and infant.* St. Louis: Mosby Year Book; 1997:586–508.
5. Rigo J, Salle BL, Picaud J-C, Putet G, Senterre J. Nutritional evaluation of protein hydrolysate formulas. *Eur J Clin Nutr* 1995;49:S26–38.
6. Micheli JL, Schutz Y. Protein. In: Tsang RC, Lucas A, Uauy R, Zlotkin S, eds. *Nutritional needs of the preterm infants.* Baltimore: Williams & Wilkins; 1993:29–46.
7. Hamosh M. Digestion in the newborn. *Clin Perinatol* 1996;23:191–209.
8. Lindberg T, Engberg S, Jakobsson I, Lonnerdal B. Digestion of proteins in human milk, human milk fortifier, and preterm formula in infant rhesus monkeys. *J Pediatr Gastroenterol Nutr* 1997;24:537–543.
9. Axelsson I, Jakobsson I, Lindberg T, Polberger S, Benediktsson B, Raiha N. Macromolecular absorption in preterm and term infants. *Acta Paediatr Scand* 1989;78:532–537.
10. Neu J, Koldovsky O. Nutrient absorption in the preterm neonate. *Clin Perinatol* 1996;23:229–243.
11. Putet G, Senterre J, Rigo G, Salle B. Nutrient balance, energy utilization and composition of weight gain in very-low-birth-weight-infants fed pooled human milk or preterm formula. *J Pediatr* 1984; 105:79–85.
12. Putet G, Rigo J, Salle B, Senterre J. Supplementation of pooled human milk with casein hydrolysate: energy and nitrogen balance and weight gain composition in very-low-birth-weight infants. *Pediatr Res* 1987;21:458–461.
13. De Curtis M, Brooke OG. Energy and nitrogen balances in very low birth weight infants. *Arch Dis Child* 1987;62:830–832.
14. Senterre J, Vouer M, Putet G, Rigo J. Nitrogen, fat and mineral balance studies in preterm infants fed bank human milk, a human milk formula, or a low-birth-weight infant formula. In: Baum JD, ed. *Human milk processing, fractionation, and the nutrition of the low birth-weight baby.* Nestlé nutrition Workshop Series, vol 3. New York: Raven Press; 1983:102–111.
15. Senterre J, Rigo J. Nutritional requirements of low birthweight infants. In: Gracey M, Falkner F, eds. *Nutritional needs and assessment of normal growth.* Nestlé Nutrition Workshop Series, vol 7. New York: Raven Press; 1985:45–49.
16. Picaud JC, Putet G, Rigo J, Salle BL, Senterre J. Metabolic and energy balance in small- and appropriate-for-gestational age very low-birth-weight infants. *Acta Paediatr* 1994;[Suppl]405:54–59.
17. Rudloff S, Lonnerdal B. Solubility and digestibility of milk proteins in infant formulas exposed to different heat treatments. *J Pediatr Gastroenterol Nutr* 1992;15:25–33.
18. Hay WW. Nutritional requirements of extremely low birthweight infants. *Acta Paediatr Scand* 1994;402:94–99.

19. Lonnerdal B. Nutritional importance of non-protein nitrogen. In: Raiha NCR, ed. *Protein metabolism during infancy*. Nestlé Nutrition Workshop Series No 33. New York: Raven Press; 1994:105–120.

20. Cooke R, Watson D, Werkman S, Conner C. Effects of type of dietary protein on acid-base status, protein nutritional status, plasma levels of amino acids, and nutrient balance in the very low birth weight infant. *J Pediatr* 1992;121:444–451.

21. Donovan SM, Lönnerdal B. Non-protein nitrogen and true protein in infants formulas. *Acta Paediatr Scand* 1989;78:497–504.

22. Hanning RM, Zlotkin SH. Amino acid and protein needs of the neonate: effects of excess and deficiency. *Semin Perinatol* 1989;13:131–141.

23. Polberger S, Axelsson I, Räihä N. Amino acid concentrations in plasma and urine in very low birth weight infants fed non-protein-enriched or human milk protein-enriched human milk. *Pediatrics* 1990;86:909–915.

24. McIntosh N, Rodeck CH, Heath R. Plasma amino acids of the mid trimester human fetus. *Biol Neonate* 1984;45:218–224.

25. Atkinson SA, Hanning RM. Amino acid metabolism and requirements of the premature infant: does human milk feeding represent the gold standard? In: Atkinson SA, Lonnerdal B, eds. *Protein and non-protein nitrogen in human milk*. Boca Raton: CRC Press; 1989.

26. Rigo J. Azote et acides aminés. In: Ricour C, Ghisolfi J, Putet G, Goulet O, eds. *Traité de nutrition pédiatrique*. Paris: Maloione; 1993:852–866.

27. Rigo J, Senterre J. Significance of plasma amino acid pattern in preterm infants. *Biol Neonate* 1987;52:41–49.

28. Rigo J. Les besoins en acides aminés des prématurés alimentés par voie orale ou parentérale. Liège: University of Liège (Derouaux Ordina eds); 1991:1–181. [Thesis.]

29. Rigo J. Azote et acides aminés. In: Ricour C, Ghisolfi J, Putet G, Goulet O, eds. *Traité de nutrition pédiatrique*. Paris: Maloione; 1993:853–866.

30. Rigo J, Senterre J, Putet G, Salle B. Various human milk fortifiers in low birth weight infants fed pooled human milk: plasma and urinary amino acid concentrations. In: Koletzko B, Okken A, Rey J, Salle B, Van Biervliet JP, eds. *Recent advances in infant feeding*. Stuttgart: Georg Thieme Verlag; 1992:164–170.

31. Janas LM, Picciano MF, Hatch TF. Indices of protein metabolism in term infants fed either human milk or formulas with reduced protein concentration and various whey/casein ratios. *J Pediatr* 1987;110:838–848.

32. Kashyap S, Okamoto E, Kanaya S, *et al*. Protein quality in feeding low birth weight infants: a comparison of whey-predominant versus casein-predominant formulas. *Pediatrics* 1987;79:748–760.

33. Priolisi A, Didato M, Gioeli R, Fazzolari-Nesci A, Räihä NCR. Milk protein quality in low birth weight infants: effects of protein-fortified human milk and formulas with three different whey-to-casein ratios on growth and plasma amino acid profiles. *J Pediatr Gastroenterol Nutr* 1992;14:450–455.

34. Järvenpää A-L, Räihä NCR, Rassin DK, *et al*. Milk protein quantity and quality in the term infant. I. Metabolic responses and effects on growth. *Pediatrics* 1982;70:214–220.

35. Rassin DK, Gaull GE, Heinonen K. Milk protein quantity and quality in low birth weight infants. II. Effects on selected alphatic amino acids in plasma and urine. *Pediatrics* 1977;59:407–422.

36. Rassin DK, Gaull GE, Räihä NCR, *et al*. Milk protein quantity and quality in low birth weight infants. IV. Effects on tyrosine and phenylalanine in plasma and urine. *J Pediatr* 1977;90:356–360.

37. Rigo J, Senterre J. Metabolic balance studies and plasma amino acid concentrations in preterm infants fed experimental protein hydrolysate preterm formulas. *Acta Paediatr Suppl* 1994;405:98–104.

38. Boehm G, Cervantes H, Georgi G, *et al*. Effect of increasing dietary threonine intakes on amino acid metabolism of the central nervous system and peripheral tissues in growing rats. *Pediatr Res* 1998;44:900–906.

39. Rigo J, Nyamugabo K, Studzinski F, Senterre J. Reduction of hyperthreoninemia in preterm infant fed whey predominant formula without kappa-casein. ESPGAN, 29th annual meeting, Munich; 1996 (abst.).

40. Rigo J, Picaud JC, Lapillonne A, Salle B, Senterre J. Metabolic balance and plasma amino acid concentrations in VLBW infants fed a new acidic whey hydrolysate preterm formula. *J Pediatr Gastroenterol Nutr* 1997;24:A459 (abst.).

41. Rigo J, Senterre J. Optimal threonine intake for preterm infants fed on oral or parenteral nutrition. *J Parenter Enteral Nutr* 1980;4:15–17.

42. Gustafson JM, Dodds SJ, Burgus RC, Mercier LP. Prediction of brain and serum free amino acid profiles in rats fed graded levels of protein. *J Nutr* 1986;116:1667–1681.

43. Neu J, Roig JC, Meetze WH, *et al*. Enteral glutamine supplementation for very low birth weight infants decreases morbidity. *J Pediatr* 1997;131:692–699.

DISCUSSION

Prof. Lucas: Do you believe that there are adequate efficacy and safety data on hydrolyzed preterm formulas in general, or the one you are talking about in particular, to make their use recommendable in clinical care?

Dr. Rigo: Hydrolyzed formulas have been used in term infants for many years, and there have been many improvements in their composition. About 10 years ago, we made the first study on the nutritional efficiency of protein-hydrolyzed formula, and we found significant differences between some of the formulas on the market at that time and cow's milk-based formulas. Since then, however, there has been a great improvement in the quality of the hydrolyzed protein. There are still some differences from conventional formulas with respect to absorption and perhaps utilization of nitrogen. And there may also be components that are present in normal formulas but not in hydrolyzed formulas. We now have sufficient data on energy utilization and on calcium and phosphorus retention, but data on zinc and trace element accretion with hydrolyzed formulas are still insufficient. Although the quality of hydrolyzed formulas has improved, we need further nutritional studies.

Prof. Haschke: I would extend that question. Are sufficient safety data available for the presently used nonhydrolysate premature infant formulas? The long-term outcome data presently available are for premature formulas that are no longer on the market and are completely outdated. We know nothing about the long-term outcome of premature formulas that are on the market at present. In clinical practice both the hydrolysates and the nonhydrolysates are well tolerated, but we have not studied them with an adequate sample size as in pharmaceutical trials.

Dr. Rigo: There are still some differences between hydrolysate and nonhydrolysate premature infant formulas that request evaluation. The difficulties are illustrated in relation to the threonine concentration. We know that with previous whey hydrolysate formulas the threonine concentration was quite high. We had two possibilities: one was for the industry to change the composition of the formula by using acidic whey, which decreased the threonine concentration; the other issue was to carry out large developmental studies to determine the effect of a high threonine concentration. The work involved for developmental studies would be more extensive than decreasing the threonine concentration by using acidic whey.

Dr. Atkinson: In support of hydrolysate formulas for premature infants, you suggested first, improved digestibility over whole protein, though your data do not support that; second, prevention of allergy, and I wonder if you have any data showing that there is less allergy in premature infants fed on hydrolysates; and third, improved gastric motility, and again do you have any data to support that? You also said that the acidic processing of whey reduces the threonine content. Do you really feel that the level of threonine in standard whey-predominant formulas is potentially toxic?

Dr. Rigo: Protein digestibility was a little lower than for whole protein because the absorption rate was significantly different. Regarding atopic disease, there are data from Lucas suggesting that premature infants may develop atopy, but we have no follow-up data in preterm infants fed protein hydrolysate to evaluate the efficacy of whey hydrolysate protein in preventing atopic disease. Regarding gastric emptying, there is some evidence that it is more rapid with protein hydrolysate than with whole protein.

In relation to your question about threonine, there are no current data suggesting that threonine could be toxic during development. However, with whey protein hydrolysate formulas we are reaching levels not previously attained with whey-predominant formulas, and we know that there is a close relation between the threonine concentration in plasma and in brain. Thus there is a need for caution and follow-up studies.

Prof. Lucas: Our data on allergy are being misused in the context of hydrolyzed formula. We showed that it was only subjects with a positive family history of allergy who benefited from exclusion of cow's milk protein. The majority of infants with a negative family history probably benefit from being given whole protein. My other point is that we've had much experience with using whole-protein formulas but very little experience with using hydrolyzed formulas, in terms of clinical trial testing. From everything I've heard, it would seem that the use of these formulas should be regarded as theoretical and experimental (but see discussion of Ziegler's Chapter 16—ED).

Dr. Atkinson: I have another point I would like your opinion on. Traditionally, one purpose of hydrolysate formulas was to rest the gut in case of gastrointestinal problems. Do you think that the preterm infant's gut needs rest? Or maybe by giving them a hydrolysate are we doing harm by suppressing the induction of proteases?

Dr. Rigo: Such formulas have been used for quite a long time now without apparent ill effects on the gut, but I don't have the data to give you a complete answer on the effect on protease activity.

Dr. Guesry: I can give some partial answers to Dr. Atkinson's questions. With regard to the toxicity of threonine, we have no human studies, but there are animal studies that have been published [1] and show that baby rats with up to four times the normal level of threonine in the brain are perfectly normal in their behavior after 3 months. So there is no observable change in the behavior of rats submitted to high threonine levels. Your question about resting the intestine of the premature baby by giving hydrolyzed protein was also investigated in an animal experiment. We did studies in minipigs and showed that you don't rest the intestinal enzymes when you feed hydrolyzed protein—trypsin, chymotrypsin, all the pancreatic enzymes and intestinal enzymes were normal.

Prof. Moro: Does the acidic methodology influence other amino acids apart from threonine?

Dr. Rigo: The only significant difference was a small reduction in valine concentration. All the other amino acids were similar in the two groups.

Prof. Pohlandt: I would like to address the question of absorption and the derived values of efficiency. I think your data are based on nitrogen retention, but you didn't mention whether you had taken into account the different urea concentrations in human milk and formula. You tried to explain the surprisingly low absorption rate of human milk protein by the presence of immunoglobulins, but quantitatively the immunoglobulins are less important than urea. Urea accounts for about 25% of the nitrogen in breast milk but only 15% in commercially available formulas on the European market. I think this 10% difference in urea nitrogen could easily explain the apparently lower protein absorption from human milk.

Dr. Rigo: I disagree. Urea is very well absorbed. The difference in absorption must be due to a protein component of human milk that are not digested like immunoglobulins, transferrin, and so on. Urea is not well utilized, but 95% is absorbed, and some goes directly into the urine. Urea does not interfere with absorption rate but it does influence significantly the utilization rate and therefore the nitrogen balance.

Prof. Pohlandt: But you haven't taken it into account in the efficiency calculation.

Dr. Rigo: I showed you the global efficiency—that is, the ratio between nitrogen retention and nitrogen absorption. I explained that one of the differences between formula and human milk was the higher urea content of human milk, which is well absorbed but not well utilized, so it decreases the apparent efficiency of human milk.

Dr. Walker: Why were whey predominant formulas 2 and 3 so much more efficient than formula 1 with respect to absorption and retention?

Dr. Rigo: WPF1 was a very old formula that was used before 1980, and it had reduced energy content. The fat blend was also completely different, and we showed that the fat absorption was sometimes very low. So the metabolizable energy available with formula 1 was relatively poor. In addition, nitrogen content was also relatively high. There was no significant difference in protein absorption, but utilization is a function of the energy available.

Dr. Walker: Several years ago, it was suggested that certain amino acids are essential in premature infants that are not essential in term infants. Is this taken into consideration when providing nitrogen for the premature infant?

Dr. Rigo: I think the essential amino acids for the preterm infant are the same as for the term infant. The formula used by Räihä 20 years ago is completely different from the formulas we have now. There was a big difference in the protein content and also in the fat blend. There was also a higher phosphorus content. The amino acid content of the old formulas was not well balanced, and they were low in cysteine and taurine. Current formulas are much better balanced and are adequate in terms of their amino acid content.

Prof. Heird: As valuable as those earlier studies by Räihä, Gaull, and coworkers were at the time, they have one major problem: the mineral and particularly the sodium, potassium, and phosphorus contents of those formulas were the same, and also the same as in human milk. So our calculations lead us to the conclusion that there is no way that the higher protein intake could in fact have been retained. In fact, 2.25 g/kg·d was about the maximum that could have been retained, and that obviously is important in terms of this whole issue of the utilization of protein intake.

Prof. Koletzko: You referred to the disadvantages of heat-treated liquid formulas and implied that the Maillard reaction was a possible explanation. Do you believe we should not use heat-treated liquid formula, or is there a way to avoid the protein damage?

Dr. Rigo: We need to consider heat treatment not only in terms of protein absorption, but also in terms of amino acid bioavailability. There is certainly some reduction in amino acid bioavailability with heat treatment, and we need to bear that in mind. But the overall protein efficiency of the liquid formula was similar to the powdered formula, and the only difference we found was in absorption. Plasma amino acid concentrations were also similar to powdered formula; there were slight differences, but the profile was exactly the same.

Prof. Moro: If I understood correctly, your group of babies receiving fortified human milk was a mixture of those receiving supplementary human protein and those receiving supplementary bovine protein. I don't think you can make valid comparisons with such a composite group. You should separate babies receiving only human milk protein from the babies receiving human milk protein plus protein deriving from the fortifier.

Dr. Rigo: I agree with you, we could have split this group into two, but then I would also have had to present comparisons of seven groups, and since there was not a large difference between the two fortified human milk groups, I preferred to combine them. Also in the group fed cow milk human milk fortifier, the range of nitrogen intake would be smaller than in those fed human milk alone and with addition of human milk protein.

Prof. Wu: Several studies support the use of human milk. I think it would be better to use preterm human milk. Preterm milk has a higher content of total nitrogen, protein nitrogen, sodium, calcium, magnesium, zinc, copper, iron, as well as IgA and other protective factors.

Dr. Rigo: Most of the time we try to use own mother's milk, but if we don't have it, we also use banked human milk for feeding preterm infants. It may be difficult to obtain sufficient preterm mothers' milk.

Prof. Endres: A group in Berlin has shown that formulas containing hydrolyzed protein do not contain IGF-1. There have been few reports on this, but one study claimed that the endogenous production of IGF-1 was sufficient in premature babies. Do you have a definitive answer to this question?

Dr. Rigo: I have no complete answer to that question and the exact role of IGF-1 in the gastrointestinal tract is not known. This is something that probably needs studying.

Dr. Filho: You mentioned the use of glutamine as a supplement for preterm formulas. Do you have any further information on this?

Dr. Rigo: There are some data showing a reduction in sepsis in the preterm infant given supplementary glutamine [2]. However, there are serious technical difficulties because glutamine is very unstable. More work needs to be done.

REFERENCES

1. Castagne V, Maire JC, Moennoz D, Gyger M. Effect of threonine on the behavioural development of the rat. *Pharmacology Biochemistry and Behaviour* 1995;52(2):281–289.
2. Neu J, Roig JC, Meetze WH, *et al.* Enteral glutamine supplementation for very low birth weight infants decreases morbidity. *J Pediatr* 1997;131: 691–699.

Nutrition of the Very Low Birthweight Infant, edited by
Ekhard E. Ziegler, Alan Lucas, Guido E. Moro.
Nestlé Nutrition Workshop Series, Paediatric Programme, Vol. 43,
Nestec Ltd., Vevey/Lippincott Williams & Wilkins
Philadelphia, Pennsylvania © 1999.

Protein Requirement of the Extremely Low-Birthweight Preterm Infant

Jean-Léopold Micheli, Claire-Lise Fawer, and Yves Schutz

Division of Neonatology and Institute for Clinical Physiology, CHUV University Hospital, Lausanne, Switzerland

CLINICAL OBJECTIVES: WHAT ARE THE OUTCOME PRIORITIES?

In most neonatal units, the number of extremely immature infants has increased considerably over the last 15 years. Their mortality and morbidity have decreased, and more attention has been paid to their nutritional needs.

There is continuity between intrauterine and postnatal life for all processes related to growth, including protein metabolism. During the last two decades, the development of bedside investigative methods has provided new insight into the processes of whole-body protein accretion in the mother during pregnancy, in the fetus, and in the preterm infant. However, the major difficulty in evaluating the protein needs of the extremely low-birthweight (ELBW; <1,000 g birthweight) preterm infant is the lack of a generally accepted goal for feeding such infants.

For practical purposes the goals chosen here for the most appropriate protein supply for the ELBW infant are:

1. to achieve a protein gain that approximates the *in utero* protein gain of a normal fetus of the same postconceptional age (Fig. 1); and
2. to achieve long-term linear growth and psychomotor development close to the physiological ranges for normal term infants of the same corrected (postconceptional) age.

By combining the information given by the factorial, metabolic, and neurodevelopmental approaches, a range of advisable enteral and parenteral intakes can be defined. During the transitional early postnatal period, when a combination of enteral and parenteral nutrition is needed. Protein is increased in daily increments from 0.5 to 3.6 to 3.8 g/kg·d during the first 14 days. Similarly, the energy supply increases from 35 to 130 kcal/kg·d over the same period (Fig. 2). The time course of the enteral protein energy supply often has to be lengthened according to the clinical situation. Once full enteral feeding is achieved, most ELBW infants have growth rates similar to the intrauterine values.

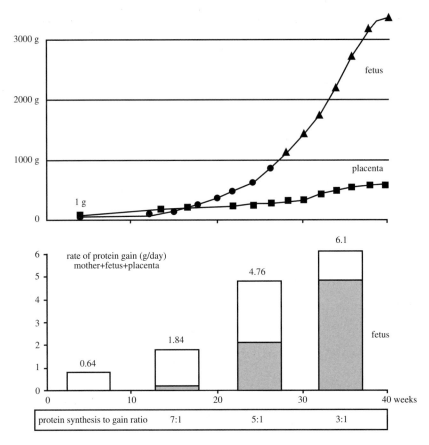

FIG. 1. Overview of weight gain of the fetus and placenta during gestation. The protein gain of the fetus (*shaded area*) is compared with the total rate of protein gain (mother + fetus + placenta). The ratio of protein synthesis to gain decreases during gestation, reflecting the fact that less protein needs to be synthesized for every gram of protein gained. Thus protein turnover seems to cycle on a less futile mode at the end of gestation. (Adapted from refs. 31, 38, and 39.)

INTRAUTERINE AND POSTNATAL GROWTH

We have no better model for growing ELBW and VLBW (very low birthweight; <1,500 g birthweight) preterm infants than the growing fetus of the same gestational age. Thus it is important to look at fetal growth curves and at the evolution of fetal whole-body composition during gestation before going into more detail about the physiological aspects of amino acid and protein metabolism. Data on the "average" fetus, obtained previously from infants born at different gestational ages, have been greatly improved over the last 15 years by serial ultrasonographic measurements during normal pregnancies. More recently, data on fetal and postnatal protein content and accretion have reached a sufficient degree of reliability and can be used at the bedside to plan the nutritional management of an extremely low-birthweight preterm infant.

Figure 3 shows the continuity between intrauterine and extrauterine growth for body length, body weight, and body content of lean mass and fat. It is apparent that for the period between 24 and 28 weeks, growth rates are extremely high (~2.5% and 1.5% per day, for weight and length gain, respectively). This growth reflects the increase in lean mass, with daily protein gains of 2.1 to 2.2 g/kg·d. The corresponding transplacental amino acid and glucose uptakes are, respectively, 3 to 3.5 g/kg·d and 7 to 10 g/kg·d.

Thus by giving intravenous amino acids as soon as possible after birth to ELBW infants, an attempt is made to minimize the effects of an acute withdrawal of amino acid supply at the postconceptional age of maximum protein gain.

BODY COMPOSITION

Measurements of body composition in preterm infants are of major importance and represent the basis for the estimation of protein needs. The total protein content of a 26-week-old fetus weighing 900 g must increase by about fivefold to reach the values observed in a term infant of 3,500 g. There is a concomitant increase in serum protein concentration and a decrease in the hydration of lean tissue from 86% at 26 weeks to 80% at term (1–3).

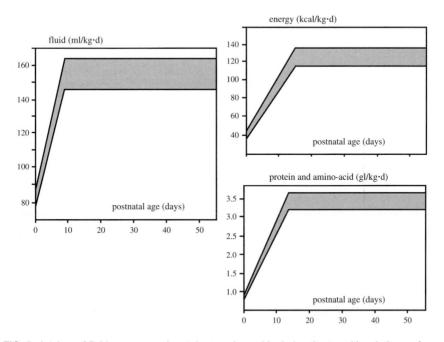

FIG. 2. Intakes of fluid, energy, and protein + amino acids during the transitional phase of extrauterine life. This figure applies to "healthy" extremely low-birthweight (ELBW) infants. (Adapted from refs. 40 and 41.)

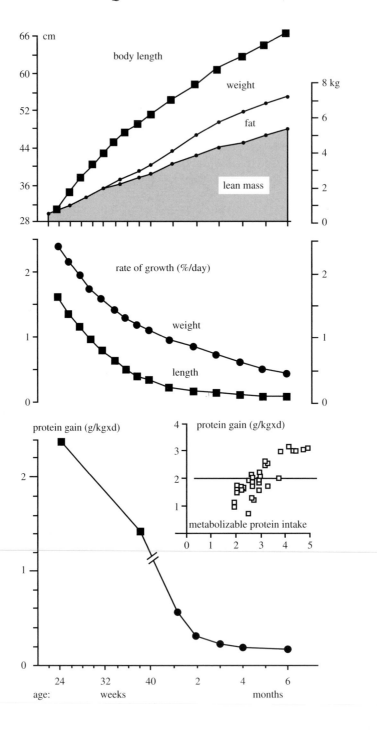

Measurements of the fetal body composition at sequential gestational ages have been published by Widdowson (1,2) and by Ziegler (3), whereas Fomon *et al.* (4) have compiled normative data on body composition for the term baby, from birth up to 10 years. Figure 3 shows the pattern of change in lean body mass and fat during growth. Lean mass is a heterogeneous compartment, composed essentially of water, protein, glycogen, and minerals. The protein content of the lean body mass increases with gestational age (1,3). It is apparent that there is a rapid growth of fat-free weight and fat weight during the intrauterine period. At 22 weeks the fetus is approximately 99% lean mass and 1% fat, compared with 86% and 14% at 40 weeks, respectively (see Fig. 3).

PHYSIOLOGY

Protein Gain to Protein Intake Relation

The simplest physiological issue related to protein metabolism and growth is the proportion of the daily protein intake incorporated into the lean tissues (protein gain). This can be determined by the nitrogen balance technique. Nitrogen balance is the difference between nitrogen intake and nitrogen excretion. In spite of several potential sources of variability (5–7), the results of several studies are in good agreement (see Fig. 3). This method is the one most extensively used for studying protein metabolism *in vivo*, even in very preterm infants (5–13).

Once nitrogen balance has been calculated (N), the protein gain can be obtained using the factor of gram $N \times 6.25$ = grams of protein.

The mean values of various neonatal studies relating protein gain to intake are shown in Fig. 3. The daily protein gain increases linearly with protein intake in the range between ~2 and ~4 g protein/kg·day. Above this level it appears that the effect on protein gain is diminished. It should be noted, however, that newborn infants receiving the highest protein intakes had altered plasma aminograms (10,11). Thus even if it were possible to achieve further protein gain with a diet providing more than 4 g protein/kg·day, this would be undesirable because of the deleterious metabolic consequences.

Coefficient of Protein Utilization

The relation between protein intake and protein gain gives an index of the efficiency whereby metabolizable protein intake can be channeled to tissue growth. This is sometimes called the *coefficient of protein utilization* or the *efficiency of protein gain*

FIG. 3. Continuity between intrauterine and extrauterine growth for body length, body weight, and body contents of lean mass and fat. It is apparent that for the period between 24 and 28 weeks, growth rates are extremely high (~2.5% and 1.5% per day, for weight and length gain, respectively). This growth reflects the increase in lean mass, with daily protein gains of 2.1 to 2.2 g/kg·day. The corresponding transplacental amino acid uptake is 3 to 3.5 g/kg·day. *Bottom inset:* Protein gain is linearly related to protein intake over a range of protein intakes extending from 2 to 4 g/kg·day. (Adapted from refs. 38 and 40.)

(ratio of protein gain to intake). Many factors are known to affect protein utilization, and these can be divided as follows:

- *Nutritional factors*—that is, the biological value of protein ingested, the energy-to-protein ratio, and the nutritional status (6,7).
- *Physiological factors*—for example, individual variations, catch-up growth in small-for-gestational-age infants (14–16).
- *Endocrine factors,* including insulin-like growth factors and others.
- *Pathological factors*—for example, sepsis and other disease states.

In "healthy" preterm infants, the efficiency of protein gain has been fairly well established at a mean value of 0.7 (70%). The mean (±SD) of the published values is 0.72 ± 0.08 for 331 infants ranging between 26 and 35 weeks of gestational age. This means that 70% of the absorbed amino acids are laid down as protein in the tissues and that the remaining 30% are oxidized and excreted. It is of interest that, according to these studies, the coefficient seems to be independent of gestational age.

Since the synthesis of protein molecules entails a considerable amount of energy, the protein–energy interaction and the *in vivo* contribution of protein gain to the energy expenditure during rapid growth both need brief discussion.

PROTEIN–ENERGY INTERACTION

Protein gain is related not only to protein intake, but also to energy intake (6,7,12,13,17–19). Therefore rapid growth is a situation in which protein-energy interrelations are of special relevance. One cannot consider the effects of protein intake and energy intake on protein gain independently of each other. Protein and energy are supplied concurrently, and it is likely that there is an optimal range of protein and energy intakes for each newborn infant. If this optimum is not achieved, the following consequences are observed:

- When energy intake is deficient, endogenous protein is used as an energy source and the nitrogen balance becomes negative.
- When energy intake reaches a suboptimal level (metabolizable energy ~50 to 90 kcal/kg·d), the newborn infant is in a very sensitive range of protein energy interaction. An increase in either the energy intake or the protein intake will result in an increase in nitrogen retention (Fig. 4). Similarly, if protein intake is suboptimal, then increasing the energy intake will spare protein for lean tissue gain. Situations of suboptimal protein energy supply are frequently met, both in ELBW infants during the postnatal transitional period and in other neonatal intensive-care situations, and have been repeatedly investigated (6,7).
- If there is a surfeit of energy for a given protein intake, the protein gain plateaus and there is no further positive effect of increasing energy intake.

By combining parenteral and enteral feeding, it is possible to maintain a positive protein gain during the transitional phase of extrauterine adaptation.

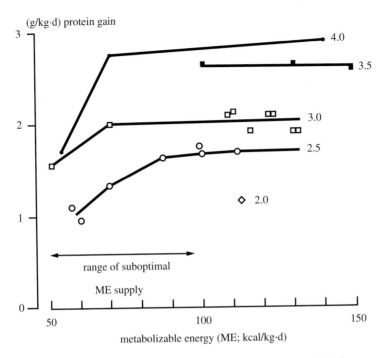

FIG. 4. Effect of increasing energy intake on protein gain at different protein intakes grouped into five categories: 2.0 (◇), 2.5 (○), 3 (□), 3.5 (■), and 4 (●) g/kg·d. Each symbol represents the mean value of a group of newborns. In the range of "suboptimal metabolizable energy supply" (50 to 90 kcal/kg·d), protein gain can be improved by increasing energy intakes, whereas above 100 kcal/kg·d there is no further positive effect on protein gain. (Adapted from refs. 7, 8, 12, 14, 18, 19, 21 25, 38, and 40.)

Metabolic Cost of Protein Gain

The energy required for protein deposition can be partitioned into the "energy content" of the gained protein (also called retained or stored energy; 4 kcal/g protein) and the extra "energy expenditure" (20) associated with the formation of new protein (called the metabolic cost of protein gain). The latter can be estimated either at the bedside, by correlating the results of nitrogen balance to measurements of energy expenditure, or theoretically on the basis of the energy equivalent of ATP.

In vivo studies have shown a linear relation between energy expenditure and protein gain. From the slope of the regression line one can infer that the metabolic cost of protein gain is approximately 10 kcal/g gain (20–23). A theoretical approach can also be used to estimate the cost of protein gain in a growing baby (20). The incorporation of 1 mole of amino acids into protein requires 6 mole of ATP. If one takes an average value of 18 kcal energy released per mole ATP, 108 kcal (6 × 18) are needed to incorporate 1 mole of amino acids into protein. Assuming that 1 mole of an average amino acid is about 110 g, the theoretical cost of protein gain is approximately 1 kcal/g.

The discrepancy between this result (1 kcal/g) and the *in vivo* data obtained at the bedside ($\sim$10 kcal/g) is striking and prompts us to re-examine the theoretical cost of protein gain. The theoretical approach makes the incorrect assumption that protein gain during growth is equal to the amount of protein synthesized. It is therefore called a *static approach.* The difference between the *in vivo* measurements and the theoretical calculations can be explained by the dynamics of protein turnover, where protein gain results from the difference between protein synthesis and breakdown, and each gram of protein gain needs five to six times more protein to be synthesized.

PROTEIN TURNOVER AND ITS CLINICAL RELEVANCE

Stable Isotope Techniques and Protein Turnover

The dynamic aspects of protein metabolism have been studied by using nonradioactive, stable 15-N or 13-C labeled amino acids as biological markers (5,8,14,24). Whole-body protein synthesis and protein breakdown in very low-birthweight preterm infants reared on human milk, reared on milk formulas, or given total parenteral nutrition were found to be increased when compared with older infants (8,20). Since the formation of peptide bonds has a high energy cost, it is of interest to determine the rate of protein synthesis and the rate of energy expenditure simultaneously. The validity of the methods used metabolism of stable isotopes, and indirect calorimetry is generally well accepted (5,20). A stable isotope enrichment technique for the *in vivo* assessment of protein turnover can be summarized in the following example.

Constant doses of 15-N glycine are added to each feed given to a preterm infant. Since this technique requires repeated feeding at short, regular intervals, preterm infants who are typically fed every 3 hours by intragastric tube represent an ideal situation for such measurements. Soon after the beginning of the experiment, the infant's urinary excretion of 15-N urea increases. Within 48 to 60 hours the enrichment of 15-N in urinary urea appears to have reached a plateau. This plateau allows the computation of the nitrogen flux through the amino acid pool as well as the rates of protein synthesis and protein breakdown (24).

Ratio of Protein Synthesis to Protein Gain

The preterm baby has a rate of protein synthesis that greatly exceeds that necessary for net protein gain (10 g protein/kg·d for synthesis *versus* 2 g protein/kg·d for gain). Energetically, the excess protein synthesis would appear to be a wasteful mechanism. However, it has been suggested that this "futile cycling" can also be considered from the evolutionary point of view as a positive adaptation. For example, in cases of suboptimal supply of protein and energy, the protein gain decreases while protein synthesis and breakdown decrease in parallel, with a concomitant reduction in energy needs (20). This dynamic mechanism of protein turnover may also be viewed as a physiological phenomenon allowing fast remodeling of body protein during rapid growth.

Cellular and Molecular Aspects

All *in vivo* tracer studies of whole protein metabolism support the conclusion that the more rapid the expected growth and expected protein gain, the higher the rates of protein synthesis and breakdown. This means that the net intracellular production of protein must be adjusted with a high sensitivity through regulated changes in the rates of protein synthesis and breakdown.

The key genes regulating protein breakdown have been cloned. Thus there is hope that information will be provided relatively soon at the molecular level to answer a series of clinical questions regarding situations of growth and nongrowth, as well as metabolic responses of "sick" neonates to stress (8,14,24–26).

Endocrinological Aspects

Insulin and insulin-like growth factors appear to be the major hormones regulating fetal growth. During intrauterine life and during early postnatal life in very preterm infants, the secretion of insulin depends on the plasma concentration of certain amino acids (e.g., arginine and leucine) as much as, or perhaps more than, on the concentration of glucose (27). Thus a shortage of supply in these and perhaps other amino acids not only limits protein metabolism but also, through a reduction in insulin and insulin-like growth factors, directly limits glucose transport and energy metabolism.

A particularly interesting group of proteins with a high turnover rate is the family of glucose transporters. Their molecular physiology and regulation have recently been fairly well established. Briefly, a shortage in amino acid can rapidly have the following effects:

• Reduce insulin and insulin-like growth factors.
• Downregulate glucose transporters at the cell membrane level.
• Result in intracellular energy failure.

By giving intravenous amino acids as soon as possible after birth a step is taken toward preventing downregulation of glucose transporters, hyperglycemia, hyperkalemia, and intracellular energy failure.

FACTORS AFFECTING PROTEIN TURNOVER

Postconceptional Age

A significant inverse relation was observed between postconceptional age and the ratio of protein synthesis to gain; thus the more immature the infant, the higher the rate of protein turnover (14). This relation is also apparent in the interstudy comparison effect of gestational age (Fig. 5). Similar studies of animal fetuses show that the rate of protein synthesis per unit body weight decreases throughout gestation. It appears that besides energy and protein intakes, postconceptional (or postmenstrual) age plays a major role in the regulation of whole-body protein metabolism. This age-

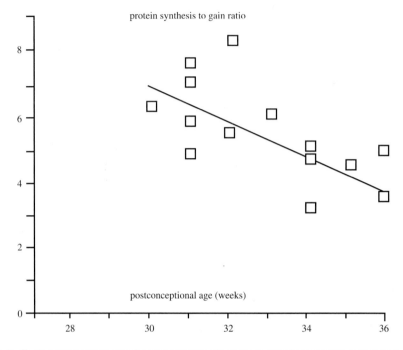

FIG. 5. Each symbol represents the mean results of protein-synthesis-to-protein-gain ratio in appropriate-for-gestation (AGA) premature infants, obtained by using 15–N glycine as tracer and 15–N urea as end product. The ratio of protein synthesis to protein gain decreases with postconceptional age. As the same trend can be observed *in utero* (see Fig. 1), it is reasonable to assume that very immature infants (<28 weeks) have very high protein turnover rates, need to synthesize (and break down) much more protein than needed for their gain, and thus have a high metabolic cost of growth. (Adapted from refs. 38–40.)

related effect may influence the optimal percentage of protein energy to be given to very immature infants below 27 weeks of gestation.

Nutritional Status

It has been observed that the protein turnover, synthesis, and breakdown rates are higher during catch-up growth in infants born small for gestational age than in normally grown infants of the same gestation. These observations are consistent with the studies on the rate of protein turnover in malnourished infants during and after the completion of refeeding.

On the other hand, when the protein turnover of a group of small-for-gestational-age infants was compared with that of a group of identically fed preterm infants of the same birthweight, the former had the lower values and the better protein-synthesis-to-gain ratio. This may explain why small-for-gestational-age infants have a faster rate of postnatal growth than identically fed, normally grown preterm infants (14,25).

Route of Feeding

Amniotic fluid is swallowed throughout most of gestation. It is therefore unphysiological to completely deprive an ELBW preterm infant of enteral feeding, since this deprivation would never normally occur *in utero*. The problems linked to enteral feeding in very immature infants have been thoroughly reviewed (28–37). Large gastric aspirates and abdominal distention are common, leading to frequent interruptions or decreases in enteral feeds. Thus several days may pass during which the nutrient intake is grossly deficient, with the risk of a further reduction in gut function.

It has been well established in experimental animals that the growth of the intestinal tract in the neonate is dependent on enteral feeding. Infants who are fed intravenously have changes in their gut hormones and significantly lower protein turnover rates in the intestinal tract. It appears that this lower turnover is probably linked to differences in visceral protein metabolism and gut hormones (38–40). For these reasons it makes biological sense to try to avoid a complete interruption in enteral feeding and to give small, subnutritional feeds, since these should stimulate gut development. The concept of "minimal enteral feeding" has been coined by Lucas (41). Indeed, it has been proven successful, because it dissociates the nutritional from the nonnutritional or subnutritional effects of enteral feeding. Minimal enteral feeding may stimulate insulin release and decrease glucose intolerance, which is a significant problem in extremely low-birthweight preterm infants.

The primary purpose of making an early start to enteral feeding would not be to achieve complete enteral feeding as soon as possible, but to initiate the postnatal adaptive events in the gut and intermediary metabolism at an "unphysiological" time of development (41).

CLINICAL ASPECTS

Hyperglycemia

Hyperglycemia is a common problem in very low-birthweight preterm infants with reported incidences as high as 20% to 86%, particularly during the first few days of life. It is often associated with nonoliguric hyperkalemia. The risks linked to this problem are partly the result of hyperosmolality, glucosuria, and dehydration; the major risks, however, are intracellular energy failure and Na^+/K^+-ATPase deficiency (41,42).

Classically, high glucose concentrations in neonates are attributed to both increased secretion of hormones with counterregulatory effects on hypoglycemia (catecholamines, glucagon, and, longer term, cortisol) and diminished end organ sensitivity to insulin. This does not apply to very preterm infants, as they have low catecholamine secretion rates and respond normally to exogenous insulin (41).

The cause appears to be reduced insulin secretion in response to glucose, characteristic of extreme immaturity, and reduced insulin secretion in response to a fall in the plasma concentration of those circulating amino acids responsible for stimulating insulin (arginine and leucine, for example). Giving amino acids as soon as possible after birth stimulates endogenous insulin secretion and can prevent to a certain extent the need for intravenous insulin infusions.

Potential Toxicity of Protein and Amino Acid Linked to Biochemical Immaturity of the Preterm Infant

Premature infants have incomplete development of several amino acid metabolic pathways. This biochemical immaturity substantially narrows the margin between an adequate protein intake and the possible adverse effects of deficiency or excess. Many of the amino acids previously thought to be nonessential may be essential for the immature organism and must be supplied by the diet (e.g., taurine and glycine). Incomplete amino acid catabolism, in case of an excessive protein intake, may result in increased concentrations of amino acids, hydrogen ion, and ammonia (12). It is still a matter of discussion whether these metabolic changes are harmful or benign; indeed, similar values have been found in fetal blood at fetoscopy and from the umbilical cord at birth (26,31,38,40).

At least three different gold standards have been proposed for assessing plasma amino acid responses to feeding in the prematurely born infant: the amino acid concentrations of mid-trimester fetal blood, the concentrations in rapidly growing preterm infants receiving their own mother's milk, and the concentrations in healthy breastfed term infants. In general, the blood amino acid levels of preterm infants fed either preterm milk or protein-enriched human milk fall within the broad range of plasma amino acids reported for breastfed term infants (26,38,40).

METHODS FOR DETERMINING IF THE PROTEIN NEEDS OF ELBW INFANTS ARE MET

Weight gain is a fundamental expression of growth, and although it is nonspecific and provides no information on changes in body composition, it remains the cornerstone of growth assessment. Length gain is less susceptible to the confounding effects of changing body composition and should be a better estimate of gain in lean body mass. However, the practical limitation is that measurements of length, unless they are taken over long observation periods, are difficult to perform reproducibly (40).

More specific indicators of the adequacy of protein intake include serum concentrations of albumin, total protein, prealbumin, and retinol binding protein (5). The usefulness of these serum biochemical indices is severely limited by the difficulties in interpretation. Severe deficiencies are easily classified as abnormal, but borderline values are not (40). Serum and urine urea concentrations, however, have proved to be of real clinical interest. Inadequate or excessive protein intakes can be detected by measurement of urea concentrations in serum or urine. The latter obviates blood sampling.

The physiological approach appears to be the most logical at present: an adequate protein intake results in rates of weight gain and protein gain approximating *in utero* growth. Protein intake must be considered in conjunction with energy intake since the energetic cost of growth is mainly dependent upon protein metabolism. To illustrate this point, 10 metabolic studies were selected on the basis that the rates of protein gain measured in these studies were very similar to intrauterine values (38,40). Interestingly, this effect was obtained in a relatively narrow range of protein and energy intakes, and served as a basis for guidelines (38,40).

However, the weight gains of the infants studied, as well as the composition of their weight gains, were different, as evidenced by various energy densities (retained energy/unit weight). The highest energy and the lowest protein intakes led to the greatest fat deposition. The highest protein and lowest energy intakes had the opposite effect (38,40).

A comparison between the results of the previously mentioned studies (41–43) and the estimated values of the American Academy of Pediatrics (44) strongly emphasizes the fact that "healthy" low-birthweight infants can accommodate various levels of protein intake, provided the energy intake is not limiting.

The amino acid profile in plasma and the coefficient of protein utilization can help assess the type of protein most suitable for growth. Premature infants fed whey/casein protein ratios of 60/40 (similar to that of breast milk) have reasonably well-balanced plasma amino acids (40) and have a coefficient of protein utilization (protein gain/intake) of 0.7, as shown in the median part of Fig. 3. Higher proportions of casein cannot be handled with the same efficiency, as evidenced by the development of metabolic acidosis and higher plasma tyrosine and phenylalanine concentrations reported with 18/82 whey/casein ratio formulas.

The major proteins supplied in enteral nutrition to preterm infants are derived either from human milk (70% human whey, 30% human casein) or from bovine milk (60% or 18% bovine whey and 40% or 82% bovine casein). Bovine casein proteins are particularly rich in phenylalanine and tyrosine, so infants fed formulas in which bovine casein predominates typically have higher concentrations of plasma phenylalanine and tyrosine than infants fed formulas with a predominance of bovine whey or infants fed human milk. Bovine whey proteins are very rich in threonine, in contrast to bovine casein proteins or human milk whey proteins. Infants fed bovine whey protein–predominant formulas have increased plasma threonine concentrations over those fed either bovine casein protein–predominant formulas or human milk (28,31,38). At present, it is difficult to know the implications of this for protein metabolism in preterm infants, particularly ELBW infants.

AVAILABLE FOODS AND RECOMMENDATION FOR THE STABLE GROWING PERIOD

Recommendations for intakes during the stable growth period are given in Tables 1 and 2.

Human Milk

The protein content of mature human milk is about 1.2 g/dl (1.8 g/100 kcal) when expressed as total nitrogen $\times$ 6.25; about 25% of the total nitrogen is nonprotein nitro-

TABLE 1. *Recommendations for the stable growing period*

	g protein/kg·d	
American guidelines (1985)		
Gestational age (weeks)	26–28	29–31
Body weight (g)	800–1200	1200–1800
Advisable intake	4.0	3.5
European guidelines (1987)		
Gestational age (weeks)	28–32	
Body weight (g)	1001–1800	
	upper limit	lower limit
Advisable intake	3.6	2.9
International guidelines (Tsang, Lucas, Uauy, Zlotkin 1993)		
Gestational age (weeks)	≤27	28–34
Body weight (g)	≤1000	1000–1750
Gross intake (= advisable intake)	3.8–3.6	3.6–3.0

gen. Not all human milk proteins are fully absorbed from the gut, and thus the nutritionally available protein may be less than expected (11,37,42). Colostrum (milk produced in the first 5 days postpartum) contains 2.3 g protein/dl, and transitional human milk (6 to 10 days postpartum) contains 1.6 g protein/dl. It has been reported that the milk of women delivering prematurely contains approximately 20% more nitrogen than the milk of mothers delivering at term. However, the higher nitrogen content decreases rapidly postnatally, and after the first 14 days there is no, or only a minimal, difference between preterm and term milk. The whey proteins represent more than 70% of the total proteins in human milk (28). Unfortified human milk from milk banks is usually inadequate in protein content for VLBW preterm infants, and its use may result in growth failure and other long-term handicaps (29). Banked milk can be used successfully when enriched with human milk protein or with bovine milk preparations (38,40,41).

Cow's Milk–Based Formula

Formulas designed for VLBW infants have a higher protein content (1.8 to 2.4 g/dl) and a higher energy density (75 to 85 kcal/dl) than the formulas generally used for term infants. They provide about 2.8 to 3.2 g protein/100 kcal.

Own Mother's Milk

A daily intake of about 250 ml/kg of banked human milk (containing 1.2 g protein/dl) would be necessary to provide a protein intake of 3.0 g/kg·d in a preterm infant, but such high intakes are not commonly used. Intakes of 185 to 200 ml/kg·day of own mother's fresh milk are not unusual in moderately low-birthweight preterm infants (around 1,500 g) but are very unusual in ELBW infants. They may be considered an

TABLE 2. Practical application: protein and fluid supply during the transitional period of the first postnatal days. ELBW <1000 g, <27 weeks. All these figures have to be modified according to individual needs

Postnatal days	1	2	3	4	5	6	7	8	9	10	11	12	13	14	15	16
Total fluids (ml/kg)	80	100	120	140	160	160	160	160	160	160	160	160	160	160		
Enteral feeding (ml/kg) Preterm formula or Enriched mother's milk	—	10	20	30	40	50	60	70	80	90	100	120	140	160		
Enteral protein (g/kg)	—	0.25	0.5	0.75	1.0	1.2	1.4	1.7	1.9	2.2	2.4	2.9	3.4	3.8		
Parenteral fluids (ml/kg)	80	90	100	110	120	110	100	90	80	70	60	40	20	stop		
Amino acid (g/kg)	0.5	0.75	1.0	1.25	1.5	1.5	1.5	1.5	1.5	1.5	1.2	1.0	0.5	—		
Total protein + a. acid enteral + parenteral (g/kg)	0.5	1.0	1.5	2.0	2.5	2.7	2.9	3.2	3.4	3.4	3.4	3.4	3.4	3.8		

Modify intakes if:
Unexplained metabolic acidosis (check ammonia, reduce protein intake, investigate metabolism)
Weight loss >10% of birthweight : increase fluids, watch glucosuria.
Infant on a ventilator (fluid reduction around 20 ml/kg)
Weight gain during the first 3–4 postnatal days (fluid reduction around 20 ml/kg)
As long as body weight < birthweight take the latter as reference for calculations
Preterm formula   2.4 g protein/dl; 85 kcal/dl; 2.8 g protein/100 kcal
Enriched mother's milk   2.1 g protein/dl; 85 kcal/dl; 2.45 g protein 100 kcal
(approximative values)

"ideal" intake. The amino acid profile of such infants has been proposed as the gold standard. However, when own mother's milk is not available in such large quantities or if the mother's milk is heat-treated, this ideal situation ceases to hold (40).

In early life, when the protective factors of maternal milk may be of greatest value, it is an advantage to provide the mother's own fresh preterm milk, especially for very immature ELBW infants (41). Soon after this critical period for survival is over, the metabolic needs of growth and development have to be met. For such matching to occur, the mother's milk needs to be enriched or a preterm formula needs to be provided. Owing to the many advantages of nonnutritional components in human milk, fortified mother's milk or fortified donor milk (if available) should be the diet of first choice. However, if human milk is not available, special preterm formulas can be used.

Parenteral Amino Acids

The optimum concentration and composition of parenteral amino acids for preterm infants are unknown. However, the current amino acid formulations come close to meeting their needs, as far as can be observed on the basis of growth, nitrogen retention, plasma amino acid profile, and acid/base status. From recent reviews of the subject (40) one can conclude that preterm infants receiving total parenteral nutrition require more than 70 kcal/kg of nonprotein energy daily and more than 2.5 g/kg of amino acids to achieve acceptable (albeit not optimal) protein gain. Parenteral amino acids are used not only for total parenteral nutrition in preterm infants who cannot be fed enterally, but also as an obligatory adjunct to enteral feeding during the first postnatal days in ELBW infants.

CLINICAL CONDITION AFFECTING THE PROTEIN REQUIREMENT

Protein Requirements of "Sick," Nongrowing, Very Low-Birthweight Infants

Very commonly, the clinician has to deal with life-threatening illnesses that severely stress the infant, so that growth does not occur even when all nutrients are provided. The goal of nutritional management is limited to a nitrogen balance close to equilibrium. A pragmatic approach suggests that about 1.0 to 1.5 g/kg·d of protein, given as intravenous amino acids, would be a reasonable estimate. These figures may even be too high in some critically ill ELBW infants. Another approach stems from physiological studies in stable, growing preterm infants. The idea is to define "minimum intakes" of protein and energy that would prevent net protein loss by keeping protein synthesis and breakdown in balance. An extrapolation of the regression lines of protein gain *versus* intake (20,38,40) shows that a protein intake of 0.5 g/kg·d is associated with zero net protein gain. However, the relevance of these findings to the situation of the unstable, nongrowing ELBW infant is unknown.

A reasonable way of solving the issue is to start with a "minimum protein intake" of 0.5 g/kg·d and to increase this gradually if the sick neonate seems free of adverse effects. So long as the infant is critically ill, the intakes should not go beyond the "pragmatic limit" of 1.0 to 1.5 g/kg·d. An intake of this order may be expected to maintain the infant at zero protein gain. In this situation net synthesis of protein equals protein breakdown.

Protein Requirements of Small-for-Gestational-Age, Extremely Low-Birthweight Infants

Neither the American nor the European recommendations (28,40,44) differentiate small-for-gestational-age (SGA) from appropriate-for-gestational-age (AGA) ELBW infants. In fact, in many neonatal units SGA infants receive higher protein and energy intakes than AGA infants to facilitate their catch-up growth.

Published studies comparing the protein metabolism of a group of SGA infants with a group of AGA infants (13,16) used feeding schedules that were not the same in the two groups and thus did not answer the clinical question of whether SGA infants should be fed differently from AGA infants. A study comparing a group of AGA infants with a group of SGA infants under the same feeding conditions showed that the latter have a slower rate of protein turnover (20). This means that for the same gain of protein, the rates of synthesis and breakdown are smaller in SGA infants than in AGA infants (13,38,40).

Thus, being more mature in various physiological and biochemical systems, SGA infants have a lower protein-synthesis-to-gain ratio than AGA infants of the same birthweight and are consequently better able to handle protein efficiently. They may be able to tolerate higher protein intakes without adverse effects. However, even during catch-up growth, there is no conclusive evidence that protein intakes beyond the recommended values should be beneficial.

EARLY DIET AND LONG-TERM OUTCOMES OF EXTREMELY LOW-BIRTHWEIGHT PRETERM INFANTS

Growth

In "healthy" ELBW (without major problems during the first postnatal months), growth rates are in the lower range of normal values during the first 3 years of life (41). Although genetic and parenting factors may explain these findings, there is evidence that the reduced growth rates are linked with an inadequate protein energy supply during the early postnatal period (42).

Neurodevelopment

In parallel with the successful regionalization of perinatal care, various neonatal centers have reported a decline in mortality and major neurological impairment in ELBW infants (45–47). The results shown in Fig. 6 illustrate this trend.

Major Impairments

Major impairments include cerebral palsy, mental retardation, severe visual and auditory disorders, epilepsy, and multiple handicap. Because of the many neurological

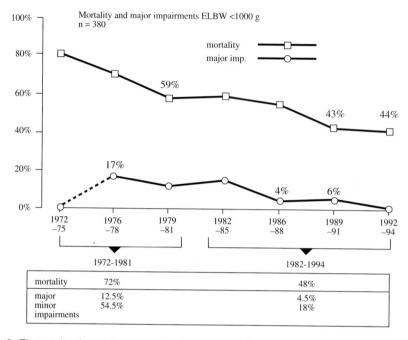

FIG. 6. The results of our reference center for a geographically well-defined population of 1 million residents (9,000 to 10,000 deliveries/year) are shown. The data cover a period of 22 years. Since the mid-1970s, nearly all preterm infants <32 weeks and very low-birthweight infants have been born in the university hospital. *Upper panel:* In parallel with the steady decline in mortality, there has been a decrease in major handicap. *Lower panel:* The data have been divided into two periods (1972–1982 and 1982–1994). The year 1982 was chosen as a break point because several advances (improved perinatal care, improved neonatal intensive-care technology, and cerebral ultrasound) were taking place around that time. The comparison between the two periods shows that overall there has been a decrease in mortality and a lower incidence of major and minor handicaps among survivors. The possibility that early diet, at a potentially vulnerable period of brain development, could have an impact on long-term developmental outcome and prevent minor handicaps, the so-called new morbidities, is a key question with important implications for practice.

risk factors associated with very preterm delivery, it is unlikely that postnatal nutritional interventions *per se* can achieve a reduction in major neurological sequelae.

Minor Impairments

Roughly one in five surviving ELBW infants has "minor" neurodevelopmental impairment (see Fig. 6). These include moderate visual/auditory disorders, mild neuromotor signs, and language, learning, and behavior problems. The possibility that an improvement in early postnatal diet, including substances that influence neurodevelopment (e.g., amino acids, long-chain lipids, hormones, and growth factors), might prevent these handicaps requires further investigation.

REFERENCES

1. Widdowson EM. Changes in body composition during growth. In: Davis JA, Dobbing J, eds. *Scientific foundation of paediatrics,* 2nd ed. London: Heinemann Medical Books; 1981:330–342.
2. Widdowson EM. Protein needs during infancy. In: Fomon SJ, Heird WC, eds. *Energy and protein needs during infancy.* San Diego: Academic Press; 1986:99–104.
3. Ziegler EE. Protein requirements of preterm infants. In: Fomon SJ, Heird WC, eds. *Energy and protein needs during infancy.* San Diego: Academic Press; 1986:69–85.
4. Fomon SJ, Haschke F, Ziegler EE, Nelson SE. Body composition of reference children from birth to age 10 years. *Am J Clin Nutr* 1982;35:1169–1175.
5. Yudkoff M, Nissim I. Methods for determining the protein requirement of infants. *Clin Perinatol* 1986;13:123–132.
6. Zlotkin SH, Bryan MH, Anderson GH. Intravenous nitrogen and energy intakes required to duplicate *in utero* nitrogen accretion in prematurely born human infants. *J Pediatr* 1981;99:115–120.
7. Zlotkin SH. Protein-energy interactions in humans. In: Fomon SJ, Heird WC, eds. *Energy and protein needs during infancy.* San Diego: Academic Press; 1986:157–174.
8. Catzeflis C, Schutz Y, Micheli J-L, Welsch C, Arnaud MJ, Jéquier E. Whole body protein synthesis and energy expenditure in very low birth weight infants. *Pediatr Res* 1985;19:679–687.
9. Fenton TR, McMillan DD, Sauve RS. Nutrition and growth analysis of very low birth weight infants. *Pediatrics* 1990;86:378–383.
10. Benevenga NJ, Steele RD. Adverse effects of excessive consumption of amino acids. *Annu Rev Nutr* 1984;4:157–161.
11. Räihä NCR. New perspectives in the nutrition of very low birthweight infants. In: Domenech E, Castro R, Ormazabal C, Mendez A, Moran J, eds. *Neonatal nutrition and metabolism.* Barcelona: Editiones Cientificas y Technicas; 1991.
12. Senterre J, Voyer M, Putet G, Rigo J. Nitrogen, fat and mineral balance studies in preterm infants fed bank human milk, a human milk formula, or a low birth-weight infant formula. In: Baum D *Human milk processing, fractionation, and the nutrition of the low birth-weight baby.* Nestlé Nutrition Workshop Series, vol 3. New York: Raven Press; 1983:102–111.
13. Senterre J, Rigo J. Nutritional requirements of low birthweight infants. In: Gracey M, Falkner F, eds. *Nutritional needs and assessment of normal growth.* Nestlé Nutrition Workshop Series, vol 7. New York: Raven Press; 1985:45–49.
14. Cauderay M, Schutz Y, Micheli J-L, Calame A, Jéquier E. Energy–nitrogen balances and protein turnover in small and appropriate for gestational age low birthweight infants. *Europ J Clin Nutr* 1988;42:125–136.
15. Chessex Ph, Reichman BL, Verellen GJE, *et al.* Influence of postnatal age, energy intake, and weight gain on energy metabolism in the very low-birth-weight infant. *J Pediatr* 1981;99:761–776.
16. Chessex Ph, Reichman B, Verellen G, *et al.* Metabolic consequences of intrauterine growth retardation in very low birthweight infants. *Pediatr Res* 1984;18:709–713.
17. De Curtis M, Senterre J, Rigo J, Putet G. Carbohydrate derived energy and gross energy absorption in preterm infants fed human milk or formula. *Arch Dis Child* 1986;61:867–870.
18. Gudinchet F, Schutz Y, Micheli J-L, Stettler E, Jéquier E. Metabolic cost of growth in very low-birth-weight infants. *Pediatr Res* 1982;16:1025–1030.
19. Moro GE, Minoli I, Heininger J, Cohen M, Gaull G, Räiha N. Relationship between protein and energy in the feeding of preterm infants during the first month of life. *Acta Pediatr Scand* 1984; 73:49–54.
20. Micheli JL, Schutz Y. Protein metabolism and postnatal growth in very low birthweight infants. *Biol Neonate* 1987;[Suppl 1] 52:25–40.
21. Putet G, Senterre J, Rigo J, Salle B. Nutrient balance, energy utilization, and composition of weight gain in very-low-birth-weight infants fed pooled human milk or a preterm formula. *J Pediatr* 1984;105:79–85.
22. Reichman B, Chessex PH, Putet G, *et al.* Diet, fat accretion, and growth in premature infants. *N Engl J Med* 1981;305:1495–1500.

23. Reichman BL, Chessex Ph, Putet G, *et al.* Partition of energy metabolism and energy cost of growth in the very low-birth-weight infant. *Pediatrics* 1982;69:446–452.

24. Bier DM, Young VR. Assessment of whole-body protein–nitrogen kinetics in the human infant. In: Fomon SJ, Heird WC, eds. *Energy and protein needs during infancy.* San Diego: Academic Press; 1986.

25. Micheli J-L, Schutz Y, Cauderay M, Calame A, Jéquier E. Catch-up growth in small for date, low birthweight infants. *Dev Physiopathol Clin* 1990;1:97–108.

26. Hanning RM, Zlotkin SH. Amino acid and protein needs of the neonate: effects of excess and deficiency. *Semin Perinatol* 1989;13:131–41.

27. Gaull GE, Wright CE. Proteins and growth modulators in human milk. In: Fomon SJ, Heird WC, eds. *Energy and protein needs during infancy.* San Diego: Academic Press; 1986.

28. Committee on Nutrition of the Preterm Infant, European Society of Paediatrics, Gastroenterology, and Nutrition. In: Bremer HJ, Brooke OG, Orzalesi M, *et al.,* eds. *Nutrition and feeding of preterm infants.* Cambridge, MA: Blackwell Scientific Publications; 1987.

29. Lucas A, Morley R, Cole TJ, *et al.* Early diet in preterm babies and developmental status at 18 months. *Lancet* 1990;335:1477–1481.

30. Fomon SJ, Thomas LN, Filer LJ, Ziegler EE, Leonard MT. Food consumption and growth of normal infants fed milk-based formulas. *Acta Paediatr Scand* 1971;223 [Suppl]:1–36.

31. Micheli J-L, Schutz Y, Jéquier E. Protein metabolism in new borns. In: Polin RA, Fox WW, eds. *Textbook of neonatal and fetal medicine: physiology and pathophysiology.* Philadelphia: Grune & Stratton; 1991.

32. Anderson TL, Muttart CR, Bieber MA, Nicholson JF, Heird WC. A controlled trial of glucose versus glucose and amino acids in premature infants. *J Pediatr* 1979;94:947–951.

33. Freymond D, Schutz Y, Decombaz J, Micheli J-L, Jéquier E. Energy balance, physical activity, and thermogenic effect of feeding in premature infants. *Pediatr Res* 1986;20:638–645.

34. Kashyap S, Forsyth M, Zucker C, Ramakrishnan R, Dell RB, Heird WC. Effects of varying protein and energy intakes on growth and metabolic response in low birth weight infants. *J Pediatr* 1986;108:955–963.

35. Kashyap S, Schulze K, Forsyth M, Dell RB, Ramakrishnan R, Heird WC. Growth, nutrient retention, and metabolic response of low- birth-weight infants fed supplemented and unsupplemented preterm human milk. *Am J Clin Nutr* 1990;52:254–262.

36. Schulze KF, Stefanski M, Masterson J, *et al.* Energy expenditure, energy balance, and composition of weight gain in low birth weight infants fed diets of different protein and energy content. *J Pediatr* 1987;110:753–759.

37. Lucas A, Gore SM, Cole TJ, *et al.* Multicentre trial on feeding low birthweight infants: effects of diet on early growth. *Arch Dis Child* 1984;59:722–730.

38. Micheli J-L , Schutz Y, Jéquier E. Protein metabolism of the newborn. In: Polin RA, Fox WW, eds. *Textbook of fetal and neonatal medicine: physiology and pathophysiology,* 2nd ed. Philadelphia: WB Saunders; 1998.

39. Willomet L, Schutz Y, Whitehead R, Jéquier E, Fern EB. Whole body protein metabolism and resting energy expenditure in pregnant Gambian women. *Am J Physiol* 1992;263:E624–31.

40. Micheli J-L, Schutz Y. Protein. In: Tsang RC, Lucas A, Uauy R, Zlotkin S, eds. *Nutritional needs of the preterm infant: scientific basis and practical guidelines.* Baltimore: Williams & Wilkins; 1993.

41. Micheli J-L, Pfister R, Junod S, *et al.* Water, energy and early postnatal growth in preterm infants. *Acta Paediatr Suppl* 1994;405:35–42.

42. Lucas A. Enteral nutrition. In: Tsang RC, Lucas A, Uauy R, Zlotkin S, eds. *Nutritional needs of the preterm infant: scientific basis and practical guidelines.* Baltimore: Williams & Wilkins; 1993.

43. Putet G. Energy. In: Tsang RC, Lucas A, Uauy R, Zlotkin S, eds. *Nutritional needs of the preterm infant: scientific basis and practical guidelines.* Baltimore: Williams & Wilkins; 1993.

44. Committee on Nutrition American Academy of Pediatrics. Nutritional needs of low-birthweight infants. *Pediatrics* 1985;75:976–986.

45. Hack M, Fanaroff A. Outcomes of extremely-low-birth-weight infants between 1982 and 1988. *N Engl J Med* 1989;321:1642–1647.

46. Monset-Couchard M, de Bethmann O, Kastler B. Mid- and long-term outcome of 89 premature infants weighing less than 1000 g at birth—all appropriate for gestational age. *Biol Neonate* 1996;70:328–338.

47. Hagberg B, Hagberg G, Olow I, Wendt L. The changing panorama of cerebral palsy in Sweden. VII. Prevalence and origin in the birth year period 1987–90. *Acta Paediatr* 1996;85:954–960.

DISCUSSION

Dr. Putet: You said that 63% of your infants weighing less than 1,000 g were fed according to the guidelines. Have you done any follow-up on them? Did they grow better than the others?

Dr. Micheli: Babies fed according to the guidelines do better, but they are still below the normal centile range.

Prof. Ziegler: You said that 63% of the babies were fed according to guidelines. How did you define this? Do you have energy guidelines, protein guidelines, guidelines for other nutrients? And how did you define that the baby was in compliance? Was it compliance on all days or on certain days? Could you explain this a bit more?

Dr. Micheli: It was a very pragmatic approach. Every day on rounds, we would check if the energy and protein intakes fell within the acceptable zone. If not, that was one day on which the guidelines were not met.

Prof. Ziegler: I think that the percentage meeting such guidelines in our nursery would be much lower than in yours. Why do you think that authoritative guidelines are so widely ignored?

Dr. Micheli: In general, I think the guidelines are not followed because the infants are perceived to be intolerant of enteral feeding, which may not always be the case. The fear of necrotizing enterocolitis also plays a major role.

Prof. Heird: I was interested that although 63% of the babies met the guideline, at discharge they were still well below the normal centile range. Does this mean the guidelines are not optimal, or does it mean that it is futile to attempt to achieve catch-up growth during this period?

Dr. Micheli: The guidelines are designed for stable growing periods. There is a gray area covering the periods of intermediate feeding, where you combine intravenous and enteral feeding during the first 12 postnatal weeks. I often wonder why we still keep depriving these fetuses of nutrients, because they are still fetuses—if they had stayed *in utero*, they would be receiving their full amino acid load every day. But we, on the other hand, suddenly decrease it to a fraction of what they should be getting, which constitutes acute deprivation of amino acids. Certainly this has consequences.

Prof. Heird: As I read them, the guidelines don't really allow for catch-up growth; the magnitude of nutrient losses during this early period can be pretty staggering.

Dr. Guesry: As I understand it, the important fact is not that 63% of the babies received the guidelines but that during 2,700 days of hospital treatment of 79 babies they were fed only during 1,800 days. This means that as a group the babies received only two-thirds of the guidelines. There is no question that they were underfed. If you give only 2 g/kg of protein instead of 3 g/kg, they will be short of protein!

Dr. Micheli: I agree with you. I think it was clear that I was referring to days of care and not babies. Certainly there is a strong correlation between intake and growth. But other factors may be important in this kind of situation too. For example, why do ELBW babies so often have glucose intolerance? They get less glucose than they would receive *in utero* and fewer amino acids. One hypothesis from animal experiments concerns glucose transporters and the idea that these could be linked more to certain of the amino acids than to glucose itself. Insulin-like growth factor may also play an important role. Certainly it is no wonder that these infants grow less, but there are factors other than purely protein.

Prof. Moro: You mentioned that you had nine cases of NEC, or a rate of approximately 10% to 12%. Did the NEC occur before or after enteral feeds were begun, and do you use a regimen of minimal enteral feeding with human milk?

Dr. Micheli: All the cases occurred after the start of enteral feeding, and we begin minimal enteral feeding on day 2.

Prof. Haschke: You showed that you had an 18% incidence of minor handicap. Is this related to inadequate feeding? Do you have data that there is an interaction between not meeting the guidelines and developing handicap?

Dr. Micheli: No. The only thing I can say is that in half of these minor handicaps there was no documented hypoxic/hypotensive episodes and the cerebral ultrasonography was perfectly normal. We have to look for something else, and of course the first thing you think of is the impact of suboptimal nutrition.

Dr. Debauche: You told us that the babies stayed in the unit for about 4 weeks. Did you find any difference in compliance with the guidelines during the four separate weeks?

Dr. Micheli: Yes, of course, the number of episodes where the nurses stopped feeding was greater early on. But we still had surprises—babies who suddenly start having large gastric residuals at 15 days or 17 days. But most of the problems were in the first week.

Dr. Debauche: What are good guidelines for the first week?

Dr. Micheli: At present the guidelines don't fix rules for the first postnatal days.

Prof. Lucas: I imagine that it was the smallest, sickest infants who were most likely to fail to meet the guidelines, because they were the ones causing most concern. Since those infants have the worst outcome for other reasons, it's very difficult to disentangle whether failing to meet the guidelines does have adverse consequences or not. This is another reason for doing aggressive intervention trials on a randomized basis.

Dr. Micheli: I agree. Interventional studies need to be done to settle this point. We also need to know more about the growth of the brain, particularly the hippocampus, in relation to nutrition.

Dr. Lauterbach: What is the minimum weight of your babies when you decide to discharge them from hospital?

Dr. Micheli: We have no weight limit for discharge. We discharge in peripheral hospitals once the infants are stable and feeding well, with no apneic episodes or supplemental oxygen requirement. Some of them leave our unit at quite low weights compared with 10 or 15 years ago, when we discharged them once they reached 2 kg. Now we sometimes discharge infants as small as 1.2 kg.

Dr. Lightdale: Are you using indomethacin prophylaxis and is there a problem with persistent ductus arteriosus (PDA)?

Dr. Micheli: We use indomethacin early when there are clinical and/or echographic signs of PDA. This occurs in the majority of our ELBW infants, but we don't use it prophylactically.

Prof. Ziegler: The main reason that it's difficult to meet guidelines, or a reasonable protein intake, is that preterm formulas have too low a protein content for our very small premature babies, and the same is true for human milk fortifiers. They are too low in protein to meet a reasonable protein intake for the very small premature baby. I don't know how you managed to achieve an intake of 3.6 or 3.8 g/kg·d, but in our nursery it would be very unusual to achieve such an intake. We have volume restrictions in our nursery that are imposed by other factors and considerations, and this means that we cannot achieve the volumes necessary to achieve a protein intake of 3.6 or 3.8 g/kg. So it's not just that the resident withholds the feeding during the night because the abdomen gets distended; the other reason is that our feeding regimens across the board are too low in protein.

Prof. Lucas: The only preparations we have for increasing nutrient density, other than fortifiers that contain everything, are energy sources. We don't in general add extra protein to the diet when volume is limited. That might be a positive suggestion for industry—it would be really useful to have a commercially available protein supplement that could be added to either formula or human milk as protein alone. You would need to use it in various combinations with energy supplements, of course.

Prof. Heird: I think there is a larger problem, and that's the rather general impression that the most important thing is the energy intake. When you're dealing with a ready-made formula, that emphasis is fine, because the formula provides sufficient protein and other nutrients, and if you judge the intake by the calories, it will probably be reasonably adequate in other respects. But the automatic impression that you should do something to increase the energy intake completely ignores the important concept of the linkage between protein and energy that took years to work out. Maybe an even better suggestion would be to re-educate people in the equal importance of both energy and protein.

Dr. Schanler: There are at least two protein supplements available in the United States, and probably elsewhere around the world—a casein and a whey protein supplement. We would recommend using those in our nursery when we are concerned about poor growth.

Nutrition of the Very Low Birthweight Infant, edited by
Ekhard E. Ziegler, Alan Lucas, Guido E. Moro.
Nestlé Nutrition Workshop Series, Paediatric Programme, Vol. 43,
Nestec Ltd., Vevey/Lippincott Williams & Wilkins
Philadelphia, Pennsylvania © 1999.

Protective Nutrients for the Immature Gut

W. Allan Walker and Dingwei Dai[a]

Mucosal Immunology Laboratory, Combined Program in Pediatric Gastroenterology and Nutrition, Massachusetts General Hospital and The Children's Hospital, Boston, Massachusetts, USA; [a]Shanghai Institute for Pediatric Research, Shanghai Second Medical University, China

Humans live in close association with vast numbers of microorganisms that are present on the skin, in the mouth, and in the gastrointestinal tract. Although fecal bacteria were first observed microscopically some 300 years ago by Van Leeuwenhoek, the degree of microbial colonization of the lower intestinal tract was not appreciated until relatively recently. That this is considerable is evidenced by the observation of Savage that there are approximately 10^{14} cells associated with the human body and that 90% of these are microorganisms, the vast majority of which reside in the colon (1). One gram of large intestinal contents contains about 10^{12} bacteria. Biologically important functions of the large gut include absorption and secretion of certain electrolytes and water, as well as the storage and excretion of waste materials. However, it is now recognized that the gut microflora is very important in the health of the human host. Through the process of fermentation, intestinal bacteria are able to produce a wide range of compounds that have both positive and negative effects on gut physiology, as well as other systemic influences (2–4). For example, the metabolism of complex carbohydrates to short-chain fatty acids (SCFA) may result in an increased energy yield from the system, whereas proteolytic species can produce toxic compounds. There is therefore considerable interest in the manipulation of the composition of the gut flora toward the most salutary relationship—that is, an increase in numbers of health-promoting genera, such as bifidobacteria and lactobacilli. In this review, we describe the role of nutrients in the protection of the human immature gut and their effects on the modulation of human colonic flora and its activities.

THE GUT MICROFLORA AND ITS HEALTH EFFECTS

The human colon is an extremely complex ecosystem in which individual bacteria exist in a multiplicity of different microhabitats and metabolic niches. The microbiota consist of several hundred different bacterial species. Information regarding the composition of the gut microbiota has largely arisen as a result of studies on feces. Several studies have shown that Gram-negative anaerobes of the genus *Bacteroides* are the single most numerous group in the large gut, accounting for up to 3% of the

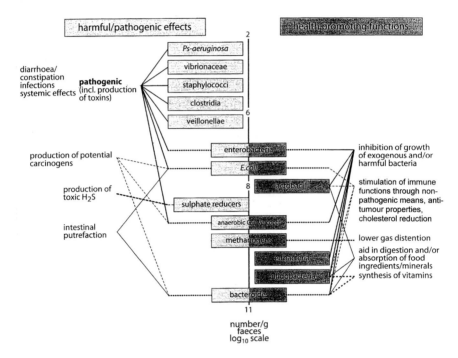

FIG. 1. Generalized scheme of the human gut microbiota composition. The different bacterial groups are divided on the basis of whether they exert properties that are potentially damaging or health promoting for the host. The central vertical line gives approximate numbers of organisms in feces. (Reproduced with permission from ref. 6.).

total fecal flora. Other numerically predominant groups are Gram-positive rods (bifidobacteria, eubacteria, clostridia, lactobacilli) and Gram-positive cocci (ruminococci, peptococci, peptostreptococci). Chief among these are the bifidobacteria, which may constitute as much as 25% of total fecal counts. Several other groups exist in lower proportions, including enterococci, coliforms, methanogens, and dissimilatory sulfate-reducing bacteria (5,6) (Fig. 1).

In general, intestinal bacteria may be divided into species that exert either harmful or beneficial effects on the host (see Fig. 1). Pathogenic effects include diarrhea, inflammation, necrosis and ulceration, liver damage, carcinogenesis, and intestinal putrefaction. Health-promoting effects may be caused by the inhibition of growth of harmful bacteria, stimulation of immune functions, decrease of gas production, improved digestion and absorption of essential nutrients, and synthesis of vitamins B and K.

FEEDING AND GUT MICROFLORA

At birth, colonization of the previously germ-free human gut begins. Normally, the first microbes to be established are derived from the mother during delivery and subsequently from other external environments (e.g., neonatal intensive-care unit personnel). There have been many reports on the establishment of intestinal microflora (7–12). Numerous factors affect the nature of intestinal microflora, especially the local environment and diet. It has been recognized that profound differences exist with respect to the composition of the gut microbiota in response to the infant's feeding (Fig. 2). The newborn intestine is first colonized with enterobacteria, and their number reaches 10^9 per gram of feces. Yoshioka *et al.* (7) reported that by day 6 bifidobacteria were the predominant organisms in the stool of breastfed infants, exceeding enterobacteria by a ratio of 1,000:1, whereas enterobacteria were the predominant organisms in formula-fed infants, exceeding bifidobacteria by approximately 10:1. At 1 month of age, bifidobacteria were the most prevalent organisms in both groups. But the number of these organisms in the stool of formula-fed infants

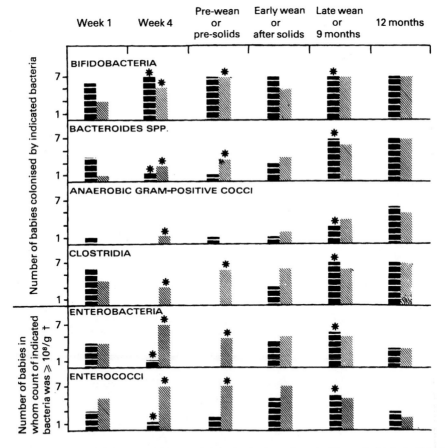

FIG. 2. The succession of bacterial populations in the large bowel of breastfed infants (*filled columns*) and formula-fed infants (*hatched column*).
˙When fewer than seven babies were examined the results have been adjusted to a fraction of seven.
†Counts of facultative anaerobic bacteria $\geq 10^8$/g feces are raised in comparison with counts in normal adults.
(Reproduced with permission from ref. 10.)

was approximately one-tenth that of breastfed infants. A diet of breast milk creates an environment favoring the development of a simple flora of bifidobacteria and few other anaerobic and small numbers of facultatively anaerobic bacteria. In contrast, formula-fed infants have a more complex microbiota, which contains bifidobacteria, bacteroides, clostridia, and streptococci (8,9).

The introduction of solid food to breastfed infants causes a major disturbance in the microbial ecology of the large bowel as numbers of enterobacteria and enterococci rise sharply and colonization by *Bacteroides* spp., clostridia, and anaerobic streptococci occurs. This was not observed when formula-fed infants began to take solids; instead, counts of facultative anaerobes remained high while colonization by anaerobes other than bifidobacteria continued. At 12 months, the anaerobic bacterial populations of the large bowel of both groups of infants are beginning to resemble those of adults in number and composition, and there is a corresponding decrease in the number of facultative anaerobes (10).

The studies discussed earlier were on normal, healthy newborns. Bell *et al.* (11) found that the incidence of pure cultures of aerobic bacteria was higher in the stool of the premature neonate and critically ill infants than in normal full-term infants.

The reasons for the differences in the fecal flora of breastfed and formula-fed infants are not yet fully known but appear to be related to the following:

1. *The type of protein*—whey-based formula produces a flora more like that of the breastfed baby (9);
2. *The availability of iron,* which is determined by the amount of iron in infant formula and the presence of lactoferrin in human milk. Bifidobacteria and lactobacilli do not need iron, whereas *Bacteroides* species and enterobacteria require iron for growth. Lactoferrin supplementation may suppress the growth of facultative organisms in the infant gut (12);
3. *The presence of oligosaccharides*—some N-acetylglucosamine-containing oligosaccharides in breast milk are shown to be "growth factors" for bifidobacteria (13);
4. *The pH*—human milk is thought to be necessary to maintain an acidic pH in the gut owing to its poor buffering capacity compared with cow's milk and formula milks, with their high calcium and phosphate content. Bullen and Willis (14) noted that the pH of stool in breastfed infants was 5.1 at age 7 days, whereas it was as high as 6.5 in formula-fed infants. The low pH level promotes the growth of bifidobacteria and lactobacilli but inhibits other bacteria. In addition, secretory IgA (SIgA) may act to suppress the growth of coliforms in the infant gut.

PROTECTIVE NUTRIENTS FOR THE IMMATURE GUT

Because of immaturities of intestinal host defenses, the preterm neonate is more susceptible to pathological colonization leading to intestinal infection. The incomplete development of host defense at the mucosal level could explain this increased susceptibility (15–17). Nutrition may play an important role in the development of the mucosal barrier. Bacteria colonize the gut by adhering to a receptor of glycoprotein or glycolipid in the microvillus membrane. Pathological bacteria are defined in part by their expression of adhesins on their surface and the capacity of these adhesins to bind to the microvillus glycoconjugates in a lectinlike fashion (18). Thus inhibiting bacterial colonization may reduce the risk for bacterial infection.

Feeding preterm infants may include supplements of age-appropriate maternal milk (milk secreted after birth in mothers who deliver prematurely). Human preterm milk may provide near optimal nutrition for the preterm infant, and its role in meeting preterm infants' host defense needs may be equally important. Human preterm milk appears to be qualitatively different from term milk and may, as such, be uniquely suited to the host defense needs of the preterm infant (16). There are various growth factors, hormones, and nutrients in human milk (16,19) that are thought to promote gastrointestinal maturation and strengthen mucosal barriers (Table 1).

Apart from these trophic factors, there are many immunological components and nonimmunological factors in human milk, which are thought to be anti-infective agents for the newborn (13,16,20). Compared with milk from other species, human milk is unique with regard to its content of complex oligosaccharides (13,20). For many years, these components have been thought to play a role only in the development of a normal gut flora in breastfed infants. Now there is striking evidence that free oligosaccharides and glycoconjugates are potent inhibitors of bacterial adhesion to the microvillus membrane, an initial stage of the infective process (13,20). *In vitro* assays have shown the ability of these molecules to competitively inhibit microbial adhesion and enterotoxin binding by acting as receptor analogs (20). Gangliosides have been shown to act as receptor analogs for the heat-labile toxins from *Escherichia coli* and *Vibrio cholerae* (21). Other oligosaccharides in human milk have also been shown to inhibit *in vitro* attachment of the classic and E1 Tor strain of *V. cholerae* (22), *Streptococcus pneumoniae,* and *Haemophilus influenzae* (23), and inhibit localized adherence of enteropathogenic *E. coli* to HEp-2 cells (24). Glycoproteins and glycolipids also interfere with the binding of enterotoxigenic *E. coli* to epithelial cells (25). Many protective oligosaccharide and glycoconjugate components in human milk are now known. We list the prominent ones in Table 2.

It is known that glycosylation in the microvillus membrane is under developmen-

TABLE 1. *Nutrients and hormones that may promote gastrointestinal maturation*

Nutrients	Hormone and growth factors	Others
Iron	Growth hormone	Nucleotides
Zinc	Glucocorticoids	Polyamines
Vitamin A	Insulin	
Vitamin B_{12}	Thyroxine	
Folic acid	Bombesin	
Glutamine	Somatomedin	
Arginine	Intestinal peptide YY	
Taurine	Epidermal growth factors	
Lactose	Nerve growth factors	
Amino sugars	Insulin-like growth factors	
	Transforming growth factors	

TABLE 2. *Oligosaccharides and glycoconjugates in human milk that inhibit enteropathogen adhesion or its toxin binding*

Receptors	Pathogens
Fucosylated pentasaccharide	Enteropathogenic *E. coli*
Fucosylated oligosaccharide	*E. coli* (the heat stable enterotoxin)
	Campylobacter jejuni
Gal(1-4)GlcNAc(1-3)Gl(-4)Glc	*Streptococcus pneumoniae*
Ganglioside GM$_1$	*Vibrio cholerae* (toxin)
	E. coli (the heat labile enterotoxin)
	C. jejuni (toxin)
Glycolipid Gb$_3$	*Shigella* (toxin)
	Enterohemorrhagic *E. coli* (verotoxin)
Mannosylated glycopeptide	Enterohemorrhagic *E. coli*

tal regulation (15,26). In the adult animal, mature glycosylation results in mature carbohydrate side chains on microvillus membrane glycoproteins and glycolipids. In contrast, the newborn intestine has immature glycosylation, which results in differences in the availability of glycoconjugates and may account for enhanced pathogen toxin binding (15). We have previously reported in an animal model that sialyltransferase activity is increased in newborns and that fucosyltransferase and galactosyltransferase activities are decreased (27,28). We have also shown that these and other glycosyltransferases may be developmentally regulated by pretreatment with cortisone (27,28). Previous studies have suggested that the human neonatal intestine may show pathological colonization of bacteria because of immaturity in glycosylation of the mucosal surface molecules (glycoconjugates) (29), and preliminary studies have suggested that cortisone can modify these immature glycoconjugates to cause a more mature pattern of bacterial colonization (15,26,29). Many factors other than cortisone affect the developmental regulation of glycosylation in the intestine, including nutritional factors such as vitamin A deficiency (30) and nutrient composition differences in the diet (31). However, further studies are needed to clarify the nutritional regulatory mechanism of glycosylation and to define the nutrient requirements for this process.

PROBIOTICS, PREBIOTICS, AND THE GUT MICROFLORA

It is becoming increasingly accepted that the intestinal microbiota may play an important role in the maintenance of host health. Keeping the equilibrium of microflora seems to be a contributory factor. *Bifidobacterium* is the numerically predominant bacterial genus in the feces of breastfed infants, and this may contribute to the protection which breastfeeding provides against intestinal infections. Because of their potentially beneficial properties (Table 3), there have been attempts to increase the numbers of these bacteria in the human intestine. Diet can influence microbial colonization in two ways: (i) administration of live microorganisms by mouth (probiotics); or (ii) the oral intake of bacterial stimulants that are directed toward specific components of the endogenous flora (prebiotics). The two approaches are more formally defined as follows:

- *Probiotics* are live microbial food supplements that beneficially affect the host animal by improving its intestinal microbial balance (32).
- *Prebiotics* are nondigestible food ingredients that beneficially affect the host by selectively stimulating the growth or activity of one or a limited number of bacteria in the colon that can improve host health (5).

Both probiotic and prebiotic supplements are targeted toward beneficial microorganisms and therefore tend to operate through that part of the gut flora containing lactic acid bacteria and bifidobacteria. Lactobacilli (e.g., *Lactobacillus acidophilus, L. casei, L. delbruekii*) and bifidobacteria (e.g., *Bifidobacterium adolescentis, B. bifidum, B. longum, B. infantis*) are commonly used as probiotics. Feeding yogurt containing putative probiotic organisms may introduce more bifidobacteria or lactobacteria into the intestine. Bifidobacteria given in this way can pass through the terminal ileum and may be detected in the feces at 10^9 organisms per gram (33). However, they rapidly disappear from the feces when oral supplementation is discontinued. Similar results have been obtained with *L. casei* strain GG (34). These studies indicate that long-term colonization with probiotics did not occur. These invading species need to compete for nutrients and colonization sites with a previously established microflora comprising several hundred other bacterial strains and species that already occupy the available physical, physiological, and metabolic niches.

Those prebiotics that have hitherto been described are specifically used to stimulate the growth and activities of bifidobacteria. Among the natural nondigestible oligosaccharides that fulfill these criteria as colonic food, fructo-oligosaccharides are the only products presently recognized and used as food ingredients that meet all the criteria allowing classification as prebiotics (5). In a recent *in vitro* study using both pure strains of colonic bacteria and mixed human fecal cultures, Wang and Gibson (35) showed that in comparison with other simple or complex carbohydrates, fructo-oligosaccharides selectively stimulate bifidobacterial growth, while restricting the growth of potential pathogens such as *E. coli* and clostridia to some extent. This effect was subsequently confirmed *in vivo*, when human volunteers were given a strictly controlled diet supplemented with oligofructose or insulin at a level of 15 g/d (36). Moreover, in defined co-culture experiments, various species of bifidobacteria inhibited the growth of *E. coli* and *Clostridium perfringens* owing to secretion of an anti-

TABLE 3. *The beneficial effects of bifidobacteria on human health*

Inhibits the growth of potential pathogens
Lowers blood ammonia levels
Produces vitamins B and folic acid
Promotes immunological attack against malignant cells
Improves host resistance to pathogens
Reduces blood cholesterol levels
Restores the normal microflora during antibiotic therapy

microbial substance that was independent of changes in the culture pH. Plating experiments also showed that this antimicrobial substance variably suppressed several other groups of pathogenic organisms, including species belonging to the genera *Salmonella, Listeria, Campylobacter,* and *Shigella,* as well as *V. cholerae* (37).

BACTERIAL FERMENTATION IN THE HUMAN COLON

Many different substrates reach the large intestine and are utilized by bacteria. The principal nutrient substrates for bacterial growth are resistant starches, plant cell wall polysaccharides, and host mucopolysaccharides, together with various proteins and peptides (2,4). Most of the simple sugars and oligosaccharides ingested and digested by humans are absorbed in the small intestine. However, some low-molecular-weight carbohydrates such as lactose, raffinose, and stachyose, together with fructo-oligosaccharides (such as oligofructose or inulin), sugar alcohols, sorbitol, and xylitol, pass into the colon and are rapidly fermented (38).

The most numerous, as well as the most versatile, polysaccharide utilizers in the colon belong to the genus *Bacteroides.* Other bacteria able to grow on carbohydrates are saccharolytic species belonging to the genera *Bifidobacterium, Ruminococcus, Eubacterium, Lactobacillus,* and *Clostridium.* Because of the extremely complex nature of the gut ecosystem, many groups of bacteria are unable to degrade polymerized carbohydrates directly. These species grow by crossfeeding on fragments produced by primary polysaccharide degraders. Saccharolytic bacteria are highly adapted for growth on complex carbohydrates by means of their ability to produce a variety of polyhydrolases and glycosidases. Although some bacteria in the colon can synthesize many different types of saccharolytic enzymes, carbohydrate metabolism is likely to be dependent on the cooperation of different enzymes and various bacterial species taking part in the process.

The principal end products of carbohydrate fermentation are short-chain fatty acids (SCFA), which include acetate, propionate, and butyrate in the molar ratio of 60:20:18, respectively (2,4). Several gases (hydrogen, carbon dioxide, and methane) and bacterial cell mass (bacterial mass) are also produced in this process (2,39). Protein fermentation also leads to SCFA, H_2, CO_2, and bacterial mass and to the generation of branched-chain fatty acids (BCFA) such as isobutyrate, isovalerate, and α-methylbutyrate, ammonia, amines, and phenols, together with various other organic acids. In some circumstances other fermentation intermediates accumulate, such as ethanol, lactate, succinate, and pyruvate, and these may, in addition, be further fermented to SCFA. Carbohydrate metabolism is quantitatively more important than amino acid fermentation in the colon, particularly in the proximal bowel, where substrate availability is greatest.

Every bacterial species has its own characteristic profile of SCFA products, and these are often used in species identification. *Bacteroides* produce mainly acetic, propionic, and succinic acids. Bifidobacteria and eubacteria produce mainly acetic and lactic acids. It is not known which bacteria are responsible for each SCFA in the final colonic fermentation mixture, and in particular it is not known which species contribute to butyrate production. Rasmussen *et al.* (40) have described differences in fecal SCFA of neonates and adults that were expressed in a high relative contribution of acetic acid in the fecal SCFA of infants. A higher contribution of acetic acid to the SCFA spectra has also been observed in breastfed as compared with bottle-fed infants (40–42).

The intestinal microflora functions through fermentation. Many physicochemical factors can influence the pattern and extent of fermentation of particular substrates. These include nutrient substrate availability, the physicochemical environment of the colon, various host conditions, metabolic interaction among bacteria, and individual dietary preferences (2,3).

THE PHYSIOLOGICAL ROLE OF SCFA

The primary function of human colon microbiota is to salvage energy from carbohydrates not digested and absorbed in the upper gut. This is achieved through fermentation and absorption of its major products, SCFA, which represent around 40% to 50% of the available energy of the carbohydrates (4). The principal SCFA—acetate, propionate, and butyrate—are metabolized by the colonic epithelium (butyrate), liver (propionate), and muscle (acetate). In recent years the physiological significance of SCFA has been receiving considerable attention. These observations are summarized later.

Energy Supply

SCFA contribute to total energy requirements. Theoretically, it is estimated that around 300 to 800 mmol SCFA are formed by intestinal bacteria in the human colon each day (43). This amount of SCFA would provide 400 to 1,000 kJ (90 to 240 kcal), representing 5% to 10% of the host's total daily energy requirements. The SCFA load could be much greater in those individuals consuming very-high-fiber diets or in those with malabsorption. Large quantities of malabsorbed carbohydrate may be fermented to SCFA, and therefore in patients with malabsorption the colon could have a significant role in meeting total energy needs.

Effect on Colonic Epithelial Cell Transport

SCFA are absorbed rapidly, primarily by passive diffusion of the nonionized acid. SCFA absorption promotes the absorption of sodium, potassium, and water, and an increase in luminal bicarbonate concentration. This process appears to occur by the following mechanism, described by Binder *et al.* (44). After absorption, the SCFA are ionized at the intracellular neutral pH to hydrogen (H^+) and fatty acids (FA^-). The H^+ is exchanged for sodium (Na^+) by an antiport transport mechanism, and the FA^- (particularly butyrate) is exchanged for chloride (Cl^-) by a similar mechanism. In addition, FA^- are metabolized to bicarbonate (HCO_3^-) in the cell, which is also exchanged for Cl^-. Thus the net effect is that SCFA stimulate Na^+ and Cl^- absorption and bicarbonate secretion. SCFA do not therefore appear to contribute to the osmotic load and may actually constitute an important protection against diarrhea through the removal of sodium and water from the colon.

Substrate Supply for Enterocytes

The human colonic epithelium derives 60% to 70% of its energy from bacterial fermentation (45). SCFA are partly metabolized to CO_2 and ketone bodies that act as precursors for lipid biosynthesis in the mucosa. Roediger (45) found that more than 70% of oxygen consumption by colonocytes grown *in vitro* was caused by butyrate metabolism. SCFA also stimulate mucosal proliferation both in the large bowel and, when instilled into the isolated cecum, in the small bowel. The mechanisms of their trophic effects on the jejunal epithelium are currently being actively investigated (46).

Modulation of Nucleic Acid

The role of butyrate in modulation of nucleic acid is of particular interest, especially its effects on the regulation of gene expression and cell growth. Butyrate can reversibly alter the *in vitro* properties of human colorectal cancer cell lines by prolonging doubling time and slowing growth rates. Low concentrations of SCFA reduce DNA synthesis and suppress proliferation in a variety of cell types (2). Smith's work has indicated that butyrate inhibits the enzyme histone deacetylase in the cell nucleus, thereby allowing the hyperacetylation of histone proteins (47). This has the effect of opening up the DNA structure, thus facilitating better access by DNA repair enzymes. Recently, Ohno *et al.* (48) showed that butyrate increased the secretion of macrophage inflammatory protein-2 (MIP-2) in stimulated rat small intestinal epithelial cells (IEC-6) by increasing histone acetylation. Shah *et al.* (49) found that *n*-butyrate reduced the expression of β-galactoside α2,6-sialyltransferase mRNA in Hep G2 cells by a post-transcriptional mechanism. In addition, butyrate is well established as a growth inhibitor and inducer of differentiation in many cell lines.

Antibacterial Effect

Production of SCFA and the anaerobic flora that fermentation supports prevents the establishment of pathogenic bacteria such as *Salmonella* species. Recently, Jacewicz and his colleagues (50) reported that butyrate enhanced the expression of Gb3, the Shiga toxin receptor, and its synthetic enzyme (UDP-galactose: lactosyl ceramide galactosyltransferase) in human cultural intestinal cells (CaCo-2A cells). Moreover, butyrate suppresses the expression of α2,6-sialyltransferase but promotes the expression of β1,4-galactosyltransferase and N-acetylglucosyltransferase in cultured T84 colonic cells (51). Since some pathological bacteria and toxins use glycoconjugates on the microvillus membrane of the intestine as acceptors before invasion and cell destruction, it may be hypothesized that SCFA protect the intestine by regulating glycosylation.

Effects on Carbohydrate and Lipid Metabolism

Animal experiments have shown that acetate infusions reduce plasma glucose concentrations. However, acetate given either orally or intravenously has little effect on glucose metabolism and does not stimulate insulin release in man. Propionate-supplemented diets have been shown to lower blood cholesterol in rats and pigs (52,53), but in man the effects are less apparent. More research is needed to determine the exact effects of SCFA on glucose and cholesterol homeostasis in humans.

In the light of the growing interest in the physiological actions of SCFA in the human host, it may become worthwhile to manipulate SCFA in the colon for specific clinical situations such as the treatment and prevention of intestinal disease. To achieve the ideal SCFA profile for each situation, it is necessary to do further studies on the bacteria responsible for producing individual SCFA and their preferred nutrient substrates.

GUT MICROFLORA AND NECROTIZING ENTEROCOLITIS

Necrotizing enterocolitis (NEC) is one of the leading causes of morbidity and mortality in newborn infants, with some reports estimating an incidence of more than 10% among very low-birthweight infants weighing less than 1,500 g and with an associated mortality as high as 35% among affected infants (54,55). Although the etiology of NEC is still unclear, impaired intestinal barrier function and the resultant translocation of bacteria and their products seem to be the most consistent risk factors (56,57).

The human host has developed multiple defense mechanisms that harmonize to prevent intestinal bacteria and endotoxins from reaching systemic organs and tissues (17). These defenses include mechanical barriers, the stabilizing influence of a normal intestinal microflora, and the immune system. Many, if not all, of the defenses that prevent bacterial translocation are impaired in patients at risk of developing NEC. For example, the combination of an immature gastrointestinal mucosal barrier and an underdeveloped gastrointestinal immune system would certainly predispose the premature or low-birthweight infant to bacterial translocation.

Bacterial overgrowth in the intestine is one of the major factors that promotes bacterial translocation. In an animal model, even with a normal intestinal barrier function, bacterial translocation will occur if certain enteric bacteria reach or exceed intestinal population levels of 10^{9-10} bacteria per gram of cecum content or stool (57). Based on studies in germ-free mice colonized with single strains of bacteria, it appears that not all bacteria are able to translocate equally well (58). Although indigenous Gram-negative enteric bacilli translocate in large numbers to mesenteric lymph nodes, Gram-positive bacteria translocate at intermediate levels and obligate anaerobes at only very low levels. These results suggest that enteric bacilli such as *E. coli*, proteus, pseudomonas, and enterobacter are associated with a higher incidence of bacteremia in high-risk patients because these bacteria translocate more efficiently from the gastrointestinal tract than other bacteria, especially obligate anaerobes (57). Bell *et al.* (11) found that the incidence of pure cultures of aerobic bacteria was higher in the stools of infants nursed in neonatal intensive-care units than in normal full-term infants. Therefore it appears that NICU infants are at increased risk for bacterial translocation owing to the high levels of Gram-negative aerobic bacteria and low levels of anaerobic bacteria in their gut microflora. The term *colonization resistance* is used to describe the phenomenon whereby certain members of the normal gut microflora (e.g., strict anaerobes, lactobacilli) protect the host against intestinal colonization and subsequent infection with potential bacterial pathogens.

Many diverse bacteria can elicit an intestinal infection in the newborn period (Table 4). The presence of a mechanism that suppresses the growth of these organisms in the intestine is obviously favorable in preventing disease in young infants. It has been repeatedly documented that the occurrence of disease caused by enteropathogenic *E. coli*, salmonellae, or shigellae is significantly more likely in formula-fed than in breastfed infants (59,60).

The incidence of NEC was noted to vary in relation to variation in the intestinal microflora cultured from infants in neonatal intensive-care units. Increased colonization with *E. coli* and *K. pneumoniae* was associated with an increased incidence of NEC, which suggests that these organisms are related to the pathogenesis of NEC (61–63).

Panigrahi *et al.* (64) showed that NEC-associated bacteria (*E. coli*) have a greater propensity than non-NEC-associated bacteria of the same species to prevent adherence of Gram-positive bacteria to the enterocytes and to cause pathological changes typical of NEC in an animal model, and the injury could be prevented by co-infection with Gram-positive isolates from the homologous infant. The same investigators' recent results have shown that the same *E. coli* isolates can cross Caco-2 cell monolayers in the absence of ultrastructural change or damage. The transcytosis of *E. coli* was reduced three- to fivefold in the presence of *Enterococcus faecium,* previously shown to prevent NEC-like injury in the animal model. There was a mild increase in the rate of *E. coli* transcytosis when studies were conducted with younger, undifferentiated cells; these immature cells had no brush border, but retained well-defined tight junctions. A further reduction or complete blockage of *E. coli* transcytosis was observed when *E. faecium* was used as the co-infection in studies with these undifferentiated cells (65). These data suggest that bacterial translocation and the microflora in the neonatal gut play a pivotal role in the development of NEC.

Despite the lack of direct evidence for bacterial overgrowth resulting in NEC, it

TABLE 4. *Bacterial enteropathogens in newborn period*

Escherichia coli
Staphylococcus epidermidis
Clostridium difficile
Klebsiella pneumoniae
Salmonella
Shigella
Campylobacter
Yersinia enterocolitica

was noted that oral antibiotics (66), formula acidification (67), and IgG/IgA administration (68) could decrease bacterial translocation and reduce the incidence of NEC.

Several factors that are involved in NEC are beyond the control of the neonatologist and pediatrician, the most important of which would be the prevention of premature birth. Nevertheless, there is clinical and laboratory evidence to suggest that certain therapeutic approaches directed at improving intestinal mucosal immunity, hastening mucosal maturation, and promoting the development of a normal gut flora will decrease the incidence of NEC.

SUMMARY AND CONCLUSIONS

The normal human microflora is a complex ecosystem in part dependent on enteric nutrients to establish colonization. The gut microbiota is important to the host in respect of many metabolic functions and in resistance to bacterial infection. Normal intestinal microflora are relatively constant during a lifetime, but certain factors may affect this equilibrium. Diet and environmental conditions can influence this ecosystem. A breastfed infant has a preferred intestine microbiota in which bifidobacteria predominate over potentially harmful bacteria. Oligosaccharides and glycoconjugates, natural components in human milk, may prevent intestinal attachment of enteropathogens by acting as receptor homologs. Probiotics and prebiotics modulate the composition of human intestine microbiota to the benefit of the host. Bifidobacteria and lactobacilli are commonly used as probiotics. Nondigestible oligosaccharides in general, and fructo-oligosaccharides in particular, are used as prebiotics. The beneficial effects may result in the suppression of harmful microorganisms or the stimulation of bifidobacterial growth. In the future, control and manipulation of the intestinal mircroflora may be an approach to both therapeutic and preventive medicine.

REFERENCES

1. Savage DC. Microbial ecology of the gastrointestinal tract. *Annu Rev Microbiol* 1977;31:107–133.
2. Cummings JH, Macfarlane GT. A review: the control and consequences of bacterial fermentation in human colon. *J Appl Bacteriol* 1991;70:443–459.
3. Macfarlane GT, Macfarlane S. Human colonic microbiota: ecology, physiology and metabolic potential of intestinal bacteria. *Scand J Gastroenterol* 1997;32[Suppl 222]:3–9.
4. Cummings JH, Macfarlane GT. Role of intestinal bacteria in nutrient metabolism. *J Parenter Enteral Nutr* 1997;21:357–365.
5. Gibson GR, Roberfroid MB. Dietary modulation of the human colonic microbiota: introducing the concept of prebiotics. *J Nutr* 1995;125:1401–1412.
6. Fuller R, Gibson GR. Modification of the intestinal microflora using probiotics and prebiotics. *Scand J Gastroenterol* 1997;32 [Suppl 222]:28–31.
7. Yoshioka H, Iseki K, Fujita K. Development and difference of intestinal flora in the neonatal period in breast-fed and bottle-fed infants. *Pediatrics* 1983;72:317–321.
8. Balmer SE, Wharton BA. Diet and faecal flora of newborn: breast milk and infant formula. *Arch Dis Child* 1989;64:1672–1677.
9. Balmer SE, Scott PH, Wharton BA. Diet and faecal flora of newborn: casein and whey proteins. *Arch Dis Child* 1989;64:1678–1684.
10. Stark PL, Lee A. The microbial ecology of the large bowel of breast-fed and formula-fed infants during the first year of life. *J Med Microbiol* 1982;15:189–203.

11. Bell MJ, Rudinsky M, Brotherton T, Schroeder K, Boxerman SB. Gastrointestinal microecology in the critically ill neonate. *J Pediatr Surg* 1984;19:745–751.
12. Roberts AK, Chierici R, Sawatzki G, Hill MJ, Volpato S, Vigi V. Supplementation of an adapted formula with bovine lactoferrin. 1. Effect on the infant faecal flora. *Acta Paediatr* 1992;81:119–124.
13. Kunz C, Rudloff S. Biological functions of oligosaccharides in human milk. *Acta Paediatr* 1993;82:903–912.
14. Bullen CL, Willis AT. Resistance of the breastfed infant to gastroenteritis. *Br Med J* 1971:3:338–343.
15. Chu SW, Walker WA. Development of the mucosal barrier: bacterial toxin interaction with the immature enterocytes. *Immun Invest* 1989;18:405–416.
16. Groer M, Walker WA. What is the role of preterm breast milk supplementation in the host defenses of preterm infants? Science vs fiction. *Adv Pediatr* 1996;43:335–358.
17. Insoft RM, Sanderson IR, Walker WA. Development of immune function in the intestine and its role in neonatal diseases. *Pediatr Clin North Am* 1996;43:551–571.
18. Sharon N, Lis H. Lectins as cell recognition molecules. *Science* 1989;246:227–246.
19. Carver JD, Barness LA. Trophic factors for the gastrointestinal tract. *Clin Perinatol* 1996;23:265–285.
20. Newburg DS. Do the binding properties of oligosaccharides in milk protect human infants from gastrointestinal bacteria? *J Nutr* 1997;127[Suppl 5]:S980–984.
21. Otnaes AK, Laegrid A, Ertresval K. Inhibition of enterotoxin from *Escherichia coli* and *Vibrio cholerae* by gangliosides from human milk. *Infect Immun* 1983;40:563–569.
22. Holmgren J, Svennerholus AM, Lindblad M. Receptor like glycocompounds in human milk that inhibit classical and El Tor *Vibrio cholerae* cell adherence. *Infect Immun* 1983;39:147–154.
23. Anderson B, Porras O, Hanson LA, Lagergard T, Svanborg–Eden C. Inhibition of attachment of *Streptococcus pneumoniae* and *Haemophilus influenzae* by human milk and receptor oligosaccharides. *J Infect Dis* 1986;153:232–237.
24. Cravito A, Tello A, Villafan H, Ruiz J, del Vedovo S, Neeser JR. Inhibition of localized adhesion of enteropathogenic *Escherichia coli* to HEp 2 cells by immunoglobulin and oligosaccharides fractions of human colostrum and breast milk. *J Infect Dis* 1991;163:1247–1255.
25. Newburg DS, Pickering LK, McCluer RH, Cleary TG. Fucosylated oligosaccharides of human milk protect sucking mice from heat-stable enterotoxin of *Escherichia coli*. *J Infect Dis* 1990;162:1075–1080.
26. Chu SW, Walker WA. Bacterial toxin interaction with the developing intestine. *Gastroenterology* 1993;104:916–925.
27. Chu SW, Walker WA. Developmental changes in the activities of sialyl- and fucosyltransferases in the rat intestine. *Biochim Biophys Acta* 1986;740:170–175.
28. Ozaki CK, Chu SW, Walker WA. Developmental changes in galactosyltransferase activity in the rat intestine. *Biochem Biophys Acta* 1989;991:243–247.
29. Chu SW, Ely IG, Walker WA. Age and cortisone alter host responsiveness to cholera toxin in the developing gut. *Am J Physiol* 1989;256:G220–226.
30. Deluca L, Schumacher M, Wolf G. Biosynthesis of a fucose-containing peptide from small intestine in normal and vitamin A-deficient conditions. *J Biol Chem* 1970;245:4551–4558.
31. Biol MC, Martin A, Louisot P. Nutritional and developmental regulation of glycosylation processes in digestive organs. *Biochimie* 1992;74:13–24.
32. Fuller R. A review: probiotics in man and animals. *J Appl Bacteriol* 1989;66:365–378.
33. Bouhnik Y, Pochart P, Marteau P, Arlet G, Goderel I, Rambaud JC. Fecal recovery in humans of viable *Bifidobacterium* sp ingested in fermented milk. *Gastroenterology* 1992;102:875–878.
34. Goldin BR, Gorbach SL, Saxelin M, Barakat S, Gualtiere L, Salminen S. Survival of *Lactobacillus* species (strain GG) in human gastrointestinal tract. *Dig Dis Sci* 1992;37:121–128.
35. Wang X, Gibson GR. Effects of the *in vitro* fermentation of oligofructose and inulin by bacteria growing in the human large intestine. *J Appl Bacteriol* 1993;75:373–380.
36. Gibson GR, Beatty EB, Wang X, Cummings JH. Selective stimulation of bifidobacteria in the human colon by oligofructose and inulin. *Gastroenterology* 1995;108:975–982.
37. Gibson GR, Wang X. Regulatory effects of bifidobacteria on the growth of other colonic bacteria. *J Appl Bacteriol* 1994;77:412–420.
38. Roberfroid M. Dietary fibre, inulin and oligofructose: a review comparing their physiological effects. *CRC Crit Rev Food Sci Technol* 1993;33:103–148.
39. Christl SU, Murgatroyd PR, Cummings JH. Production, metabolism and excretion of hydrogen in the large intestine. *Gastroenterology* 1992;102:1269–1277.

40. Rasmussen HS, Holtug K, Ynggard C, Mortensen PB. Faecal concentrations and production rates of short chain fatty acids in normal neonates. *Acta Paediatr Scand* 1988;77:365–368.

41. Midvedt A-C, Carlstedt-Duke B, Norin KE, Saxerholt H, Midvedt T. Development of five metabolic activities associated with the intestinal microflora of healthy infants. *J Pediatr Gastroenterol Nutr* 1988;7:559–567.

42. Siigur U, Ormisson A, Tamm A. Faecal short-chain fatty acids in breast-fed and bottle-fed infants. *Acta Paediatr* 1993;82:536–538.

43. Royall DR, Wolever TMS, Jeejeebhoy KN. Clinical significance of colonic fermentation. *Am J Gastroenterol* 1990;80:1307–1312.

44. Binder HJ, Mehta P. Short-chain fatty acids stimulate active sodium and chloride absorption *in vitro* in the rat distal colon. *Gastroenterology* 1989;96:989–996.

45. Roediger WEW. Role of anaerobic bacteria in the metabolic welfare of the colonic mucosa of man. *Gut* 1980;21:793–798.

46. Frankel WL, Zhang W, Singh A, *et al.* Mediation of the trophic effects of short-chain fatty acids on the rat jejunum and colon. *Gastroenterology* 1994;106:375–380.

47. Smith PJ. *n*-Butyrate alters chromatin accessibility to DNA repair enzymes. *Carcinogenesis* 1986;7:423–429.

48. Ohno Y, Lee J, Fusunyan RD, MacDermott RP, Sanderson IR. Macrophage inflammatory protein-2: chromosomal regulation in rat small intestinal epithelial cells. *Proc Natl Acad Sci USA* 1977;94:10279–10284.

49. Shah S, Lance P, Smith TJ, *et al.* *n*-Butyrate reduces the expression of β-galactoside α2,6-sialyl-transferase in Hep G2 cells. *J Biol Chem* 1992;267:10652–10658.

50. Jacewicz MS, Acheson DWK, Mobassaleh M, Donohue-Rolfe A, Balasubramnian KA, Keusch GT. Maturational regulation of globotriaosylceramide, the Shiga-like toxin receptor, in cultured human gut epithelial cells. *J Clin Invest* 1995;96:1328–1335.

51. Li M, Andersen V, Lance P. Expression and regulation of glycosyltransferase for N-glycosyl oligosaccharides in fresh human surgical and murine tissues and cultured cell lines. *Clin Sci* 1995;89:397–404.

52. Illman RJ, Topping DL, McIntosh GH, *et al.* Hypocholesterolaemic effects of dietary propionate studies in whole animals and perfused rat liver. *Ann Nutr Metab* 1988;32:97–107.

53. Thacker PA, Bowland JP. Effects of dietary propionic acid on serum lipid, and lipoproteins of pigs fed diets supplemented with soybean meal or canola meal. *Can J Animal Sci* 1981;61:439–448.

54. Kliegman RM, Walker WA, Yolken RH. Necrotizing enterocolitis: research agenda for a disease of unknown etiology and pathogenesis. *Pediatr Res* 1993;34:701–728.

55. Stoll BJ. Epidemiology of necrotizing enterocolitis. *Clin Perinatol* 1994; 21: 205–218.

56. Scheifele OW. Role of bacterial toxins in neonatal necrotizing enterocolitis. *J Pediatr* 1990;117:S44–46.

57. Deitch EA. Role of bacterial translocation in necrotizing enterocolitis. *Acta Paediatr Suppl* 1994;396:33–36.

58. Steffen EK, Berg RD, Deitch EA. Comparison of translocation rates of various indigenous bacteria from the gastrointestinal tract to the mesenteric lymph node. *J Infect Dis* 1988;157:1032–1038.

59. France GL, Marmer DJ, Steele RW. Breastfeeding and Salmonella infection. *Am J Dis Child* 1980;134:147–152.

60. Mata LJ, Wyatt RG. Host resistance to infection. *Am J Clin Nutr* 1971;24:976–986.

61. Bell MJ, Schackelford PG, Feigin RD, Ternberg JL, Brotherton T. Epidemiologic and bacteriologic evaluation of neonatal necrotizing enterocolitis. *J Pediatr Surg* 1979;14:1–4.

62. Bell MJ, Feigin RD, Ternberg JL. Changes in the incidence of necrotizing enterocolitis associated with variation of the gastrointestinal microflora in neonates. *Am J Surg* 1979;138:629–631.

63. Hoy C, Miller MR, Mackey P, Godwin PGR, Langdale V, Levene MI. Quantitative changes in faecal microflora preceding necrotising enterocolitis in premature neonates. *Arch Dis Child* 1990;65:1057–1059.

64. Panigrahi P, Gupta S, Gewolb IH, Morris JG. Occurrence of necrotizing enterocolitis may be dependent on patterns of bacterial adherence and intestinal colonization: studies in Caco-2 tissue culture and weanling rabbit models. *Pediatr Res* 1994;36:115–121.

65. Panigrahi P, Bamford P, Horvath K, Morris JG, Gewolb IH. *Escherichia coli* transcytosis in a Caco-2 cell model: implications in neonatal necrotizing enterocolitis. *Pediatr Res* 1996;40:415–421.

66. Fast C, Rosegger H. Necrotizing enterocolitis prophylaxis: oral antibiotics and lyophilized enterobacteria vs oral immunoglobulins. *Acta Paediatr Suppl* 1994;196:86–90.
67. Carrion V, Egan EA. Prevention of necrotizing enterocolitis. *J Pediatr Gastroenterol Nutr* 1990;11:317–323.
68. Eibl MM, Wolf HM, Furnkranz H. Prevention of necrotizing enterocolitis in low-birth-weight infants by IgA IgG feeding. *N Engl J Med* 1988;319:1–7.

DISCUSSION

Prof. Haschke: What do you think about the safety of probiotics in premature infants? Adding probiotics means adding living bacteria to a formula. The preterm gut might react differently from the term gut. If there was inflammation, bacteria might cross the gut and enter the bloodstream. Are there any animal models that could simulate this?

Dr. Walker: That is a very pertinent question. We don't want to run before we can walk in these studies. We're trying to do basic science experiments in our laboratory—to simulate as far as we can both *in vivo* and *in vitro* conditions in which bacteria interact with the intestine. If these studies prove to be as helpful as I think they might, then we have to cautiously do some clinical trials. What happens in a transplanted human intestine is not necessarily what is happening in the infant itself. Eventually, we are going to have to try some probiotics on the living infant, even if they do cross the epithelium. This is a multistep process, and I don't mean to infer from my comments that we should start feeding probiotics to infants at risk of necrotizing enterocolitis immediately. In the long run, though, this approach may turn out to be a much better approach than using antibiotics, because antibiotics eventually result in overgrowth of resistant organisms and may cause more harm than good.

Prof. Haschke: But what will your approach be before going into clinical trials?

Dr. Walker: First we need to do more studies in our model systems. Then we need to be able to show that probiotics are beneficial and that they can displace pathogenic organisms. And then I would use probiotic bacteria already available in yogurt and other products, to see if a beneficial effect can be shown.

Dr. Guesry: You presented very nice *in vitro* data on lactoferrin and nucleotide, but nobody has ever been able to show any significant reduction in morbidity with either lactoferrin or nucleotides. How do you explain that?

Dr. Walker: It's possible that in infants lactoferrin is not metabolized *in vivo* in the intestine to produce the conjugates that interfere with bacterial colonization. It's also possible that lactoferrin as an intact molecule does not get across the epithelium to interact with its receptor on TH1 helper cells. You're absolutely right. We need to pursue this in a manner that is beneficial to the patient. We may have to use different dosages or different modifications of intraluminal events.

Dr. Schanler: You mentioned the effect of corticosteroids on bacterial colonization. I know that the data on steroids in NEC are equivocal, but were you talking about an antenatal steroid effect, or about the pharmacological effect of steroids? And how does that affect bacterial colonization?

Dr. Walker: What I alluded to is that using our pretreatment model system—that is, treating before the animal delivers or immediately after—we can modify the nature of bacterial colonization and translocation and alter glycosyltransferases that we believe affect that colonization process. It's a big step from those observations to what has actually been done. I quoted the Bauer study, which suggested that the use of prenatal steroids in mothers at risk for delivering prematurely reduced the incidence of NEC [1], but there are also studies contradicting that finding [2]. I was just pointing out that there is an experimental basis for accepting the initial observations that prenatal steroids might help prevent NEC.

Dr. Schanler: Another comment. We talk about single nutrient additives—single proteins like lactoferrin by itself or one oligosaccharide—but don't you think that the most protective effect would be the whole mixture? I don't understand why we should expect one protein to be the magic protein. That's one of the reasons why human milk is unique—it is so complex!

Dr. Walker: You're absolutely right. I don't believe that NEC is caused by a single mechanism or a single organism, so we need multiple protective mechanisms. Lactoferrin has not been shown to be effective as a single molecule, but collectively, oligosaccharides, lactoferrin, and nucleotides added to premature formulas may be effective in helping to protect the intestine from infection and inflammation.

Dr. Berseth: Can you suggest how your research at the cellular level will be translated into clinical reality?

Dr. Walker: We're trying to answer questions at the cellular level, and this does not necessarily translate to the living infant. The points that have been made about clinical trials are very important. We need to continue our studies in human fetal model systems to the point where we think we should take the next step, which would be clinical trials. Your own studies, where epidermal growth factor and its influence on the intestine, illustrate yet another component of this complex process. For example, growth factors affect the intestinal cell differently at different stages of development, so how do we choose the right time for their introduction? We need to have more information about these very complex problems, and it is necessary for someone to coordinate the basic science observations. We've made a step closer to the human by going away from cancer cells and animal models to human *in vitro* models. Now we need to work with our clinical investigator colleagues to come up with the best recommendations for clinical studies. Invariably, what we see *in vitro* or even "simulated" *in vivo* is not necessarily what is happening in the human infant *in vivo*.

Dr. Baibarina: Which is more important, secretory IgA or specific immunization?

Dr. Walker: They are not mutually exclusive. I did not talk about IgA because its protective properties are thought to be immunologic rather than nutritional. IgA is a unique immunoglobulin for the mucosal surface and is produced in response to antigens or microorganisms that cross the epidermal surface. The IgA content of breast milk under prolactin stimulation is a direct and specific response to organisms that might cause harm to the infant. In general, immunoglobulin specifically responds to an epitope on an antigen or a microorganism, and it prevents binding of the antigen or the microorganism to the epithelial surface. Thus it's a specific process. Other substances such as oligosaccharides may have a more generalized effect on bacterial colonization.

Prof. Wu: One of your slides stated that NEC only occurred in premature infants. In our hospital, many cases occur in term infants. So the statement is not true, in China at least.

Dr. Walker: I meant to imply that being premature is a major risk factor. It is my understanding that most reported cases of NEC, about 90%, occur in premature infants. I'm aware that full-term infants can develop it, and that may or may not be a different process. I was just attempting to give some clinical relevance to what I talked about experimentally.

Dr. Putet: What changes in gut colonization occur when pasteurized human milk is used, or when milk is supplemented with protein or lactose? And does hydrolyzed protein affect gut colonization?

Dr. Walker: When you pasteurize and freeze milk, you affect many of its protective properties. You end up with maybe 75% of the immunoglobulin, all the cells killed, and many cytokines modified. In other words, if freezing may strikingly affect the protective properties of the milk. My personal bias would be that the mother should express her milk for her own infant. However, when you give humanized supplemental formula you probably encourage colonization with bifidus lactobacilli. So there may be some beneficial effects, but not as much as when the infant is given mother's own expressed milk. I don't know what hydrolysis of protein does to colonization in the premature infant, though there are studies suggesting that the bacterial flora is altered by the presence of hydrolyzed nutrients in the gut or by using parenteral rather than enteral feeding [3]. I don't know if anyone has specifically studied immune responsiveness with hydrolysates compared with nonhydrolysates.

Prof. Ziegler: I have a question about butyrate. You showed data suggesting that butyrate increases the release of IL-8. Butyrate is of course regularly produced from lactose as a byproduct of fermentation in the colon, especially in the breastfed infant. I know of other data—for instance, in the piglet—showing that butyrate can serve as a major energy substrate and even has trophic effects [4]. So where is the balance here in terms of positive and negative effects?

Dr. Walker: That's an important point. The studies we've been doing have been on small intestinal cells. You're absolutely correct in suggesting that butyrate, as a fermentation product, acts as an energy source in the colon; it is particularly important under conditions such as short bowel syndrome. In the small intestine, butyrate affects histone acetylation and upregulates the production of cytokines a hundredfold. This does not mean that it is not functioning differently in the colon, or in the small intestine, when used as an energy source.

Prof. Cooper: When there are outbreaks of necrotizing enterocolitis I imagine these must be related to specific bacterial colonization at those times. Do you have any idea of what specific organisms may be involved?

Dr. Walker: We mainly see NEC shortly after feeding has been introduced. I tried to show that by the nature of the feeding you modify the nature of the organism, and that the immature intestine tends to not handle pathological organisms very well; in particular, the release of toxins may cause an inappropriate response. I believe the combination of inappropriate colonization and an abnormal inflammatory response to the interaction of bacteria with epithelial cells is the major contributor to the pathogenesis of NEC. I don't think there is any specific organism, because epidemiologic studies have shown many different types of organisms involved. The problem lies in the conditions of colonization and the reaction of the immature intestine.

Prof. Cooper: There seems to be a difference sometimes in the epidemic form of NEC, which seems to follow a specific pattern, and the background cases that one sees intermittently.

Dr. Walker: Some of that has to do with the nature of how infants with NEC are handled. They are put into a hospital environment where specific organisms exist from the hospital personnel and they are given antibiotics, because they're thought to be septic, so you are modifying some of the other gut organisms. I was suggesting that if we could use another nonpathogenic organism to interfere with the colonization, we might prevent some of the other processes that occur.

Prof. Lucas: You've touched on the idea of using breast milk biological proteins, such as lactoferrin, in formula. How important do you think it might be that these are actually synthesized in the breast, in terms of surface components or packaging that might subsequently influence their handling or activity in the gut?

Dr. Walker: I don't know the answer to that. It could very well be that the nature of glycosylation or the glycoprotein components might be important in what is going on in the intestine. That's another area of research.

Prof. Haschke: I should like to discuss nucleotides. In your opinion, which nucleotides are active and at what concentrations? At present, we add them in the amounts considered to be present in breast milk, but do we need more? And if so, is there any possibility that they might be toxic?

Dr. Walker: We've studied this in the experimental setting. We've been able to show that for general responses, such as proliferation and differentiation, using the concentrations and combinations of nucleotides that exist in breast milk seems to be effective. The fortuitous response shown with organ culture was when we were trying to see if single nucleotides had an effect, and we showed that adenosine monophosphate affected apoptosis. Now AMP is a very important component with a host of cell functions, so further work is needed to clarify this. Pickering's study [5] used nucleotides added to formula at the concentrations that occur early on in breastfeeding (nucleotide levels in breast milk decline with time). This was a human study done under controlled conditions that made some important observations.

I don't believe there is toxicity effect. However, we have preliminary data to show that nucleotides may enhance some of the inflammatory cytokine responses, which might represent a potential negative effect.

Prof. Berger: There is preliminary evidence that free radicals may play a role in necrotizing enterocolitis. We know that bacteria, depending on whether they're anaerobic or aerobic, have an antioxidant enzyme capacity. Is there a possibility of synergism in antioxidant protection? In other words, is it possible that the bacterial flora help in the catabolism of various reactive oxidant species? For example, I do know that clostridium species have xanthine oxidase, which could therefore increase the input of free radicals. If there were some synergism in the antioxidant capacity of the bacteria, there could be a relationship to the type of flora in NEC.

Dr. Walker: We're just at the beginning of our understanding of this. Like most paradigms, the more you get into it, the more complex it becomes. The immaturity of the intestine is sometimes protective for the neonate, and when you mention clostridia, it reminds me that the receptor for clostridium A toxin is underexpressed in the neonate. That's why neonatologists can grow clostridia in the stools of neonates, but they don't get pseudomembranous colitis. So Nature is not totally against the neonate. But your point is very well taken and we need to look more carefully at that.

REFERENCES

1. Bauer CR, Morrison JC, Poole WK, *et al.* A decreased incidence of necrotizing enterocolitis after prenatal glucocorticoid therapy. *Pediatrics* 1984;73:682–688.
2. Dai D, Walker WA. Role of bacterial colonization in neonatal necrotizing enterocolitis and its prevention. *Acta Pediatr Sin* 1998;39:357–365.
3. Walker WA, Duffy LC. Diet and bacterial colonization: role of probiotics and prebiotics. *J Nutr Biochem* 1998;9:668–675.
4. Kripke SA, Fox AD, Berman JM, *et al.* Stimulation of intestinal mucosal growth with intracolonic infusion of short-chain fatty acids. *J Parenter Enteral Nutr* 1989;13(2):109–116.
5. Pickering LK, Granoff DM, Erickson JR, *et al.* Modulation of the immune system by human milk and infant formula containing nucleotides. *Pediatrics* 1998;101:242–249.

Nutrition of the Very Low Birthweight Infant, edited by
Ekhard E. Ziegler, Alan Lucas, Guido E. Moro.
Nestlé Nutrition Workshop Series, Paediatric Programme, Vol. 43,
Nestec Ltd., Vevey/Lippincott Williams & Wilkins
Philadelphia, Pennsylvania © 1999.

Feeding and Neonatal Necrotizing Enterocolitis

Firmino F. Rubaltelli, Roberto Biadaioli, M. Francesca Reali

Department of Pediatrics, Division of Neonatology, University of Florence, Azienda Ospedaliera Careggi, 85, viale Morgagni, 50134 Firenze, Italia

Necrotizing enterocolitis (NEC) is an acquired syndrome affecting the gastrointestinal tract defined as "ischemic-inflammatory necrosis of neonatal bowel." This syndrome is one of the most serious problems affecting newborns, and its frequency is greatest among premature and low-birthweight (LBW) infants (increased between fourfold and 10-fold compared with full-term infants) (1). A multifactorial pathogenesis has been proposed, but the pathogenesis remains obscure. Nevertheless, the theory that NEC could be the final result of several etiological and pathophysiological events has been suggested. We know that there are at least three factors other than prematurity essential for developing NEC:

1. intestinal ischemia,
2. the presence of bacteria in the intestinal lumen, *and*
3. the availability of substrates (formula or human milk) to support bacterial growth. These three factors can coexist and influence one another in a vicious cycle.

The mechanism by which all these events interplay in initiating an inflammatory cascade leading to NEC is not clear. However, raised concentrations of various proinflammatory cytokines, including interleukin-6 (IL6), tumor necrosis factor-alpha (TNF-α), and platelet-activating factor (PAF) have been reported in infants with NEC (2,3). Recently, it has also been found that nitric oxide (NO) is produced in large quantities by enterocytes in the intestinal wall of infants with NEC; this probably leads to abnormal apoptosis of enterocytes in apical villi through peroxynitrite formation (3).

At present, prematurity and enteral feeding are believed to represent the only primary risk factors in NEC development, with bowel ischemia playing only a secondary role. For this reason, feeding is associated with NEC in approximately 90% of cases (4). Therefore better knowledge of the strategy of feeding can improve the overall health of premature infants and reduce the NEC rate.

199

WHEN AND WHY TO START ENTERAL FEEDING

In 1960, Bauman introduced the concept of early enteral feeding in preterm infants (5). Initially, the early enteral feeding of sick preterm infants was thought to increase the risk of aspiration syndrome and failure to thrive (because of inefficient energy absorption and functional bowel immaturity), to cause mechanical damage (from the orogastric feeding tubes) and to make the development of NEC more likely. Hence, parenteral nutrition techniques were introduced and adapted for newborns with the intention of delaying enteral nutrition.

Now we know that both parenteral and enteral nutrition may cause morbidity in preterm infants; nevertheless we can achieve the goal of good nutrition in even the smallest preterm by the well-balanced use of both modes of nutritional support.

To reduce major complications, the concept of "early" enteral feeding must be related to the concept of "minimal" feeding—that is, small volumes (varying from 0.1 to 20 ml/kg·d) of enteral nutrition are given as early as 1 day after birth, whereas in the following days parenteral nutrition is used simultaneously to supply most of the nutrients intake (6). The amount of feeding must be advanced gradually to minimize the risk of NEC, while tolerance is carefully monitored. A daily rate of no more than 1 ml/kg·h is considered safe (7).

Various recent studies have proved that small volumes of nutrients introduced early in the gastrointestinal tract can have several benefits in premature infants. This initial enteral experience seems to support gut morphological and functional maturation, leading to an increase in mucosal thickness and villi height, increased plasma concentrations of gastrointestinal peptides, and better coordination of gastrointestinal motility (6). Moreover, the early presence of intraluminal nutrients allows the development of normal bacterial colonization, representing a further trophic stimulus for the immature neonatal bowel. Early-fed infants showed greater weight gain, fewer episodes of feeding intolerance, and more rapid achievement of full enteral feeding than late-fed infants. There have been no reports of an increase in the incidence of NEC after early minimal enteral intake (8).

A recent retrospective report from the National Institute of Child Health and Human Development Neonatal Research Network recommends the early introduction of enteral feeding and the early achievement of full enteral nutrition to reduce late-onset sepsis in very low-birthweight (VLBW) newborn infants (9).

WHAT KIND OF FEEDING? HUMAN MILK VERSUS FORMULA

As commented earlier, even if enteral alimentation is thought to be an important risk factor in the pathogenesis of NEC, some aspects related to feeding can be considered equally important in *reducing* the NEC rate.

Prospective randomized controlled trials have examined milk feeding and NEC. In a large, prospective, multicenter study, Lucas and Cole (10) enrolled 926 premature infants with birthweight below 1,850 g (mean weight 1,300 g; mean gestation 31 weeks): 253 were fed only human milk, either raw milk or pasteurized donor milk; 437 on breast milk plus an infant formula; and 236 on formula only. Clinical NEC developed in 5.5% of all infants studied (51 of 926). In the exclusively formula-fed group, the risk of NEC was three to five times higher than in infants fed breast milk and formula combined, and 10 times higher than in the group fed only breast milk. Hence human milk seems to be protective even when associated with formula. Only in formula-fed infants delaying the start of enteral feeding seem to reduce the incidence of NEC substantially.

Apart from clinical studies emphasizing the protective role of human milk against NEC, it is well known that this disease is very rare in those countries where almost all premature infants are fed human milk. Because in Italy more than 85% of all newborn infants are fed on breast milk, the incidence of NEC is very low (about 2.4% among VLBW infants). This was shown by a prospective multicenter study in which the occurrence of complications associated with acute respiratory disorders was examined (unpublished data). The NEC rate data are shown in Table 1.

How breast milk could exert such a protective role is not fully understood. Nevertheless, we know that human milk is rich in various specific and nonspecific immunoprotective factors. These factors confer passive protection against pathogenic microorganisms in the respiratory and alimentary tracts and modulate the mucosal immune system of neonatal bowel, counteracting the physiological systemic and local immune impairment. The immune system of human milk is composed of soluble factors and living cells, changing in quantity according to the time of delivery; in fact, the quantity of host defense factors in preterm milk is greater than that in term milk (11). Moreover, the daily production of many defense agents changes as lactation proceeds, in a way that is inversely proportional to the infant's ability to produce them endogenously in the gastrointestinal tract (12). The complex of soluble factors can be subdivided into three groups of compounds with synergistic activity:

1. antimicrobial factors (such as lactoferrin, oligosaccharides, and specific antibody),

TABLE 1. *The relations between the necrotizing enterocolitis (NEC) rate and gestational age and birthweight* [a]

Weeks	NEC	Birthweight	NEC
25	3/57 (5.3)	<1000	9/364 (2.5)
26	1/77 (1.3)	1000–1499	7/672 (1.0)
27	4/98 (4.1)	1500–2499	6/3864 (0.15)
28	3/127 (2.4)	2500–4000	2/55159 (0.03)
29	2/148 (1.4)	>4000	0/3487
30	3/217 (1.4)		
31	2/257 (0.8)		
32	2/344 (0.6)		
33	1/435 (0.2)		
34	1/636 (0.15)		
35	0		
36	0		
>36	2/57688 (0.03)		

Values in parentheses are percentages.
[a] A one year prospective study of the Italian Group of Neonatal Pneumology.

2. anti-inflammatory factors (such as protease antagonists, PAF acetylhydrolase, epithelial growth factors, antioxidant agents, soluble receptors for inflammatory cytokines, anti-inflammatory cytokines), and
3. other immunomodulating factors (such as some cytokines, nucleotides) (12).

The dominant immunoglobulin in human colostrum and milk is secretory IgA (sIgA), which has been linked epidemiologically with protection against several respiratory and enteric pathogens. Secretory IgA has high antigenic specificity, generated by the migration of immunologically-triggered B cells from Peyer's patches and lymphoid centers in the small intestinal tract and bronchial tree, respectively, to the mammary gland. Hence, sIgA of human milk coats the intestinal villi of recipient infants, providing a specific passive immunity against antigens of the infant/mother dyad environment. The function of the entero-mammary immune system in the premature infant/mother dyad is even more relevant if the mother is able to produce specific antibody against the nosocomial pathogens of her infant's nursery (13). Most sIgA remains intact after milk pasteurization (14), assuring efficient protection even in banked breast milk–fed infants.

Oligosaccharides account for the third main component of human milk, after lactose and lipids; they are increased in colostrum and decrease progressively in mature milk (15). The quantity of oligosaccharides is higher in preterm milk than in term milk (16). By contrast, mature bovine milk,which is currently used to produce infant formulas, has a low level of oligosaccharides (17). Some oligosaccharide fractions stimulate the bifidus flora, resulting in control of the growth of pathogenic strains (15). Other milk oligosaccharides, having structures that mimic specific bacterial antigen receptors, inhibit the binding of several viral and bacterial agents by blocking their adherence to epithelial surfaces, preventing enteric infections (18,19).

Among immunomodulating factors, nucleotides are widely present in human milk. Nucleotides are thought to enhance immune function by stimulating natural killer and antibody activity while maintaining intestinal mucosal integrity. This reduces the incidence of diarrhea (20). On such premises, supplementation of starter infant formulas with sialyl-oligosaccharides and nucleotides is recommended to provide broad-based protection against gastrointestinal infections when breastfeeding is impossible.

Some investigators have suggested that circulating platelet-activating factor (PAF) may play a part in NEC pathogenesis by inducing profound vasoconstriction or changes in microvascular compartment (2,21). PAF acetylhydrolase (PAF-AH), a degradation enzyme, has been found in human milk (22). This enzyme may serve to metabolize PAF produced by inflammatory cells and intestinal flora, and thus may exert a protective role against the development of NEC. Recently, it has been reported that levels of PAF-AH activity are higher in preterm human milk than in term milk. Such activity remains unchanged in preterm milk with advancing lactational age, opposite to what happens in term milk (23).

A peculiarity of human colostrum and milk is that they are rich in living neutrophils, lymphocytes, macrophages, and monocytes, which exert several complex and protective functions (24). These cells survive in the gastrointestinal tract and can pass through the epithelial surface, providing not only local immunity but also systemic immunity.

Pitt and colleagues (25) were able to prevent klebsiella-induced NEC by feeding rats with colostral macrophages but not by feeding them with the soluble colostral factors. Such findings do not confirm previously reported data about poor activity of milk leukocytes and macrophages (26).

FEEDING AND GUT COLONIZATION

NEC has never been observed *in utero* (4). This shows that gut colonization plays an important, if not definitive, role in NEC pathogenesis (8). It is well known that there is a close correlation between the type of infant feeding and the type of intestinal flora derived from it. In fact, the fetus is germ-free until shortly before birth, if the amniotic membrane remains intact. After birth, the gastrointestinal tract is soon colonized by commensal bacteria.

In the ecosystem of breastfed babies, there is a predominance of Gram-positive organisms such as enterococci, bifidobacteria, and particularly lactobacilli. Among Gram-negative bacilli, *Escherichia coli* is the most frequent but is present in relatively small numbers. Other Gram-negative bacilli rarely colonize breastfed infants. In bottle-fed neonates, there are fewer bifidobacteria and relatively larger numbers of *E. coli*; moreover, bacteroides and other anaerobes are detected in higher numbers, as in adult intestinal flora (27).

As previously reported, colostrum and human milk contain a bifidus factor that might allow selective growth of nonpathogenic bacteria. In addition, the presence of other antimicrobial factors—such as lactoferrin and lysozyme—is essential in regulating the growth of intestinal pathogens. In the breastfed infant bowel, lactose-fermenting bifidobacteria lower intraluminal pH. As a result, the growth of potentially pathogenic bacteria, such as *E. coli*, is considerably reduced (27).

In a prospective, double-blind study, Carrion and Egan showed that gastrointestinal acidification decreased bacterial colonization and reduced the incidence of NEC in preterm infants (28).

FEEDING AND PREVENTION STRATEGIES

Human milk feeding, especially from mothers delivering preterm neonates, is the primary step in reducing NEC risk in preterm infants. As this is not always possible, formula milk should be supplemented with agents that play a role in the anti-infective properties of human milk, particularly nucleotides and oligosaccharides. At the same time, other strategies may be used to prevent NEC, such as those based on the pathogenic hypothesis developed since the 1960s.

In a randomized clinical trial, Eibl and coworkers have evaluated the efficacy of an oral immunoglobulin preparation containing IgA and IgG in reducing the incidence of NEC (29). They enrolled 179 low-birthweight (LBW) infants fed formula alone or formula plus pasteurized human milk. These were randomly assigned to receive an oral IgA/IgG preparation daily as a supplement to their feeds. NEC developed in six of 91 control infants during the 4-week study period, while no cases occurred in the IgA/IgG-treated infants. We obtained similar results in Padova (30), in a randomized clinical trial involving 132 formula-fed LBW infants. During the first 15 days of life, the infants in the treatment group were fed 500 mg/d of monomeric IgG (Sandoglobulin®), subdivided into five doses, as a supplement to their feeds. Four infants in the control group developed NEC, but none of the 65 treated infants developed it (Table 2).

Abnormal intestinal gas production, probably caused by carbohydrate fermentation by gut microflora, has been observed in most NEC patients studied radiologically. This suggests that it might be possible to prevent NEC by employing probiotic agents that stabilize the gut ecosystem. Such probiotics have been shown to play a positive role in the prevention and treatment of gastrointestinal disorders (31). *Lactobacillus casei* GG, a strain of human origin, is normally found in the bowel of healthy term and preterm infants, though it disappears when antibiotics are given. On the other hand, the intestinal flora of sick preterm infants treated in neonatal intensive-care units is predominantly represented by enterobacteriaceae and coagulase negative staphylococci. In a study of the administration of *Lactobacillus casei* GG to such infants, a dose of 5×10^8 colony-forming units (cfu) a day did not affect the degree of intestinal colonization by potential pathogens (32). However, in a preliminary study of our own, we found that a larger dose (10^9cfu/d) was capable of inhibiting the pathogenic strains. Those findings led us to initiate a wider collaborative study to identify which, if any, infants might benefit from the treatment. The study was a placebo-controlled multicenter trial of *Lactobacillus casei* GG (Dicofarm, Italy), given to premature infants admitted to neonatal intensive-care units. The protocol

TABLE 2. *Morbidity and mortality among infants treated with oral monomeric-IgG and controls*

	Placebo group	Monomeric-IgG group
Causes of morbidity		
NEC	4	0
Sepsis	4	4
Meningitis	0	0
Peritonitis	0	0
Pneumonia	0	2
Enteritis	1	0
Total	9/67 (13%)	6/65 (8.9%)
Causes of mortality		
Infection	0	0
Respiratory distress	4	2
Pneumothorax	2	0
Intraventricular hemorrhage	5	5
NEC	1	0
Total	12/67 (18%)	7/65 (10.4%)

NEC = necrotizing enterocolitis.
Modified from Rubaltelli et al. (30).

was double blind, using sealed envelopes to ensure randomization. Between March and November 1997, 202 premature infants, consecutively admitted to neonatal intensive-care units in the participating hospitals with birthweight of less than 1,500 g and/or gestational age of less than 33 weeks, were enrolled in the study. From the first day of enteral feeding until discharge, 10^9 cfu/d of *Lactobacillus casei* GG (a freeze-dried preparation dissolved in raw or pasteurized human milk) were given to the infants. We recorded two cases of NEC in the control group and none in the study group (unpublished data). These findings suggest the need for a larger-scale multicenter study.

REFERENCES

1. Covert RF, Neu J, Elliott MJ, *et al.* Factors associated with age of onset of necrotizing enterocolitis. *Am J Perinatol* 1989;6:455–459.
2. Caplan MS, Hsueh W. Necrotizing enterocolitis: role of platelet activating factor, endotoxin, and tumor necrosis factor. *J Pediatr* 1990;117:S47–51.
3. Ford H, Watkins S, Reblok K, Rowe M. The role of inflammatory cytokines and nitric oxide in the pathogenesis of necrotizing enterocolitis. *J Pediatr Surg* 1997;32:275–282.
4. Kliegman RM, Fanaroff AA. Necrotizing enterocolitis. *N Engl J Med* 1984;310:1093–1103.
5. Bauman WA. Early feeding of dextrose and saline solutions to premature infants. *Pediatrics* 1960;26:756–761.
6. Berseth CL. Minimal enteral feedings. *Clin Perinatol* 1995;22:195–205.
7. Vasan U, Gotoff SP. Prevention of neonatal necrotizing enterocolitis. *Clin Perinatol* 1994;21:425–435.
8. La Gamma EF, Browne LE. Feeding practice for infants weighting less than 1500 g at birth and the pathogenesis of necrotizing enterocolitis. *Clin Perinatol* 1994;21:271–306.
9. Stoll BJ, Gordon T, Korones SB, *et al.* Late-onset sepsis in very low birth weight neonates: a report from the National Institute of Child Health and Human Development Neonatal Research Network. *J Pediatr* 1996;129:63–71.
10. Lucas A, Cole TJ. Breast milk and neonatal necrotizing enterocolitis. *Lancet* 1990;336:1519–1523.
11. Goldman AS, Garza C, Nichols B. Effect of prematurity on the immunologic system in human milk. *J Pediatr* 1982;101:901–905.
12. Goldman AS. The immune system of human milk: antimicrobial, antiinflammatory and immunomodulating properties. *Pediatr Infect Dis J* 1993;12:664–671.
13. Schanler RJ. Suitability of human milk for the low-birthweight infant. *Clin Perinatol* 1995; 2:207–222.
14. Evans TJ, Ryley JC, Neale LM. Effect of storage and heat on antimicrobial proteins in human milk. *Arch Dis Child* 1978;53:239–241.
15. Coppa GV, Gabrielli O, Pierani P, *et al.* Changes in carbohydrate composition in human milk over 4 months of lactation. *Pediatrics* 1993;91:637–641.
16. Coppa GV, Pierani P, Zamoini L, *et al.* Contenuto di carboidrati nel latte di madri che partoriscono prima del termine: risultati preliminari. *Riv Ital Ped* 1996;22:357–359.
17. Nesser JR, Golliard M, Del Vedovo S. Quantitative determination of complex carbohydrates in bovine-milk and milk-based infant formulas. *J Dairy Sci* 1991;74:2860–2871.
18. Yolken RH, Petersen JA, Vonderfech SL, Midthun K, Newburg DS. Human milk mucin inhibits rotavirus replication and prevents experimental gastroenteritis. *J Clin Invest* 1992;90:1984–1991.
19. Teneberg S, Willemsen P, De Graaf FK. Characterization of gangliosides of epithelial cells of calf small intestine, with special reference to receptor-active sequences for enterophatogenic Escherichia coli K99. *J Biochem* 1994;116:560–573.
20. Brunser O, Espinoza J, Araya M, *et al.* Effect of dietary nucleotide supplementation on diarrhoeal disease in infants. *Acta Paediatr Scand* 1994;83:188–191.
21. Furukawa M, Lee E, Johnston JM. Platelet-activating factor-induced ischemic bowel necrosis: the effect of PAF acetylhydrolase. *Pediatr Res* 1993;34:237–241.
22. Furukawa M, Narahara H, Yasuda K, *et al.* The presence of platelet-activating factor-acetylhydrolase in milk. *J Lipid Res* 1993; 34: 1603–1609.
23. Moya FR, Eguchi H, Zhao B, *et al.* Platelet-activating factor acetylhydrolase in term and preterm milk: a preliminary report. *J Pediatr Gastroenterol Nutr* 1994;19:236–239.

24. Xanthou M. Human milk cells. *Acta Paediatr* 1997;86:1288–1290.
25. Pitt J, Barlow B, Weird WC. Protection against experimental necrotizing enterocolitis by maternal milk: role of milk leukocytes. *Pediatr Res* 1977;11:906–909.
26. Thorpe LW, Rudloff HE, Powell LC, *et al.* Decreased response of human milk leukocytes to chemoattractant peptides. *Pediatr Res* 1986;20:373–375.
27. Goldmann DA. Bacterial colonization and infection in the neonate. *Am J Med* 1981;70:417–422.
28. Carrion V, Egan EA. Prevention of necrotizing enterocolitis. *J Pediatr Gastroenterol Nutr* 1990; 11:317–320.
29. Eibl MM, Wolf HM, Fürnkranz H, Rosenkranz A. Prevention of necrotizing enterocolitis in low-birth-weight infants by IgA-IgG feeding. *N Engl J Med* 1988;319:1–7.
30. Rubaltelli FF, Benini F, Sala M. Prevention of necrotizing enterocolitis in neonate at risk by oral administration of monomeric IgG. *Dev Pharmacol Ther* 1991;17:138–143.
31. Fuller R. Probiotics in human medicine. *Gut* 1991;32:439–442.
32. Gronlund MM. Lactobacillus GG supplementation does not reduce faecal colonization of Klebsiella oxytoca in preterm infants. *Acta Paediatr* 1997;86:1–2.

DISCUSSION

Dr. Schanler: I was intrigued by your IgG feeding study. What do you know about the integrity of the IgG? Is it digested and absorbed by the infant, or does it line the gastrointestinal tract?

Prof. Rubaltelli: No, it is not absorbed. We showed that serum IgG was the same in treated and control groups. We have not performed studies in the feces, but Blum showed that IgG is excreted intact [1]. IgG has a role in treating infants with rotavirus infection, as reported in *Lancet* some years before our study [2].

Dr. Koletzko: What do we know about the role of feed osmolality? Are there any data to show that osmolality above a certain threshold level would increase the risk of necrotizing enterocolitis?

Prof. Rubaltelli: There have been cases reported where NEC appears to have occurred in association with the use of hyperosmolar formulas. In Italy we are very aware of this problem and are very cautious about using milk fortifiers or anything that can increase the osmolality of the feed. There are data on experimental animals to show that hyperosmolar nutrients can induce NEC. An osmolality of more 400 mOsm/kg is dangerous [3].

Prof. Ziegler: I'd like to make a comment on the osmolality question, because it is always mentioned. The only human data in existence are the results of a study carried out in Salt Lake City by Book and coworkers [4]. They compared a then new formula, in which the sole carbohydrate was glucose and which had an osmolality of 650 mOsm/kg, with a control group. Significantly more babies fed the new formula developed necrotizing enterocolitis. That is the grand total of human clinical data on osmolality and NEC. No current formula has an osmolality anywhere near 650 mOsm/kg, and we don't even know whether it was the osmolality or something else in that formula that caused the NEC—for example, the high glucose concentration. So I think it is unjustified to worry about whether an osmolality of, say, 350 or 380 mOsm/kg water could cause NEC.

Prof. Rubaltelli: Yes, but if drugs such as antibiotics are given in the feeds they can cause a large increase in the osmolality, which may then certainly exceed 400, or even 500, mOsm/kg [5].

Dr. Schanler: Fortified human milk in the United States has an osmolality of between 400 and 450 mOsm/kg water, and we see less NEC with that than with formula. I don't advocate that the osmolality of all milk be that high, but I think we know that this is within the safe range.

Prof. Rubaltelli: The approach is quite different in Italy from that in the United States. We

only use banked human milk, without fortifier, during the first 2 to 3 weeks of life, until the infant is getting 60% of the total energy intake enterally. Then, if the mother is not producing milk, we gradually shift to a preterm formula. Growth may not be as good as we would like on this regimen, but the risk of NEC is very low.

Prof. Lucas: Your data compared fortified human milk with formula, but when we did an internal randomized comparison of fortified *versus* unfortified human milk, we found a higher incidence of NEC six cases in fortified group *versus* two cases in the unfortified group. Our interpretation was that this was an effect of adding cow's milk proteins to human milk and influencing the protective factors, but the other interpretation is that it was the increased osmolality. There are very few randomized trials that allow one to look at the effects of osmolality. Very few experimental studies have addressed the question. So we simply don't know.

Dr. Walker: There have been some studies on the degree of osmolality liable to damage cells [6–8]. It requires levels of more than 600 mOsm/kg water to cause direct cell damage. This is thought to be the basis for gut damage from elemental formulas. Lower levels of osmolality only cause changes in fluid shifts across the epithelium.

Prof. Berger: I seem to recall from my physiology textbooks that osmolality was an important factor in gastric emptying and that the gastric contents were first made iso-osmolar before being released. Is this correct? Maybe this doesn't happen in the normal way in the preterm baby. Shouldn't we expect more problems in the stomach rather than further down the intestine if osmolality was playing a role?

Prof. Rubaltelli: I have no idea whether gastric emptying depends on osmolality, but I do know that emptying is much more rapid with modern whey-protein-predominant formulas than with the older casein-predominant types. I don't know whether that depends on osmolality or not. However, we sometimes find that very preterm infants can't accept even a small amount of saline, so gastric emptying must depend on other factors as well, such as the clinical situation of the infant.

Prof. Moro: I think we are overestimating the problem of osmolality. We routinely use human milk fortifiers, and the final osmolality is between 300 and 315 mOsm/kg water. When we use bovine fortifiers, the level is around 400 to 450 mOsm/kg water. We have not had a single case of NEC for more than 5 years in our unit. So if human milk is used with caution, starting with minimal enteral feeding, and if fortification is begun when the baby is able to tolerate a volume of around 100 ml/kg·d, then I think we are safe.

Dr. Rashwan: We know that some ELBW babies are born with a degree of asphyxia, and this may affect the gut. Do you still advise early feeding under these conditions? And if pre-NEC signs develop, do you advise stopping oral feeds?

Prof. Rubaltelli: Our protocol in asphyxiated newborns, who are mostly full term, is not to feed these babies orally for the first few days of life. In preterm newborns, the Apgar score is of course always lower than in full-term infants, but if we feel there is good evidence of severe asphyxia, we defer enteral feeds. If infants develop abdominal distention, we stop enteral feeding, and we restart it after 12 or 24 hours, using very small quantities of human milk. With this very cautious approach, I have not seen a genuine case of NEC in our unit in the last 3 years. We believe we can probably prevent NEC by stopping feeding at the first clinical signs.

Prof. Wu: About 10% of our patients develop NEC without having been fed, though abdominal distention is less severe in these cases. During the passage through the birth canal, the baby swallows maternal blood. I believe this can be a substrate for bacteria in the gut and lead to NEC.

Prof. Lucas: Several studies have shown that NEC occurs in about 10% of babies who've received no enteral feeding at all. This must mean that other factors are involved.

Prof. Polberger: This is a puzzling issue. In Sweden, NEC is very rare and has almost no

mortality. We routinely start enteral feeding with human milk during the first hours of life, even in very sick infants on ventilators. However, in the recent past we have seen a few cases of focal spontaneous perforation, though still with no mortality. I wonder whether this is in fact NEC or some other entity.

Prof. Rubaltelli: We have also seen a few cases of spontaneous perforation. One happened after indomethacin treatment, and we thought that this had caused damage to the intestinal mucosa. In another case, the perforation was thought to have resulted from a congenital malformation. I don't think either case was true necrotizing enterocolitis. Our approach to feeding babies is the same as the Swedish approach.

Prof. Ziegler: I'd like to make a comment about the diagnosis of NEC, because I think what we call NEC is almost certainly more than one disease. We appear to have only one diagnosis in premature neonates for any acquired gastrointestinal disease, and that includes isolated punched-out lesions, and even indomethacin-induced perforations. When our colleague from China describes NEC as occurring in 10% of term infants, he is probably referring to a condition with intestinal distention, but it's almost certainly not the same disease that kills premature babies. Therefore all the statistics we are currently using are suspect and confounded by this nonuniformity of diagnosis.

Dr. Berseth: We see babies in our nursery who do not have pneumatosis intestinalis, yet when they go to surgery the surgeon finds flagrant NEC. On the other hand, we have cases where we will clinically make a diagnosis of NEC but when the baby dies the pathologist tells us that we were really dealing with a baby who had ileus secondary to sepsis, and that there is no evidence of NEC at all. All these permutations suggest that we need refinement in diagnosis. It is obvious that we are dealing with a variety of clinical diseases and situations.

Prof. Rubaltelli: May I ask you what is your indication for surgery in an infant without any clinical or radiological signs of NEC?

Dr. Berseth: These are babies who have continued to deteriorate and who have symptoms related to the gastrointestinal tract, such as abdominal distention. If there is rapid clinical deterioration, the surgeons will sometimes agree to evaluate the problem.

Dr. Walker: Presumably, one begins enteral feeding early to stimulate the intestine. Has anyone looked at hormone release from epithelial cells in the intestine under conditions of enteral feeding in the very premature infant? Do we know what actually happens?

Prof. Rubaltelli: I don't know. Maybe Dr. Lucas can comment?

Prof. Lucas: We coined the term *minimal enteral feeding* after looking at gut hormone release in preterm infants. We discovered that if you did not feed preterm babies at all after birth, they had the same hormone levels as in cord blood. But if you fed them, then they got a massive release of gut hormones. We then discovered that even trivial amounts of enteral feeds, 0.5 ml for a couple a days, was all that was required to produce maximal gut hormone release [9,10].

Dr. Costalos: We did a study a couple of years ago concerning premature babies and NEC. We found a disturbed pattern of peptide hormones in these babies. We know that the hormones can be affected by asphyxia, so I think it would be worth exploring whether there really is a close relation between the hormone pattern and NEC.

Prof. Rubaltelli: I think gut hormones play a role in promoting maturation of the intestines. I don't believe they have anything to do with NEC *per se.*

Dr. Costalos: In our studies, we showed that babies with NEC had a different pattern of gut hormones from controls. We don't know whether this is an effect of the NEC or whether these disturbances contribute to its cause. I think this should be looked into further.

Dr. Da Silva: When starting to feed extremely low-birthweight infants, with or without

asphyxia, is there any role for diluted formulas or semielemental formulas if you have no human milk available?

Prof. Rubaltelli: I can only give my advice, without scientific support. You can start giving distilled water and then move to diluted preterm formula, assessing tolerance by distention and gastric residual volume. Generally, we give parenteral nutrition to very sick preterm babies, with a very small amount of enteral nutrition. If human milk is unavailable, we start with diluted preterm formula. I have no experience of semielemental diets in very low-birthweight infants.

Dr. Al-Siyud: What is the effect of sedation on gut motility?

Prof. Rubaltelli: We don't sedate our infants, even if they are on ventilators, so I have no experience with the effects of sedation on the gut motility. However, in full-term infants who are severely asphyxiated and who are treated with phenobarbital, there is no decrease in intestinal motility.

Prof. Cooke: In your talk, you emphasized the importance of prematurity and feeding practices in the etiology of NEC, but you rather dismissed the importance of gut ischemia. But there is really quite a lot of evidence that abnormal gut blood flow in the fetus before birth that can be demonstrated on Doppler studies is associated with later enterocolitis, as are problems with persistence of the ductus arteriosus, umbilical vessel catheters, recurrent apnea, and so on. These all point to a primary ischemic problem rather than, as you were suggesting, to a secondary one. I wonder whether the modified feeding regimes—minimal enteral feeding or simply delaying feeding—and their effect on reducing clinically evident NEC is simply that we are providing an opportunity for the gut to recover from an earlier ischemic insult rather than overloading it too early, thus producing florid NEC.

Prof. Rubaltelli: My topic was feeding related to NEC, so I concentrated on the feeding aspects. But I agree with you that intestinal ischemia plays an important role in the pathogenesis. If we are very prudent with our feeding practices in these babies, probably giving only minimal enteral feeding during the first days of life, I accept that this allows time for the intestinal situation to improve so the infant doesn't develop clinical symptoms.

Prof. Cooke: I just wonder whether some of the cases of isolated perforation described earlier are simply the extreme end of the asphyxia spectrum, where recovery has not occurred even though you have not fed the child; lesser degrees with asphyxia recover without symptoms using the more modern feeding approach that you've been describing.

Prof. Rubaltelli: Theoretically, that is possible, but the cases I described were definitely connected with indomethacin administration and a congenital malformation. Ischemia may have played a role, but not on its own.

Prof. Lucas: I like the idea of human milk and minimal enteral feeding exerting a protective effect in a damaged gut. I think that is a very good synthesis of the available data.

Prof. Rubaltelli: It is possible that not feeding at all is worse than giving a small amount of human milk, because of the atrophic effect on the gut mucosa. A study by a colleague in Padova, Dr. Carnielli, which has not yet been published, showed that there was no difference in the rate NEC between parenterally fed infants and formula-fed infants, so it seems that withholding oral feeding and using only parenteral nutrition does not provide any additional protection.

Dr. Berseth: I'd like to comment on blood flow. There is a very intimate relation between enteral feeding and vascular responses. We need to be aware of hyperemia as much as of ischemia. One of the physiological responses that occurs with feeding is a decrease in splanchnic resistance and an increase in blood flow. There is some work from Sweden showing that this obligatory change does in fact occur in preterm infants, but it may occur at the expense of

redistribution of blood flow, specifically to the cerebral circuitry. We have to look at what we are doing in the gastrointestinal tract in terms of the whole organism.

REFERENCES

1. Blum PM, Phelps DL, Ank BJ, Krautman HJ, Stiehm ER. Survival of oral human immune serum glob-ulin in the gastrointestinal tract of low birth weight infants. *Pediatr Res* 1981;15:1256–1261.
2. Barnes GL, Doyle LW, Hewson PH, Knoches AML, McLellan JA, Kitchen WH. A randomised trial of oral gammaglobulin in low weight infants infected with rotavirus. *Lancet* 1982;1:1371–1373.
3. La Gamma EF, Browne LE. Feeding practices for infants weighing less than 1,500 g at birth and the pathogenesis of necrotizing enterocolitis. *Clin Perinatol* 1994;21:271–306.
4. Book LS, Herbst JJ, Atherton SO, Jung AC. Necrotizing enterocolitis in low-birth-weight infants fed an elemental formula. *J Pediatr* 1975;87:602–605.
5. White KC, Harkavy KL. Hypertonic formula resulting from added oral medications. *Am J Dis Child* 1982;136:931–933.
6. Wheeler PG, Menzies IS, Creamer B. Effect of hyperosmolar stimuli and coeliac disease on the per-meability of human gastrointestinal tract. *Clin Sci Molec Med* 1978;54:495–498.
7. Laker MF, Menzies IS. Increase in human intestinal permeability following ingestion of hypertonic solutions. *J Physiol* 1977;265:881–883.
8. Kameda H, Abei T, Nasrallah S, *et al.* Functional and histological injury to intestinal mucosa pro-duced by hypertonicity. *Am J Physiol* 1968;214:993–995.
9. Lucas A, Bloom SR, Aynsley-Green A. Metabolic and endocrine consequences of depriving preterm infants of enteral nutrition. *Acta Paed* 1983;72:245–249.
10. Lucas A, Bloom SR. Aynsley-Green A. Postnatal surges in plasma gut hormones in term and preterm infants. *Biol Neonate* 1982;41:63–67.

Nutrition of the Very Low Birthweight Infant, edited by
Ekhard E. Ziegler, Alan Lucas, Guido E. Moro.
Nestlé Nutrition Workshop Series, Paediatric Programme, Vol. 43,
Nestec Ltd., Vevey/Lippincott Williams & Wilkins
Philadelphia, Pennsylvania © 1999.

Feeding and Maturation of Gut Motility

Carol Lynn Berseth

*Newborn Section, Department of Pediatrics, Baylor College of Medicine, Houston, Texas
USA*

Motor function is exerted by the three muscle layers that comprise the outer layers of
the intestine. These muscle layers must contract in a coordinated fashion:

1. to mix and churn intraluminal nutrients during the process of digestion and
2. to move the unused materials aborally for expulsion.

Motor activity is responsible for the movement of nutrients from the posterior phar-
ynx to the stomach through the esophagus, the emptying of gastric contents into the
proximal duodenum, the movement of nutrients distally through the small and large
intestines, the storage of fecal material, and the expulsion of waste. This muscle activity is under neural regulation. The most direct neural regulation is exerted by the
enteric nervous system (ENS), which is considered to be part of the autonomic nervous system. Although the central nervous system, sympathetic nervous system, and
parasympathetic nervous system can modulate motor function, neural regulation of
intestinal motor function by the ENS occurs when input from any of these three other
systems is interrupted. Thus the ENS can function independently of the other systems. In addition, the ENS has a unique, intimate relationship with the mucosal surfaces of the gastrointestinal tract. First, primary afferent nerves provide input concerning events related to the intraluminal nutrients, such as distention of the luminal
wall. Second, local neural reflexes may be triggered by physical or chemical properties of the intraluminal nutrient, such as osmotic load or the presence of fat. Finally,
the presence of intraluminal nutrients triggers the release of gastrointestinal hormones and peptides, which may exert endocrine, paracrine, or neurocrine regulation
of motor function. In summary, the regulation of motor activity in the small intestine
is very complex, and the quantity and the quality of the nutrients present in the lumen
of the gut exert significant influence or motor function.

Despite the complexity of neural and hormonal regulation of motor activity in the
small intestine, two basic patterns of activity are described in the adult (1). During
fasting, motor activity cycles through three types of patterns every 60 to 90 minutes.
First, there is motor quiescence, or an absence of motor contractions. This pattern in
turn is gradually replaced by one of irregular contractions. These irregular contractions in turn are replaced by a series of intense, phasic contractions that are initiated

in the distal antrum and sweep distally through the duodenum, jejunum, and ileum in a coordinated, sequential fashion. This latter event is called the migrating motor complex, or MMC, and the complete cycle of all three patterns is called the interdigestive cycle (Fig. 1). It is the MMC that is responsible for propelling intraluminal nutrients forward, and as such is called the intestinal housekeeper (2). When a meal is ingested, this cyclical pattern is disrupted by the presence of persistent uncoordinated contractions occurring at all levels of the intestine. This pattern is called the fed response (Fig. 2). The duration of the fed response is dependent upon the volume and the characteristics of the meal ingested.

In adults there is a reciprocal relation between motor function and the type of foods or nutrients ingested. When loss of neural regulation of motor function occurs, as the result of diabetic neuropathy for example, the process of emptying foods from the stomach or the overall time required to move the food from the mouth to the rectum may be significantly delayed. Conversely, the presence of specific nutrients may slow gastric emptying or hasten intestinal transit. Thus it has been shown that when fats are not completely digested or absorbed, their presence in the distal intestine may stimulate the release of peptide YY, which in turn may slow gastric emptying (3). Although many aspects of gastrointestinal function are immature in the preterm and term neonate, there are many that are partially or fully present. Thus certain aspects of the intimate relation between feeding and motor function may be exploited in designing enteral feeding strategies for these high risk infants.

It has been well recognized that motor function in the preterm infant differs from that seen in the adult as well as in the term infant. The ability to suck does not appear

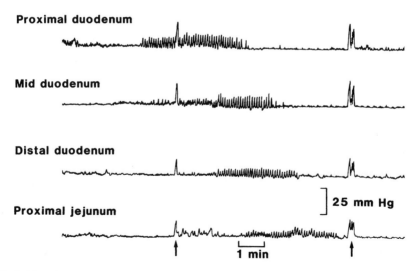

FIG. 1. Migrating motor complex in a term infant. Motor activity recorded from the proximal duodenum is displayed on the top line; patterns shown in the second line were recorded 2.5 cm distally to that shown in the top line; patterns shown in the third line were recorded 5.0 cm distally; patterns in the fourth line were recorded 7.5 cm distally. A series of phasic contractions occurs in the proximal duodenum and appears sequentially in each more distally located recording.

FED PATTERN IN A TERM INFANT

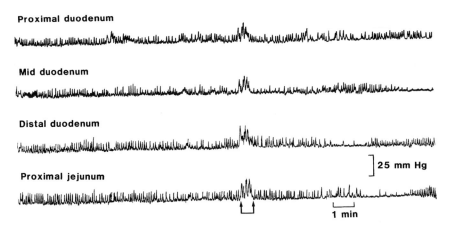

FIG. 2. The magnification and configuration of this tracing are similar to those in Fig. 1. Continuously recurring contractions are seen at all four levels of the intestine. (Reproduced with permission from ref. 9.)

until 32 weeks of gestation (4). Lower esophageal tone and function is immature in the preterm infant compared with that seen in older infants (5). Gastric emptying is more delayed in the preterm infant than in the term infant (6), and overall intestinal transit is slower in the preterm infant (7). Although enteral feeds can be given by orogastric or transpyloric tubes, immaturity of gastric emptying and intestinal transit often precludes the use of enteral feeding. Thus the major focus of this discussion will be on motor function of the stomach and small intestine.

Motor patterns during fasting and feeding have been described in preterm and term infants. While characteristics of antral motor patterns are similar, the patterns seen in the duodenum differ in preterm and term infants (8,9). Though adults display full interdigestive cycles during fasting, few infants with gestational ages of less than 34 to 35 weeks do so. Instead, preterm infants display short episodes of motor quiescence that alternate with irregular contractions. In addition, infants display a pattern that is not commonly seen in adults, called the *cluster* (Fig. 3). Clusters consist of regular, phasic contractions that do not migrate. They are arbitrarily defined as short if they have a duration of less than 2 minutes and long if their duration exceeds 2 minutes. This pattern occupies 40% of the manometric recordings of preterm infants. Although term infants show complete interdigestive cycles, they also display a prominence of clusters. Characteristics of clusters change with increasing gestational age, in that the duration of individual episodes increases and the overall occurrence decreases. These maturational changes can be used to assess the level of functional maturation of the neonate's intestine in order to assess feeding strategies.

Motor responses to feeding are also immature in the preterm infant. Neonates most commonly ingest feeds over 15 to 20 minutes whether they are being breast-fed or

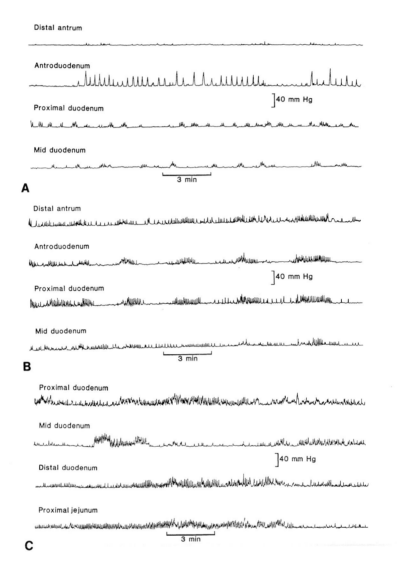

FIG. 3. Motor pattern recorded in the same preterm infant at 32 weeks of gestation (**A**), 34 weeks (**B**), and 36 weeks (**C**). The orientation is similar to that seen in Fig. 1. Phasic contractions that do not migrate distally are seen in the duodenum of all three tracings. Individual clusters are of short duration and occur more frequently at 32 weeks than at 34 or 36 weeks of gestation. (Reproduced with permission from ref. 8.)

ingesting an artificial formula. The term infant who is fed over 15 minutes displays a brisk fed response, in that the overall occurrence of contractions increases and interrupts the presence of the interdigestive cycle. When the preterm infant is fed over 15 minutes, only 40% will display an increase in contractions to interrupt the fasting pattern. The others will display a *decrease* in motor activity (10).

EFFECTS OF FEEDING ON MOTOR ACTIVITY

Exposure of the gut to intraluminal nutrients hastens maturation of motor function. A series of clinical trials has demonstrated that characteristics of duodenal motor activity in the preterm infant evolve quickly when infants are given routine feeds, in that the complete interdigestive cycle emerges and the duration of individual episodes of clusters increases, while the overall occurrence decreases (11). When infants are given parenteral nutrition supplemented with small feeds of 24 ml/kg·d of regular formula or an equal volume of sterile water, motor activity matures faster in those given the formula feeds. In addition, plasma concentrations of gastrointestinal peptides that modulate motor function—such as gastrin, motilin, and gastric inhibitory peptide—increase in infants who receive these small feeds. This enhancement of maturation of gut function is in turn reflected clinically, as these infants make a faster transition to full enteral feeding and have fewer days of feed intolerance compared to the unfed babies. This effect of feeding appears to be related to the presence of nutrient and not volume, as babies who receive "feeds" containing sterile water do not show the maturation of motor function and plasma hormone release that occurs in babies fed nutrients (12).

Studies in animals have provided some additional insight into the volume of nutrient that is necessary to trigger maturation of motor activity. When newborn dogs are given chronic parenteral nutrition and their energy intake is supplemented with varying levels of enteral feeding, only feed volumes that provide in excess of 30% of daily estimated energy intake cause an increase in gut growth, as assessed by bowel weight and DNA and protein content (13). On the other hand, enteral feed volumes that provide as little as 10% of daily estimated energy intake cause an increase in the maturation of the appearance of migrating motor activity. We speculate from these findings that feeding strategies that provide enteral feed volumes of 10% or more of daily estimated energy intake are sufficient to trigger the maturation of gut motility if there are clinical indications to limit the volume of enteral feeding given to the preterm infant.

Just as in the adult, the composition, volume, and rate of feeding can all affect the type of motor responses seen in preterm infants when they are given feeds. As noted earlier, when preterm infants are fed by bolus over 15 minutes, about half will show a decrease in duodenal motor activity (11). This decrease in motor activity is associated with a decrease in the rate at which gastric contents are emptied from the stomach into the upper intestine. When these same infants are fed the same volume over 120 minutes, they show an increase in motor activity similar to that seen in term infants, and they empty their gastric contents more quickly. Thus this subgroup of infants may tolerate enteral feeds better if they are given as a slow, intermittent infusion.

The presence of a small volume of feed (e.g., 4 ml/kg) is as capable as a larger feed volume (e.g., 10 ml/kg) of eliciting a motor response to feeding (14). Therefore when one is using minimal feed volumes to enhance gut maturation, small volumes appear to be able to achieve the same level of stimulation of motor function as larger ones. This effect can be elicited when using enteral feed volumes that provide as little as 10% of the infant's daily estimated energy intake.

Feeding diluted formula to preterm infants results in a diminished motor response (14,15). However, the intestine responds similarly to feeds given intragastrically or transpylorically. As in the adult, warming or chilling formula does not result in any alteration in motor activity or gastric emptying.

EFFECT OF MOTOR FUNCTION ON FEEDING

Because motor function is regulated by neural and hormonal input, the administration of drugs or nutrients that alter the release of neurotransmitters or hormones can in turn alter motor function. The administration of antenatal steroids has been shown to induce maturation of the central nervous system as well as intestinal mucosal enzyme release. Therefore one could postulate that preterm infants exposed to antenatal steroids might show more mature motor function. Morriss demonstrated that duodenal motor contraction rate was higher in preterm infants who had been exposed to antenatal steroids than in those who had not (16). Similarly, we have recently shown in a large retrospective study that infants exposed to one or more doses of steroids antenatally show more motor quiescence and less cluster activity than infants who had not received antenatal steroids (17). These infants also experienced better feeding tolerance. Others have reported that infants exposed to antenatal steroids have a lower incidence of necrotizing enterocolitis, but this finding has not been confirmed.

Opioids are commonly used to sedate preterm infants who require ventilator support. The gastrointestinal tract is richly populated with opioid receptors. In another study we have shown that recordings of motor activity in babies who are fed within 24 hours of their most recent dose of morphine show significantly more motor quiescence than babies fed 48 to 72 hours after the most recent dose of morphine. As a result, the former infants have a more rapid rate of gastro-anal transit, suggesting that they have not had as good an opportunity to absorb nutrients.

Mydriatics instilled for routine screening for retinopathy of prematurity alter parasympathetic and sympathetic input. When preterm infants receive eyedrops before their first eye examination, they show a profound decrease in gut motor activity, and this results in a delay in gastric emptying (18).

The antrum and upper duodenum possess receptors for the hormone motilin. When motilin binds to these receptors, an episode of migrating activity is initiated. The antibiotic erythromycin binds competitively to the motilin receptor. Intragastric administration of erythromycin can trigger the initiation of migrating activity in preterm infants whose gestational ages exceed 32 weeks, and it can be used to increase gastric emptying in these infants (19).

THE INTERRELATION OF NUTRIENTS AND MOTOR FUNCTION IN DEVELOPMENT OF FEEDING STRATEGIES

An improved understanding of the interrelation between motor function and the presence of intraluminal nutrients may enable a more pragmatic approach to decisions about feeding preterm infants. For example, providing small enteral feeds to extremely premature infants may permit the bowel to mature faster, smoothing the transition to larger feed volumes later on. It appears that a volume as small as 10% of daily estimated energy intake, or approximately 15 to 20 ml/kg·d, can achieve this goal. If there are clinical reasons to limit the volume fed to the baby—such as concerns about the association between higher feeding volumes and necrotizing enterocolitis, or the need to reduce fluid intake in a baby who has chronic lung disease—current studies suggest that the benefits of enteral feeding on motor function can still be achieved using small volumes. In infants who have immature responses to bolus feeds, one may wish to consider the use of intermittent slow infusions to improve gastric emptying and feed tolerance.

Many different drugs are given to preterm infants as part of their routine care, including opioids, methylxanthines, prostaglandin inhibitors, mydriatics, and antibiotics. All these drugs may have unintended effects on gastrointestinal motor function. Thus the neonatologist may wish to withhold or alter feeding strategies while infants are receiving these drugs. Alternatively, as more information on the control of developing motor function has become available, the intentional use of agonists or antagonists of neural input to the intestine may be useful in enhancing the ability to provide nutrients enterally. Feeding selective nutrients enterally may also trigger the endogenous mechanisms for neural or hormonal regulation of motor function.

REFERENCES

1. Malagelada JR, Camilleri M, Stanghellini V, eds. Systematic approach to reading gastrointestinal manometric tracings. In: *Diagnosis of motility disorders.* New York: Thieme; 1986.
2. Szurszewski JH. A migrating electric complex of the canine small intestine. *Am J Physiol* 1969;217:1757–1763.
3. Wen J, Phillips SF, Sarr MG, Kost LJ, Holst JJ. PYY and GLP-1 contribute to feedback inhibition from the canine ileum and colon. *Am J Physiol* 1995;269:945–952.
4. Herbst JJ. Development of suck and swallow. *J Pediatr Gastroenterol Nutr* 1983;2 (Suppl): S131–135.
5. Gryboski JD. The swallowing mechanisms of the neonate. I. Esophageal and gastric motility. *Pediatrics* 1965;35:445–452.
6. Siegel MM. Gastric emptying time in premature and compromised infants. *J Pediatr Gastroenterol Nutr* 1983;2 [Suppl]:S136–140.
7. Berseth CL. Chronic therapeutic morphine administration alters small intestinal motor patterns and gastroanal transit in preterm infants. *Pediatr Res* 1996;39:305A (abst.).
8. Berseth CL. Gestational evolution of small intestinal motility in preterm and term infants. *J Pediatr* 1989:115:646–651.
9. Amarnath PR, Berseth CL, Malagelada JR, *et al.* Postnatal maturation of small intestinal motility in preterm infants. *J Gastrointest Motil* 1989;1:138–143.
10. Al-Tawil Y, Berseth CL. Gestational and postnatal maturation of duodenal motor responses to intragastric feeding. *J Pediatr* 1996;129:374–381.
11. Berseth CL. Early feedings induce functional maturation of preterm small intestine. *J Pediatr* 1992;12:947–953.
12. Berseth CL, Nordyke C. Enteral nutrients promote postnatal maturation of intestinal motor activity. *Am J Physiol* 1993;264:G1046–1051.
13. Owens L, Burrin D, Berseth CL. Enteral nutrition has a dose-response effect on maturation of neonatal canine motor activity. *Gastroenterology* 1996;110:828A.
14. Koenig WJ, Amarnath RP, Hench V, Berseth CL. Manometrics for preterm and term infants: a new tool for old questions. *Pediatrics* 1995;38:133–139.
15. Baker JH, Berseth CL. Duodenal motor responses in preterm infants fed formula with varying concentrations and rates of infusion. *Pediatr Res* 1997;42:618–622.

16. Morriss FH, Moore M, Weisbrodt NW, *et al.* Ontogenetic development of gastrointestinal motility. IV. Duodenal contractions in preterm infants. *Pediatrics* 1986;78:1106–1113.
17. Baker-Wills E, Berseth CL. Antenatal steroids enhance maturation of small intestinal motor activity in preterm infants. *Pediatr Res* 1996;39:193A (abst.).
18. Bonthala S, Sparks JW, Musgrove C, Berseth CL. Mydriatics decrease gastroduodenal motor function after routine eye exams in preterm infants. *Pediatr Res* 1996;39:125A (abst.).
19. Jadcherla SR, Berseth CL. Prokinetic effects of erythromycin in preterm and term infants are related to gestational age. *Pediatr Res* 1995;37:124A (abst.).

DISCUSSION

Dr. Da Silva: In relation to pharmacological manipulations, do you have any information about the use of cisapride, in animal models, for example?

Dr. Berseth: There has been very little work done on cisapride in neonates. My concern with many drugs is that we don't know what receptors are present, or what neural mechanisms. We know from work on erythromycin that there is a gestational evolution of response to that drug, and there is a very precise dose/response effect in neonates that is significantly different from what one sees in the older child. Based on those data, I would certainly speculate that we would see differences in the way cisapride is handled. However, a group in Europe demonstrated increased gastric emptying with cisapride [1], though I don't know the gestational ages of the babies. We need a lot more information. One should keep in mind that the intestinal tract may be telling us that it is not ready. When we force it by using such agents, we may be doing more harm than good.

Dr. Costalos: We have just completed a study on preterm babies where we measured gastric emptying ultrasonically. We found much faster gastric emptying with cisapride.

Dr. Walker: As you know, there is an intimate relation between the enteric immune system, the enteric nervous system, and by implication the muscles within the intestine. What do you know about inflammatory cytokines and their role on motility in the immature intestine? I'm referring particularly to studies that Scott reported a number of years ago, though not on premature infants, suggesting that inflammatory cytokines released under conditions of mast cell stimulation can enhance peristaltic movement in the intestine [2]. I wonder if there is anything known about this in the context of the very small infant?

Dr. Berseth: I don't think this has been looked at specifically in the human infant. It's an important issue that needs study, particularly in view of the pathophysiology of necrotizing enterocolitis, which is usually heralded by abdominal distention.

Dr. Rashwan: Could you summarize the advantages of continuous *versus* intermittent feeding? And did you study position? Previous studies mentioned that positioning the infant at 45°, for example, enhances gastric emptying.

Dr. Berseth: I want to make clear that when we did our studies, we were not looking at continuous infusions. We looked at an intermittent infusion given slowly *versus* an intermittent infusion given rapidly. We found that emptying was incomplete with the slow, intermittent infusion regimen, suggesting that when continuous infusions are used we may not be allowing the intestine to clear material completely. But I don't want to give the impression that we were assessing continuous infusions; we weren't. When I'm feeding babies, I prefer some sort of cycling where there is a period of feeding and a period of fasting. Both cyclical fasting activity and the feeding response may be important for normal physiological gut activity.

With reference to position, we often don't have the ability to choose this, because the position is dictated by the needs of pulmonary care. When we do our gastric emptying studies as a research tool, we are careful about making sure that the babies are positioned the same way, to minimize posture as an additional variable, but we haven't specifically investigated that aspect.

Dr. Rashwan: But does position enhance emptying or not?

Dr. Berseth: Yes, Victor has shown that the position does influence emptying [3]. If one were just concerned with emptying, one would place the baby right side down.

Prof. Cooke: One of the reasons usually given for delaying feeding sick newborn infants is that their gastric motility is likely to be abnormal when they're hypotensive or acidotic or hypoxic. Do you have any evidence from your studies that any of these abnormal physiological conditions alter gastric motility in preterm infants, or can we actually ignore the fact that the infant is sick and carry on feeding?

Dr. Berseth: We know that the central nervous system and the parasympathetic and sympathetic systems can have a tremendous effect on gut motor function. We don't choose to study babies when they are in a stressed condition, but there are some who develop difficulties while we are doing the studies, and in those instances we can see their activity tapering off. I don't think we have any way of being able to assess the effect directly in any given clinical situation, but in general one would anticipate that any stress is going to have an inhibitory effect on motor function.

Dr. Sedaghatian: Have you done any studies on breast milk *versus* formula? Most of your babies seem to have been on Similac.

Dr. Berseth: Studies were done comparing breast milk with formula some years ago in a very small number of babies [4]. There was some evidence of a faster return to the prefeeding pattern when babies were fed breast milk. We have not repeated those studies, but that would be of interest.

Prof. Lucas: From our own studies, human milk and formula have a profoundly different effect on gastrointestinal hormones, so I think that would be a fruitful area to pursue. Do you think that motilin has any promise as a therapeutic agent for stimulating gut maturation or gut motility in clinical situations where there is a functional ileus or where immaturity seems too great for enteral feeding? I am aware of one case report, but you may know of more data on this.

Dr. Berseth: To remind those who may be rusty on the subject, motilin is a hormone that is released cyclically into the blood. It binds to motilin receptors in the distal stomach and upper intestine and triggers the migrating motor complexes. Our original reason for looking at erythromycin was specifically that its amino acid structure makes it a competitor for the motilin receptor. We found that there is no cyclical release of motilin in preterm babies; however, beyond about 32 weeks of gestation they will respond to erythromycin, so it does appear that the receptor is present. In the older infant therefore there may be opportunities to use motilin or an analog as a prokinetic agent, and there are some reports of its use in postoperative babies with feeding difficulties. A nonantibiotic analog of erythromycin has been developed and is undergoing clinical trials in adults. If this were to become available for pediatric use, it would be a very interesting drug to evaluate.

Dr. Costalos: We measured gut hormone levels in babies fed intragastrically or naso-jejunally, and we found almost identical hormone patterns.

Dr. Berseth: The only difference we found in our studies was the release of gastrin. When we use transpyloric feeding, we are not able to show gastrin release.

Dr. Horpaopan: In your study of mydriatics for eye examination, how long does the effect last?

Dr. Berseth: We did not continue to record throughout the day after the eye examination, so I don't know. However, it seems that even with the low doses now in use, we are getting systemic absorption and we are seeing gastrointestinal effects as a result. Neonatologists need to be aware of this in terms of possibly altering the feeding regimen on the day of the examination.

Dr. Devane: Do you have information on day-to-day variability in a given baby in gut motor patterns?

Dr. Berseth: We don't record from day to day. Most of our babies had records on three separate occasions. Despite the fact that there is a maturational change going on, every baby has a very characteristic pattern, so I think there is consistency over time in a given baby. But obviously there are things that change every day in the nursery—babies develop infections, they may have apnea, bradycardia, and so on, so there are many other factors that may cause day-to-day variation.

Prof. Moro: There seem to be two different ways of feeding VLBW infants, practically speaking. One is to use continuous feeding 24 hours a day, and the other is to use small bolus feeds every 1 or 2 hours. According to what you have told us, there could be a third option—to feed continuously for periods of several hours, interspersed with some hours of rest. Could you comment on this?

Dr. Berseth: Schanler has just finished a very large trial looking specifically at the use of continuous feeding *versus* bolus feeding. I have been using the third alternative you describe—that is, 1- or 2-hour infusions followed by 2 hours of fasting. The reason I used 2 hours of fasting was that from earlier studies it appeared that a small number of babies took about 90 minutes to return to the fasting pattern; thus I chose 2 hours to ensure that they all returned to a prefeeding pattern. Now that we have some of our gastric emptying data available, we have some concern about the use of continuous infusions, even though the overall outcome in terms of weight gain and the establishment of feeding were not different between the two feeding strategies.

Prof. Ziegler: Bile aspirates are obtained every now and then and they usually cause alarm. Am I correct in saying that retrograde paradoxical duodenal motility may explain these bile stained aspirates?

Dr. Berseth: Some babies certainly have retrograde migration, though others may have episodes of ileus that account for the finding.

REFERENCES

1. Kneepens CMF, van Weissenbruch MM, Kalick W, Touw DJ, Cranendonk A, Laeseber HN. Effect of cisapride on gastric emptying preterm infants: corrections for ^{13}C recovered of voids needs for standardized meals in the ^{13}C-octanoic acid breath test. *J Pediatr Gastroenterol Nutr* 1998;26:552.
2. Insoft RM, Sanderson IR, Walker WA. Development of immune function in the intestine and its role in neonatal diseases. *Pediatr Clin North Am* 996;43(2):551–571.
3. Victor YH. Effect of body position on gastric emptying in the neonate. *Arch Dis Child* 1975;50(7):500–504.
4. Tomomasa T, Hyman PE, Itoh K, et al. Gastroduodenal motility in neonates: response to human milk compared with cow's milk formula. *Pediatrics* 1987;80(3):434–438.

Nutrition of the Very Low Birthweight Infant, edited by
Ekhard E. Ziegler, Alan Lucas, Guido E. Moro.
Nestlé Nutrition Workshop Series, Paediatric Programme, Vol. 43,
Nestec Ltd., Vevey/Lippincott Williams & Wilkins
Philadelphia, Pennsylvania © 1999.

Actual Nutrient Intakes of Extremely Low-Birthweight Infants

Susan J. Carlson

*Department of Food and Nutrition Services, Children's Hospital of Iowa,
Iowa City, Iowa, USA*

Nutrient requirements have been described for the extremely low-birthweight infant (ELBW; less than 1,000 g birthweight) (1–3). These requirements serve as goals for the nutritional plan of care. Many factors may influence the ability to meet these nutritional goals. Complications of prematurity—including hyperglycemia, respiratory distress, sepsis, patent ductus arteriosus, and necrotizing enterocolitis—influence medical decisions about nutritional therapy. The initiation of nutritional therapy, type of nutrients provided (enteral or parenteral), amount of fluid to be given, and rate of nutrition advancement are all affected by the infant's medical condition. It is assumed that eventually nutritional goals are met and growth begins. While studies have been done describing the growth of the very low-birthweight (VLBW) and ELBW infant, there is little information describing the actual nutrient intakes these infants receive.

Beginning in September 1994, routine nutrient intake and growth data were collected on all infants admitted to the Children's Hospital of Iowa with birthweights of less than 1,300 g. Results of the first monitor interval, September 1994 to May 1995 (interval A), have been published previously (4). Data collection has continued to the present day to monitor changing trends in nutrition therapy and identify areas in which nutrition management of the VLBW infant may be improved. The effects of changes in nutritional practices can be evaluated by comparing monitor intervals over time. My purpose here is to describe changes in nutrient intakes and growth of infants born in interval A with those born from January to December 1997 (interval B). For the purposes of this chapter, only data from those infants of birthweight less than 1,000 g will be described.

DATA COLLECTION

A standard method of collecting nutrient intake and growth data was initiated in September 1994 and continues through the present time. All infants of birthweight less than 1,300 g and admitted to the University of Iowa Hospitals and Clinics spe-

TABLE 1. *ELBW infants in interval A (9/94–5/95) vs. interval B (1/97–12/97) (median; range)*

Infant characteristics	Interval A	Interval B
Number of infants	35	51
Birthweight (g)	790; 427–1000	736; 349–983
Gestational age (weeks)	26; 23–31	26; 22–30
SGA/AGA/LGA	26% / 74% / 0%	36% / 64% / 0%
Breast milk/combination/formula	44% / 27% / 29%	31% / 47% / 21%
Days to regain birthweight (d)	13; 3–28	13; 3–23
Days to first enteral feed (d)	4; 1–18	3; 0–7
Days to start of human milk fortification (d)	24; 11–51	26; 11–73
Days to all enteral feeds (d)	28; 14–70	34; 11–92
Length of stay (d)	89; 41–203	78; 31–221
Discharge weight (g)	2060; 1250–3170	2240; 950–4530

AGA = appropriate weight for gestational age; LGA = large for gestational age; SGA = small for gestational age.

cial-care nurseries within 48 hours of life are monitored. Infants discharged before 21 days of age are removed from the data summary. Data are collected throughout the infant's stay in the special-care nurseries, ending upon discharge or transfer to another hospital or unit within the University of Iowa Hospitals.

General descriptive information collected on the infants includes birthweight; days to regain birthweight; gestational age by dates, ultrasound, or physician's examination; and weight for gestational age (5). Infants are classified as small for gestational age (SGA) if they weigh less than the 10th centile for gestational age, and large for gestational age (LGA) if they weigh more than the 90th centile for adjusted age when compared with weight curves published by Arbuckle *et al.* (6). Routine feeding information is gathered, including the type of feeding (breast milk, combination of breast milk and formula, or formula alone); other feeding information collected includes the age enteral feeding is initiated, age intravenous fluids are first discontinued, and age human milk fortification is started. The use of concentrated feeds and the energy density used (27, 28, or 30 kcal/oz; 90, 93, or 100 kcal/dl) is recorded as well. Discharge information—including length of stay, weight at discharge, and type of discharge (to home, local hospital, or other University of Iowa hospitals nursing units)—completes the general information collected. Comparison of the general characteristics of ELBW infants in interval A and interval B is seen in Table 1.

Nutrient intake data are calculated by gathering actual nutrient intakes, from midnight to midnight, every seventh day of life. The nutrient content of the parenteral and enteral feeds is determined from nursing flowsheets and from pharmacy and nutrition records. Parenteral intake includes parenteral nutrition, intravenous lipids, and any carbohydrate intake from dextrose/electrolyte solutions, medication drips, and routine flushes. Energy intake from parenteral fluids is calculated using values of 3.4 kcal/g for carbohydrate and 4 kcal/g for amino acids. Nutrient content of intravenous lipids and enteral formulas and human milk fortifier is based on manufacturer's product information. The nutrient content of human milk is estimated using data for mature human milk—that is, 67 kcal/dl and 1 g protein/dl. Actual weight of infants is recorded every seventh day of life. For those infants who are weighed more than once in the 24-hour period, the first recorded weight of the day is used.

DATA CALCULATIONS

Because nutritional goals and anticipated weight gains change as the infant matures, the data are divided into four feeding periods: the parenteral period (age 0 to 14 days), the transitional period (age 15 to 35 days), and the early and late feeding periods (age 36 to 56 days and 57 days to term adjusted age, respectively). Nutrient intakes calculated during a feeding period are averaged for that period (e.g., intakes calculated at age 21 days, 28 days, and 35 days are averaged to determine the mean nutrient intake during the transitional period). Table 2 compares the nutrient intakes for fluid, energy, and protein by feeding period in interval A *versus* interval B. Weight gains are calculated by subtracting weight at the beginning of the period from the weight at the end of the period and dividing by number of days in the period. Weight gains (g/kd·d) are calculated by dividing this number by the average weight during the feeding period. Table 3 compares the weight gain (g/d and g/kg·d) in intervals A and B to fetal growth rate at the same gestation. Fetal growth for the same feeding periods were calculated from 50th centile weights, using 26 weeks of gestation as age 0 days, 28 weeks of gestation as age 7 days, and so on (6).

TABLE 2. *Nutrient intakes by feeding period for ELBW infants, interval A (9/94–5/95) vs. interval B (1/97–12/97) (mean ± SD)*

Feeding interval	Interval A	Interval B
Parenteral period (age 0–14 days)		
Number of infants	35	51
Fluid intake (ml/kg)	128 ± 18	135 ± 24
Energy intake (kJ/kg)	310 ± 50	343 ± 54
(kcal/kg)	74 ± 12	82 ± 13
Protein intake (g/kg)	1.8 ± 0.5	2.5 ± 0.6
Transitional period (age 15–35 days)		
Number of infants	35	50
Fluid intake (ml/kg)	129 ± 10	125 ± 15
Energy intake (kJ/kg)	406 ± 50	410 ± 63
(kcal/kg)	97 ± 12	98 ± 15
Protein intake (g/kg)	2.4 ± 0.4	2.8 ± 0.4
Early enteral period (age 36–56 days)		
Number of infants	32	46
Fluid intake (ml/kg)	136 ± 15	129 ± 16
Energy intake (kJ/kg)	452 ± 58	456 ± 58
(kcal/kg)	108 ± 14	109 ± 14
Protein intake (g/kg)	2.7 ± 0.5	2.9 ± 0.4
Late enteral period (age 57 days to term)		
Number of infants	27	35
Fluid intake (ml/kg)	133 ± 18	133 ± 15
Energy intake (kJ/kg)	456 ± 58	494 ± 50
(kcal/kg)	109 ± 14	118 ± 12
Protein intake (g/kg)	2.7 ± 0.4	3.1 ± 0.4

TABLE 3. *Weight gain of ELBW infants by feeding period,*
interval A (9/94–5/95) vs. interval B (1/97–12/97) (mean ± SD)

Feeding interval	Interval A	Interval B	Fetal growth rate
Parenteral period (age 0–14 days)			
Weight gain (g/d)	1.9 ± 4.7	3.1 ± 4.7	17.5
Weight gain (g/kg · d)	2.1 ± 5.6	4.1 ± 6.6	17.1
Transitional period (age 15–35 days)			
Weight gain (g/d)	12.2 ± 4.7	15.7 ± 5.8	24.5
Weight gain (g/kg · d)	13.1 ± 4.5	16.5 ± 4.3	17.5
Early enteral period (age 36–56 days)			
Weight gain (g/d)	16.8 ± 5.7	21.3 ± 7.4	30.2
Weight gain (g/kg · d)	13.5 ± 4.3	16.3 ± 4.2	15.3
Late enteral period (age 57 days to term)			
Weight gain (g/d)	20.3 ± 6.2	26.9 ± 7.8	28.8
Weight gain (g/kg · d)	12.0 ± 4.0	14.3 ± 3.6	9.9

RESULTS

General Characteristics

The median gestational age of ELBW infants was similar in both monitor intervals, although a higher percentage of SGA infants in interval B made the median birthweight lower than interval A. More than 70% of ELBW infants in both monitor intervals began with breast milk feeds. Despite the extended length of stay, nearly 40% of the infants continued on breast milk feeds throughout their hospital stay. Minimal changes between interval A and interval B were seen in days to regain birthweight, age to initiate enteral feeds or human milk fortifier, and age when intravenous fluids were first discontinued (full enteral feeds). Despite minimal changes in the age when enteral feeds were initiated, the range was substantially smaller, indicating a more consistent use of early enteral feeds. Length of stay in the special-care nurseries declined in interval B, showing the increased number of transfers to other hospitals or nursing units (62% in interval B *versus* 49% in interval A) and decreased number of discharges to home (38% in interval B *versus* 51% in interval A). Despite the shorter length of stay and lower median birthweight, the median discharge weight in interval B was 180 g higher than the median discharge weight in interval A.

Nutrient Intakes

Fluid restriction remains a standard component of medical management for infants at risk for bronchopulmonary dysplasia (BPD). Fluid intake varied minimally from interval A to interval B. During the early enteral feeding period, approximately 60% of infants born weighing less than 750 g had average fluid intakes ≤135 ml/kg. Fifty percent of infants born weighing 750 to 1,000 g had mean fluid intakes of ≤135 ml/kg in the same feeding period. In response to the need for fluid restriction, concentrated feeds were often used, with 47% of infants in interval A and 63% of infants in interval B receiving concentrated formulas or fortified human milk.

Energy

Energy intake during the parenteral period overestimated actual energy intakes during the period, as the days of measurement were age 7 and 14 days. Improving energy intakes from interval A to interval B were seen in the parenteral period and late enteral feeding period. In the former, increased energy intake probably reflected the use of higher concentrations of dextrose and amino acid solutions in parenteral feeding. Increased use of concentrated feeds and the extended use of preterm formula and human milk fortifiers in infants weighing 2,000 to 3,000 g increased energy intake in the late enteral feeding period.

Protein

Protein intake may be underestimated in both intervals A and B owing to the high percentage of breast milk-fed infants and the use of mature human milk protein content for nutrient intake calculations. In addition, actual mean protein intake in interval B was underestimated as some of the infants were involved in a protein supplementation study. Because the study protocol is double blind, it is unknown which infants received protein supplementation. Therefore this protein intake could not be included in the nutrient intake calculations. However, a review of protein intakes in interval B *versus* interval A showed a trend toward improved protein intakes in all but the early enteral feeding period. Protein intakes in interval B were increased by using higher amino acid concentrations in parenteral nutrition and by extending the use of preterm formulas and human milk fortifiers for infants weighing 2,000 to 3,000 g.

Growth

The weight gain of infants in interval B surpassed that of infants in interval A in all feeding periods both in g/day and in g/kg·d. When compared with fetal growth calculated from the 50th centile weight for gestational age starting at 26 weeks of gestation, infants in intervals A appeared to exceed fetal growth (g/kg·d) in the late enteral period, whereas those in interval B appeared to exceed fetal growth in both the early and late enteral periods (6). Early growth failure results in a smaller denominator in the g/kg·d equation and thereby exaggerates weight gains in infants of less than the appropriate weight for age. When growth rates were converted to total weight gain (g/d), the growth of infants in both monitor intervals was below fetal growth rate throughout their hospital stay. Figure 1 shows the mean weight of infants in intervals A and B compared with the 50th centile weight of infants at similar gestational ages. This figure demonstrates the increasing growth deficit occurring in ELBW infants throughout the period of hospital admission.

DISCUSSION

Results of nutrition monitoring completed in September 1994 to May 1995 showed a deficit in both energy and protein intake of VLBW infants throughout their

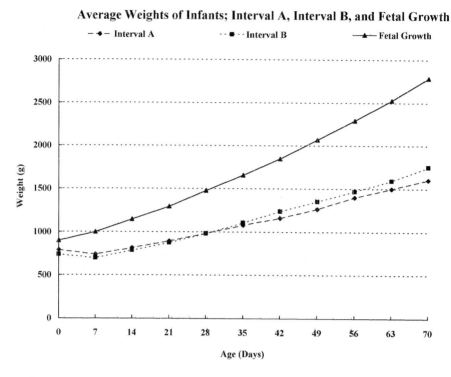

FIG. 1. Mean weights of infants in intervals A and B compared with 50th centile fetal weight starting at 26 weeks of gestation.

hospital stay (4). Subsequently, nutrition interventions were initiated to improve awareness of nutrition deficits and to modify nutrition practices in the special-care nurseries at the University of Iowa Hospitals and Clinics. Interventions included routine review of nutrition monitoring results with health care team members, increased use of high-nutrient-density parenteral nutrition solutions through percutaneous central catheters, extended use of premature formulas and human milk fortifiers in infants weighing 2,000 to 3,000 g, and development of nutrition guidelines and references for medical residents and nurse practitioners. In addition, a routine electrolyte monitoring and supplementation protocol was established and a double-blind randomized controlled trial of protein supplementation was initiated. As a result of these interventions, nutrition monitoring completed in January 1997 to December 1997 showed increases in energy and protein intake as well as improved weight gains and fewer days in a level III nursery.

Despite these improvements, infants continue to fall below estimated goals in energy and protein intakes as well as in weight gain. It has been estimated that preterm infants require nutrient intakes of 110 kcal/kg·d for growth (7). During interval B, this goal was achieved only in the late enteral interval. Barriers to achieving energy goals include fluid restrictions and slow advancements in enteral feeds to adjust for growth. A recent review of 10 ELBW infants on full enteral feeds found the mean number of days between enteral feeding advancement was 3.8. Nine of the 10 infants had at least one feeding period when enteral feeds were held at the same volume for ≥7 days.

Estimated protein goals of ELBW infants are 4 g/kg·d using the factorial method (3). As the infants grow, protein requirements decline but still remain at 3.5 g/kg in infants weighing 1,500 to 2,000 g. Despite improvements in protein intakes from interval A to B, protein intake remained below goals throughout special-care nursery admission. Potential causes for this protein deficit included fluid restrictions and the use of concentrated feeds made from the addition of term formula concentrates. The predominant reason for reduced protein intakes is likely to be the protein energy ratio of current preterm infants feeds. Although it is estimated that infants weighing less than 1,000 g require a protein-to-energy ratio of 3.6 g/100 kcal, preterm infant formulas contain at best 3.0 g/100 kcal, and fortified human milk is even lower.

Wilson *et al.* described improved growth and earlier hospital discharge in 64 VLBW infants fed an aggressive nutrition regimen (8). Berry *et al.* showed a positive correlation between energy and protein intakes and growth in 109 ELBW infants (9). In addition, they found a negative correlation between birthweight ratio and growth. Improved growth rate from interval A to interval B may be due to the higher percentage of SGA infants in interval B but also is probably related to improvements in energy and protein intake. Increased intake of protein in particular may have contributed to the increased growth. Kashyap and Heird have shown a relation between increasing protein intakes and growth (10). Infants meeting estimated protein requirements in their studies met or exceeded fetal growth rates. The greatest improvement in energy and protein intake occurred in the parenteral period, whereas the biggest improvements in weight gains occurred in the transitional period. It is reasonable to assume that early adequate nutrition may affect growth and nutritional status well beyond the first weeks of life.

Despite improvements in weight gain, growth of ELBW infants remained significantly below fetal growth. By the late enteral interval, weight gain rates (g/kg·d) exceeded those of the fetus; however, total weight gain (g/d) continued below fetal growth. Therefore a weight deficit continued to accrue throughout the period in the hospital. The mean weight of infants in interval B at 36 weeks of gestation-adjusted age was 1,036 g less than the weight of a 36-week-gestation fetus growing at the 50th centile. Because interval B had a large number of SGA infants, the infants started with a weight deficit. However, the weight deficit at birth was only 164 g, substantially lower than the weight deficit 10 weeks later.

CONCLUSION

Extremely low-birthweight infants remain at high risk of nutritional deficits. Although improvements in nutrient intakes, particularly protein, were shown to improve growth rate in this study, ELBW infants continued to fall behind fetal growth curves throughout their hospital stay. Various factors in prematurity may influence growth. Berry *et al.* found a negative correlation between dexamethasone use and growth and between respiratory support duration and growth (9). The multiple medical challenges facing the ELBW infant may make it impossible to achieve fetal growth outside the womb. However, every effort should be made to improve nutrition therapy, achieve nutrition goals, and thereby improve nutritional status and growth of these infants.

REFERENCES

1. Pereira GR. Nutritional care of the extremely premature infant. *Clin Perinatol* 1995;22:61–75.
2. Ziegler EE, Biga RL, Fomon SJ. Nutritional requirements of the premature infant. In: Suskind M, ed. *Textbook of pediatric nutrition.* New York: Raven Press; 1981:29–39.
3. Ziegler EE. Protein in premature feeding. *Nutrition* 1994;10:69–71.
4. Carlson SJ, Ziegler EE. Nutrient intakes and growth of very low birth weight infants. *J Perinatol* 1998;18:252–258.
5. Ballard JL, Khoury JC, Wedig K, Wang L, Eilers Walsman BL, Lipp R. New Ballard Score, expanded to include extremely premature infants. *J Pediatr* 1991;119:417–423.
6. Arbuckle TE, Wilkins R, Sherman GJ. Birth weight percentiles by gestational age in Canada. *Obstet Gynecol* 1993;8:38–48.
7. Bell EF. Nutritional support. In: Goldsmith JP, Karotkin EH, eds. *Assisted ventilation of the neonate.* Philadelphia: WB Saunders; 1996:381–395.
8. Wilson DC, Cairns P, Halliday HL, *et al.* Randomised controlled trial of an aggressive nutritional regimen in sick very low birthweight infants. *Arch Dis Child* 1997;77:F4–F11.
9. Berry MA, Abrahamowicz M, Usher RH. Factors associated with growth of extremely premature infants during initial hospitalization. *Pediatrics* 1997;100:640–646.
10. Kashyap S, Heird WC. Protein requirements of low birthweight, very low birthweight, and small for gestational age infants. In: Raiha NCR, ed. *Protein metabolism during infancy.* Nestlé Nutrition Workshop Series, vol 33. New York: Raven Press; 1994.

DISCUSSION

Prof. Lucas: You posed so many important practical questions that we could have spent the whole rest of the day addressing them. These are immensely important matters for clinical practice. It seems that the failure to meet the infant's needs is caused by two main factors. One is not prescribing enough, and the other is not giving what you actually prescribe. It is the latter I want to discuss. We recommend that when babies are not growing well, a neonatologist should record the prescribed protein and energy intake, and not the achieved protein and energy intake, and they are often radically different. One of the reasons for that difference is that when feeds are discarded, because of gastric aspirate or distention, they are not replaced, or when an intravenous infusion tissue ceases for a couple of hours because the resident is busy, the amount lost is not replaced. What is the solution to that? Should we recalculate after a missed feed so that we give an increased amount? Should we overprescribe deliberately to account for likely losses? What is your policy for dealing with that?

Ms. Carlson: Our policy is not well established. Perhaps we should set our goals a little bit higher with the understanding that we may not provide the full amount. Then I think we need to be more attentive at ensuring that if feeds are withheld, they are withheld for a reason. Another thing that I did not bring up but which I think is important is that often feeds are not advanced as the children grow. The residents feel that if the baby is continuing to gain weight, why should the feeds be increased. We need to be rather more proactive with advancing feeds as the babies grow.

Prof. Moro: You said that you are giving electrolyte supplementation orally? Why do you give oral electrolytes, rather than intravenously? Do you measure the osmolality of the solution?

Ms. Carlson: I was referring to electrolyte supplementation given after the children are no longer receiving intravenous fluids. We find that many preterm infants on full enteral feedings have hyponatremia or hypokalemia and require some electrolyte supplementation. I agree that it is important to consider the effect on osmolality, because oral electrolyte solutions are certainly hyperosmolar. We are very careful to give small amounts with many feeds rather than large amounts with just a single feed. We find the babies tolerate electrolyte supplements well.

Prof. Ziegler: For clarification, Ms. Carlson calls it supplementation when it is given enterally. While the baby is on parenteral nutrition, the electrolytes are of course adjusted to maintain normal serum values. The criteria for when supplementation is necessary are not well established. Sometimes we supplement when the serum sodium reaches 130 mmol/l, and sometimes only when it is way below 130. A high proportion of the babies who require electrolyte supplementation are receiving diuretics and that may be the main reason. Another important reason is that our feeds, whether human milk with fortifier or formula, are all low in sodium.

Dr. Rashwan: Were these babies receiving multivitamins or other oral supplements?

Ms. Carlson: We did not give additional vitamin supplementation to infants fed fortified human milk or preterm formula, though babies on fortified breast milk did receive iron supplementation.

Dr. Sedaghatian: We also use oral electrolytes and sometimes bicarbonate when the infants are on enteral feeding. I think this is necessary. But I was amazed by the amount of fluid you give to babies of less than 1,000 g sometimes up to 300 or 400 ml/kg body weight. Is that correct?

Ms. Carlson: There certainly were babies who received substantially higher fluid intakes than are generally accepted as the norm. But remember that those intakes of 300 ml/kg were given during the first 3 to 4 days of life, before the babies developed a satisfactory skin barrier. By day 7, our fluid intake was quite low, which probably reflected our concern about preventing patent ductus arteriosus.

Dr. Sedaghatian: Do you think we should try to achieve intrauterine growth rates at any cost? Maybe we should be content with lesser amounts of growth and give more attention to other factors in their care. In the past, it has been accepted that babies grow slowly under these conditions, and neurodevelopmental outcome has been satisfactory.

Ms. Carlson: I don't think we know what the potential of our babies is for growth. It may be unreasonable to expect a 25-week-gestation infant ever to grow at the intrauterine rate outside its mother. But from the data we have collected we know that our nutrient intakes did not even meet our goals. Although many babies may have a good neurological outcome despite poor growth, is it not possible that we could enhance the outcome by providing better nutrition?

Dr. Georgieff: Your study raises the question of the role of "nutrition support service police" in an intensive-care nursery, particularly where you have residents prescribing the daily nutrient intakes. Have you had a chance to compare intakes and compliance in a prenutrition support and a postnutrition support era? Do we do better when we have somebody coming round once a week to check on intakes, particularly when the service tends to be pulmonary oriented?

Ms. Carlson: There has been a dietitian at the University of Iowa Hospital Special Care Nurseries since long before I came, so it's hard for us to do a pre- and postevaluation. But I'm hoping to show that with more attention to methods of feeding there will be improved intakes and improved growth.

Dr. Georgieff: In our institution this has been looked at in the adult ICU with a nutrition support service. There were substantial cost savings to the hospital such that the administration now makes nutrition support consultations mandatory.

Ms. Carlson: There are institutions that don't have dietitians actively involved in the special-care nurseries, and those might be the sort of place to do that kind of evaluation in neonates.

Dr. Micheli: Your postnatal protein intake figures were similar to the ones showed by Prof. Heird and by myself yesterday. I do wonder, though, why we are depriving these fetuses of amino acids and protein during the first 14 days. Their intakes during this period are far below what they would have received *in utero*.

Ms. Carlson: I agree that by day 14 we still aren't providing the protein goal that we think preterm infants need. I'm not certain that I can identify all the reasons. In the first week or so, babies who are on parenteral nutrition may become septic so the catheter is removed and they are placed on dextrose, electrolyte solutions; we then lose 24 hours of intravenous amino acids while we wait for the next bag of TPN to come up. The low protein intakes that you see in the later intervals may be related to the low protein content of preterm formula and fortified breast milk. Many of our babies start on breast milk feeds, but we don't start fortifiers until the babies are about a month old. Even after increasing the amino acids in our parenteral solutions we may not be able to achieve our protein guidelines.

Dr. Micheli: But during this early adaptive phase we all prescribe protein intakes that are much lower than the supply that would be given through the placenta at the same gestational age. I don't know why.

Ms. Carlson: Maybe as we feel more comfortable with managing ELBW infants, we'll feel more comfortable about giving protein early.

Prof. Lucas: In our study comparing term formula with preterm formula, we randomly assigned those diets for a month and saw a major difference in neurodevelopmental outcome. If we just assume for one moment that this could be something to do with protein intake for essential tissue growth like brain growth, we are looking at 0.6 g/kg·d difference in protein intake between the two groups, yet we prescribe deficits of way over 0.6 g/kg·d of protein intake during the first month. I think Dr. Micheli has raised a critically important point. I can't help feeling that in 30 years' time, we will look back on this period of protein restriction in the early life of preterm infants as an extraordinary folly of late-twentieth-century neonatal practice.

Ms. Carlson: I completely agree.

Prof. Heird: It seems clear now that babies who are getting less than 1 g/kg·d of amino acids are in negative balance, and they are in approximate balance at 1 g/kg. Thus even if they receive 1 g/kg·d of protein over the first two weeks, which they may not, by the end of that time they will already have incurred a protein deficit of around 52 g compared with what they should have received *in utero*, and this is going to take a while to make up.

Prof. Ziegler: If we look back to 8 years ago, we would probably see intakes in the first week of life averaging less than 1 g/kg. It used to be standard practice not to provide TPN in the first 4 or 5 days, and then to start at 0.5 g/kg. Nobody knows where this came from, but it was standard practice. Now we are starting with 1.5 g on the first day of life. I think we are doing much better than we did only a few years ago, but I agree with you—we are not doing well enough.

Dr. Rigo: I'd like to ask about fluid restriction. You said that there was a fluid restriction policy in your unit aimed at preventing bronchopulmonary dysplasia. But the incidence of

BPD seems to be decreasing in most units, even in ELBW infants, with or without a policy of fluid restriction. It also seemed from your results that you were not increasing the fluid intake the first month of life, even in babies without BPD. Do you continue with fluid restriction right to the end of the stay in the neonatal unit, or do you have two populations that you can analyze separately—babies with fluid restriction and babies without fluid restriction?

Ms. Carlson: There are some babies without significant lung disease who receive more fluids. However, our unit policy may represent a particular way of managing lung disease— the residents believe that fluid restriction is good for preventing bronchopulmonary dysplasia, and many babies have fluid restrictions, even those who would probably tolerate more fluids. It is clear that much higher fluid volumes are given in some other units. It would be interesting to compare outcomes between units that give low and high fluid volumes with respect to BPD.

Prof. Cooper: As far as I'm aware, the data relating increased fluids to bronchopulmonary dysplasia and persistent ductus arteriosus relate to the early neonatal period. It's not scientific to extrapolate that beyond the first month or to the child who's already got established lung disease. Do you know of any data to support this policy? Otherwise, it would sound like a good subject for a randomized controlled study, since one could postulate the opposite—better nutrition and better growth might actually improve BPD regardless of the fluid intake.

Prof. Ziegler: Please don't hold our neonatal dietitian responsible for the policies of some neonatologists! Some of our neonatologists strongly believe in fluid restriction. That's the simple explanation for those low fluid volumes.

Prof. Lucas: We have monitored fluid intake of premature babies once they go home. Within 4 weeks of going home, a significant proportion of premature babies are spontaneously consuming between 250 and 350 ml/kg. I think we have probably been far too restrictive of volume in the well-growing baby. We have missed an opportunity of increasing dietary intake by manipulating volume.

Dr. Atkinson: Did you do any length measurements?

Ms. Carlson: No, we didn't. We don't feel very comfortable with the accuracy of length measurements within our institution in our ELBW infants, so we did not feel that those measurements would provide us with accurate data.

Dr. Atkinson: In our neonatal unit, our dietitian does them once a week. My second question is relating to your oral supplements. You did not list phosphorus supplements. I wondered whether you have much hypophosphatemia in these tiny babies, especially the ones on steroids.

Ms. Carlson: Not that we've noticed. We occasionally give calcium and phosphorus supplementation, but always together. This would be for babies who are at risk of rickets of prematurity. We concentrate our preterm formula by adding term formula concentrates, which not only dilutes protein but also dilutes calcium and phosphorus intake. Often these infants require additional calcium and phosphorus supplements to meet their needs for bone mineralization.

Dr. Rashwan: We have no dietitian in our hospital, in common with most of the Middle East area. I want to ask you about the nature of your work. Does your role start before oral feeding begins or after? And is your collaboration with the neonatologists on a daily basis? Do you plan the regimen with the neonatologists?

Ms. Carlson: I am involved with the infants from their admission into the neonatal intensive-care unit. Some institutions have a pharmacist who deals with the parenteral feeding and a dietitian who deals with the enteral feeds. I work with both. In our neonatal intensive-care unit, I help the staff write the parenteral prescriptions daily and recommend changes in enteral feeding regimens. In our intermediate unit, my involvement is less frequent, but I try to see what the babies are receiving on a daily basis. If I see any baby whose intake is far below our goal, I interact with the residents to get changes made.

Prof. Ziegler: The issue of what the dietitian is allowed to do and what neonatologists reserve for themselves is an interesting one. In our case the neonatologist determines the total fluid volume, the age at which feeding is started, and when feeding is withheld. Practically everything else is left to the dietitian, and because of that, Ms. Carlson has had a considerable impact on, for example, how much amino acids are given from the beginning. So in our case the dietitian has almost total autonomy in some areas, while in other areas she has no say at all.

Dr. Rashwan: Why is your role limited to the ICU? Surely it is also very important to be involved after discharge?

Ms. Carlson: As the dietitian, I am involved with the infants in the step-down nursery and after discharge. So we do try to continue to maintain optimum nutrition throughout those periods as well.

Prof. Polberger: Your title was "actual nutrient intakes," but it seems that you did not do any milk analyses. You estimated the human milk energy and protein to be the values accepted for mature human milk—that is, 67 kcal and 1 g protein per deciliter. But weren't you using mother's own milk, so shouldn't you have used data for preterm milk?

Ms. Carlson: We don't do nutrient analysis of the breast milk, so we don't really know what it contains. It's also difficult to identify when a baby is getting preterm milk or mature milk in our unit, so overall I felt it was better to underestimate than overestimate the nutrient content by using the mature milk value.

Prof. Devlieger: In our unit, we have designed with the help of a pharmacist a fixed standard TPN solution with different degrees of dilution, depending on the fluid tolerance of the baby. We are able to reach the required intake of energy and protein within 5 days. What is the role of the pharmacist in your parenteral feeding procedure?

Ms. Carlson: At our institution, we do not have a pharmacist who is actively involved in our neonatal intensive-care unit. Therefore I assist with parenteral nutrition orders. In our pediatric intensive-care unit, there is a pharmacist involved in helping to determine appropriate parenteral regimens, but that does not occur in our neonatal ICU.

Dr. Chessex: I'd like to return to the fundamental question that has been raised these last days by Prof. Ziegler, Dr. Micheli, and Prof. Lucas: Why aren't we following the recommendations? One reason may be that people outside this room don't believe it is important. This may be because there is not enough solid information showing that it is important. When Dr. Morley's studies are published it will perhaps be easier for people to believe in the importance of nutrition. If you see a brain echo with a large bleed, you have no difficulty in accepting that this may cause long-term problems, but when you hear talk about negative nitrogen balance, it is more difficult to make the connection. We need more solid evidence, and we are going slowly in that direction.

Prof. Lucas: I agree with that, but it is possibly a little unfair. There is a huge amount of accumulated data on malnutrition and adverse outcome. The major problem is the failure to communicate it rather than the failure to generate it. Obviously, we need more clinical trials, but making babies malnourished does not make sense on the basis of the information that we've already got.

Nutrition of the Very Low Birthweight Infant, edited by
Ekhard E. Ziegler, Alan Lucas, Guido E. Moro.
Nestlé Nutrition Workshop Series, Paediatric Programme, Vol. 43,
Nestec Ltd., Vevey/Lippincott Williams & Wilkins
Philadelphia, Pennsylvania © 1999.

Trophic Feeds

Ekhard E. Ziegler

The Fomon Infant Nutrition Unit, Department of Pediatrics, University of Iowa, Iowa City, Iowa, USA

The question of when to start enteral feeding confronts the caretaker of very low-birthweight (VLBW) infants on a daily basis. Seemingly conflicting objectives enter into consideration. The desire to minimize the risk of necrotizing enterocolitis (NEC) argues for the delayed introduction of feeds. Or so it did until recently. On the other hand, the desire to provide nutrients argues in favor of the early introduction of feeds. In the 1960s and 1970s the argument for delayed introduction was considered compelling and regimens calling for the prolonged withholding of feeds were widely adopted. In more recent years, the focus of attention has shifted to the prevention of gut atrophy as an important consideration. Consequently, early feeding regimens have been devised and successfully tested.

Undernutrition is common in the preterm infant (1) and is perhaps to some degree unavoidable. Its potential for long-term adverse effects is generally not fully appreciated by neonatologists, who face the challenge of providing nutritional support while battling with a host of usually more pressing medical problems. In the overall nutrition of the VLBW infant, enteral feeding during the early days of life constitutes but one facet of a complex situation (2). What follows is a brief description, from a decidedly nutritional point of view, of the delayed feeding as practiced until recently. A review of the controlled studies of trophic (early) feeds shows that this modality is not only effective in preventing gut atrophy, but also appears safe in that it does not seem to increase the risk of NEC. Finally, the results of a survey of feeding practices at my own institution are presented, showing that gastric residuals are a common occurrence in the first week of life without being harbingers of NEC.

DELAYED FEEDING REGIMENS

With the advent of neonatal medicine in the 1960s and the increased survival of premature infants came NEC—until then an uncommon disease entity. Because this often devastating disease almost always occurred in infants who were being fed enterally and hardly ever in infants who were not fed, feeds were suspected of causing NEC. Although the exact role of feeds in the etiology of NEC (obligatory bystander *versus* causative agent) remains unclear to this day, the fact that feeds are always

233

being given when NEC strikes is not in dispute. It is therefore understandable that preventive strategies focused on enteral feeding. Regimens were developed that called for graded periods of withholding of feeds, with infants at highest risk for NEC having feeds withheld for the longest time.

A prominent example is the regimen of Brown and Sweet (3). For low-birthweight infants with illness or a history of problems during delivery, they withheld feeds for the first 5 to 7 days of life before gradually introducing them. Frequent episodes of apnea or of bradycardia required cessation of feeds until 1 week after the last such episode. Marked abdominal distention, or occult fecal blood associated with other untoward signs, similarly necessitated withholding of feeds until a week after the abnormalities had cleared. If there were any gastric residuals of formula, a reduction in feed volume was mandatory, and persistent residuals required the cessation of feeding for 1 week. Brown and Sweet reported that before the introduction of their delayed feeding regimen, the incidence of NEC among low-birthweight babies had been 1.5%, but that it dropped to 0.11% after the introduction of the new regimen.

Only one prospective controlled trial tested the efficacy of delayed feeding regimens with regard to the incidence of NEC. In the study by La Gamma and colleagues (4), one group of infants with a birthweight of less than 1,500 g received only parenteral nutrition but no intragastric feeds for the first 2 weeks of life, whereas another group received parenteral nutrition plus intragastric feeds in gradually increasing amounts. A diagnosis of NEC required the presence of the clinical triad of abdominal distention or ileus, hematochezia, and bilious vomiting; radiologic confirmation was accepted but was not required. Using this definition, the incidence of NEC episodes was 60% in the group receiving no feeds for 2 weeks and 22% in the group receiving early oral feeds. The difference was statistically significant at $p < 0.02$. Although one might argue whether, in the absence of radiologic confirmation, all these episodes represented NEC, it is clear that the specific delayed feeding regimen that was tested did lead to an increase, rather than a decrease, in the incidence of NEC episodes.

Despite the absence of controlled trials showing the efficacy of delayed feeding regimens, such regimens were adopted widely and underwent a variety of modifications. Acceptance was probably facilitated by the soundness of the physiological principles invoked by proponents of delayed feedings, such as Brown and Sweet (3). The basic concept that any event causing gut ischemia increases the risk of NEC in a susceptible subject (e.g., a preterm infant) is certainly valid. What one may disagree about, however, is whether withholding of feeding is an effective countermeasure. Furthermore, from today's perspective, one must ask whether, even if withholding were effective, its adverse effects might not outweigh its possible beneficial effects.

ADVERSE EFFECTS OF DELAYED FEEDING

Undernutrition

When enteral feeding is withheld, nutrients must be provided by the parenteral route. Brown and Sweet (3) stressed that parenteral nutrition must be provided during periods when enteral feeds are withheld, but they provided no specifics concerning nutrient intakes, either recommended or actually achieved. Since in those days peripheral veins were used almost exclusively, one has to assume that intakes of energy and specific nutrients were limited. It is not unreasonable to presume that VLBW infants subjected to delayed feeding regimens incurred a substantial price in terms of nutrients not received and complications of parenteral nutrition incurred. Although a quantitative risk/benefit assessment is, of course, impossible, it appears that a definite risk was incurred in exchange for uncertain and unknown benefits.

Gut Atrophy

There is a sizable body of data from animal studies describing the effects of the prolonged withholding of luminal nutrition (5). In the adult rat, parenteral nutrition in the absence of luminal nutrition leads to a decrease in gut weight, mucosal height and thickness, reduced crypt cell proliferation, shortened villus height, and lowered antral gastrin concentration (6,7), as well as to diminished disaccharidase and peroxidase activities (8). In the suckling rat, withholding of luminal nutrition leads to profound alterations of gut size and villus height (9), although these changes are readily reversible upon refeeding (10). Small amounts of luminal nutrients were shown to be required for prevention of gut atrophy in the rat (11). In the rabbit, Rothman *et al.* (12) showed that withholding luminal nutrition increased the permeability of the gut to macromolecules. Changes in permeability may play a role in the increased bacterial translocation observed during parenteral nutrition (13). Intestinal cellular immunity is also decreased (14). In children with protein/energy malnutrition, decreased local secretion of IgA has been reported (15). Groër and Walker (16) have pointed out that feeding is necessary for the normal maturation of the gut secretory immune system. Table 1 summarizes the important changes observed during luminal starvation.

TROPHIC FEEDS

In the early 1980s neonatologists began to question the wisdom of routinely withholding feeds. Some questioned its efficacy in reducing NEC (17), some were

TABLE 1. *Effect of starvation on the gut*

Morphological changes:	↓ Mucosal mass
	↓ Cell production
	↓ Villus height
Functional changes:	↑ Permeability
	↓ Amino acid absorption
Enzymes:	↓ Sucrase
	↓ Lactase
Immunity:	↓ Number of lymphocytes
	↓ IgA secretion
	↑ Bacterial translocation

concerned about the adverse effects of prolonged parenteral nutrition (18), and many were concerned about the intestinal atrophy resulting from a prolonged absence of luminal nutrition (18–20). They began to explore ways by which the alleged benefits of delayed feeding (i.e., a reduced risk of NEC) could be retained while at the same time preserving gut integrity. This explains the various terms applied to enteral feeds introduced earlier than had become standard practice. These terms include *minimal enteral feedings* (21), *gastrointestinal priming* (20), *early hypocaloric feeding* (18), *trophic feeding*, or *early feeding*. The terminology reflects the notion that small amounts of feed are sufficient to prevent gut atrophy while at the same time being small enough to keep the risk of NEC low. This belief rested in part on the finding by Lucas and colleagues (22) that small amounts of feed produce marked increases in plasma gut hormone levels in preterm infants, and in part on results of animal studies showing that small amounts of nutrients are sufficient to prevent intestinal atrophy (see earlier).

The effects of the early introduction of feeds were examined in several prospective controlled trials. In addition to looking for potential beneficial effects, investigators were careful to look for possible adverse effects (e.g., an increase in the incidence of NEC). The results of these controlled studies of early feeding are summarized in Table 2. It is worth pointing out that the age at which feeds introduced in control subjects ranged between 7 and 18 days. Most probably these were the ages at which feeding was started in the respective nurseries as a matter of policy at the time. Table 2 shows that early feeding generally led to improved intestinal function, which may be interpreted as showing that gut atrophy was prevented or ameliorated. Most important, in none of the trials was there an increase in the incidence of NEC, nor were any other adverse effects noted.

In the trials listed in Table 2 the initial feeds consisted of water, various formulas (both dilute and full strength), and breast milk. No conclusions regarding an optimal type of feed can be drawn from these trials. However, breast milk must be considered the preferred type of feed for all the reasons normally put forward in support of breast milk, including the documented protection it affords against NEC (24) and sepsis (25) in the LBW infant.

TABLE 2. *Controlled studies of trophic feeds*

Author(s)	Age at start: experimental	Age at start: control	Adverse effects	Beneficial effects
Ostertag et al. (17)	1 d	7 d	None	↑ Nutrient intakes
Slagle & Gross (19)	8 d	18 d	None	↑ Feeding tolerance
				↓ Serum bilirubin
Dunn et al. (18)	2 d	9 d	None	↑ Feeding tolerance
				↓ Serum bilirubin
				↓ Osteopenia
Berseth (23)	3-5 d	10-14 d	None	↑ Gut motility maturation
				↑ Feeding tolerance
Meetze et al. (20)	3 d	15 d	None	↑ Feeding tolerance
				↑ Serum gastrin

EARLY FEEDING—IOWA 1997

Although most neonatologists have now abandoned regimens involving prolonged withholding of feeds as a matter of routine and have moved toward the early introduction of enteral feeding, there is no documentation of actual contemporary feeding practices in VLBW infants. A survey was therefore conducted at my institution, one purpose of which was to obtain data on the actual feeding practices during the first week of life. Because gastric residuals are often the earliest sign of illness in NEC and precede other manifestations of the disease, their occurrence is usually considered to indicate NEC until proven otherwise. However, in the first week of life gastric residuals seem to be common and without apparent connection to NEC. A second purpose of the survey was therefore to obtain data on the volume and color of gastric residuals.

Methods

The records of all 101 infants with birthweights of less than 1,250 g who were admitted in 1997 were reviewed. We excluded 11 infants who died within the first week of life, three who were admitted after the first week of life, one who had atresia of the sigmoid colon requiring surgical resection, and a set of conjoined twins born after a gestation of 32 weeks. The records of one infant could not be located. From the records of the remaining 83 infants the following information was extracted for each of the first 7 days of life:

- Type and amount of any feeding
- Mode of administration (bolus or continuous drip)
- Periods of withholding of feeds
- Volume and color of gastric residuals

Where recorded, actions taken in response to gastric residuals and reasons for withholding of feedings, where applicable, were ascertained. The records were also searched for episodes of NEC, or suspected NEC, during the first week of life, as well as during the entire hospital stay.

At the University of Iowa there is not an established feeding protocol. Rather, decisions regarding feeding are individualized and are made by the attending neonatologist. However, there is a consensus that feeding should be started early and that feed volumes should be increased slowly. Prevention and early recognition of NEC are overriding concerns, and in infants considered to be at increased risk of NEC, enteral feeding may be withheld for some period of time. The presence of signs compatible with NEC naturally prompts the usual steps, including temporary cessation of feeding until matters are resolved. Transpyloric feeding is not used. Feeds are mainly given as boluses, continuous feeding only being used occasionally.

The nursing staff are highly supportive of breastfeeding, and 75% to 85% of mothers initiate lactation and provide expressed breast milk for at least some period of time. During treatment with indomethacin, feeds are withheld for 48 to 72 hours. With few exceptions, VLBW infants receive parenteral nutrition, starting within 24 to 36 hours of birth. As a nursery routine, all infants have nasogastric or orogastric feeding tubes inserted soon after admission, and gastric contents are routinely aspirated every 3 hours whether the infant is fed or not. Volume and color of residuals, if present, are recorded.

Results

We found that the first feed was given at a mean age of 60 hours of age (range 9 to 156 hours). The reason for late initiation was often the continued presence of gastric residuals (see later), but in some cases a history of birth asphyxia was noted as the reason. The vast majority of infants received bolus feeds. Initial feed volume ranged from 0.2 to 5 ml per feed. The starting feed volume was most commonly 1 ml. The frequency of feeds ranged from one a day to one every 3 hours, the most common frequency being every 8 hours. Continuous-drip feeding was used as the initial feeding mode in only two infants, at an initial rate of 0.5 ml/h.

In 63 infants (76%) breast milk was the intended feed. It was not uncommon for mothers to provide little or no milk (colostrum) during the first 3 to 5 days. In four of these cases and at the explicit request of the mother, some supplemental formula was fed until sufficient breast milk became available. In two cases the breast milk supply remained low and the feeding of formula was started, at the mother's request, during the first week of life. At their mothers' decision, 20 infants received only formula.

Gastric residuals were considered to be present if any volume of 0.1 ml or more was recorded, or to be absent if the record indicated 0 or trace. Gastric residuals were a common occurrence before the first feed was offered. Thirty-nine infants (47%) had one or more records of a gastric residual volume of more than 0.1 ml. On the other hand, most infants ($n = 44$) had no gastric residual before feeds were initiated. Most residuals were of modest size (1.0 ml or less), but in 21 infants larger residuals were obtained on one or more occasion. The largest aspirate was 4 ml. Bilious residuals (green or yellow) were recorded in 17 infants on one or more occasion before feeds were initiated, including seven infants with residuals that were of trace volume but were nevertheless described as green. It appears likely that the preponderance of nonpropagating clusters characteristic of the preterm infant's duodenal motor activity pattern (26) is responsible for the frequent bile-stained gastric residuals.

Although the size and color of residuals undoubtedly influenced decisions about the initiation of feeding, documentation is for the most part not readily available. Nevertheless, in infants with no residuals, feeding was started at a mean age of 53 hours, compared with 68 hours in those with residuals, and this difference was statistically significant ($p < 0.05$). Infants who had bilious residuals were started on feeds somewhat later (mean age of 73 hours) than infants who did not have bilious residuals (mean age of 58 hours); this difference was not statistically significant.

Although after the first feed there was almost always a residual, in most infants ($n = 55$), there was no appreciable change in the overall size or frequency of residuals after the start of feeds. On the other hand, in 22 infants there was a marked increase in size or frequency of residuals. Although the increase was transient in most infants, in a few cases it prompted temporary discontinuation of feeds. In seven infants there was a definite decrease in the size or frequency of residuals once feeding was started. Bilious residuals were recorded in 28 infants (33%) on one or more occasions. Bolus feeds were changed to continuous-drip feeds in three infants as a matter of routine and in two infants because of sizable residuals with bolus feedings.

In 39 infants, feeds were discontinued for 24 hours or longer on at least one occasion during the first week of life. Although in 15 infants the reason for withholding was treatment of a persistent ductus arteriosus with indomethacin, in 24 infants there were other reasons. In 12 of these infants, bilious residuals preceded withholding of feeding. This represented 43% of the 28 infants with bilious residuals, whereas only 22% of infants without bilious residuals had feeds withheld for longer than 24 hours. Feeds were withheld once or twice for periods of less than 24 hours in 15 infants. Thus only 29 infants (35%) did not have feeds withheld for one reason or another during the first week of life.

In Table 3, data are summarized by chronological age (24-hour intervals). It is evident that the proportion of infants who were fed at a given age plateaued from about the fourth day. This illustrates the fact that, although all infants were started on feeds by 156 hours of age (6.5 days), by that time some infants had had feeds withheld for the reasons listed earlier. The average number of daily feeds and the total amount of milk or formula received increased throughout the first week of life. On the other hand, the proportion of infants with residuals, as well as the frequency and size of the residuals, essentially did not change during the first week of life.

Necrotizing Enterocolitis

None of the infants (including those who died in the first week of life) had signs suggestive of NEC, and in no infant was this diagnosis made during the first week of life. It is thus evident that none of the many gastric residuals was associated with NEC. Three infants had signs compatible with NEC when they were between 26 and 36 days old. None had radiologic evidence of pneumatosis intestinalis, although in two of these infants other clinical signs were suggestive of NEC and feeds were withheld for 10 days. One additional infant was admitted from another hospital at age 22 days with a radiologically confirmed diagnosis of NEC.

TABLE 3. *Feeds and gastric residuals by chronologic age during first week of life in 83 very low birthweight infants (successive 24 hour periods)*

	1	2	3	4	5	6	7
Number of infants fed	6	36	61	67	70	66	73
Number of feeds (mean)*	1.2	2.9	3.1	4.0	4.7	5.3	5.3
Feed volume (mean, ml/d)*	1.4	2.9	5.3	8.4	12.4	18.0	20.6
Number of infants with residuals	29	23	38	42	41	35	38
Number of residuals (mean)†	1.6	1.6	1.9	1.5	1.8	1.7	1.9
Residual volume (mean, ml/d)†	1.4	1.2	1.1	1.1	1.1	1.4	1.4

* Among fed infants.
† Among infants with residuals.

Conclusion

Gastric residuals were a frequent occurrence in VLBW infants during the first week of life, whether the infants were fed or not and regardless of age. Since none of the infants had NEC, gastric residuals must have had other, more benign explanations (e.g., immature motility). Although many gastric residuals were bilious, none of the infants had intestinal obstruction. Appropriate responses to the largely benign gastric residuals during the first week of life have yet to be defined. Because immature intestinal motility is most likely to be responsible for the frequent gastric residuals, and because feeding has been shown to promote the maturation of intestinal motor activity (23,27), it may not be advisable to withhold feeds in response to benign gastric residuals.

Feeds were started on average at 60 hours of age. This is early by the standards of just a few years ago. An obstacle to the still earlier introduction of feeds, apart from the frequent presence of residuals, is that breast milk is often not available during the first few days of life. Feed volumes were increased very slowly, a practice that is designed to keep the risk of NEC low (28).

SUMMARY

Feeding regimens involving delayed introduction of feeding in VLBW infants were designed to reduce the risk of NEC. Because they were never shown convincingly to be effective in this regard, and because of concerns over the adverse effects of prolonged withholding of enteral feeding, including the adverse effects of prolonged parenteral nutrition, the earlier introduction of feeding (trophic feeding) has been proposed. A series of controlled trials showed that early (trophic) feeds not only are safe with regard to NEC but also seem to be effective in forestalling gut atrophy. Although documentation is not available, the impression is that early feeding protocols of one form or another have been widely adopted in nurseries across the country. At my own institution, early feeding has generally been adopted. The frequent occurrence of gastric residuals prevents early feeding in many infants. Strategies to overcome this obstacle need to be developed.

REFERENCES

1. Carlson SJ, Ziegler EE. Nutrient intakes and growth of very low birth weight infants. *J Perinatol* 1998;18:252–258.
2. Ziegler EE. Malnutrition in the preterm infant. *Acta Paediatr Scand* 1991;374:58–66.
3. Brown EG, Sweet AY. Preventing necrotizing enterocolitis in neonates. *JAMA* 1978;240: 2452–2454.
4. La Gamma EF, Ostertag SG, Birenbaum H. Failure of delayed oral feedings to prevent necrotizing enterocolitis: results of study in very-low-birth-weight neonates. *Am J Dis Child* 1985;139:385–389.
5. Jackson WD, Grand RJ. The human intestinal response to enteral nutrients: a review. *J Am Coll Nutr* 1991;10:500–509.
6. Johnson LR, Copeland EM, Dudrick SJ, Lichtenberger LM, Castro GA. Structural and hormonal alterations in the gastrointestinal tract of parenterally fed rats. *Gastroenterology* 1975;68:1177–1183.
7. Levine GM, Deren JJ, Steiger E, Zinno R. Role of oral intake in maintenance of gut mass and disaccharide activity. *Gastroenterology* 1974;67:975–982.

8. Castro GA, Copeland EM, Dudrick SJ, Johnson LR. Intestinal disaccharidase and peroxidase activities in parenterally nourished rats. *J Nutr* 1975;105:776–781.
9. Castillo RO, Pittler A, Costa F. Intestinal maturation in the rat: the role of enteral nutrients. *J Parenter Enteral Nutr* 1988;12:490–495.
10. Castillo RO, Feng JJ, Stevenson DK, Kwong LK. Altered maturation of small intestinal function in the absence of intraluminal nutrients: rapid normalization with refeeding. *Am J Clin Nutr* 1991;53:558–561.
11. Dworkin LD, Levin GM, Farber NJ, Spector MH. Small intestinal mass of the rat is partially determined by indirect effects of intraluminal nutrition. *Gastroenterology* 1976;71:626–630.
12. Rothman D, Udall JN, Pang KY, Kirkham SE, Walker WA. The effect of short-term starvation on mucosal barrier function in the newborn rabbit. *Pediatr Res* 1985;19:727–731.
13. Lipman TO. Bacterial translocation and enteral nutrition in humans: an outsider looks in. *J Parenter Enteral Nutr* 1995;19:156–165.
14. Marrei HVL, Rodrigues MAM, DeCamargo JLV, Campana AO. Intraepithelial lymphocytes in the jejunal mucosa of malnourished rats. *Gut* 1980;21:32–36.
15. Reddy V, Raghuramulu N, Bhaskaram C. Secretory IgA in protein calorie malnutrition. *Arch Dis Child* 1975;51:871–879.
16. Groër M, Walker WA. What is the role of preterm breast milk supplementation in the host defenses of preterm infants? Science *versus* fiction. *Adv Pediatr* 1996;43:335–358.
17. Ostertag SG, LaGamma EF, Reisen CE, Ferrentino FL. Early enteral feeding does not affect the incidence of necrotizing enterocolitis. *Pediatrics* 1986;77:275–280.
18. Dunn L, Hulman S, Weiner J, Kliegman R. Beneficial effects of early hypocaloric enteral feeding on neonatal gastrointestinal function: preliminary report of a randomized trial. *J Pediatr* 1988;112:622–629.
19. Slagle TA, Gross SJ. Effect of early low-volume enteral substrate on subsequent feeding tolerance in very low birth weight infants. *J Pediatr* 1988;113:526–531.
20. Meetze WH, Valentine C, McGuigan JE, Conlon M, Sacks N, Neu J. Gastrointestinal priming prior to full enteral nutrition in very low birth weight infants. *J Pediatr Gastroenterol Nutr* 1992;15:163–170.
21. Berseth CL. Minimal enteral feedings. *Clin Perinatol* 1995;22:195–205.
22. Lucas A, Bloom SR, Aynsley-Green A. Gut hormones and minimal enteral feeding. *Acta Paediatr Scand* 1986;75:719–723.
23. Berseth CL. Effect of early feeding on maturation of the preterm infant's small intestine. *J Pediatr* 1992;120:947–953.
24. Lucas A, Cole TJ. Breast milk and neonatal necrotising enterocolitis. *Lancet* 1990;336:1519–1523.
25. El-Mohandes AE, Picard MB, Simmens SJ, Keiser JF. Use of human milk in the intensive care nursery decreases the incidence of nosocomial sepsis. *J Perinatol* 1997;17:130–134.
26. Berseth CL. Gestational evolution of small intestine motility in preterm and term infants. *J Pediatr* 1989;115:646–651.
27. Berseth CL, Nordyke C. Enteral nutrients promote postnatal maturation of intestinal motor activity in preterm infants. *Am J Physiol* 1993;264:G1046–1051.
28. Anderson DM, Kliegman RM. The relationship of neonatal alimentation practices to the occurrence of endemic necrotizing enterocolitis. *Am J Perinatol* 1991;8:62–67.

DISCUSSION

Prof. Polberger: If we are using bolus feeding during the first weeks of life, do you have any comments on how often we should supply the feeds—every 2 or 3 hours, perhaps every hour?

Prof. Ziegler: We start by giving 1 ml every 8 hours on the first day of life. Then we increase the frequency. Don't ask whether that is rational; it's just the practice in our nursery! Quite possibly shorter feeding intervals might be better.

Dr. Walker: To what do you attribute your success in having no cases of necrotizing enterocolitis?

Prof. Ziegler: I think giving colostrum may play a big part in that.

Prof. Lucas: Many people think that babies below 26 weeks of gestation are very difficult to feed, even minimally, so they are compelled to go on for weeks and weeks with intravenous feeding. If you say that atrophic changes start to be significant within a few days, then I would regard it as failure of minimal enteral feeding if it is not established by, say, 4 or 5 days. On that basis, what is the failure rate in your unit in babies below 26 weeks of gestation? That is, where you actually give up minimal enteral feeding because of unacceptable aspirates or because something happens to make you feel you can't go on with it. I'm told all the time by neonatologists that they have failed to establish minimal enteral feeds in babies of that gestation.

Prof. Ziegler: There were no cases of outright failure the way you describe it. But feeding was frequently stopped for short or longer periods because of gastric residuals. There was one baby who had aspirates of some quantity over 5 or 6 days, but then it was decided to feed the baby anyway, and from that moment on there were no more aspirates. Neonatologists are scared of necrotizing enterocolitis. Every gastric aspirate constitutes NEC until proven otherwise. Because of that, babies are often not fed for as long as there are any aspirates at all.

Dr. Rashwan: What is your policy about the quantity of aspirate?

Prof. Ziegler: We have a rule that if the residual volume is greater than 20% of the feed volume, that requires a medical decision. It's a purely arbitrary rule. I think a more important distinction is the type of aspirate—is it pure gastric juice, is it pure milk, is it mixed?

Dr. Chessex: As a neonatologist, I'm one of the bad guys. But like every neonatologist in this room I'm the one who has to go and explain to parents who have just lost a child that increasing the feeds on the day before had no relationship with the death of the child on the next day. It is difficult to make the parents believe it. The principal point of my comment is to say that there is a Canadian multicenter trial on trophic feeding that started about 18 months ago. The protocol has tried to tackle all the points you have raised. The endpoints of the study are necrotizing enterocolitis and the frequency of feeding stops. The study is ongoing and we'll have to await the results.

Prof. Ziegler: I applaud you for undertaking such a task. It is very difficult to identify all the reasons feeds are withheld. When there is an aspirate, feeds may be held automatically for one or two cycles. That is certainly not the same as withholding feeds until a radiographic examination of the baby's abdomen has been done.

Prof. Pohlandt: I'm not happy with using the term *early trophic feeding* synonymously with any early feeding. We would need a third term for those neonatologists who like to feed the baby early for real nutrition, not in these very small amounts for trophic purposes. What should we call that type of feeding? You gave the impression that most of the American neonatologists are afraid of early feeding. On this side of the Atlantic, at least in Germany, many neonatologists think that it is advantageous to give early feeding. We conducted a multicenter randomized trial 5 years ago where babies between 500 and 1,000 g birthweight were fed from the second day on according to a strict feeding protocol. By day 10, 62% of these babies were able to accept 100 ml of undiluted preterm formula, which is much more than trophic feeding. I think the majority can be fed.

Prof. Ziegler: I said at the outset that my remarks were colored by experience in the United States. I would not say that all neonatologists are afraid of early feeding. There is the notion that feeding babies increases the risk of NEC. I've been aware that in Germany and other countries, feeding is begun earlier.

Prof. Nem-Yun Boo: We recently completed an analysis of a case control study looking at predictors of food intolerance on VLBW babies. We started feeding at a volume of at least 0.5 ml per feed at 3-hour intervals. If the feed volume was less than 6 ml/feed, we defined intolerance as an aspirate of 2 ml or more at the time of the next feed; if the feed volume was more than 6 ml/feed, we defined intolerance as an aspirate of more than 33% of the feed volume. On this basis we found a very high rate of feed intolerance, around 64%. We looked at a number of potential risk factors, including the age of initiation of feeding, the volume fed, and a whole variety of neonatal management factors. On logistic regression analysis, the only significant predictor of feed intolerance was the age when the first feed was given—the later we fed the baby, the greater the risk of intolerance. We are preparing the data for publication.

Prof. Ziegler: Thank you very much for that interesting contribution. I look forward to seeing the data.

Dr. C. Kind: Did you look at the relation between tolerance of early feeding and the passage of meconium?

Prof. Ziegler: That's a good idea. I haven't looked at that, but I will.

Prof. De Vonderweid: Is there any sound reason for stopping minimal enteral feeding in babies who receive indomethacin or inotropes?

Prof. Ziegler: In our nursery, it's been a rule for many years that babies must not be fed until 24 hours after the last dose of indomethacin. The rationale is that if the baby perforates and is being fed, he gets worse peritonitis than if he is not being fed. In relation to inotropes, usually if there is great cardiovascular or respiratory instability, we will not feed. But it's getting more and more accepted that instability is not a contraindication to small feeds. However, this is a gradual process, and there are big differences of opinion among neonatologists.

Dr. Berseth: The major dilemma we have in dealing with necrotizing enterocolitis is that we can't predict the infants who are at risk. As a result, we're left dealing with the lowest common denominator—that is, we develop our feeding protocols for all infants in the nursery in an attempt to prevent a disease that is only going to occur in 8% of them. The price we pay as a result is that we are artificially holding back the other 92%. There were two abstracts presented last year at the pediatric research meetings indicating that if one were more aggressive with increasing the feeds, one could achieve full enteral feeding sooner at a lower cost. My other point relates to what volume to use. We approached this as a dose/response question. We used a chronically hyperalimented puppy model and gave varying small increments of enteral feeds to those puppies. We could not demonstrate increased growth, as measured by intestinal weight or DNA content, until the enteral feed volume exceeded 30% of the fluid intake of the puppies. However, we could achieve maturation of motor function and some other functional indices in the gastrointestinal tract at volumes of 7.5% or more of the daily fluid intake, which is in the range of what many of us are using when we give minimal enteral feeding. So it appears that we can probably achieve at least part of what we want to achieve using a very low volume.

Prof. Pereira: In the two hospitals of my university in Chile, we start oral feeding in the first 6 to 12 hours at a volume of between 2 and 4 ml/kg·d. This is given as a bolus every 2 or 3 hours. Colostrum is given in 90% of the newborns. We increase the feeds gradually over 4 to 5 days if the baby looks well and doesn't have more than 30% of gastric aspirate. On day 7, more than 90% of our babies are receiving feed volumes of about 60 to 80 ml/kg·d. More than 70% of the feed is own mother's milk. We have about five or six cases of NEC per 10,000 live births each year.

Prof. Ziegler: Those are very impressive figures.

Prof. Koletzko: One explanation for the apparent difference in feeding routines between the United States and Europe could be the marked difference in the cost of malpractice insurance. This might make American neonatologists a bit more defensive. Another possible reason for the difference could be the more common use of breast milk for establishing enteral feeding in Europe, and when formulas are used, the predominance of hydrolysates, which give more rapid intestinal transit and less hard stools. Maybe that could be an advantage in establishing early feeding. My other comment relates to NEC incidence. Published data on NEC rates seem to show a lower incidence in Europe than in the United States, though this may reflect different diagnostic criteria. Do you have any comment on this?

Prof. Ziegler: I'm very cautious when I compare incidence data of NEC, since the criteria for diagnosis vary so widely. I don't think malpractice costs have anything to do with our feeding policies, nor do I think the type of feeds currently used are likely to be a factor in NEC incidence. I do think the claim of the early studies that postponing enteral feeding reduces the incidence of NEC was uncritically accepted as proven fact, and this is the reason why feedings were withheld in the United States. You Europeans probably never accepted that at face value, and maybe that is the reason you have persisted with early feeding.

Prof. Lucas: There is very little experience of using hydrolyzed formulas in America and Britain, but I understood that about 90% of the preterm formulas used in Germany are partially hydrolyzed. Prof. Koletzko therefore raised an important issue, that maybe there is a reduction in one particular sort of morbidity as a result of using that kind of formula. I'd be interested to hear of any more evidence on the use of these in preterm infants. There has evidently been much more clinical experience of their use than many of us are aware of.

Prof. Pohlandt: One of the main problems with feeding ELBW infants is constipation, and linked with that, how to establish faster transit of the stools. Gastric emptying is thought to be facilitated by hydrolysates, so we did a randomized prospective study in 19 (babies that was the precalculated sample size) and found that the transit time of the hydrolysate was 9 hours shorter than that of whole cow's milk protein. But that doesn't prove that we can move up to a full enteral intake more rapidly on a hydrolyzed formula. That study has not yet been done.

Dr. Sedaghatian: We use only breast milk for early feeding in infants of less than 1,000 g. We start at 24 hours with 0.5 ml every three hours, not every eight hours, but we don't give any foreign protein for at least 2 or 3 days. Do you think you should specify in your protocol that early feeding should only be with human milk, or do you think it is acceptable to use a formula from the start?

Prof. Ziegler: I do not see a reason for not introducing a milk-based formula in the first 24 hours. I would still start with very small feeds. It is possible that milk formulas carry a higher risk of necrotizing enterocolitis, but it's still unproven whether it makes a difference when we start feeding very early. I don't see a reason for withholding a formula when breast milk is not available.

Nutrition of the Very Low Birthweight Infant, edited by
Ekhard E. Ziegler, Alan Lucas, Guido E. Moro.
Nestlé Nutrition Workshop Series, Paediatric Programme, Vol. 43,
Nestec Ltd., Vevey/Lippincott Williams & Wilkins
Philadelphia, Pennsylvania © 1999.

Milk-Borne Growth Factors and Gut Development

Bohuslav Dvorak, Anthony F. Philipps, and Otakar Koldovsky[*]

Department of Pediatrics and Steele Memorial Children's Research Center, University of Arizona, Tucson, Arizona, USA
[*] Deceased April 5, 1998

The gastrointestinal tract undergoes substantial changes during the period of development. Profound growth, morphological changes, and functional maturation are observed during this developmental period in the small intestine. Differentiation of the gastrointestinal tract during the late gestation period prepares it for its many extrauterine tasks. Birth represents possibly the most critical period in gastrointestinal tract development, when placental supply of macro- and micronutrients is replaced by enteral nutrition. Enteral nutrition initiates changes in mucosal structure and function required for utilization of milk feeds. Finally, this process is concluded by the weaning phase, when the transition from milk to solid food occurs. Physiological changes in digestive and absorptive processes are well described (1), but regulation of these changes is still not clearly understood. For example, the intestinal mucosal surface undergoes nearly complete turnover of the epithelial population every 24 to 96 hours in man and other species. The processes of constitutive growth and proliferation of the intestinal mucosa occur in a highly organized spatial context of proliferation, followed by differentiation and maturation of epithelial cells. Cell production in each crypt is maintained by a few stem cells, and the organization of this process is vertical, from the intestinal crypt to the villus.

Understanding of the mechanisms whereby intestinal growth and epithelial turnover are regulated remains fragmentary. However, it is clear that biologically active peptides play a critical role. The number of biologically active peptides important for regulation of intestinal growth is still increasing. Research studies have documented the essential role of peptide growth factors in intestinal development. These factors include both growth factors that are produced locally within the small intestine and exogenously produced growth factors delivered into the intestinal lumen.

In this review we will summarize recent understanding of the role of milk-borne epidermal growth factor (EGF) and transforming growth factor alpha (TGFα) on the developing gut.

EGF AND TGFα IN THE GASTROINTESTINAL TRACT DURING PERINATAL DEVELOPMENT

EGF and TGFα belong to a group of diverse low-molecular-weight polypeptide growth factors (2). EGF was first characterized by its mitogenic activity (3) and inhibition of gastric acid secretion (4). TGFα, described originally as a sarcoma-derived growth factor, was found to be structurally related to EGF and is now accepted as an integral physiological regulator of growth in normal tissues (5). Both EGF and TGFα share the same EGF receptor (2,5).

Expression of EGF receptor has been demonstrated in the intestine of developing rats (6–9), mice (10–12), pigs (13,14), and human fetus (15,16). Whereas in fetal rats EGF receptors are detectable, in suckling rats they were not detected (8,17). This could be due to the potential binding of the milk-borne EGF to this receptor.

Transcript levels of EGF and TGFα in developing small intestine have not been well characterized. Originally, the presence of TGFα mRNA transcripts was found in the gastrointestinal tract from adult rodents only, and the expression of EGF mRNA was not detected at all in either adult (18–21) or suckling gastrointestinal tract (22). Miettinen (23) detected the presence of TGFα and EGF mRNAs in human fetal intestine. Her observation suggested a higher abundance of TGFα transcripts in human fetal intestine in comparison with EGF mRNA. Previous studies from our laboratory have shown the presence and cellular localization of both EGF and TGFα mRNAs in the small intestine of suckling and adult rats (24). Using an *in situ* hybridization technique, we have shown that the intestinal crypt epithelium is the major site of EGF and TGFα transcripts in both suckling and adult rats. In suckling rats, however, the EGF mRNA signal was very low or absent, whereas TGFα mRNA signal was markedly higher. Since gene expression of growth factors in developing small intestine is, in general, very low, the reverse transcription (RT) competitive polymerase chain reaction (PCR) assay was established to measure mRNA levels quantitatively (25). In suckling rats, the intestinal TGFα mRNA level was about 10-fold higher than that of EGF mRNA. The expression of EGF-R mRNA in suckling rat jejunum was the highest, about sixfold more than TGFα mRNA, and about 60-fold higher than the EGF mRNA level (26).

The presence of EGF peptide in the stomach and duodenum of the human fetus, newborn, and child was demonstrated first by immunochemistry (27). Later, EGF and TGFα immunoreactivity was detected after the sixteenth gestational week in the human fetal small intestine (28,29). By radioreceptor assay, the fetal intestine contained 10 times more EGF receptor binding substance than EGF, as measured by immunofluorometric assay. Chromatographic analysis suggests that TGFα-like peptides account for at least part of this activity (28). EGF levels in the small intestine were several times higher in suckling rats than in adults; however, the intestinal concentrations of TGFα in suckling and adult rats were similar (30). The large amount of EGF present in the small intestinal mucosa and lumen of suckling rats depends on the intake of milk-borne EGF (31,32), whereas TGFα content is influenced much less (30). Furthermore, EGF peptide was demonstrated in the small intestine of fetal and neonatal mice (12). Presence of TGFα peptide was also detected in the small intestine of suckling pigs at 1, 2, and 3 weeks of postnatal age (33) and in a high density in duodenum of fetal mice (34).

EGF AND TGFα IN MILKS

Numerous papers have reported the presence of EGF in human milk as well as in milk of other species (13,35). However, in infant formulas the EGF concentration is very low or undetectable (36). Human milk does contain high-molecular-weight EGF complexes, but these are unstable at neutral and acidic pH levels (37). Rat milk-borne EGF is present in several forms (38,39). In contrast to this, TGFα peptide was detected in low amounts in human milk (40,41) but could not be detected in rat milk (30).

EFFECTS OF ADMINISTRATION OF EGF AND TGFα

The effect of the administration of EGF and TGFα on the developing gastrointestinal tract has been studied using either *in vitro* organ cultures or *in vivo*. The administration of these growth factors to animals was performed either parenterally or orogastrically. With few exceptions, all the doses used must be considered pharmacological. The question of physiological doses is discussed in the review of the orogastric effects of these peptides.

In organ culture studies, addition of EGF to fetal jejunal explants (11–14 weeks of gestation) increased lactase activity, but surprisingly repressed the normally occurring increase of sucrase activity. Furthermore, EGF inhibited hydrocortisone-stimulated DNA synthesis (42). In fetal colon (14–17 weeks of gestation), EGF evoked a significant decrease of [^{3}H]-thymidine incorporation into DNA and a decrease of sucrase and activities digesting maltose (called maltase) (43). In rodent studies, Beaulieu and Calvert (44) have shown that addition of EGF to the medium accelerated differentiation of rough endoplasmic reticulum in duodenal explants from fetal mice. EGF added to mouse duodenal explants (17 days of gestation, 48 hours' cultivation) increased levels of alkaline phosphatase, maltase, and trehalase activities, whereas sucrase activity and DNA content were unchanged (44). In the jejunum of 8-day-old mice (48 hours of incubation), no effect of EGF addition was seen in activities of microvillus disaccharidases and DNA synthesis. It is not clear if the differences between these two experiments from the same laboratory are due to the age of donors or to the intestinal segments used. No EGF effect was seen on DNA and protein synthesis in duodenojejunal explants obtained from rat fetuses taken 5 and 3 days before birth as well as on postnatal days 4 and 7. Interestingly, in 1-day prenatal and 1-day postnatal rats, an EGF effect on DNA and protein synthesis was demonstrated (45).

Parenteral Effects

In the postnatal period, parenteral administration of EGF increased intestinal proliferation in human infants with a congenital microvillus atrophy (46) or necrotizing enteritis (47) who were treated intravenously with recombinant EGF. Suckling rats injected with EGF showed increased weight of the whole stomach; increased DNA, RNA, and protein content of the oxyntic gland mucosa; and higher rates of basal acid secretion and pentagastrin stimulated acid secretion (48). Odaka *et al.* (49) reported increased small intestinal weight in suckling rats injected with EGF for 4 days. Administration of EGF caused intestinal hypertrophy in fetal rhesus monkeys (50).

Injections of EGF into newborn rats also caused a large decline in lactase activity in the colon (51) but did not affect the incorporation rate of [^{3}H]-thymidine (52). Arsenault and Menard (53) reported an increase in thymidine incorporation into DNA of the small intestine of 3- to 8-day-old suckling mice treated with high doses of EGF. Hormi and Lehy (54) found that the proliferative effect of EGF and TGFα differed quantitatively in various segments of the gastrointestinal tract of suckling rats. Oka *et al.* (55) have shown that EGF given for 3 days subcutaneously in high doses inhibited body weight gains by 13% but increased the protein content of the duodenum by 32% in the brush border, increased the concentration of calbindin by 35% to 65%, and increased sucrase activity two- to sixfold.

With regard to absorptive processes, Greene *et al.* (56) reported an increase in calcium transport in rats treated in the same way as in the study by Oka *et al.* (55). Harada *et al.* (57) have shown that giving EGF subcutaneously to suckling rats suppressed intestinal absorption of IgG. Giving mouse EGF (mEGF) intraperitoneally to rabbits from postnatal day 3 to day 17 upregulated intestinal absorption of H_2O, Na^+, and glucose and caused alterations in the membranes of the microvilli (58). Parenteral administration of EGF into 3-day-old piglets increased sucrase and maltase activities in the small intestine, whereas alanine uptake was not affected (59). Subcutaneous administration of EGF inhibits gastric evacuation and intestinal propulsive motility acutely in suckling rats; interestingly, administration of antibodies against EGF in amounts sufficient to block the estimated amount of EGF present in the suckling rats accelerated intestinal propulsive motility (60). Similarly, TGFα affected the gastric evacuation and intestinal propulsive motility in suckling rats (Shinohara H, unpublished results).

Lastly, several other studies have explored the EGF effect on disaccharidases in more depth. Harada *et al.* (57) found no effect on sucrase activity, whereas Foltzer-Jourdainne and Raul (52), Foltzer-Jourdainne *et al.* (61), and Odaka *et al.* (49) showed an increase of intestinal sucrase activity in suckling rats after administration of EGF. Since this effect was not inhibited by adrenalectomy or co-administration of RU 38486 (a glucocorticoid antagonist), Foltzer-Jourdainne *et al.* (61) concluded that EGF acts in a glucocorticoid-independent manner. Later from the same laboratory the interaction between EGF and other maturational factors was analyzed by Emvo *et al.* (62) in suckling rats, starting on day 12. EGF evoked an increase of sucrase activity and sucrase mRNA in both normal and adrenalectomized rats.

Orogastric Effects

The impetus for all studies related to the role of milk-borne EGF was the work of Cohen and Taylor (63), who reported that oral administration of mEGF caused precocious eyelid opening in newborn mice. Various laboratories were able to demonstrate effects of orogastrically administered hormones on the suckling using high pharmacological doses. This led us to define the physiological dose of a milk-borne hormone as the amount (DD = daily dose) that corresponds to that taken in milk by the suckling per day, as calculated from the daily milk intake (64) and the known concentration of the hormone in milk. We have calculated for the suckling rat that the dose of EGF is about 2 μg/100 g body weight. Another important fact to realize is that under normal conditions (i.e., suckling), milk-borne hormones are presented to the suckling as a cocktail containing agonistic, antagonistic, and neutral hormones, growth factors, and binding proteins. Before discussing the orogastric effect, the gastrointestinal handling of EGF in suckling should be mentioned.

If an ingested peptide hormone is to function within the gastrointestinal tract and beyond, its survival in the gastrointestinal tract (i.e., its resistance to proteolytic degradation) is necessary. Britton *et al.* (65) have shown that *in vitro* degradation of [^{125}I]-EGF by the gastric juices of preterm infants is negligible. Interestingly, degradation of EGF was found to be greater in gastric and intestinal juices from adult subjects (66). Similar animal studies show low degradation in suckling and a decrease in degradation after weaning (65,67).

[^{125}I]-EGF given orogastrically to suckling rats, using doses in the range of calculated daily intake, was degraded very little in the stomach and small intestinal lumen (68,69); similar results were seen in suckling mice (22,70) and lambs (71). [^{125}I]-EGF given orogastrically or into the lumen of the small intestine was detected in the gastric and small intestinal wall by biochemical methods and by autoradiography (68,69,72,73). In lambs, EGF (71) is absorbed into the bloodstream, but not into lymph. Intravenously administered [^{125}I]-EGF appears in bile of suckling rats, thus suggesting the possibility of reabsorption of orogastrically delivered EGF (74). The significance of an intake of milk-borne EGF was strongly suggested in experiments where suckling rats were fed pooled rat milk to which antibody against EGF was added; the intestine of these rats had lower wet weight, lower DNA synthesis and content, and lower RNA content (75). *In vitro* studies showing the presence of inhibitors protecting EGF from degradation by luminal contents in the suckling gastrointestinal tract indicate enhanced survival of milk-borne as well orogastrically delivered EGF in the presence of milk (73). Absorption of [^{125}I]-EGF from the gastrointestinal tract of suckling animals was demonstrated in rats (68,69,72,73) and mice (22). Importantly, in another study, luminally added EGF stimulated rapid tyrosine phosphorylation of the EGF receptor in the jejunum of suckling rats; the response was rapid (within several minutes), and EGF doses used were within the physiological range (8).

Newborn rats fed between 0 and 39 hours of age with an artificial milk that contained high doses of EGF (25 to 120 × DD) showed an increase in DNA synthesis and content in the small intestine (75) and an increase of DNA synthesis in the liver (76). Stomach wet weights of newborn rats fed artificial formula to which EGF (10 × DD) was added were greater than in those fed formula only (77). Orogastrically instilled EGF (3 × DD) given to suckling rats between day 11 and day 13 increased the cell-labeling indices of fundic, antral, and ileal mucosa, and of the exocrine pancreas (78). In suckling rats fed rat milk substitute (RMS) from 11 to 14 days of age with added EGF ($1.6 \times DD$), the protein content of the colon was significantly lower and the DNA content was significantly higher than that in rats fed RMS only. Supplementation of RMS with a similar amount of EGF normalized the development of Kupffer cell functions in suckling rats (79). Orogastric administration of EGF ($8 \times DD$) to suckling rabbits for 2 weeks evoked an increase in wet weight of the stomach and pancreas, and of DNA content in the ileum, and an increase in sucrase activity concomitant with a decrease in lactase activity in the proximal segments of the small intestine (80). Absorption of H_2O, Na^+, and glucose was increased owing to the intestinal mucosal hyperplasia (58). Similar treatment caused precocious maturation of liver functions—that is, the bile salt pool and the secretion and activity of glucokinase (81). Luminally administered EGF did not affect gastric acid secretion in suckling rats (82), although EGF-specific receptors were detected in the stomach mucosal membranes from 8- to 30-day-old rats (82).

The effect of milk-borne hormones during the suckling period, both in experimental mammals and in human neonates, might be not only physiological (i.e., enabling normal development) but also protective against noxious factors (cytoprotection), a role previously demonstrated for EGF (83). In this respect, we may speculate about the significance of growth factors such as EGF as protectors and healers in the case of necrotizing enterocolitis (35).

CONCLUSIONS

We hypothesize that EGF may play multiple roles during postnatal development. During the suckling period, when suckling EGF production is low, milk-borne EGF provides important maintenance. After weaning, when the offspring's EGF production dramatically increases, endogenous EGF is likely to be involved with induction of developmental changes in the gastrointestinal tract. Moreover, we hypothesize that EGF and other growth factors present in milk are important for gastrointestinal development and for the development of specific organs such as liver, muscle, and skin. Studies on the EGF effects (after both parenteral and enteral administration) have direct relevance not only to a general understanding of neonatal growth, but also to specific problems relating to feeding of low-birthweight infants in intensive-care nursery settings. Recent advances in technology and respiratory physiology have allowed a marked improvement in survival of the premature neonate, but the ability to feed low-birthweight babies enterally has been drastically limited owing to the extreme immaturity of their gastrointestinal tracts. Studies in experimental animals are important to gain a more complete understanding of the effects of milk-borne EGF for suckling mammals before recommending trials of altered formulas for human premature newborns.

REFERENCES

1. Koldovsky O. Digestive-absorption functions in fetuses, infants, and children. In: Polin RA, Fox WW, eds. *Fetal and neonatal physiology,* 2nd ed. Philadelphia: WB Saunders; 1998:1401–1418.

2. Goustin AS, Leof EB, Shipley GD, Moses HL. Growth factors and cancer. *Cancer Res* 1986;46: 1015–1029.
3. Carpenter G, Cohen S. Epidermal growth factor. *Annu Rev Biochem* 1979;48:193–216.
4. Gregory H, Bower JM, Willshire IR. Urogastrone and epidermal growth factor. In: Kastrup KW, Nielson JH, eds. Growth factors. *FEBS Colloquium B3, 1977;*48:75–84.
5. Derynck R. Transforming growth factor-α. *Cell* 1988; 54: 593–595.
6. Rao RK, Thornburg W, Korc M, Matrisian L, Magun BE, Koldovsky O. Processing of epidermal growth factor by suckling and adult rat intestinal cells. *Am J Physiol* 1986;250:G850–885.
7. Toyoda S, Lee PC, Lebenthal E. Interaction of epidermal growth factor with specific binding sites of enterocytes isolated from rat small intestine during development. *Biochim Biophys Acta* 1986; 886:295–301.
8. Thompson JF. Specific receptors for epidermal growth factor in rat intestinal microvillus membranes. *Am J Physiol* 1988;254:G429–435.
9. Thompson JF, Van Den Berg M, Stokkers PC. Developmental regulation of epidermal growth factor receptor kinase in rat intestine. *Gastroenterology* 1994;107:1278–1287.
10. Gallo-Payet N, Pothier P, Hugon JS. Ontogeny of EGF receptors during postnatal development of mouse small intestine. *J Pediatr Gastroenterol Nutr* 1987;6:114–120.
11. Menard D, Pothier P, Gallo-Payet N. Epidermal growth factor receptors during postnatal development of the mouse colon. *Endocrinology* 1987;121:1548–1554.
12. Shigeta H, Taga M, Katoh A, Minaguchi H. Ontogenesis and distribution of epidermal growth factor immunoreactivity and binding activity in the mouse fetal and neonatal tissues. *Endocrine J* 1993; 40:641–7.
13. Jaeger LA, Lamar CH. Immunolocalization of epidermal growth factor (EGF) and EGF receptors in the porcine upper gastrointestinal tract. *Am J Vet Res* 1992;53:1685–1692.
14. Kelly D, McFadyen M, King TP, Morgan PJ. Characterization and autoradiographic localization of the epidermal growth factor receptor in the jejunum of neonatal and weaned pigs. *Reprod Fertil Dev* 1992;4:183–191.
15. Pothier P, Menard D. Presence and characteristics of epidermal growth factor receptors in human fetal small intestine and colon. *FEBS Lett* 1988;228:113–117.
16. Menard D, Pothier P. Radioautographic localization of epidermal growth factor receptors in human fetal gut. *Gastroenterology* 1991;101:640–649.
17. Gallo-Payet N, Hugon JS. Epidermal growth factor receptors in isolated adult mouse intestinal cells: studies *in vivo* and in organ culture. *Endocrinology* 1985;116:194–201.
18. Malden LT, Novak U, Burgess AW. Expression of transforming growth factor alpha messenger RNA in normal and neoplastic gastrointestinal tract. *Int J Cancer* 1989;43:380–384.
19. Barnard JA, Polk WH, Moses HL, Coffey RJ. Transforming growth factor α in the normal gastrointestinal tract. *Am J Physiol* 1991;261:C994–1000.
20. Koyama S, Podolsky DK. Differential expression of transforming growth factor α and β in rat intestinal epithelium. *J Clin Invest* 1989;83:1768–1773.
21. Beauchamp RD, Barnard JA, McCutchen CM, Cherner JA, Coffey RJ. Localization of transforming growth factor α and its receptor in gastric mucosa cells: implications for a regulatory role in acid secretion and mucosal renewal. *J Clin Invest* 1989;84:1017–1023.
22. Popliker M, Shatz A, Avivi A, Ullrich A, Schlessinger J, Webb CG. Onset of endogenous synthesis of epidermal growth factor in neonatal mice. *Dev Biol* 1987;119:38–44.
23. Miettinen PJ. Transforming growth factor-α and epidermal growth factor expression in human fetal gastrointestinal tract. *Pediatr Res* 1993;33:481–486.
24. Dvorak B, Holubec H, LeBouton AV, Wilson JM, Koldovsky O. Epidermal growth factor and transforming growth factor-α mRNA in rat small intestine: *in situ* hybridization study. *FEBS Lett* 1994; 352:291–295.
25. Dvorak B, Stephan AL, Holubec H, Williams CS, Philipps AF, Koldovsky O. Insulin-like growth factor-I (IGF-I) mRNA in the small intestine of suckling and adult rats. *FEBS Lett* 1996;388:155–160.
26. Dvorak B, Kolinska J, McWilliam DL, *et al.* The expression of epidermal growth factor and transforming growth factor-α mRNA in the small intestine of suckling rats. *FEBS Lett* 1998;435:119–124.
27. Kasselberg AG, Orth DN, Gray ME, Stahlman, MT. Immunocytochemical localization of human epidermal growth factor/urogastrone in several human tissues. *J Histochem Cytochem* 1985;33:315–322.
28. Miettinen PJ, Perheentupa J, Otonkoskit, Lahteenmaki A, Panula P. EGF- and TGF-alpha-like peptides in human fetal gut. *Pediatr Res* 1989;26:25–30.
29. Poulsen SS, Krygerbaggesen N, Nexo E. Immunohistochemical localization of epidermal growth factor in the second-trimester human fetus. *Histochem Cell Biol* 1996;105:111–117.

30. Dvorak B, Koldovsky O. The presence of transforming growth factor-α in the suckling rat small intestine and pancreas and the absence in rat milk. *Pediatr Res* 1994;35:348–353.
31. Schaudies RP, Grimes J, Davis D, Rao RK, Koldovsky O. EGF content in the gastrointestinal tract of rats: effect of age and fasting/feeding. *Am J Physiol* 1989;256:G856–861.
32. Grimes J, Schaudies P, Davis D, *et al.* Effect of short-term fasting/refeeding on epidermal growth factor content in the gastrointestinal tract of suckling rats. *Proc Soc Exp Biol Med* 1992;199:75–80.
33. Jaeger LA. Immunohistochemical localization of transforming growth factor-alpha in suckling porcine intestine. *Acta Anat* 1996;155:14–21.
34. Hormi K, Onolfo JP, Gres L, Lebraud V, Lehy T. Developmental expression of transforming growth factor-alpha in the upper digestive tract and pancreas of the rat. *Regul Peptides* 1995;55:67–77.
35. Koldovsky O. Hormones in milk. In: Litwack G, ed. *Vitamins and hormones,* vol 50. New York: Academic Press; 1995:77–149.
36. Koldovsky O. Hormones and growth factors in milk. *Ann Nestle* 1996;54:105–112.
37. Azuma N, Hosaka E, Kamiogawa S, Yamauchi K. Occurrence of high molecular weight EGF complexes in human milk. *Agric Biol Chem* 1989;53:1043–1050.
38. Raaberg L, Nexo E, Tollund L, Poulsen SS, Christensen SB, Christensen MS. Epidermal growth factor reactivity in rat milk. *Regul Peptides* 1990;30:149–157.
39. Schaudies RP, Grimes J, Wray HL, Koldovsky O. Identification and partial characterization of multiple forms of biologically active EGF in rat milk. *Am J Physiol* 1990;259:G1056–1061.
40. Okada M, Ohmura E, Kamiya Y, *et al.* Transforming growth factor (TGF)-α in human milk. *Life Sci* 1991;48:1151–1156.
41. Connolly JM, Rose DP. Epidermal growth factor-like proteins in breast fluid and human milk. *Life Sci* 1988;42:1751–1756.
42. Menard D, Corriveau L, Arsenault P. Differential effects of epidermal growth factor and hydrocortisone in human fetal colon. *J Pediatr Gastroenterol Nutr* 1990;10:13–20.
43. Menard D, Arsenault P, Pothier P. Biologic effects of epidermal growth factor in human fetal jejunum. *Gastroenterology* 1988;94:656–663.
44. Beaulieu JF, Calvert R. The effect of epidermal growth factor (EGF) on the differentiation of the rough endoplasmic reticulum in fetal mouse small intestine in organ culture. *J Histochem Cytochem* 1981;29:765–770.
45. Conteas CN, DeMorrow JM, Majumdar AP. Effect of epidermal growth factor on growth and maturation of fetal and neonatal rat small intestine in organ culture. *Experientia* 1986;42:950–952.
46. Walker-Smith JA, Phillips AD, Walford N, *et al.* Intravenous epidermal growth factor/urogastrone increases small intestinal cell proliferation in congenital microvillous atrophy. *Lancet* 1985; iii: 1239–1240.
47. Sullivan PB, Brueton MJ, Tabara ZB, Goodlad RA, Lee CY, Wright NA. Epidermal growth factor in necrotising enteritis. *Lancet* 1991;338:53–54.
48. Dembinski AB, Johnson LR. Effect of epidermal growth factor in the development of the gastric mucosa. *Endocrinology* 1985;116:90–94.
49. Odaka K, Hiramatsu Y, Eguchi K, Kudo T. Effects of epidermal growth factor on neonatal growth of rat intestines. *Acta Med Okayama* 1994;48:47–50.
50. Read LC, Tarantal A, George-Nascimento C. Effects of recombinant human epidermal growth factor on the intestinal growth of fetal rhesus monkeys. *Acta Paediatr Scand* 1989;351:97–103.
51. Freund JN, Duluc I, Foltzer-Jourdainne C, Gosse F, Raul F. Specific expression of lactase in the jejunum and colon during postnatal development and hormone treatments in the rat. *Biochem J* 1990;268:99–103.
52. Foltzer-Jourdainne C, Raul F. Effect of epidermal growth factor on the expression of digestive hydrolases in the jejunum and colon of newborn rats. *Endocrinology* 1990;127:1763–1769.
53. Arsenault P, Menard D. Stimulatory effects of epidermal growth factor on deoxyribonucleic acid synthesis in the gastrointestinal tract of the suckling mouse. *Comp Biochem Physiol B Comp Physiol* 1987;86:123–127.
54. Hormi K, Lehy T. Transforming growth factor-alpha *in vivo* stimulates epithelial cell proliferation in digestive tissues of suckling rats. *Gut* 1996;39:532–538.
55. Oka Y, Ghishan FK, Greene HL, Orth DN. Effect of mouse epidermal growth factor/urogastrone on the functional maturation of rat intestine. *Endocrinology* 1983;112:940–944.
56. Greene HL, Moore MC, Oka Y, Moran JR, Ghishan FK, Orth DN. Epidermal growth factor in human milk and the effects of systemic EGF injection on intestinal calcium transport in suckling rats. *Endocrinol Exp* 1986;20:189–198.

57. Harada E, Hashimoto Y, Syuto B. Epidermal growth factor accelerates the intestinal cessation of macromolecular transmission in the suckling rat. *Comp Biochem Physiol Physiol* 1990;97:201–204.
58. Opleta-Madsen K, Meddings JB, Gall DG. Epidermal growth factor and postnatal development of intestinal transport and membrane structure. *Pediatr Res* 1991;30:342–350.
59. James PS, Smith MW, Tivey DR. Dexamethasone selectively increases sodium-dependent alanine transport across neonatal piglet intestine. *J Physiol (Lond)* 1987;393:569–582.
60. Shinohara H, Williams C, Yakabe T, Koldovsky O. Epidermal growth factor delays gastric emptying and intestinal transit in suckling rats. *Pediatr Res* 1996;39:281–286.
61. Foltzer-Jourdainne C, Garaud JC, Nsi-Emvo E, Raul F. Epidermal growth factor and the maturation of intestinal sucrase in suckling rats. *Am J Physiol* 1993;265:G459–466.
62. Emvo EN, Raul F, Koch B, Neuville P, Foltzer-Jourdainne C. Sucrase-isomaltase gene expression in suckling rat intestine hormonal, dietary, and growth factor control. *J Pediatr Gastroenterol Nutr* 1996;23: 262–269.
63. Cohen S, Taylor JM. Epidermal growth factor: chemical and biological characterization. In: Maibach HI, Rove DT, eds. *Epidermal wound healing.* Chicago: Year Book Medical Publishers; 1972: 203–218.
64. Hahn P, Koldovsky O. *Utilization of nutrients during postnatal development.* Oxford: Pergamon Press; 1966.
65. Britton JR, George-Nascimento C, Udall JN, Koldovsky O. Minimal hydrolysis of epidermal growth factor by gastric fluid of preterm infants. *Gut* 1989;30:327–332.
66. Playford RJ, Marchbank T, Calnan DP, et al. Epidermal growth factor is digested to smaller, less active forms in acidic gastric juice. *Gastroenterology* 1995;108:92–101.
67. Shen WH, Xu RJ. Stability of epidermal growth factor in the gastrointestinal lumen of suckling and weaned pigs. *Life Sci* 1996;59:197–208.
68. Thornburg W, Matrisian L, Magun B, Koldovsky O. Gastrointestinal absorption of epidermal growth factor in suckling rats. *Am J Physiol* 1984;246:G80–85.
69. Thornburg W, Rao RK, Matrisian LM, Magun BE, Koldovsky O. Effect of maturation on gastrointestinal absorption of epidermal growth factor in rats. *Am J Physiol* 1987;253:G68–71.
70. Rao RK. Luminal processing of epidermal growth factor in mouse gastrointestinal tract *in vivo*. *Peptides* 1995;16:505–513.
71. Read LC, Gale SM, George-Nascimento C. Intestinal absorption of epidermal growth factor in newborn lambs. In: Goldman AS, Atkinson SA, Hanson LA, eds. *Human lactation 3.* New York: Plenum Press; 1987:199–204.
72. Gonnella PA, Siminoski K, Murphy RA, Neutra MR. Transepithelial transport of epidermal growth factor by absorptive cells of suckling rat ileum. *J Clin Invest* 1987;80:22–32.
73. Rao, RK, Koldovsky O, Korc M, Pollack PF, Wright S, Davis TP. Processing and transfer of epidermal growth factor in developing rat jejunum and ileum. *Peptides* 1990;11:1093–1102.
74. Kong WY, Koldovsky O, Rao RK. Appearance of exogenous epidermal growth factor in liver, bile, and intestinal lumen of suckling rats. *Gastroenterology* 1992;102:661–667.
75. Berseth CL. Enhancement of intestinal growth in neonatal rats by epidermal growth factor in milk. *Am J Physiol* 1987;253:G662–665.
76. Berseth CL, Go VLW. Enhancement of neonatal somatic and hepatic growth by orally administered epidermal growth factor in rats. *J Pediatr Gastroenterol Nutr* 1987;7:889–893.
77. Falconer J. Oral epidermal growth factor is trophic for the stomach in the neonatal rat. *Biol Neonate* 1987;52:347–350.
78. Puccio F, Lehy T. Oral administration of epidermal growth factor in suckling rats stimulates cell DNA synthesis in fundic and antral gastric mucosae as well as in intestinal mucosa and pancreas. *Regul Peptides* 1988;20:53–64.
79. McCuskey RS, Nishida J, McDonnell D, Williams C, Koldovsky O. Effect of milk-borne EGF on the hepatic microcirculation and Kupffer cell function in suckling rats. *Biol Neonate* 1997;71:202–206.
80. O'Loughlin EV, Chung M, Hollenberg M, Hayden J, Zahavi I, Gall DG. Effect of epidermal growth factor on ontogeny of the gastrointestinal tract. *Am J Physiol* 1985;249:G674–678.
81. Opleta K, O'Loughlin EV, Shaffer EA, Hayden J, Hollenberg M, Gall DG. Effect of epidermal growth factor on growth and postnatal development of the rabbit liver. *Am J Physiol* 1987;253:G622–626.
82. Rao RK, Chang H-H, Levenson S, et al. Ontogenic differences in the inhibition of gastric acid secretion by epidermal growth factor. *J Pharmacol Exp Ther* 1993;266:647–654.
83. Konturek SJ, Radecki T, Brzozowski T, et al. Gastric cytoprotection by epidermal growth factor: role of endogenous prostaglandins and DNA synthesis. *Gastroenterology* 1981;81:438–443.

DISCUSSION

Prof. Haschke: How mature is the gut of the suckling rat compared with humans?

Prof. Dvorak: It corresponds to a highly premature baby, but I could not tell you how many weeks.

Prof. Haschke: Has anybody studied the interaction between growth factors in breast milk?

Prof. Dvorak: There have been studies showing interaction between IGF-1 and EGF. Injection of EGF to neonatal rats regulates IGF-1 serum levels, hepatic gene expression of IGF-binding proteins and IGF BPs serum levels [1,2].

Dr. Debauche: You said that EGF in milk is stable in an acidic environment, but you also said that milk EGF has a high molecular weight that would be unstable at acidic pH. Can you comment on that?

Prof. Dvorak: It is true that there is partial degradation, but in suckling rats, about 80% to 90% survives passage through the stomach.

Dr. Walker: As you pointed out, the preweaned rat is comparable to the quite premature human infant. In the late 1980s an investigator named Menard from Sherbrook looked at the effect of EGF on 12-week gestation and 19- to 22-week-gestation fetal intestinal cells from the human and found striking differences [3]. My question is, "Do you see similar results in comparing, let's say, 2-day-old rats with 14-day-old? Growth factors have different effects at different times in development, and that is a very important area to study if we are going to be able to apply the data to humans.

Prof. Dvorak: Though we did not specifically do developmental studies, I measured the expression of mRNA in 4-day-old, 10-day-old, 12-day-old, and 14-day-old animals, and did not see significant changes. There were differences, but they were not sufficient to allow me to say there was a trend to increase or decrease.

Dr. Sedaghatian: Have you investigated EGF in premature mother's milk and compared it with full-term mother's milk?

Prof. Dvorak: We are comparing these term rat babies with premature human infants, so it's a difficult comparison. The milk we used in our experiments was mature rat milk, harvested from day 8 to day 12 of lactation. We were not using colostrum or early milk. We were also using animals between 8 and 12 days old, but we believe there may be a time window when it is most important to have this growth factor. We are now going to see whether EGF has a greater effect if it is added between, say, day 0 and day 4, instead of day 8 to 12. Of course there are many growth factors and other biologically active substances in milk, and we are trying to target them one by one. Another option is to develop antibodies against individual growth factors and knock them out of the milk, and then compare the effects.

Dr. Walker: There is a large amount of EGF in preterm milk, and there is a fairly high level in term colostrum, but the concentration falls off with time.

Prof. Lucas: Presumably, growth factors are present in cow's milk and have biological effects on the calf. How species-specific are growth factors of this nature in their activity, and how well preserved or not preserved are they in the production of an infant formula? Could you preserve them, and would they have an effect on the infant?

Prof. Dvorak: It would be difficult to preserve them in a formula. There are differences in the level of these growth factors from species to species. TGFα, for example, is present in human milk but we couldn't detect it in rat milk, while EGF is present in both. Insulin-like growth factor is present attached to a binding protein, so it is protected. But to my knowledge, there are no formulas containing growth factors in comparable amounts to human milk.

Dr. Guesry: I don't know whether TGFβ2 is comparable to other growth factors, but it is very well preserved during processing and large amounts are present in infant formula.

Prof. Dvorak: We have focused more on the EGF and IGF families, and those growth factors are not very well preserved during processing.

Prof. Haschke: As far as I know, growth factors from cow's milk colostrum are commercially available. They are not species-specific, because they also work in the rat. So even if there is a difference in binding or whatever, it seems that growth factors from cow's milk could be effective in the human infant.

Prof. Dvorak: I think that is true. We actually used human EGF for a long time, since it was cheaper than rat EGF. We switched to rat EGF to be on the safe side, but there were no significant differences in activity. There are changes in structure—there are two different amino acids, and the human EGF molecule is a little longer than the rat molecule, but biologically there are no significant differences in activity.

Dr. Walker: In relation to the structure, the receptor may be the same, but I'm not sure that the programming is the same. We need to do a lot more studies before we can infer that the TGF present in cow's milk has an appropriate effect on human intestine.

Prof. Dvorak: It needs a very high level of biochemical expertise to do such studies, and then convert them into animal models.

Prof. Moro: Do you know if heat treatment of human milk can have any effect on these growth hormones?

Prof. Dvorak: It reduces the biological activity of these growth factors significantly.

Prof. Endres: If IGF-1 is destroyed by hydrolysis, will EGF and TGF also be destroyed by this procedure?

Prof. Dvorak: Yes, I believe so.

Prof. Berger: Over the last few years there has been increasing interest in parathyroid related protein, which apparently has protean effects—on cell maturation, immunity, surfactant induction in the lung, and so on. I am intrigued by the fact that the concentration in human milk is apparently 1,000 times higher than in the maternal plasma. Do you know anything about this in relation to gut maturation? I know people have been looking at that in relation to calcium absorption.

Prof. Dvorak: I am unable to comment on this.

REFERENCES

1. Chernausek SD, Dickson BA, Smith EP, Hoath SB. Suppression of insulin-like growth factor-I during epidermal growth factor-induced growth retardation. *Am J Physiol* 1991;260:E416–421.
2. Murray MA, Dickson BA, Smith EP, Hoath SB, Chernausek SD. Epidermal growth factor simulates insulin-like growth factor-binding protein-1 expression in neonatal rat. *Endocrinol.* 1993;133: 159–163.
3. Murphy SM, Walker WA. Development of the small intestine. *Pediatric gastroenterology,* 3rd ed. Cambridge, MA: Blackwell; 1993:113–130.

Subject Index

Page number followed by *f* indicates a figure; a page number followed by *t* indicates a table.